A PERSISTENT
PEACE

Merry Christmas!
With blessings of
Peace,

John Dear

Also by John Dear:

Disarming the Heart

Jean Donovan and the Call to Discipleship

Our God Is Nonviolent

Christ Is with the Poor

Seeds of Nonviolence

Oscar Romero and the Nonviolent Struggle for Justice

The God of Peace

The Sacrament of Civil Disobedience

Peace Behind Bars

The Sound of Listening

Jesus the Rebel

Living Peace

Mohandas Gandhi

Mary of Nazareth, Prophet of Peace

You Will Be My Witnesses

The Questions of Jesus

Transfiguration

The Advent of the God of Peace

Put Down the Sword

A PERSISTENT PEACE

ONE MAN'S STRUGGLE FOR A NONVIOLENT WORLD

JOHN DEAR, SJ

LOYOLA PRESS.
A JESUIT MINISTRY
Chicago

LOYOLA PRESS.
A JESUIT MINISTRY

3441 N. Ashland Avenue
Chicago, Illinois 60657
(800) 621-1008
www.loyolapress.com

Author photo by Jill Williams
Cover design by Think Design Group LLC
Interior design by Kathryn Seckman Kirsch

Library of Congress Cataloging-in-Publication Data
Dear, John, 1959–
  A persistent peace : one man's struggle for a nonviolent world / John Dear.
    p. cm.
  ISBN-13: 978-0-8294-2720-2
  ISBN-10: 0-8294-2720-1
  1. Dear, John, 1959– 2. Catholic Church—United States—Clergy—Biography. 3. Jesuits—United States—Biography. 4. Nonviolence—Religious aspects—Catholic Church. 5. Peace—Religious aspects—Catholic Church. I. Title.
  BX4705.D2849A3 2008
  271'.5302—dc22
  [B]
                                                                      2008019699

Printed in the United States of America
08 09 10 11 12 13 Bang 10 9 8 7 6 5 4 3 2 1

CONTENTS

回 FOREWORD 図

Although I was unable to attend my friend John Dear's ordination to the priesthood (due to travel misconnections from South Africa), I did arrive in time to attend his first mass, celebrated on Sunday, June 13, 1993, in the packed basement of St. Aloysius Roman Catholic Church in Washington, D.C., just a few blocks from the Capitol.

Ordained only twenty-four hours earlier, this brilliant young Jesuit stood in front of the largely black and mostly poor congregation, which he had faithfully served during his Jesuit formation years, and gave his first blessing to begin his first mass: "May the grace and peace of God our Creator, the fellowship of the Holy Spirit and the love of the nonviolent Jesus be with all of you."

Normally a congregation would respond, "and also with you," but there was nothing normal about this blessing or the priest who gave it. On the contrary, this astonishing reference to the Son of God as "the nonviolent Jesus" was greeted with wild enthusiastic cheering and sustained applause, and for good reason; this blessing was the "good news" preached to the poor: Our God is loving and nonviolent. What a revelation! Let's celebrate!

By choosing such a concept to begin his priesthood, John Dear confirmed what all of us in that church, what his government prosecutors, and what his Jesuit superiors had come to expect from this fiercely independent, spiritually disarming young man. Despite the special occasion, today would be no different from all the ones preceding it, since John began his extremely difficult and often lonely journey on "the long road to peace." And he would continue to confront every wretched form of violence and injustice with loving nonviolent resistance in every thought, word, and deed.

While this path is the chosen purpose of his life's work and the major source of his joy, it is not possible to fully comprehend John Dear's journey without comprehending the journey of his fellow Jesuit, mentor, and our mutual friend, Daniel Berrigan, SJ. There is no one John has admired more than Dan Berrigan, who has been a living example of everything John aspired to become: a committed Jesuit and a peace-and-justice advocate willing to risk his life and freedom by confronting the institutionalized violence and corruption of the state as well as the complacency of the Church and his own Jesuit order.

With faithful adherence to the command of the prophet Isaiah to "beat swords into plowshares and make war no more" and the command of Christ to "love your enemies," Dan's entire life has been a witness for peace and justice. And while his courageous activism earned him the long promised blessing reserved for the peacemakers, it also flew in the face of America's hot-and-cold war policies and the nuclear arms race and earned him, as well, a long stretch in a federal penitentiary and criticism from within the Church and from some of his fellow Jesuits.

Clearly John knew what lay in store for him if he chose to follow Dan's path, yet he did not hesitate to do so. In fact, he embraced it wholeheartedly with his own personal vow of nonviolence taken long before he took the three standard Jesuit vows (poverty, chastity, and obedience). He, too, would suffer a similar fate of prison, sharp criticism, and the misunderstanding of others.

Since the mid 1980s I have been drawn to share a portion of John's peace journey, which has led to sharing a few jail cells along the way. Public demonstrations with John have always been deeply personal and spiritually nourishing experiences that enriched my life immeasurably. Whenever I've appeared with him at any peace march, protest rally, or direct nonviolent confrontation where civil disobedience and arrest occurred, John always assumed a prayerful leadership role, was often among the first taken into custody, and always remained calm, nonviolent, and even joyful throughout the process.

Our first arrest together happened in New York City while protesting Reagan's effort to place nuclear weapons in outer space, the "Missile Defense Shield." This hare-brained scheme was popularly referred to as "Star Wars" and never quite got off the ground—thank heaven!

Many more demonstrations and protests would follow through the years, including arrests in Washington, D.C. at the Pentagon, the Capitol, and the White House for opposing U.S. policy in Central America—such as Reagan's "Contra War" in Nicaragua. There were arrests at Fort Benning, Georgia, protesting the presence there of the School of the Americas (S.O.A.), where many soldiers from Central and South America were trained by the U.S. Army and the C.I.A. to murder and oppress their own people throughout Central America and the Southern hemisphere.

John and I shared several arrests in downtown Los Angeles at the federal building, protesting U.S. involvement in El Salvador's civil war, the assassination of Archbishop Romero, the murder of the four American church women, and the brutal massacre of the six Jesuits and their coworker and her fifteen-year-old daughter, all in El Salvador.

There were numerous demonstrations and arrests with John at the nuclear test site in Mercury, Nevada, where nuclear weapons were stored and tested, and at Livermore Lab in Livermore, California, where enough nuclear weapons and their delivery systems are designed and built to destroy the world endlessly.

I came to know and love John Dear through these intense actions, and we developed a unique relationship. I traveled with him through El Salvador and Guatemala, visited him during his peacemaking service in Northern Ireland during the violent troubles there, supported him during his long prison stay in North Carolina, and despite being twenty years older than him, I came to regard him as a big brother.

All the while I was becoming known as a peace and justice activist, but my personal commitment proved only a shadow of John's—this made clear by his courageous participation in a risky "Plowshares Action" with Philip Berrigan, which John describes in detail in this book. This action alone changed forever the direction of John's life and proved to be a point of no return on his long road to peace.

Courage is often described as the first virtue from which so many other virtues flow. It is certainly the most admired virtue and the one most devoutly wished for, and while its source remains a mystery, courage is universally acknowledged as the very best part of the human character. Courage is breathtakingly abundant in John Dear.

How he arrived at such an enviable level of moral and physical courage—reflected in numerous acts of civil disobedience, carried out with disarming nonviolence and joy, and often met with harsh consequences—is simply astonishing. Even more astonishing is that his life's commitment to peace and justice appears instinctive, springing from an unfathomable source. Surely it is a reflection of John's deep spirituality. And while he credits the examples of Mahatma Gandhi, Dr. Martin Luther King Jr., and Robert F. Kennedy as the chief inspirations for his own life, we all have these examples; yet, the vast majority of us remain dull by comparison.

I suspect that much of John's character was formed, as it is for all of us, during adolescence, that critical period when every level of physical, emotional, physiological, sexual, and spiritual development begins to emerge. It is then that we glimpse the first real possibility of our independence with an equal measure of joy and dread; we are consumed by a mysterious energy. Then the reality of peer pressure emerges as a powerful common denominator, and while each of us is unique unto ourselves we are nevertheless instinctively drawn together for mutual recognition and acceptance. It is here (I believe) where we come to know ourselves in deeply revealing ways, which often set the course of our future. It is here where the first small conscious act of heroism often occurs, bringing us rejection from the crowd, and we decide to subtly "go it alone." It is here where the ego befriends the truth and the first small step is taken, whether consciously or unconsciously, on a lifelong journey to unite the will of the spirit with the work of the flesh. It is here where I believe a very young John Dear began to identify himself independently of his peers so that for the rest of his life he would never quite be comfortable unless he was at the very least slightly uncomfortable. And it is here where (I believe) he began to slip out of the grip of fear and into the uncertain freedom of faith.

Mahatma Gandhi is frequently acknowledged by John Dear as a principle source of inspiration for his own life. What was said of Gandhi can perhaps be equally applied to John: "Future generations will scarce believe that such a one actually existed."

Martin Sheen
January 20, 2008

▣ INTRODUCTION ▣

I was born on the eve of the 1960s, on August 13, 1959, in Elizabeth City, North Carolina, not far from where the Wright Brothers first flew at Kitty Hawk. My earliest memories are happy: generous parents, three brothers, a brown pony named Lucky, a big white house with a long wide front lawn and the spectacular beaches nearby—wonder and beauty and a new adventure every day.

Everything went smoothly until my uncle died in early 1967, and my father, publisher of the local newspaper, was suddenly named head of the family newspaper chain. We moved to Bethesda, Maryland so he could work full-time at the National Press Club in Washington, D.C. My mother, a nurse, began a doctorate in sociology and a teaching career at Johns Hopkins and George Mason universities.

We became news junkies, watching every evening the grim newscasts about the war in Vietnam. When Martin Luther King Jr. was assassinated, I sat glued to the TV for days, watching footage of his life and mourning his loss. Two months later, I repeated the scenario, mourning for Robert F. Kennedy. I attended Catholic grade school and a Jesuit high school, studied hard, was involved in sports, and volunteered at our local parish church. But in order to get away from the Catholic church and set out on my own, I chose to attend Duke University, back in North Carolina. Little did I know what lay in store for me.

Over the years I've committed my story to paper in fits and starts—journals now stowed away in file cabinets, scattered notes in folders, half-developed reflections lying about. Lately it seemed good to stitch the pieces together, to make of them a coherent memoir. It's an exercise that leads to introspection like nothing else. The mystery of life unfolds. The meaning of events draws near. I've enjoyed the process, returning to events and smelling the bloom of significance.

Along the way I pondered the question: Which event ranks highest? Perhaps the day I renounced all my plans, including my dream of becoming a rock star, to serve God as a Jesuit. Perhaps that day in Israel, camped by the Sea of Galilee, pondering the Beatitudes, pledging to make them mine if only I were given a sign—and then ducking as Israeli jets appeared out of nowhere, thundered overhead, and unleashed their bombs in Lebanon. That was surely a sign of something.

Maybe the key moment was when I entered the Jesuits and professed a vow of nonviolence. Or when I journeyed to the Pentagon to protest war, ended up in handcuffs, and received word from my superior that he had dismissed me from the Jesuits—a dismissal later overturned.

My most significant season could easily be one turbulent summer in El Salvador. There I made my home in a makeshift camp with long-suffering Salvadoran refugees and witnessed daily U.S. bombing raids. In El Salvador, I met the visionary Jesuits at the University of Central America who were assassinated a few years after.

Or perhaps my most important days were still to come—days in Iraq, India, Haiti, the Philippines, Nicaragua, Guatemala, Colombia, Northern Ireland, and Palestine. Or my years of banishment to a Jesuit high school in Scranton for challenging Jesuit authority. Or my stretch at a homeless shelter blocks from the U.S. Capitol. Or later at Berkeley, ostensibly studying theology, but spending more time organizing demonstrations against U.S. military actions.

Certainly, one would think my ordination to the priesthood ranks high—ordained at last despite Jesuit annoyance with me. But so did my 1993 Plowshares action, during which I entered an Air Force base in North Carolina and hammered on an F15—in biblical terms, to "beat swords into plowshares," the most notorious of some seventy-five arrests for peace. Or my years as director of the Fellowship of Reconciliation, the oldest interfaith peace group in the U.S. Or perhaps when I paddled a canoe down Connecticut's Thames River to block a Trident submarine. Or my work for the New York Red Cross consoling grieving family members and rescue workers at Ground Zero after the terrorist attacks of September 11, 2001. Or the morning National Guard Battalion 515 arrayed itself outside my rectory door in the high desert of New Mexico and chanted, "One bullet, one kill!"

I've asked myself, How do these events line up in terms of importance? And it dawned on me: discrete events aren't important; the journey itself is the real story. Meaning in life is found on the long road to peace. Though I'm nobody, I've tried to undertake a lifelong journey into Gospel nonviolence, and I have discovered a taste of life's meaning: love, compassion, service, resistance, and peace.

Mahatma Gandhi titled his autobiography, *The Story of My Experiments in Truth*. I find that helpful. I've conducted experiments in the truth of nonviolence. Early on, I decided I wanted to do what the rich young man of the Gospel couldn't do—give away my wealth to the poor and follow Jesus—with disregard for the consequences. To "lose my life in order to save it." To "seek first God's reign and God's justice" and let everything be provided for me. I've discovered that the Gospel works. The promises come true. Jesus' promise to his disciples has been fulfilled in my life: "Amen, I say to you, there is no one who has given up house or brothers or sisters or mother or father or children or lands for my sake and for the sake of the gospel who will not receive a hundred times more now in this present age: houses and brothers and sisters and mothers and children and lands, with persecutions" (Mark 10:29–30).

Living this way thrust me into the midst of the world's suffering— refugees, prisoners, the homeless, the poorest, and death row inmates. And it has allowed me to be among the privileged and influential— presidents, a pope, a queen, Nobel peace prize winners, and more, the saints of our time: Mother Teresa, Thich Nhat Hanh, Dom Hélder Câmara, Coretta Scott King, Desmond Tutu, Mairead Maguire, César Chávez, and Daniel and Philip Berrigan.

This journey toward peace creates a life of deep contrasts. I've observed protocol in palaces and moldered in prisons. I've stalked the halls of power and lived months at a time in a refugee camp. I want to follow the nonviolent Jesus, and so I try in a modest way to enter the Gospel story and proclaim the gospel of peace, even to a world of war.

Over the years I've crisscrossed the continent and spoken to hundreds of thousands of people. I urge them to oppose war. I invite them to embrace Jesus' way of peace and nonviolent love. My authority, I believe, springs from my story.

I share this story in the hope that others will undertake their own experiments in Gospel nonviolence, in pursuit of a new world without war, poverty, or nuclear weapons. I can promise difficulties beyond number, but blessings beyond your wildest dreams. In the end, the blessings are all that matter.

John Dear

Frat Boy
(1978–79)

If you had stopped in Durham, North Carolina, on a Friday night in 1979 and walked across the green lawns of Duke University, past the gothic buildings and the towering cathedral, under the stone arches, across the quad, and through Kappa Sigma's wooden door into the din of the never-ending fraternity party, you would have found me—the life of the party, in the center of the throng of men and women drinking, eating, singing, and dancing—getting the beer-chugging contest under way and tossing pints down the hatch. My record: thirty-two in one night.

At the time, it seemed like fun. But the hangovers! They lasted for days. Such was the life of the best and the brightest, the cream of the crop, the spoiled, wealthy frat boy. I arrived at Duke, in January 1978, much more temperate. I spent my first semester learning the ropes and finding my way around campus. People at Duke were friendly but serious, focused, and smart. I decided early on to sign up with the professors who had the best reputations, and whatever subject I ended up having the most credits in would be the subject I would declare as my major. I ended up majoring in African-American history.

Duke didn't allow juniors and seniors to live in campus dorms. To stay on campus, you had to move into a fraternity house; otherwise, you had to move off campus and rent an apartment in Durham. The autumn of my sophomore year, my roommate Doug and I made the rounds of the frat houses and attended the weekend rush parties. We decided on Kappa Sigma. In January 1979, we moved in as pledges, and the partying began in earnest.

Kappa Sigma made John Belushi's *Animal House* seem like kindergarten. I studied all day, spent hours at the piano, and stayed up late into the next morning doing more than my share of drinking. I don't know when I ever slept.

The fraternity brothers treated us pledges as lackeys. We had to jump through hoops to get every fraternity brother's signature in our pledge books, a process that lasted the whole semester. To earn a signature, we had to fulfill some demeaning task for the brothers: clean their rooms, wash their cars, type their papers, or fetch tennis balls during their matches. They ordered us around and called us names, and we obediently complied—up to a point. The pledges appointed me "Secretary of War," and my job was to strategize battle against the brothers. Under my command we waged mischief and mayhem, risking demerits and at times expulsion. Still the brothers held the upper hand, gathering us pledges once a month for an evening of humiliation and abuse, lining us up against the wall for hours and calling us every name in the book. Our pledging ordeal ended with the infamous Hell Night, held in April. The following week, with the necessary signatures collected—and grateful to be alive—we were blindfolded, sworn to secrecy, and initiated.

I never did understand how my fraternity brothers managed to do so well in school. They partied all night, every night and still got straight As. Our fraternity had the highest grade point average on campus. We had a file cabinet full of stock term papers, available to anyone who wanted to copy them, but that doesn't entirely explain why the brothers were so successful. They were hard partying, hard drinking, hard studying, hardworking, and brilliant. When I was still a pledge, a senior frat brother reproached me for being insouciant. *Insouciant?* What did that mean? Who *were* these guys? Today, most of them are CEOs, lawyers, bankers, and doctors, some of them millionaires. One uses a private jet.

The most fascinating of all was Paul Farmer. He came from a large family that lived on a houseboat in Florida. Paul was a flat-out genius. A premed student who also majored in anthropology, Paul wrote his mother every day, composed theater and book reviews every week for the Duke newspaper, *The Chronicle,* and produced displays for the main entrance to Perkins Library, one of the largest in the country. Each evening he hosted marathon parties in his rooms for dozens of students. It seemed that Paul never studied, yet he earned straight A's. He went on to Harvard Medical School, became a leading researcher there, and founded a clinic for the poor in Haiti. His example inspires countless other doctors to serve the third world poor. His story was told in the best-selling book, *Mountains beyond Mountains: The Quest of Dr. Paul Farmer.* He has become our own Albert Schweitzer. But even back then in college, we were in awe of him.

回   回

In those days, I pondered three possible careers. I could become a newspaper publisher like my father, his father, and his grandfather or a lawyer like my high school friends Chas and Mark. Mostly, though, I wanted to be a rock star.

My friends still laugh at my grandiose ambition, but I was serious. I wanted to compose my own songs, record as a solo artist, and move to

Los Angeles and live like Jackson Browne or James Taylor. I had been playing the piano seriously since I was six and had taken up the guitar at ten. At Duke, I spent a lot of time in their new music building, with its more than forty music studios, two performance spaces, recording studio, and extensive music library. Years earlier, one of my brothers and I had built a primitive recording studio in our basement by connecting tape players and attaching microphones to them. He played drums and bass guitar; I played piano and acoustic guitar and sang.

At Duke I studied classical piano, learning my way around Beethoven, Mozart, Rachmaninoff, and Brahms. I spent four hours a day practicing. I also played pop music and wrote my own songs. I loved the Beatles and the Beach Boys and all the singer-songwriters of the 1970s—Billy Joel, Jackson Browne, Elton John, James Taylor, Dan Fogelberg, and Graham Nash—and I tried to write like them. After a few months, I had several dozen good songs, and in the midst of my busy class schedule and crazy fraternity life, I drove off one night to a recording studio about two hours west of Raleigh. It was an unimpressive building, its interior walls lined with orange shag carpeting. But it was filled with the latest musical recording equipment, and there in the center of the studio was a magnificent grand piano. I recorded seven or eight songs, handling all the parts myself. Afterward, my friend Margaret and I bought a bottle of wine, and stayed up late in my fraternity room listening to the tapes. The experience of recording my own music was one of the most exciting of my life. That night, I dreamt of becoming a successful singer-songwriter.

It was through my love of music that I befriended one of the most influential people in my life, the legendary jazz pianist Mary Lou Williams. During my time at Duke, she was artist in residence, and her jazz classes were the most popular on campus. I signed up, and on the first day of class, nearly a hundred of us crowded nervously in the seashell auditorium where the orchestra rehearsed. Down below in the center was a gleaming black grand piano. Mary Lou was late. When she finally walked in, the room became quiet. She was a big woman with dark skin and black hair. She was dressed in black, and pinned to her dress was a large black papier-mâché rose. Without saying a word, she ambled toward the piano, looked around the room, and threw us a smile. Then she sat down and started to play. We were instantly mesmerized.

Her story is just as extraordinary as her music. She started playing piano at the age of three and joined a jazz tour at twelve. She played with Duke Ellington when she was sixteen. She joined Andy Kirk's band, Twelve Clouds of Joy, in the 1930s, leaving in the 1940s to settle in Harlem, where she played at every well-known jazz club. She counted Billie Holiday and Dizzy Gillespie among her best friends and appeared with Dizzy at the Newport Jazz Festival. Plus, she composed and arranged music. She wrote for Louis Armstrong, Tommy Dorsey, and Benny Goodman, compiling a body of work that included more than 350 pieces. At the height of her career, she performed three movements of her classic *Zodiac Suite* with the New York Pops Orchestra at Carnegie Hall.

Then, in the mid-1950s, she converted to Catholicism and gave up music. She decided not to have a family but to spend the rest of her life in contemplative prayer and humble service to the poor. Her musician friends were stunned. But at St. Ignatius Loyola Church on Park Avenue, where she attended daily Mass, she met an astute Jesuit who convinced her to return to music as a way to serve people and inspire them to love one another. So she scored a Catholic Mass with jazz music that became the first jazz Mass performed at St. Patrick's Cathedral. Every year she performed for Dorothy Day at the Catholic

Worker farm in New Jersey. All the while, she continued to pray for several hours each day.

"Jazz is love," she told us that first day of class. "You have to feel the love in the music. It will make you into a more loving person and bring joy into your life." We were beguiled. Through her music, Mary Lou taught us jaded Duke students about the spiritual life. She imparted love through boogie-woogie.

I wanted to learn from Mary Lou, so I went up to her after class one day, introduced myself, and asked if she would give me private lessons. She agreed on the spot.

For several months, I took the bus each week to her house, on the outskirts of Durham, where we sat on a small bench before her modest upright and together played jazz. Her hands stretched well over an octave. She taught me the finer points of syncopation and the emotion behind the diminished seventh chord. She showed me how to make my left hand lope along on bass while my right jingled some kind of melody. She tried to teach me improvisation. She would play a riff and then ask me to repeat it. I would try but never quite get it right.

I treasured those hours with Mary Lou, who became a true friend to me. One day, she presented me with a jazz piece she'd written for me. Her love, joy, and sense of wonder touched me deeply. Even then, early in my own spiritual formation, I recognized that this woman was filled with the Holy Spirit. And although it was her music that drew me, it was her holiness that captured me and set me spinning.

回 回

Each May as the school year came to an end, all the Duke fraternities and sororities spent a wild week at Myrtle Beach, South Carolina. When finals ended in the spring of 1979, I headed off to the party.

I remember only parts of it. We drank all night and slept all day on the beach. On one of those nights, my friend Digger and I drank ourselves sick on Schnapps. Later, the temperature dropped, and chilly strong winds blew in from the ocean. By the time I returned home to Bethesda, Maryland, for the summer, I had developed a bad case of bronchitis, and the doctor ordered prolonged bed rest. I ended up in bed for over a month. My brothers were off at camp or at work, my father downtown at the National Press Club. My mother was in Baltimore teaching at Johns Hopkins. Alone at home, I faced a long summer.

I also faced myself. Lying around gave me the space to reflect on my life. In searching the house for something to read, I came upon my father's copy of Arthur Schlesinger's massive biography of Bobby Kennedy, *Robert Kennedy and His Times*. Once I opened it, I couldn't put it down. As I read about the assassinations of Robert Kennedy and Dr. Martin Luther King Jr., the emotions I felt as a boy when those events occurred rushed over me like a tidal wave.

To be honest, I was much more interested in Bobby than in John Kennedy, because after his brother's death, Bobby Kennedy clearly changed. As Jack Newfield wrote in *Robert Kennedy: A Memoir*, Bobby Kennedy underwent an inner transformation that began with searing grief and soul-searching prayer and led to an unusual sense of compassion for the poor. He took up poetry, pondered the eternal questions, and began to expand his horizons. Eventually, he stood with César Chávez and the United Farm Workers, attended Dr. King's funeral, and spoke out vehemently against the Vietnam War. He talked about the need for justice in a way that few politicians had ever done before, or have since.

On the night of Dr. King's assassination, April 4, 1968, Bobby Kennedy spoke to a crowd of African-Americans in inner-city

Indianapolis. After he told the stunned crowd that Dr. King had been killed, he spoke extemporaneously about the need for compassion:

> Martin Luther King dedicated his life to love and to justice for his fellow human beings, and he died because of that effort. . . .
>
> In this difficult time for the United States, it is perhaps well to ask what kind of a nation we are and what direction we want to move in. For those of you who are black . . . you can be filled with bitterness, with hatred, and a desire for revenge. . . .
>
> Or we can make an effort, as Martin Luther King did, to understand and to comprehend and to replace that violence, that stain of bloodshed that has spread across our land, with . . . compassion and love. . . .
>
> What we need in the United States is not division . . . not hatred . . . not violence . . . but love and wisdom, and compassion toward one another, and a feeling of justice toward those who still suffer within our country, whether they be white or they be black. . . .
>
> Let us dedicate ourselves to what the Greeks wrote so many years ago: to tame the savageness of man and make gentle the life of this world.

The next day, in Cleveland, Kennedy gave a clear denunciation of violence. "What has violence ever accomplished?" he asked. "What has it ever created? No martyr's cause has ever been stilled by an assassin's bullet. . . . Violence breeds violence, repression brings retaliation, and only a cleansing of our whole society can remove this sickness from our soul."

As I lay there with a bad case of bronchitis blues, Kennedy's words flowered within me. He awakened in me a passion for life and peace. I could identify with him because we both came from white, upper-class, well-educated, ambitious Catholic families. But now we had something else in common: I aspired to reach the same sort of inner transformation that he had experienced between his brother's assassination and his own death. Now, a decade later, Bobby Kennedy was drawing me to a larger vision of life, to a wider compassion for humanity that he had edged toward by 1968.

And all of a sudden, I could see. I could see not only the immorality of violence, but also its impracticality. I could see the precariousness of life. I could see again how precious life is. And there in bed I made a clear decision to reject violence as best I could.

What most disturbed me was the injustice of it all. Bobby Kennedy, the nation's best and brightest, had died for declaring ideals of justice and peace, as had Dr. King. What chance did anyone have to make this country more just? How would anyone ever again offer honest political leadership? Why even go to law school? Or seek a career in politics, the media, or law? Why try to make a difference at all?

These questions only deepened with each biography I read of Kennedy and Dr. King. The stories of their lives rocked my presuppositions about life, work, purpose, and death. They turned my life plans upside down and set me on an entirely new path.

The Day of Conversion
(1979–80)

By the end of June I had recovered from bronchitis. To earn some money for my junior year, I took the first job I could find, on a construction crew. I got the grunt work: picking up trash, digging ditches, pouring cement, raking yards, and chopping down trees.

As the school year approached, I decided that I would not apply to law school. Nor would I go into the family publishing business. My heart and mind were restless, and I needed to set out on a new search. This was hard, and it made my return to classes unsettling. I continued composing and recording, but I didn't know where I was headed.

Even my musical hopes were in jeopardy. I joined the student association that organized concerts on campus, and the first concert that year featured Livingston Taylor, who was James Taylor's younger brother and had a hit song on the radio that year. After the show, I found him alone in his dressing room and introduced myself as an aspiring singer-songwriter. Then I asked, "What advice do you have for me about going professional?"

He sat down, looked me in the eye, and said, "Don't do it. The music industry is totally corrupt. It isn't at all what people think. It's very difficult to make it. You have to travel endlessly and sell yourself out. Don't do it unless you absolutely have to, unless you have no other choice." I mumbled my thanks and walked out in shocked silence. That Christmas, a musician friend, Bob, and I went to New York City and left some cassettes of our music with Elektra/Asylum Records. As I recall, they wrote us with interest, but neither of us pursued it.

Meanwhile, my class work grew more demanding. I was working hard for several extraordinary history professors. One of them, Anne Firor Scott, was a leading feminist historian. She taught American social history and spent years studying the diaries of ordinary Americans from the late 1700s. She copied dozens of them, had them bound, and assigned them as our readings instead of textbooks. The ordinary voices on those pages, written during the American Revolution, sounded like those of any struggling person today, and I was deeply moved by their humanity. But as I had during my bed rest over the summer, I was struck by the mystery of death. Those voices were long ago silenced. Where were they now? Were they alive in some distant heaven? Had they vanished forever?

The diaries drew me into further reflection, about the brevity of life and my place in the flow of history. Where would I be in two hundred years? Those writings stirred in me a desire not only to read history, but also to make it; I wanted my life to count, as had the lives of Bobby Kennedy and Martin Luther King Jr. When I declared history as my major, I asked Professor Scott to be my adviser. Over time, I began sharing with her my intense questions and ponderings. She did not blink but encouraged me to pursue them.

When I realized how hard my classes would be, I looked to round out my schedule with something easier. Someone had told me that the easiest class on campus was Abnormal Psychology, taught by Harold Schiffman, an absentminded professor who looked like Albert Einstein. I signed up. On the first day of class, I sat in the packed auditorium with my fellow students. Class was to start at 2:00; he walked in finally at 2:20 and seemed taken aback. "When does our class meet?" he asked. According to the course catalog, it met from 2:00 to 3:45 on Mondays, Wednesdays, and Fridays. But a rogue frat student raised his hand and said, "Mondays and Wednesdays from 2:00 to 3:00." Professor Schiffman replied, "Fine," and with that the class was cut in half. He made some introductory remarks, and one caught my attention. He would raise the grade by one letter for any student who performed a few hours of volunteer work for him each week. I knew an easy A when I saw one, so I volunteered.

Schiffman wanted us to help out in psychiatric clinics and homeless shelters around Durham. I was free only on Fridays, and the only Friday opportunity was in nearby Butner at the state hospital, also known as the North Carolina State Hospital for the Criminally Insane. When Friday morning came, a group of us drove out into the countryside. The mammoth facility was a former military barracks that looked more like a prison than a hospital. The institution had only recently stopped performing frontal lobotomies. The officials gave us a brief orientation and assigned each of us to a section where we would spend the day with the patients. They sent me to the Continued Treatment Unit. A guard escorted me through endless hallways that reeked of disinfectant. Along the way, we passed a woman running up and down the hallway screaming at the top of her lungs.

After passing through two sets of locked doors, we arrived at a large white room right out of *One Flew over the Cuckoo's Nest*. On every one of the some fifty cots sat a man dressed in white, his head shaved, staring off into space. Each had been found guilty of some crime and diagnosed insane. Each was drugged and more or less catatonic. They owned nothing. They had no friends. They had no life. No one cared for them. They had been left to rot in this stinking prison. The underpaid, undertrained, uneducated yet well-armed staff watched them twenty-four hours a day from a glass booth.

It was ten in the morning. The guard, who must have taken me to be a psychiatrist, looked at his watch and said, "I'll be back for you at four." He left, locking the doors behind him. There I was, alone with fifty Charles Mansons. They all turned as one and looked at me; I expected to be killed at any moment. Then one of them spoke, in a whisper, as they all did—a side effect of the drugs. His words sounded friendly, so I walked over and asked his name. He started to talk, and I sat down to listen. For the rest of the day, I listened to dozens of these forsaken men.

I sat in silence on the way back to Duke. My complacency had been shattered. How could these people be left to rot? Didn't anyone care for them? What should happen to them, and what does the state owe them given their violence and crimes? Where was God in the midst of their suffering? What did their lives mean? Or was there any meaning to life when this situation could exist?

When I arrived back at the fraternity house, the party was well under way. I stood among the country's first and best, having just left the least and worst, and the contrast hit me hard: how could humanity be so divided?

How does one respond to this great divide? What can a person do? I suddenly felt homeless myself, even in my insular world of privilege. Yet I wasn't sure I had the wherewithal to reject the selfishness around me and within me and find a home somewhere else. For the next twelve weeks, the contrast weighed on me and plunged me deeper into despair. I went to class, played music, hung out at the fraternity, and spent Fridays locked up with North Carolina's criminally insane.

One day, I led four patients outside for a walk. They were fairly "functional," I was told, and so were allowed to wander the grounds.

One woman liked to chat and went on and on about how good Jesus was to her. The others clamored for my attention, too, and I tried to make myself available to them all. But when I turned back to the woman, she was gone. I panicked and looked everywhere. Finally I notified the guards. They began a search of the grounds. An hour later, I found her alone in the gym, playing basketball. She called me over to join the fun and started telling me again about Jesus.

No matter how much I pondered the divide of humanity, new questions kept coming, and lingering. Where was God? Wasn't God aware of this sea of suffering? Why wasn't God helping? The rift in my heart widened, and my turmoil grew.

Then I came upon an answer: maybe there wasn't a God.

It almost felt good to acknowledge this. It made things easier. I could discard the church's catechism—I had been raised Catholic and had attended a Jesuit high school—and live from now on by society's anticatechism: *Life has no moral purpose. I have no obligations. There is no higher justice. There is no ultimate meaning.* I could do whatever the hell I wanted—live for myself, pursue big money, get ahead, turn my back on the poor, and join the wild crowd. I could put an end, too, to my ruminations about the brevity of life and the mystery of death. When I died, I would vanish into oblivion—finis. It was time to stop worrying and just live for myself.

This was the logic of despair, and I accepted it, hoping it would resolve my crisis. But instead it caused my inner darkness and despair to deepen. It led me to conclude that violence, starvation, execution, and war made perfect sense. Nothing matters, so by all means kill people. Send missiles against civilians. Let populations starve. From the halls of power, plot crimes against humanity. Destroy the planet. Unleash a nuclear winter. To hell with everything.

But I couldn't bear the scope of such meaninglessness. I couldn't bear meaninglessness at all. Deep down, more than anything, I craved meaning. I wanted meaning to lend dignity to the deaths of my cousin Mark Blackman and my grandfather John Regan, who both died while I was in high school. I wanted to see meaning in the suffering of the patients at the psychiatric hospital. I wanted to find meaning in the senseless assassinations of Bobby Kennedy and Martin Luther King Jr. I wanted my own existence to have meaning.

In the coming months, I befriended Diana, a psychiatric patient who smiled often and liked to talk. She seemed to be the only sane person in the institution. She welcomed me, toured me around, and facilitated my interactions with others.

On the Friday after Thanksgiving, I couldn't find her and asked one of the guards if she'd been discharged. Apparently, she had suffered a severe breakdown. I asked to see her, and the guard led me to the suicide-watch chamber. I peered into her cell through a small window. There she was, lying on the floor, drugged, naked, and crying. She didn't recognize me.

I walked through the fraternity door that night, the party in full swing: kegs full of beer, stereo blasting, couples necking on the benches outside. Suddenly all of it— the way we lived as if nothing mattered— revolted and grieved me.

▣ ▣

My questions just grew heavier. I walked about abstracted and touchy, with the attention span of a five-year-old. I forgot things and had trouble sleeping. I looked forward to nothing and felt a pit of emptiness inside me. When the new semester began, I decided to give God one last chance.

In January 1980, I enrolled in a religion class called The History of Christianity in America, taught by one of the most popular teachers on campus, Barney Jones, a Methodist minister. The class reviewed the lives of the great American preachers and Christian movements. We would be asked to write a lengthy biographical paper on a significant American Christian. The syllabus lacked any reference to Catholics, a prejudice that caught my attention, and I decided to rectify it in my paper.

My mother had taught at St. Joseph's College in Emmitsburg, Maryland, where Elizabeth Ann Seton had lived, worked, and died. We had often visited her burial place on Sundays. Mother Seton had recently been canonized, so I picked her. A classmate decided on Dorothy Day, founder of the Catholic Worker movement. My godfather, my cousin Daniel Marshall, had lived at the Catholic Worker house in Brooklyn and knew Dorothy Day. So I was interested in my peer's impressions of her. We began to talk about these great Catholic women and what it meant to be Catholic.

Still, my depression lingered. I needed a diversion, so I signed up for a seminar called The Art of Biography. It was there that I met Joe Markwordt, a sophomore from Dundalk, Maryland, who had won a full scholarship to Duke. He was wise and funny and fiercely independent. During our first class, Joe told me that his Catholic faith was the reason he had refused to join a fraternity. He lived off campus in an apartment with a few other students, and he hung out with a small group of Catholic students at the Newman Catholic Student Center, in the basement of the Duke Chapel.

At the next week's class, Joe was wearing a bright yellow button that said, "God Don't Make No Junk." I asked him about it, and he launched into a sermon, preaching that God loves everyone, that each one of us is great because we were made by a loving God, and that none of us is junk.

I was intrigued by his button and his outspokenness. No one I knew at Duke behaved this way. Joe explained his interest in Catholicism, his devotion to Jesus, and the values he tried to live by. He was unlike any of my friends in the Greek system. He had a conscience. He was appalled by the arrogance of most Duke students. He hated our classism, racism, and prejudices and thought that most of us were selfish snobs who didn't care about anything except money and careers.

I looked at Joe's button and thought of the people in Butner. They were junk, thrown away like trash. I, too, felt like a piece of junk, without meaning or purpose. But Joe, speaking with an authority and a conviction I had never before encountered in anyone my age, insisted that God exists, that God is good, that we are loved, and that every human being deserves to be treated as a priceless image of the infinitely loving God.

One cold morning in late January, I ran into Joe on campus in front of the student center. I started to complain about all the papers I had to write, the tests I had to take, and the craziness of fraternity life. I expected a sympathetic response from this self-proclaimed Christian. But he looked me in the eye and said, "You know, John, if you really believe in Jesus, then nothing else really matters that much."

His words struck me like a bolt of lightning. He walked on, but I stood there on the quad, electrified. I knew immediately that he was right. Something in me responded to the essential truth Joe had spoken, but at the time I couldn't come up with a response. Even now I look back at that moment and know that Joe's simple statement was probably the most important thing anyone had ever said to me.

I couldn't pay attention to anything for weeks afterward. My mind raced with questions. Could I believe as fearlessly as Joe? Could I make the same moral choices? Petty problems, he said, would fall into the background, and meaning and direction would become clear. Might

Jesus be the answer to my despair? Could I walk Jesus' way, against the tide of culture? This last question challenged me profoundly. More, it gave me a glimmer of hope for myself—and for the world.

回 回

A few days after the encounter with Joe, I attended the daily noon Mass in the basement of Duke Chapel. I had rarely entered the enormous cathedral, much less the basement below. The room was a mess, furnished with a few threadbare couches, a cross on the wall, and a coffee table for the bread and wine. Four or five other students gathered around the table. Father Joe Burke, a Jesuit priest, was the Catholic chaplain. Short, bald, and garrulous, he had a lively, enthusiastic, contagious spirit. At that time, it didn't seem to me that Father Joe did anything—he never organized a single retreat, guest lecture, student group, service trip, or student dinner. He sat in that room every day, all day long, listening to students. And because of his complete availability to any student at any hour, he was greatly loved. He knew everyone and, I came to realize, was the heart and soul of Duke. As far as I was concerned this lively little Jesuit was the only nonjudgmental, compassionate, attentive presence available on campus.

I sat through his simple Mass, said nothing, and left quickly.

In preparation for my paper for religion class, I was reading *Mrs. Seton*, the definitive biography of Elizabeth Ann Seton. I was impressed by the story of this successful housewife, Manhattan socialite, and busy mother who lost her husband, became an impoverished widow, converted to Catholicism, and embarked upon an extraordinary spiritual journey. In the process, she founded a religious order of nuns, started a school for the poor, and set up her community in the woods of Maryland. Seton was a contemplative, an educator, a servant of the poor, and a disciple of Jesus. As I studied her life, I felt peaceful for the first time in a long while.

One February afternoon, beams of sunlight drenched my basement room in the fraternity house while I studied in solitude. I could feel myself being drawn into this story of Elizabeth Seton—her conversion and pursuit of poverty, her selfless service to the poor, her deep contemplative prayer and most of all, her devout love of Jesus. I remember looking up from my reading, as the gears in my mind began to turn. Mother Seton had helped hundreds, had influenced thousands, and through her life with Jesus and her service to suffering humanity had found purpose and meaning. That must mean that I could, too. In the midst of a busy, difficult life, she had found personal peace; there was no reason I couldn't as well. I could take the risk, as she did, and surrender myself.

Finally I saw it: God existed. Not only because Joe said it and Mother Seton lived it; God's existence was made plain through the life of Jesus. I finally understood that the universe has purpose, the human race has value, and my own life has meaning. When I die, I won't vanish. I will stand before the God of the universe to be welcomed into the house of love and peace. I won't be junk; I will be loved.

Because I knew that all of this was true, I couldn't waste my life any longer on selfish pursuits. I couldn't throw my life away or hurt others or offend God. No, instead I must prepare myself and others for eternal life with God and, like Mother Seton, embrace the highest calling in life—selfless service to the human race, in the footsteps of Jesus.

It was an all-or-nothing choice. If God exists, I should renounce my life, surrender it to God, reach out in universal love, and take off in the footsteps of Jesus. If God does not exist, Joe was wrong, Elizabeth Ann Seton was misguided, Bobby Kennedy and Martin Luther King had wasted their time, and Jesus was a liar.

This moment has the aura of my own personal myth, with all the mystery and wonder of St. Paul's fall from the horse, St. Ignatius's revelation on his sickbed, St. Francis's realization upon kissing the leper, and Thomas Merton's discovery at Columbia University that he wanted to be a priest. My heart filled with desire to give my whole life to God. I suddenly realized that, yes, God does exist. Jesus is right, Joe is right, and Elizabeth Ann Seton is right. There *is* meaning and purpose to life. I am loved by God, my life has meaning, and everyone is being led to live in love with one another. As these thoughts raced through my mind, I wondered, *How does one give oneself to God? What great gesture can I make?*

All of a sudden, the Jesuits I had known from high school, and now Father Joe Burke, rushed to mind. And I knew. I would become a priest. I would become a Jesuit. I would spend my life following Jesus in loving service of humanity in the Society of Jesus. I jumped up from my rocking chair, terrified and exhilarated all at once.

It was Ash Wednesday, February 20, 1980.

Father Burke had planned a service of repentance for four o'clock. I suddenly remembered it and trotted over to the chapel to join the service just as it was beginning. After reading the Gospel, he spoke about the Lenten themes of repentance and conversion, of changing our lives and following Jesus.

Then he invited us to come forward. I walked up the imposing center aisle of the gothic cathedral to the stone altar. Father Burke dipped his thumb in a bowl of ashes, traced a cross on my forehead, and said, "Repent and believe the good news of Jesus."

When I stepped outside into the sunlight, everything had changed. From now on, I would be a follower of Jesus.

The Journey Begins
(1980–81)

For the next six months, everything sparkled. It was as if I had been blind and then miraculously gained sight. I noticed colors for the first time. The flowers in the Duke gardens, the green grass, the blue sky, the clouds, the sun and moon—it was as if I had never seen them before. I walked in a daze, delighted at the beauty around me, grateful to be alive, and overwhelmed by the consolation, the peace and joy I now felt.

I told no one but Father Burke, deciding to keep quiet for a while, perhaps even a year. My decision to become a Jesuit had come about suddenly, and I thought it should be put to the test. If it came from God, it would happen; otherwise, it would evaporate. Deep down, though, I knew my path was set. The anxieties that had plagued me for weeks had vanished, and I was left with this great secret. I read the Gospels and began attending daily Mass. During my occasional meetings with Father Burke, I gratefully accepted his encouragement, enthusiasm, and friendship.

My happiness crested at Easter. Joe Markwordt invited me to picnic with other Newman Center students in the Duke gardens. We sat on the grass, ate sandwiches, threw the Frisbee, told jokes, and said a few prayers; it couldn't have been plainer. But compared to the selfishness, arrogance, and violence of the fraternity, it was beautiful, refreshing, and even holy, as Easter should be. Father Burke was there, along with another student, Anne Mallory, a devout Catholic, smart and sincere, whose kindness and guidance would help me through the next years.

My elation over deciding to join the Jesuits elbowed aside everything else, even my love of music. And so, I shortly decided to stop composing and recording. But I had one more recording session scheduled and went ahead with it, knowing it would be my last. This time, I brought along a fraternity friend named Lou, a New Yorker studying to be a doctor, who played a mean drum solo.

We had a fabulous session, recording ten songs. Lou enjoyed himself so much that on the way home he practically glowed. I glowed, too, but for a different reason. During the long drive I just couldn't keep my secret any longer.

"Lou, from now on, I won't be doing any more recording. I've decided to become a priest."

"You've decided to become a what?"

"A Jesuit priest."

"You're kidding me."

"No, I'm not. About a month ago, I—"

"What a waste!" His anger startled me. "You are so talented, and now you're throwing it all away." He smoldered the whole way home. He got out of the car, slammed the door, and never spoke to me again.

回 回

That was my first taste of what my decision would cost me. Giving my life away to Jesus was bound to anger some people. Plus, there were the personal sacrifices: I would not get to do some of the things I enjoyed. I would never marry, never know intimate love, never have my own family, never pursue my own interests, never do things for my own sake. From now on, there would be no music, no riches, no success. I would pray, follow Jesus, and spend my life serving the human family.

On March 24, 1980, I heard the news that the outspoken archbishop of San Salvador, Óscar Romero, had been assassinated, fatally shot while presiding at Mass. I was devastated and yet strangely inspired. Here was another public disciple of Jesus who had walked with the poor and defended them and been killed, like Jesus, Martin Luther King Jr., and Bobby Kennedy, like the early saints and martyrs. Romero's martyrdom evoked in me a desire to risk my life for the gospel of Jesus.

During the previous weeks I had written to the Jesuits, and the vocation director sent me a package of official materials about the Society of Jesus. What I read caught my interest immediately and summed up my deepest desires and hopes. The statements of the Thirty-second General Congregation of the Society, the 1974–75 international gathering of Jesuit leaders from around the world, described the Jesuit mission as solidarity with the world's poor, discipleship to the crucified Jesus, and "faith that does justice."

> What is it to be a Jesuit? It is to know that one is a sinner, yet called to be a companion of Jesus as Ignatius was: Ignatius, who begged the Blessed Virgin "to place him with her Son," who then saw the Father himself ask Jesus, carrying his cross, to take this pilgrim into his company. What is it to be a companion of Jesus today? It is to engage, under the standard of the cross, in the crucial struggle of our time: the struggle for

faith and that struggle for justice which it includes. . . . We seek to preach the Gospel in a personal love for the person of Jesus Christ, asking daily for an ever more inward knowledge of him, that we may better love him and follow him; Jesus whom we seek, as St. Ignatius sought, to experience; Jesus, Son of God, sent to serve, sent to set free, put to death, and risen from the dead. This love is the deepest wellspring of our action and our life.

Those words confirmed my decision to become a "companion of Jesus."

▣ ▣

That summer turned out to be one of the most creative times of my life, though none of the creativity was visible. I looked for a menial job and found one as a janitor at a nearby Arby's fast-food restaurant. I wanted work that went against everything Duke stood for—riches, success, comfort, and fame. It was a humbling experience, and in that humility I discovered a new inner freedom and compassion.

When I wasn't at work, I read. I absorbed everything: the four Gospels, the lives of the saints, and biographies of Thomas Merton, Dorothy Day, and Franz Jägerstätter, the Austrian Catholic farmer who was beheaded for refusing to fight for the Nazis. The autobiography of Thérèse of Lisieux touched me powerfully, inviting me deeper into the life of contemplative prayer, suffering love, and inner trust in God. I felt close to her, asked for her intercession, and prayed to her every day.

I tried to practice Thérèse's "little way" of self-denial, unconditional love, and selfless service toward those around me. That meant first of all trying to be kinder, more loving, and more generous toward my parents and brothers. For starters, I would help out around the house. I cleaned up, did my chores, mowed the lawn, even cooked an occasional dinner. At the same time, I tried not to do everything I wanted to do; rather, I tried to do what others needed of me. This was a difficult experiment. I expected a great deal of pain and stress, but afterward I felt inner peace, even joy. I began to understand the spiritual life. Through selfless service, loving-kindness, and genuine generosity, one could experience God's love. God gives an inner sense of consolation and peace to encourage the good choices we make and the good deeds we do.

That summer, knowing of my admiration for Bobby Kennedy, my father arranged for me to meet his friend Warren Rogers, who had also been one of Kennedy's closest friends. As a journalist for *Life* magazine, he had covered Bobby Kennedy's campaign, and he was with Kennedy when he was shot. Rogers now worked on the board of the National Press Club with my father.

I drove to Georgetown and spent an afternoon with Rogers. I learned that long ago, he had entered the Jesuit novitiate in Wernersville, Pennsylvania. I described to him the effect that Bobby Kennedy's death had had on me, my struggle to locate meaning, and my questions about God. He in turn regaled me with Kennedy stories and told me of his time at the novitiate before leaving to become a journalist. Here was a new friend, someone who shared my passion and my struggle.

As summer neared its end, I spent a week on Cape Cod with my parents and one of my brothers. It was magnificent—the salty breezes, the boat, the beautiful ponds, the blue ocean, the lobster bisque. Our last day, on the island of Nantucket, was magical. And so that night, emboldened by the good feeling, I took a deep breath and divulged my secret. I told my parents I had decided to enter the Jesuits.

Their faces fell, and they exchanged uneasy glances. They didn't want to hear this. It was especially hard for my mother, for reasons dear to her heart. Her two brothers had left home as teenagers to enter the Vincentians and become priests. But they left the priesthood twenty years later, much disillusioned and disappointed, and my mother didn't want to see that happen to me. She pleaded with me to wait a few years before entering.

I hadn't anticipated this, but I chose to honor their concerns. I told them I would wait a year after graduation before entering the Jesuits.

I returned to Duke chastened and disheartened. It felt bad to step back from a decision that seemed so right. But then I learned about the Jesuit Volunteer Corps, a service program that sends young people to work for a year among the poor and to live in community under the supervision of local Jesuits. Volunteering seemed like a good way to stick close to the Jesuits and fill out that idle year, so I applied.

回 回

I would spend my senior year taking classes, bringing communion to the dying at the Duke Medical Center, and continuing the application process to the Jesuits.

Some of my classes that year sharpened and informed the convictions I was already committed to living out. The Insurgent South was taught by one of the most popular and controversial professors on campus, the leading historian on the subject, Lawrence Goodwyn. He accepted only twenty students at a time; I'd been on the waiting list for over a year. On the first day of class, he gathered us around a large wooden table and sat there silently until we became quiet. We expected a welcome, but instead he started off with "You are all racists.

Each one of you is a product of institutionalized racism." Here was a professor who dared speak the truth even to the point of criticizing the privilege of the students on whom his livelihood depended. My education was under way.

For the next four months, Goodwyn taught us the history of slavery, the abolitionist movement, Reconstruction, the Populist movement, segregation in America, and the civil rights movement embodied in the life of Martin Luther King Jr. Each class disturbed, exhilarated, and mesmerized me. He explained history to us in ways none of us had ever heard, making connections between the social reformers and injustices of the late 1800s and the present-day struggles for racial and economic justice. I gained a new vision of equality and justice as well as a new understanding of the inequalities and injustices around me. This provocative class opened my mind to humanity's yearning for civil and human rights and laid the groundwork for my commitment to Dr. King's active nonviolence.

That course led to another, the following semester, with Professor William Chafe, one of the foremost historians of the civil rights movement and its strategy of nonviolence. Nonviolence, he taught, operates by a power all its own. It insists on making the truth known and on suffering the consequences with love. And, he said, it never fails. In the end, steadfast, organized suffering love will melt opponents' hearts, inspire mutual respect, and create social justice. Nonviolence alone has the power to confront institutionalized injustice, disarm our violence, and redeem everyone—the oppressor as well as the oppressed.

Consider the Birmingham campaign of 1963, Dr. Chafe said one memorable day. Dr. King led a protest to combat segregation that grew to include hundreds of children and teenagers. They were attacked with fire hoses and police dogs, all of it caught on film and shown on television. The nation was shocked by the sheer brutality of the white authorities. Then one climactic day, the policemen balked and the firemen dramatically refused to turn the water on the marching youth. Scales fell from their eyes, they realized the immorality of their violence, and they disobeyed orders. That very occasion, Dr. Chafe said, marked the end of legalized segregation.

I remember the moment that spring day, sitting in the classroom, when I looked up from my notes and suddenly understood the methodology of nonviolence. Suffering love for the sake of the truth of our common humanity disarms and redeems, Dr. Chafe explained. In their willingness to suffer with love, insist on the truth, yet refuse to run away or retaliate, the nonviolent resisters melt the hearts of their opponents. Scales fall from their eyes, they stop their violence, they recognize new sisters and brothers, and are converted to justice and peace. A light went on as Dr. Chafe explained this new way of acting in the world, and I felt a surge of promise and hope. Here was another revelation.

▣ ▣

On November 29, 1980, Dorothy Day died. She stood head and shoulders above every North American Catholic of the century, living among the homeless and fearlessly, faithfully denouncing every war and injustice no matter what others thought, no matter what the cost. I had hoped to meet her. Now I felt compelled to take up where she had left off. On December 8, John Lennon was assassinated. That same week, four churchwomen—Ita Ford, Maura Clarke, Dorothy Kazel, and Jean Donovan—were raped and assassinated in El Salvador.

Day's peaceful death moved me, and I cried at the news of John Lennon, not just because of the loss of music and joy he had brought to the world but because of the loss of his outspoken stand for truth, justice, and peace.

But the deaths of the four churchwomen brought me face-to-face with the gravity of my call. When I picked up the *Durham Morning Herald* the next day, I gaped at the headline. The women died at the hands of El Salvador's National Guard, a militia trained and funded by the United States. Their bodies were discovered beside a dirt road in a makeshift grave about an hour and a half from the airport. Ita, Maura, Dorothy, and Jean—theirs was a sobering witness. They had persisted in their work despite the mounting danger they faced, and I recognized them immediately as heroes. Their courageous lives and sacrificial deaths further energized my plans to enter the Jesuit life.

回 回

I had accepted the invitation of Father Ralph Monk, the Catholic chaplain at the Duke Medical Center, to spend a few hours every afternoon visiting patients, bringing them communion, listening to their stories, and praying for their healing. .

Through that work, I met scores of sick people, some of whom had flown across the country for Duke's chemotherapy program. Father Monk would give me a list of Catholic patients, and I would knock on their hospital room doors and introduce myself. I offered to sit with them and give them communion. Everyone wanted communion. And most were desperate for friendship, company, and prayer. Over time, I developed relationships with many of the patients, some of them still memorable to me. One young man had attempted suicide by shooting himself in the face. Somehow, he survived, but his face was gone: no nose, no chin, no teeth, no cheekbones. He breathed through a network of tubes. I especially remember the born-again

Catholic thrown into doubt and confusion after open-heart surgery, and a young Rhodes Scholar from Australia who was on vacation in North Carolina with his parents when he was badly injured in a car crash and spent three painful months in a body cast.

Then my visits became more personal. One day, I was shocked to see Mary Lou Williams on my list; she had been diagnosed with cancer. For the next eight months, as she endured chemotherapy treatments and various setbacks, I visited her, prayed with her, sought her advice, and let her entertain me with the story of her life. She told me about her Harlem clothing center, her great friends Billie Holiday and Dizzy Gillespie, and her prayer life. She said that during the 1950s, various saints had appeared to her daily in mystical visions. I just listened and nodded as she told me, for example, about St. Martin de Porres standing at the foot of her bed one morning. After a while, she went to see her priest, a Jesuit, and told him about the visions. He told her that it was all fine and good, but she should tell the saints to stop bothering her so she could get back to her music and start serving people. She did not understand his guidance—nor did I!—but she accepted it, told the saints not to appear to her anymore, and returned to composing, recording, and performing jazz as a ministry in the church.

One day, she leaned across her hospital bed and whispered to me, "The secret of life is to love everyone." I went home and wrote that down. Eventually, she grew too weak to have visitors, and she died in May 1981, a week after my graduation from Duke.

Through all of this, I continued to explore my call to the Jesuits and the priesthood. In January 1981, I drove to the village of Wernersville, Pennsylvania, about ten miles west of Reading. A handful of Jesuit candidates gathered for the weekend for conferences and prayer.

I had lunch with Harry Geib, another Jesuit candidate, and Walter Ciszek, a legendary priest who had spent many years in Soviet prison camps. A few years after his death, proceedings began for his canonization. As it turned out, Harry hailed from Philadelphia and was attending Duke as a doctoral student. We spent time together back at Duke, he entered the Jesuits that summer, and we remain close friends today.

The Jesuits welcomed us and invited us to spend a few hours each day in silent prayer to reflect on the call we had received. I sat alone in the novitiate chapel, a simple room on the second floor with windows overlooking the green countryside. Behind the altar was a four-hundred-year-old crucifix that portrayed Christ dying in agony. The Jesuits told us to meditate on a verse from the Psalms: "Be still and know that I am God." I sat there in the silence, and slowly the silt within me began to settle, and my soul became clear and peaceful as a pool of clear water. I offered myself to God and felt my decision confirmed by a sense of profound peace.

As I wandered through the old library, I noticed a book titled *The Voice of Blood*, which told the story of five Jesuits recently martyred in Latin America and Africa. Their heroic deaths, particularly that of the extraordinary Salvadoran Jesuit Rutilio Grande, shocked and inspired me. He had dedicated his life to the poor, denounced the injustice that oppressed them, and died on March 12, 1977, at the hands of a United States–backed death squad. It was Grande's example that inspired Archbishop Romero to speak out for peace and justice. Such stories increased my desire to take up the cross for the gospel. I returned to Duke more determined than ever to enter the Society of Jesus.

Under Arrest
at the Vatican
(1981)

After graduation in May 1981, I learned I had been accepted into the Jesuit Volunteer Corps. But first I toured Europe with four of my fraternity friends. We flew out on May 14—the day after Pope John Paul II was shot in Rome, as it happened. In Europe, we traveled by bus and rail to England, France, Germany, Austria, Switzerland, Italy, and Ireland.

In Germany, we walked somberly through the Dachau extermination camp. I was astonished to find it surrounded by a beautiful middle-class suburb not unlike Bethesda. The town had changed little since the 1940s, said the guide, and I bristled at the thought of the neighbors pretending among themselves that they didn't know what was going on. In France, after touring the wine country and exploring every corner of Paris, I took a train by myself to Lisieux to pray at the tomb of St. Thérèse. Eventually, my friends and I settled down for a week in Rome, where I visited every church I found.

During one of our outings in Rome, we toured the Vatican art museums. Afterward, over lunch at a nearby café, Digger said that he wanted to see St. Peter's Basilica one more time so he could pray at the tomb of Pope John XXIII. I offered to go with him. Along the way, I noticed a sign in the Piazza del Sant'Uffizio pointing to the entrance of the underground "Tombs of the Popes." We followed the signs and wended our way along the basilica's south wall, past the Palace of the Canonicate, and through a parking lot studded with black limousines. Digger felt sure the entrance would turn up at any moment, so we kept on, our heads tilted up in awe at the basilica's sheer magnitude and grandeur. Few guards were around; most had been dispatched to the hospital across town where Pope John Paul II was recovering.

Plodding ahead, we suddenly found ourselves in a beautiful garden, with green lawns, sculpted hedges, flowers in every color, the ivied remains of medieval walls, and, just ahead, the pope's private chapel. We had roamed into the pope's private garden. When we turned around, we were overwhelmed to see the back side of St. Peter's towering over us. We could see no windows or doors on the side of the enormous building that we were facing, only the massive old brick wall that seemed to go straight up to heaven.

Digger and I sized up our situation. We were scared out of our wits: eerily alone, on sacred ground, and trespassing to boot—and so soon after the attempt on the pope's life. Just then we noticed a small weathered door in the center of the basilica wall, and, glancing at each other, we made a dash for it, hoping to escape before someone caught us in the garden.

Once inside the door, we found ourselves in a long, dark tunnel in the basement of St. Peter's. Up ahead was a white light, and we started toward it, our hearts pumping. As we picked up the pace, our scuffling feet produced a cloud of white dust. When I looked down, I could see the names of ancient popes chiseled into the stone. Digger and I were treading on papal tombs.

What should we do? We kept going forward, toward a bank of bright lights aimed right at us. As our eyes adjusted, we began to discern heavy shadows, then silhouettes. Then the silhouettes turned into tourists, hundreds of them staring right back at us in disbelief. And then I saw the red velvet cordon—we were behind it—and, right next to us, the stately white stone tomb of the recently deceased Pope John Paul I.

Immediately, the Vatican police appeared and grabbed us. They took us off to a side room, informed us that we were under arrest, and started to interrogate us. They pressed us again and again: "What were you doing there? The basement of St. Peter's is strictly off-limits. Who are you?" Digger could scarcely get out a word. I figured our only hope was to act like the dumb American kids we were. I stammered out our story as best I could: we were looking for the tombs of the popes . . . followed the sign . . . simply got lost . . . ended up in the garden . . . and found ourselves here. "We meant no harm. We're just stupid Americans." The truth worked. Thirty minutes later they let us go.

Arrested at St. Peter's in the Vatican—it was quite a mark on the record of a candidate for the priesthood. But I was young; it would get better. The seventy-five arrests for civil disobedience against war and nuclear weapons—at the White House; the Pentagon; the U.S. Capitol; the U.S. Naval Submarine Base in Groton, Connecticut; the Strategic Air Command base; the Nevada Test Site; Lawrence Livermore National Laboratory; Concord Naval Weapons Station; the U.S. Mission to the United Nations; and Seymour Johnson Air Force Base—would just have to wait.

▣ ▣

I returned home a few days after my arrest at the Vatican and learned that the Jesuit Volunteer Corps had lost my application, and by now most placements had been made. Warren Rogers recommended me to the Robert F. Kennedy Memorial, a small organization set up by the Kennedy family to promote Bobby Kennedy's vision. Its director was Kennedy's childhood friend David Hackett, who was the model for the main character in the popular novel *A Separate Peace*. During John F. Kennedy's administration, Hackett served in the Justice Department, and he later helped with Bobby Kennedy's presidential campaign.

So in September 1981, I drove to the small townhouse behind the Martin Luther King Memorial Library that served as the Kennedy Memorial's offices to meet David Hackett. Campaign memorabilia and pictures of Bobby Kennedy covered the walls.

We shook hands and sat down, and then he asked me point-blank, "Well, are you a do-gooder?" I wasn't sure what he meant, so I took a gamble and said yes. Then I told him about my volunteer work among the poor, the disabled, and the "criminally insane," recounted my interest in the life of Bobby Kennedy and the civil rights movement, and stated my desire to serve. After a short interview, he offered me a position as his assistant. I would write press releases, make contacts around the D.C. area, and promote the organization's monthly journal, *Youth Policy*. The salary was fifty dollars a week.

David Hackett was passionate, challenging, and tireless, the most committed, dedicated person I had met. He showed great respect for everyone and never stopped thinking about improving life for others, especially minorities, the poor, and young people. He embodied civic responsibility. I could see why Bobby Kennedy had been so taken with him.

My first day in the office, I hung Kennedy's words from a speech in South Africa on the wall over my desk:

Each time a person stands up for an ideal, or acts to improve the lot of others, or strikes out against injustice, he sends forth a tiny ripple of hope, and crossing each other from a million different centers of energy and daring, these ripples build a current that can sweep down the mightiest walls of oppression and resistance.

Over the next few months, on behalf of the memorial, I visited almost every government office in D.C. I solicited their help, gathered the latest legislative updates, and kept Hackett's contact list up to date. I walked the halls of Congress, the Justice Department, the Treasury Department, and the Department of Health and Human Services. As I traveled the streets and walked those hallways, I thought about the Gospel, became appalled by our government's bureaucracy, and tried to understand this institution. Everything seemed so far from Jesus of Nazareth, who came to serve and heal, not to dominate or oppress.

To detox from so much exposure to government institutions, I volunteered to serve meals at a soup kitchen in the city called SOME (So Others Might Eat). The organization had been founded by the Jesuit Horace McKenna, whom the media had labeled "Washington's saint." He had fought racism and the Klan in southern Maryland, supported various shelters and soup kitchens in D.C., and in the process inspired every "do-gooder" in the nation's capital.

By the end of the year, I decided, despite David Hackett's inspiring dedication, that I didn't want to spend my last few months before entering the Jesuit novitiate stalking the halls of power. I had thought long and hard about how to spend those remaining months, and I realized that if I was going to spend my life following Jesus of Nazareth, I should go and see where he had lived. So I made arrangements to travel to Israel. St. Ignatius and St. Francis had made similar pilgrimages; shouldn't I do the same? I said good-bye to David Hackett and prepared for Israel.

During Holy Week of 1982, I received my long-awaited letter. The Jesuits had accepted me into the Society of Jesus. The letter was short and to the point: Report to Wernersville, Pennsylvania in August. In the meantime, I bought a ticket to Israel and devoured as many books as I could get my hands on—on the Jesuits and their saints, the Gospels and Jesus, and Óscar Romero, Horace McKenna, and Dorothy Day, as well as tour books on the Middle East.

In June, I said good-bye to my parents and took the train to New York City. I left Penn Station, threaded my way through the crowds, and headed around the corner to St. Francis of Assisi Church. Inside, I knelt and prayed for blessings on my journey, my family, and my life ahead with the Jesuits. Then I summoned my little courage and hailed a cab to JFK Airport.

Pilgrimage to the
Holy Land
(1982)

The plane sailed quietly through the night. Peering into the dark, I could see only my reflection in the window. Everyone had told me I was crazy to be making this trip. The tourist traps had ruined the place, they said. Trouble lay hidden around every corner; I'd be liable to get blown up on a bus. The week before I left, Israel invaded Lebanon. But I was determined to make the trip.

All looked well from the air—enchanted Greece, the calm blue waters of the Mediterranean—and then Tel Aviv appeared in the distance, long and narrow, on the edge of the sparkling sea. As we came down, I looked out the window and saw the tarmac—and the regions beyond—dotted with tanks and with soldiers toting machine guns. We were not touching down in the land of shalom. We had landed in a war zone.

The Israelis were in full battle mode. In February, Israel's Major General Yehoshua Saguy had met with Pentagon officials to get approval for invading Lebanon. The United States not only approved but also funded and participated in the action, handing over more than two million dollars' worth of weapons and equipment. The Pentagon manipulated the docile U.S. media with a canard sure to foment support for the invasion, that the Soviet Union supplied bombs to the Lebanese branch of the Palestine Liberation Organization.

On June 5, 1982, under Defense Minister Ariel Sharon, Israel invaded southern Lebanon and then launched a massive land, sea, and air offensive. President Reagan ordered the USS *New Jersey* into the Mediterranean, where it lofted shells into southern Lebanon. The war lasted sixty-seven days and caused the deaths of some thirty thousand Lebanese civilians. Beirut was destroyed, a third of Lebanon was occupied, and more than a half-million Lebanese were driven from their homes. A thousand civilians—women, children, and old men—died taking shelter in the Sabra and Shatila Palestinian refugee camps. On the other side, 1,216 Israeli soldiers and 300 U.S. marines died. Israel came up with a beautiful name for this massacre to make it more palatable for the public: Operation Peace for Galilee.

My little pilgrimage became my own Operation Peace for Galilee. As I stepped off the plane, a soldier pointed his gun at me while others studied me closely. A few tense seconds later he waved me on. *Dear God*, I had prayed during the flight, my Bible open, *keep me safe. Help me on my journey. Bless my pilgrimage.* Now I thought, *What in the world am I doing here? What sort of Holy Land is this? Everyone carries a gun.* My tour book, *Let's Go Israel*, had painted a far rosier picture.

I took a bus to Youth Hostel Yoseph on Bograshov Street and caught a bus to Jerusalem the next morning. From the bus, I watched the beautiful desert landscape pass by, its slopes dotted with olive groves. I now felt exhilarated: Jesus saw this land. He knew these desert hills. He walked these dusty roads. He taught in this place, and I knew he had something to teach me. Filled with consolation,

I resolved to listen. Despite the military presence everywhere, I was determined to stay focused on my pilgrimage.

In Jerusalem, I switched buses and made my way into the modern section. I walked through the Jaffa Gate, the main entrance of the Old City, still surrounded by an ancient stone wall, and explored the narrow stone streets and breathed in the smells of exotic spices on sale everywhere I looked. I had never before experienced such intense aromas. Booths and tiny shops crowded every spare corner and overflowed with carpets, clothing, trinkets, and food. Overhead, stone arches linked the narrow street walls. The men wore head cloths. Some rode donkeys. Many of the women wore traditional black garments, while others wore modern Western apparel. Children ran through the streets. Stray cats prowled underfoot.

I followed my map into the Christian quarter, to the Armenian Catholic Church Youth Hostel, at the third station of the Via Dolorosa, the Way of the Cross. I checked into a small room for five dollars a night. Back down on the Via Dolorosa, I made my way to my first destination, the Church of the Holy Sepulchre, where historians say Jesus was crucified and buried. This old, ugly church has been fought over by every Christian denomination from the earliest centuries of Christianity, through the Crusades, and until now has been reconstructed many times. The interior was dark and damp, with candle lamps hanging from the ceiling and dirty icons covering the walls. Pilgrims crowded together, taking pictures and speaking quietly. But I found it hard to feel prayerful in such a cluttered mess. Like Palestine in miniature, the church was controlled by competing groups, and competing traditions vied for the tourists' attention.

I found it harder still to imagine the place as Golgotha, Calvary— the place where Jesus reconciled humanity with God through his perfect, nonviolent, forgiving, suffering love. Still, the Old City of

Jerusalem wasn't large and Jesus surely died, if not here, then in this vicinity. And I wanted just to be near it. I stood quietly in the church, thinking, *This is holy ground*. But the crassness, the crowds, and the bickering were ultimately too much for me to bear. I left quickly and walked out into the busy narrow streets.

I made my way through the Old City to the Wailing Wall, the remnant of Herod's temple, and watched the men bow and pray and insert their messages in the cracks between the massive stones. I wrote my own intentions on a scrap of paper and jammed it into a crack. I knew this was a solemn, holy place, and I was focused on the life that I was beginning, so I prayed that God would bless me, use me, and help me follow Jesus. I wrote down the names of each member of my family and asked for blessings upon them and the whole human race. Then I visited the Church of the Redeemer and, finally, the Ecce Homo Convent, where ancient stone slabs bear emblems of the Roman procurator. Tradition holds that Jesus was sentenced to death at the Ecce Homo Arch. I stood there trying to imagine facing the Roman Empire, as Jesus did, helpless yet determined to confront imperial might with the power of humble love, with the truth of one's own vulnerable presence. Afterward, at Uncle Moustache's, my new hangout, I bought a pita packed with vegetables, meat, potatoes, and exotic spices. That night, my first in Jerusalem, I gave thanks to God for bringing me safe thus far.

For the next week, I walked twelve hours a day through the Old City, crisscrossing every street, visiting every shrine, taking it all in. Those were quiet days of prayerful reflection on the life and death of Jesus. In the morning, I attended Mass at the Jesuit house next to the Hotel David. In the afternoon, I returned to the Church of the Holy Sepulchre, trying to grasp the reality of Calvary. I was beginning to break through the dirt, the smoke, the crowds, and the religious authorities to ponder the paschal mystery. Jesus had practiced perfect love, boundless compassion, and infinite mercy, spending his days healing the sick, teaching the crowds, and making peace. Yet he was tortured and executed, and I was planning to spend my life following him. I was overwhelmed by the prospect.

In modern Jerusalem, I rode the buses, shopped in the stores, and listened to the Hebrew being spoken on the streets. I toured the Cenacle, which commemorates the Last Supper; the ruined Pool of Solomon; the Pool of Bethesda; the Golden Gate; the Mount of Olives; the Basilica of the Agony; the place of the Ascension; the Church of the Pater Noster; and the Church of St. Anne, commemorating the place of Mary's birth.

At the Grotto of Gethsemane, I studied the mammoth, ancient olive trees with their twisted, knotted trunks. At Dominus Flevit, a chapel on the Mount of Olives that memorializes Jesus' weeping over Jerusalem, I sat for hours, looking through the large window behind the altar at the panoramic view of the city and the Dome of the Rock, the brilliant gold symbol of Jerusalem, rising above the old walls. I explored the Kidron Valley, Zechariah's Tomb, Dormition Abbey, and the Russian Orthodox Church of Mary Magdalene. Outside the city, I prayed among the roses at the Garden Tomb, identified in the late 1800s as the possible site of the Resurrection. "Yes, Jesus," I prayed. "You are risen. You are my Savior. You are my peace." Slowly, I was getting to know him, building a relationship with him, feeling confident in becoming his disciple.

After Jerusalem, I set out for Jericho. I boarded a crowded bus that raced out of Jerusalem along a two-lane highway through the desert hills. Let off at the main stop, I walked the two miles to the ruins of Jericho. From there, I walked several more miles and climbed the Mount of Temptation to visit the Greek Orthodox monastery, a stark place built in 325 that overlooks hundreds of miles of desert into Jordan. Six monks lived in solitude at the monastery. One of them, a frail elderly man with a long gray beard and wearing a long gray robe, greeted me. He told me that in 1920, at age sixteen, he left Greece to visit Israel as a pilgrim. When he arrived at this monastery, the life here so moved him that he decided to stay for a few weeks of prayer— and he never left. The monks lived a disciplined, spartan life. They drank only rainwater, he said, and it hadn't rained for a month. They kept a simple vegetarian diet, spent many days fasting, and prayed through the psalms all day long. I sat in silence with him, looking out toward Jordan. His cloistered mountain life sobered me. I wondered if I could ever live in the desert, if I could be as dedicated to Jesus as this holy man was, if I could renounce the world and seek God through such steadfast contemplative prayer.

I had to take two taxis to reach Bethany, near the southeastern corner of Jerusalem, where I visited the Tomb of Lazarus and the Church of St. Lazarus. The next day, I journeyed to Ein Kerem to pray in the Catholic Church of St. John the Baptist and the Church of the Visitation. Back in Jerusalem on Friday, I joined the weekly stations of the cross led by twenty Franciscans. Along with more than four hundred people, I walked along the Via Dolorosa and partici-pated in the concluding candlelight vigil at the Church of the Holy Sepulchre. There was no mention of the war in Lebanon, and it was far from my mind. I was focused on the long-ago life, suffering, and death of Jesus, not the present-day suffering and death of Christ in the Palestinian and Lebanese peoples just a few miles away.

On Sunday morning, I took bus 22 into Palestinian territory to visit Bethlehem. At Manger Square, I ducked through the narrow entrance in the high stone wall of the Church of the Nativity and climbed down into the crypt to see the silver star commemorating the birth of Christ. Dark oriental rugs covered the walls and ornate silver lanterns hung from the soot-covered ceiling.

After Mass there, I headed out through the fields and up a hill to Shepherds' Field, where I discovered a small Franciscan chapel. There I pondered the message of the angels long ago: "Glory to God in the highest and peace on earth to those of good will." I was lonely by now, with twinges of fear, sitting alone in the Middle East. I tried to grasp the mystery of the Incarnation but once again could only sit with the mystery. And I began to feel a new peace, even a sense of Christmas joy. I was alive, knowing that the God of life cares about me and the human race. This big God even came to share our journey, starting right here in these hills. *That's good enough for me*, I thought as I headed back.

After a trip to Masada, the mountain fortress where Jews are believed to have committed mass suicide as the Roman army launched an invasion, and a short dip in the Dead Sea, I took the bus north to Nazareth, in time for Mass in the grotto of the Basilica of the Annunciation, which overshadows the small, crowded, unprepossessing town. All the guidebooks warned that it was decidedly nondescript. I found it dirty, noisy, monotonous, without any distinctive charm or beauty. But it was holy ground. I studied the hill by the edge of the city. Perhaps the crowds who hated Jesus' first sermon had dragged him there to throw him off. I stayed the night, walked the streets, and breathed it all in. The next morning, I toured Cana in time for morning Mass at the Church of the Wedding and afterward made the six-mile trek along the dusty road to Nazareth. Knowing that Jesus had walked these hills gave me rich consolation.

I rode past Nain to Mount Tabor, which tradition identifies as the place of the Transfiguration. The bus let me off at the base, and I spent the morning climbing through grass, rocks, and trees until I reached the enormous Basilica of the Transfiguration at the top. The front doors were wide open, but no one was inside. I was alone on the mountaintop. I sat and pondered the words of God from the cloud to the frightened disciples standing before the transfigured Jesus: "This is my beloved. Listen to him!" God rarely appears like this in the scriptures. God does not reprimand them, punish them, or threaten them, but invites them to take the words of Jesus to heart—to take them seriously, to make those teachings the center of their life. I prayed that I too might listen to Jesus and obey his teachings. Then I walked among the ruins of an ancient Benedictine monastery in front of the basilica and sat for hours taking in the spectacular view of Galilee below me. There among those trees, in that silence, taking in the vista of fields, mountains, and sea, I felt tranquil. Perhaps this is what it felt like to be transfigured into the light of peace.

My trip was reaching its climax. More than anything else, I wanted to see the Sea of Galilee. This natural world of sea and hills would probably look just as it had two thousand years ago, and I would finally know something of Jesus' daily life. When I reached the place, the sun was setting behind me and made the water glint. Shielding my eyes, I could make out fishing boats bobbing on the water. The place was everything I had imagined. Bordering the sea were lush green hills and fields resplendent with yellow flowers, except on the far shore, opposite from where I stood. There rose stark desert hills, the Golan Heights, jarring my peace as I remembered newspaper reports of the ongoing violence somewhere out there. But near me, all was peace and beauty. Other than the men on the distant boats, not a living soul was around. I decided to camp right there, next to the large black rocks along the edge of the sea.

That night, I couldn't sleep. I lay there looking at the stars and staring at the deep blue of the sea. Moonlight seemed to dance on the water. I had never felt so consoled and peaceful. I thanked God for bringing me here, for the astonishing beauty, for this shared experience with Jesus. At five in the morning, I got up and took a swim in the cool water as a red sun rose before me. Jesus called the fishermen right here to become his disciples, taught the crowds from some boat along this shore, calmed the storm on this sea, walked on this water. When he rose from the dead, he met his disciples back here. He returned to this shore, built a fire, and made them breakfast. Now I knew this special place for myself. It was one of the holiest, most magical days of my life.

A Second Calling, in Galilee (1982)

The details of that next week are etched forever in my mind, each a memorable step along my pilgrimage to the Jesus of the Gospels. I swam in the Sea of Galilee, walked the coastline, traipsed through wheat fields, explored every nook and cranny, sat for hours under trees, and gazed at the big sky. No other tourists showed up, so I had the place to myself. For hours I sat on the black rocks, mesmerized by the beauty. I thought about Jesus; I read from the Gospels and prayed. I imagined the miraculous events of those times: Jesus healing the sick somewhere near here, giving sight to the blind, teaching in the synagogues, expelling the demons on "the other side" of the lake. I listened for his voice, his call, and prayed that I, too, might be a fisher of men and women.

At the ruins of Capernaum, I explored the Church of the Multiplication of the Loaves and Fishes and the Church of the Primacy of Peter. A young Franciscan archaeologist explained the excavation going on; they were sifting through the ruins and preparing to build a chapel over the spot where they believed the apostle Peter had lived.

They had discovered etchings on the stones beneath—an outline of a fish and the name Petros. Nearby stood a huge synagogue, hundreds of years old. Underneath that synagogue lay the ruins of the synagogue where Jesus likely preached.

One day, I came upon a group of Italian pilgrims sitting on the grass overlooking the sea and joined them for an outdoor Mass. Later, I took the bus to Tiberias and then south to the Jordan River. I was surprised at how small it was but delighted by the vivid green water and the eucalyptus trees towering over it. I went for a short swim, then toured the Kibbutz Dabanya and learned from several young Israelis about their farming work and life in community. I took the bus back past Capernaum to Vered Hagalil, where I spent an afternoon horseback riding on the hilltops overlooking the sea. I came upon the ruins of Chorazin, notorious as one of the cities cursed by Jesus in the Gospels. The day ended with another swim and a walk by the sea.

By now it was Wednesday, and my time in Galilee was drawing to a close. I would return the next day to Jerusalem and prepare for the long flight home. I hiked past the ruins of Capernaum, through the green fields, and up a steep hill to a stone church adorned with arches and columns. It was surrounded by palm trees, cacti, and shrubs and overlooked the sea. This was the Chapel of the Beatitudes. I entered the sanctuary and marveled at the lofty dome rising high in the middle, the small altar underneath, and the colorful show of sunlight pouring in through the stained-glass windows. Each wall had a high square window inscribed with a beatitude. I stood there quietly and read them slowly:

Blessed are the poor in spirit,
> for theirs is the kingdom of heaven.
Blessed are they who mourn,
> for they will be comforted.

Blessed are the meek,

> for they will inherit the land.

Blessed are they who hunger and thirst for justice,

> for they will be satisfied.

Blessed are the merciful,

> for they will be shown mercy.

Blessed are the clean of heart,

> for they will see God.

Blessed are the peacemakers,

> for they will be called [the sons and daughters] of God.

Blessed are they who are persecuted for the sake of

> righteousness,

> for theirs is the kingdom of heaven.

As I looked at those words, I recalled other words from the Sermon on the Mount (Gospel of Matthew, chapters 5—8), which I had been reading all week as I sat by the shore: "Do not store up for yourselves treasures on earth, where moth and decay destroy. . . . But store up treasures in heaven." The passages paraded through my mind now with startling freshness. "Blessed are you when they insult you and persecute you and utter every kind of evil against you [falsely] because of me. Rejoice and be glad, for your reward will be great in heaven."

As these familiar words sank in, all the religiosity associated with them withered, and the generality of Jesus' lessons faded. Suddenly I heard the words as if addressed to me: "I say to *you*, love your enemies, and pray for those who persecute you, that you may be children of [God] for [God] makes the sun rise on the bad and the good, and causes rain to fall on the just and the unjust" and "Be compassionate as your [God] is compassionate." I could see in an instant that these statements were a summary of the gospel, the answer to every worldly ill, the most profound words ever uttered. I had found the pearl of great price.

And then, I suddenly realized, *Oh, my God! I think Jesus is serious!* My knees went rubbery, my jaw dropped, and my mouth went dry. I walked out onto the balcony to puzzle things over. I gazed at the panorama before me—the deepness of the sea, the mountains in the distance, the vivid green of the hills and the sky an improbable blue—all of it visible and real from where I stood. I folded my arms, then rubbed my forehead. *What does this mean? Is this what I'm called to be—actually and truly? Meek and mournful? Merciful and poor in spirit? To hunger for justice and make peace?* I had always considered such teachings to be intended for special people, holy people, religious people— priests, nuns, bishops, saints, and popes, or great heroes such as Dorothy Day, Dr. King, and Mahatma Gandhi. Yet here those very words were knocking on the door of my heart. *Am I supposed to seek justice, make peace, even love my enemies?*

By no means did the costly implications escape me. I wasn't sure I *wanted* to mourn. I had little interest in being reviled. I was certain I didn't want to be persecuted. I didn't want to do these things, but I knew now that they were God's way. After some moments' pondering, I thought of a loophole. I would agree to pursue the Beatitudes if God gave me a sign. I didn't expect to get a sign, and would therefore be off the hook.

"Okay, God," I called out to the blue sky, "I promise to live out your Beatitudes—to hunger and thirst for justice, to work for peace, to love my enemies, to practice the Sermon on the Mount for the rest of my life, on one condition: if you give me a sign!" And to lend an air of sincerity to the proclamation, I brought my fist down hard on the balcony railing.

At that moment, a deafening roar split the air. I jumped back, ducked, and scanned the horizon in the direction of the thunder. Then I saw them—two Israeli fighter jets falling out of the blue, rocketing across the sea mere yards above the water, breaking the sound barrier and setting off sonic booms—and heading right toward me. I thought they might fly into the balcony where I crouched, but at the last instant they pulled up and blasted over the chapel. Then they vanished, leaving behind nothing but echoes. It happened in seconds. Moments later, I heard faint explosions, the sound of the jets dropping their bombs in Lebanon, just fifteen miles north.

I stood up trembling and looked into the sky and said with all due respect, "Okay, God, I promise here and now to dedicate the rest of my life to living your Beatitudes. I'll hunger and thirst for justice and love my enemies. For the rest of my life I'll work for peace and the end of war." And I thought, *I'll never ask for a sign again.*

My pledge was genuine, and once I said it out loud to myself and to the sky, everything changed. I knew that somehow God was behind this. I had embraced God's message. In fact, I had just received and accepted a second vocation, a vocation within a vocation. I would not only spend my life serving as a Jesuit, but I would also live out the Beatitudes and teach the lessons of the Sermon on the Mount. I would go forth from the Sea of Galilee forever opposing injustice, poverty, and war. I would make it my lifelong mission to take risks for justice and peace.

Everything I have done as a Jesuit stems from that afternoon by the sea.

The next day, I went north to Qiryat Shemona, a town on the Israeli-Lebanese border. I hid along a wall and watched the Israeli army in action. Soldiers scurried everywhere while enormous beige tanks and armed vehicles roared by into Lebanon. It was a scene right out of any war movie, but this was real. This was what the enterprise of killing looked like. For the first time, my eyes were opened to the reality of the Holy Land, indeed of the whole world: mass murder, the killing of other human beings, even in the name of the God of peace.

Everything I witnessed in that terrible place contradicted the divine wisdom on the chapel walls by the Sea of Galilee. My vocation seemed more daunting than ever, and yet it addressed the greatest need facing the world. I returned to the chapel one last time and offered a prayer: "Somehow, some way, may I live these Beatitudes and be a peacemaker, a true disciple of Jesus."

After a few more days in Jerusalem, I flew home to spend a week on vacation with my family, then set off for Wernersville, Pennsylvania, where I would join the Jesuits and begin my vocation.

Jesuit Boot Camp (1982)

Entrance day, August 18, 1982. My father drove me to Reading, Pennsylvania, and from there, west to the hamlet of Wernersville, where we turned right on Church Road and drove up the hill to the grandiose wrought-iron gates of the Jesuit novitiate.

Wernersville, as we novices called the novitiate itself, sits on a 250-acre estate of woods, ponds, wheat fields, cow pastures, lush rolling hills, and the occasional shrine to a Jesuit saint. It looms ponderously over the countryside like some great Titanic stalled at sea. Founded in 1930 by the wealthy New York business mogul Nicholas Brady, the complex in its heyday housed hundreds of novices. Brady and his wife, Genevieve, spared no expense, building the place in the style of the English Renaissance, with marble porticoes, ceilings of carved-oak recessed panels, and, between buildings, long arched breezeways. Inside, priceless art, some of it donated by popes, adorned the walls. In the cloister gardens, white statuary stared expressionlessly at the fountains and the trimmed hedges and the blossoming trees.

It was all supposed to bespeak the heavenly kingdom. But it also bespoke Jesuit wealth, influence, and prestige. I've since decided that resources would be better spent on refugee camps and homeless shelters, and I think our founder, Ignatius, would agree. His bronze statue stands on the south lawn, quite by itself, perennially stepping forward, carrying no belongings but the staff in his right hand and his *Spiritual Exercises* in the left.

In the early years of the novitiate, long before I arrived, none of the hundreds of cubicles in the dormitories went unoccupied. The refectory produced an endless bounty of food, and, nearby, the dark stone chapel received the "long black line"—the single file of novices in their cassocks. They went to the chapel regularly for sermons, Mass, and prayer.

But the glory days are over. Numbers have fallen drastically. Thousands left the priesthood in the late 1960s and early '70s, and few have come to take their place. I arrived in 1982 with ten other novices. On hand to greet us were twelve second-year novices, along with six others who in three days would be professing their first vows.

Preparing novices for the perpetual vows—of poverty, chastity, and obedience—is the basis of the program, which is run like a boot camp, minus the guns and the barking of orders. The program's aim, in the words of early Jesuits, is to turn out foot soldiers to serve on the front lines of the church. That means long, rigorous schooling in the Jesuit ways of prayer, study, self-denial, passion, and mission.

Today, only a few men enter the Society each year in my province. The years, in fact, have seen such a drastic shrinking of numbers that some novitiates have closed and provinces are merging. None of this surprises me. But still I took the priestly route. I needed structure, a concrete way to follow Jesus. I needed access to a network that sought to serve Christ in the poor. I may have had illusions that the Jesuit path would provide certainty once and for all, but time has disabused me of that idea. I've since learned that, priestly status or not, the search for God—and the struggle to follow Jesus—never end. And

I learned that I need the Jesuit support and way of life to continue in that search and struggle.

When my father and I walked into the building on entrance day, my Duke friend Harry Geib greeted us and showed us to my simple quarters: two adjacent rooms, each about ten feet by five feet, joined by a doorway. In one room was a desk and a chair; in the other, a bed. Quite a contrast—this scanty cell amid measureless opulence. The chair was severe. The only adornment on the walls was a wooden cross, which hung over a narrow, thin bed that creaked. There was no air-conditioning, and the novices shared a bathroom. Still, I liked the simplicity. I could imagine myself holed up for years in my monastic cell, reading, writing, and meditating. As it turned out, it was good preparation for jail.

Later, Harry gave my father and me a tour of the palatial building, and as the four o'clock Mass was beginning, my mother arrived. I was a mixture of emotions: excited, scared, happy, sad, nervous, calm, terrified to be leaving my family, yet ready to embark on a great adventure, as had the saints and heroes of old. The chapel filled with Jesuits, novices, and our relatives. Father Jim Maier, the novice master, welcomed us and delivered a sermon—not to us, but to our parents. The whole point of the Society of Jesus, he said, is love. "Your sons are embarking on a journey in the footsteps of Jesus, and you'll know how well they're progressing if you find them becoming more loving. The vows should set them free, free to take risks for God and the world."

After communion, Father Jim invited those of us who were entering the order to stand before the congregation. "These are men of courage," he announced. "These men have left everything behind and taken a great risk, the risk of a lifelong, unconditional commitment to God, of radical discipleship to Jesus, of adherence to the gospel of love. They are very rare in this day and age." Everyone applauded. It was quite a welcome, and Father Jim's affirming words gave me courage.

The second-year novices served dinner out on the stone patio overlooking green hills and a setting sun. After dinner, the moment came to say good-bye to my parents. I was so glad to have them here with me as I began this new life. They were still confused about my decision but wanted me to be happy. They drove away, and I let go of the rope. My rowboat set out into deep waters.

回 回

That evening, Father Jim gathered the novices in the conference room for our first session. He welcomed us, and we introduced ourselves. He explained the schedule for the next few days, led us in prayer, and urged us to get a good night's sleep. He invited everyone who wanted to socialize for a while to assemble in the basement lounge, where snacks and drinks awaited us. We bade him good night and then headed downstairs.

The eleven of us, along with several of the second-year novices, sat down in a circle of couches and old wooden chairs. We fidgeted in awkward silence until finally someone asked, "Well, why did you enter?"

I don't know why, but all eyes turned toward me. Energized by the liturgy and excited to finally be a Jesuit, and still high from my experience in Israel and the call I'd received to live the Sermon on the Mount, I took a deep breath and said, "Well, I want to spend my life following Jesus, serving the poor, opposing war and injustice, working for peace and justice, being poor and simple like the saints and martyrs, and really giving my life to God."

"Oh my God!" said one of the other first-year novices. "I'm going to have to live with St. Francis over here!" He stood up, walked over to the bar, and poured himself a stiff drink. The whole group got up after him and walked away, leaving me alone in the empty circle.

It was a moment that foreshadowed the road ahead. After all these years, I still do not quite understand what the gospel of Jesus meant to my fellow novices—or to many others I've encountered since. Looking back now, I see it as a blessing that on my first night as a Jesuit, I tasted a bit of the rejection Jesus knew.

"Jesus, thank you for bringing me here," I wrote that night in a leather journal a friend had given me. "I love you with all my heart, all my mind, all my soul, and all my strength. Here I am; take me. Make me your faithful servant, your disciple, your companion, your friend." I went to bed happy, determined to befriend my classmates, set on serving the community, hoping to become a faithful Jesuit.

回 回

Since the earliest days, Jesuit novitiates were run like monasteries. That became a source of confusion to me later as I discovered that Jesuits are not supposed to be monks, but gentle revolutionaries taking on the world, calling it to conversion, and disarming and transforming it for the reign of God. But the novitiate did give us a firm grounding in prayer, the Gospels, community, the sacraments, Jesuit spirituality, and the contemplative life.

Our day began at 7:00 a.m. with morning prayer, followed by classes on the vows, the life of Jesus, the New Testament, the history of the Jesuits, Catholic social teaching, recent church and Jesuit documents, and the lives of Jesuit saints and martyrs. I loved every minute of those classes. I read everything handed to me and spent countless hours holed up in the magnificent old library on the second floor poring over commentaries, biographies of Jesuit heroes, spiritual books, and texts about justice and peace.

Mass followed classes. Each liturgy was prepared by a different novice. Then we heard an inspiring homily from someone on the novitiate team—Father Jim Maier, the novice master; Father Ed O'Donnell, the assistant; Father Charlie Costello, the rector; or Father Bill Sneck, a psychologist and retreat leader who became my spiritual director and friend. After lunch, we headed off for two hours of manual labor. We swept floors and vacuumed, mopped halls, did laundry, baked Eucharistic bread, raked leaves, mowed lawns, and cleaned hundreds of windows. Late afternoons were free, so I returned to the library to explore the dusty old books.

At 5:00 p.m., we were sent out to walk the grounds for twenty minutes with two other novices for "spiritual conversation." This ancient practice dates back to St. Ignatius and the first Jesuits. These conversations were meant to help us grow comfortable talking about the gospel of Jesus, the presence of God, and our experience of prayer. Trouble was, I was shy and nervous about such talk. I was reluctant to share my true thoughts—about the connection between prayer and sacrament and war and injustice. I now thought that following Jesus meant standing up against the daily horrors of the world, but I knew that few others thought that way. I decided to bide my time and listen more than talk.

After dinner, there was usually a conference or a faith-sharing session, where one person would take fifteen minutes to tell his life story and of his personal experience of God. The faith-sharing process took four months. It was moving to hear how God had touched everyone's heart, but by the time my turn came, I was a nervous wreck. Who could understand my commitment to work for the abolition of war and make that the hallmark of a Jesuit—a Christian—vocation? I knew my story would fall on unresponsive ears and put me at odds with most of my peers. Here, the goal was to listen nonjudgmentally and compassionately to the speaker so that he would be empowered by the telling of his story. The exercise worked. It not only helped us know one another better, but it also liberated me and gave me confidence in myself and my journey.

◨　◨

A few weeks after entrance day, I passed fellow novice Ed DeBerri on the staircase during our afternoon free time. "What are you doing?" I asked. "Working on my peace ministry," he answered and walked on.

I ran to catch up to him. "What peace ministry?"

"I try to do something every day to promote peace and justice in the world," he answered. "At the moment, I'm collecting excerpts from papal documents and Catholic social teaching for an anthology that I want to publish."

Then he hurried off to the copy machine. I stood there on the staircase dumbfounded. Who told him he had a ministry for peace? What was I doing for peace and justice? I decided then and there on the staircase to get busy and find my own peace ministry. I had already made a commitment at the Sea of Galilee to work for peace, but I didn't know it was a "ministry" that I would have to engage in every day wherever I was. Later, Ed inspired me to write my first book on Gospel nonviolence. The book he was working on, *Catholic Social Teaching: Our Best Kept Secret*, remains in print some twenty-three years later.

In those early days, we were told that the novitiate had three purposes. First, it would provide a peaceful atmosphere in which to test our decision to spend our lives in the Society of Jesus. Second, it would teach us to undertake the mission of the society, to promote "the faith that does justice." Third, it would offer a context in which to test our vows and community life. Along with working toward these goals, we were invited to develop a personal prayer life under the guidance of a spiritual director, to study Jesuit and church documents and contemporary theology, and to begin our work in the world as apostles of Jesus, "contemplatives in action."

We also learned how to develop a personal relationship with Jesus through Ignatius's method of contemplative prayer. Through this ongoing, intimate daily encounter with Jesus, we were sent into the world as his friends on his mission of justice and peace.

Over the years, I would come to the painful realization that many North American Jesuits did not give the same priority to peace and justice that I was so clearly called to give. Nonetheless, I found the Jesuit mission and way of life bold and daring. Everything was infused with possibility and excitement. The daily Masses, Bible studies, reading assignments, faith-sharing sessions, and spiritual conversations all gave me occasion to reflect on the commitments I had made in Durham and Galilee, even if no one else understood my spiritual life as a mission to disarm the world.

Most of all, I fell hook, line, and sinker for this mysterious practice known as "Jesuit spirituality." Novices were instructed to spend an hour every day in silent meditation. The practice could begin with a story from the Gospels: we were to imagine the scene, notice the details, put faces on the characters, listen to their words, and place ourselves among them. We were to imagine as well what Jesus looked like, what he sounded like, what he would say to us personally. We were taught that the more we engaged our imaginations, the more we would enter the story and be transformed, as the first disciples had been. And over time, our lives would conform to Jesus' life, and we would perform the same remarkable deeds he and the apostles had performed. More, we would become his friends. He would know us and we would know him.

I found Ignatian spirituality immensely consoling. All I had to do was imagine Jesus standing before me and I would be at peace and feel a new devotion. Day after day, I contemplated his gentle words of invitation: "You are my beloved. I am with you. Don't be afraid. I want you to be my disciple. Follow me on the road to peace and justice into my reign. Advocate nonviolence like I do, and carry on my work for me."

Twenty-five years later, I still take time each day to imagine this welcoming Jesus. I've walked away from him many times, but he has never walked away from me. He continues to invite me into his life of love and to follow him on the long road to peace. Every day, this simple meditation unleashes in me new springs of energy and compassion that were not previously accessible. This contemplative prayer, as St. Ignatius taught, is where I encounter Jesus. It makes the journey of radical discipleship possible. It is the heart of the Jesuit life: to live in intimate relationship with Jesus and put his gospel into action. This is the journey of every Christian.

Learning the
Life of Peace
(1982)

A mere month after entering the novitiate, we novices embarked on an eight-day silent retreat—my first experience of strict silence. No mail or newspapers, no TV or radio, no phone calls, and no conversations at all, except with a spiritual director. Mine was Bill Sneck, a gifted psychologist, wise retreat leader, and respected teacher. Since entering the novitiate, I had met with Bill every few days. But during the retreat, I met with him each day for an hour. We talked of my life and why I had entered the Jesuits, and we discussed how I might make the most of my days as a novice.

Bill taught me to enter into five one-hour prayer periods a day, each devoted to a specific scene in Jesus' life. So I roamed the Pennsylvania countryside, which was just beginning to slip into autumnal shades, and pondered the life of Jesus. By the fifth day of silence, I had entered another world. Life decelerated into slow motion, as if I were a diver underwater. I noticed every breath, every motion, and every mood of the wild world around me and within me. I contemplated God's love and reflected on my own sinfulness. I thought again about my trip to Israel and the beckoning of the Beatitudes, and with my faculties now wide awake, I reaffirmed my commitment to struggle publicly for justice and peace.

My first sustained sense of God's presence happened during those eight silent days. On the ninth day, I came up for air a new man. I remember thinking, *So this is what the spiritual life is about.* Ever since, I've made a similar eight-day retreat each year, as do all Jesuits. I wish it were so for every person on the planet.

In the months that followed, I often hid myself away in the massive Jesuit library in a remote corner of the second floor, where I devoured stacks of books on the saints, the spiritual life, and on social issues. With the Israel's war on Lebanon fresh in my mind, I read every book I could find on war and injustice. And by the same token, I studied the path to peace as envisioned by Mahatma Gandhi, Martin Luther King Jr., Dorothy Day, Thomas Merton, and the Berrigan brothers, Philip and Daniel. I had in my hands for the first time literature about the methodology of nonviolence, and it sparked my imagination. What does a nonviolent lifestyle look like? Dare I undertake the noble endeavors of Gandhi and King?

Father Daniel Berrigan's books in particular inspired me. I consider him the quintessential Jesuit, a great prophet of peace to the nation, a blessing for the church and the world. He calls us back to the gospel through his poetry, his hard-won wisdom, and his curriculum vitae of civil disobedience, which begins in the 1960s, when he caught the world's imagination by burning draft files with homemade napalm with his brother, Phil, and the others of the Catonsville Nine. After being sentenced to prison, he went underground, popping up in the media to denounce the Vietnam War. Eventually, he was arrested on Block Island, Rhode Island, and spent two painful years in the federal prison in Danbury, Connecticut.

On September 9, 1980, he and Phil and other friends hammered on nuclear weapons at the General Electric plant in King of Prussia, Pennsylvania. The action, called the Plowshares Eight, was the first of some seventy-five Plowshares disarmament actions. Isaiah had foretold that swords would be beaten into plowshares; the Berrigans and their friends took great risks to hasten that day. Dan faced the possibility of ten more years in prison but after many appeals was sentenced to time served. To this day, he travels the nation, gets arrested, and denounces war. His fifty books of poetry, journals, essays, and scripture study spoke to me like nothing else.

I came across his name again later in the fall, in a lengthy account in the *National Jesuit News* of a conference on nuclear weapons the previous summer at Fordham University. The theme was the nuclear arms race, and the New York Province had invited several people to speak: a handful of generals, some just-war theorists, and Daniel Berrigan. The generals and theorists spoke, and then Berrigan took the podium and delivered a devastating statement against war and nuclear weapons. He called on every Christian to witness for peace and disarmament and to reclaim the practice of gospel nonviolence:

> The Christian response to imperial death-dealing is in effect a nonresponse. We refuse the terms of the argument. To weigh the value of lives would imply that military solutions had been grotesquely validated by Christians. There is no cause, however noble, which justifies the taking of a single human life, much less millions of them.
>
> "Witness of the resurrection" was a title of honor, self-conferred by the twelve apostles. They were called to take their stand on behalf of life, to the point of undergoing death as well as death's analogies—scorn and rejection, floggings

and jail. This is our glory. From Peter and Paul to Martin King and Óscar Romero, we are witnesses of resurrection. We want to test the resurrection in our bones. To see if we might live in hope. We want to taste the resurrection. May I say we have not been disappointed.

His words electrified me. He spoke unlike any other Christian I'd known. He possessed an authority that inspired, captivated, and challenged. *This is what a Jesuit is supposed to be like*, I thought. *Here is a real Christian.*

A few months later, I summoned the courage to write Dan and express my gratitude for his life witness and my timid hope to follow his example and work for peace. Then I wrote again, inviting him to visit and expressing my regret that I was told not to take part in any peace demonstration or act of civil disobedience. He wrote back, saying that the proscriptions I was under suggested to him that the ranking Jesuits in Wernersville would likely not make him feel welcome.

Each fall, first- and second-year novices drew assignments to work two days a week in pairs or in groups at a hospital, a soup kitchen, or an inner-city school. I was assigned, along with my friend, second-year novice Joe Sands, to work in Reading, Pennsylvania, at the John Paul II Center for Special Learning. This brand-new school was led by Sister Francis, a petite, charismatic, irrepressible woman. Joe and I marched into her office on our first day like Will Smith and Tommy Lee Jones in *Men in Black*. "We're the Jesuits," we announced gravely. She looked up at us and snickered. "Well, what do you want me to do—genuflect?" Joe and I laughed, even as our faces reddened a little.

Sister Francis was a no-nonsense woman. A friend of Jean Vanier, founder of the L'Arche communities, she had years of experience among the disabled. "The more you love the Lord," she told us one day, "the more you will become like the retarded. Learn from them to let go of everything and live life with love and joy."

Sixteen students, most with Down syndrome, spent their days at the school getting the best possible care and attention. Joe and I played, colored, and sang with them and assisted them with every imaginable task. Their disabilities prevented them from ever achieving any standard of cultural success, but their hearts were wide open. They practiced unconditional love and lived completely in the moment. Joe and I fell in love with them.

These so-called disabled students shaped some of my earliest lessons as a Jesuit: how to love and trust others, how to widen my heart, how to set aside my ego, and how to dwell in the peace of the present moment. They gave me more love than I could give them. Theirs was naturally unconditional, and I tasted in it something of the nature of God's love.

Later that fall, Ed DeBerri invited me to come with him to Reading to see *The Day after Trinity*, a documentary about J. Robert Oppenheimer and the atomic bombing of Hiroshima. I sat through it devastated. After the screening, Sister Anne Montgomery and Elmer Maas, both of whom had participated in the Plowshares Eight action with the Berrigans, spoke to us of the peace movement's work resisting the U.S. nuclear weapons industry.

As Ed and I drove back to Wernersville, he made an astonishing observation: "All great men and women, every saint and martyr has spent time in jail." This had never occurred to me. He went on: "All the early Christians were in and out of jail. All of them resisted evil during their lifetimes and suffered for it." I could see where the conversation was headed. "Perhaps to resist nuclear weapons, we, too, will have to go to jail. Maybe it's one of the requirements for membership in the Christian tradition," he concluded.

That night I couldn't sleep. The evening had inflamed my desire to work for peace, to help prevent another Hiroshima, and to live out the pledge I had made in Galilee. As I tossed and turned, my earlier commitments began to take on flesh and blood. It was dawning on me that in this day and age, resisting war was the best translation of carrying the cross. It was the best way to participate in the gospel. I sat up in bed and resolved, there in the wee hours, to stand against war and nuclear weapons and risk prison. I was wide awake. My heart burned to share the fate of the saints and help ensure that Hiroshima would never happen again. I couldn't get over this new flash of clarity. Saintliness and Hiroshima—a balanced contrast. Living toward one and against the other made for the perfect convergence of history and faith. It meant entering the process of transfiguring nonviolence by confronting disfiguring nuclear violence.

回 回

Father O'Donnell, the assistant novice director, taught a class on the New Testament and contemporary theology. He assigned each of us to make a presentation on a contemporary issue facing the church. Ed DeBerri and I decided we would each speak on war and peace. Ed spoke about the just-war theory—the seven conditions under which the church justifies military action—and the upcoming pastoral letter of the U.S. Conference of Catholic Bishops on the subject, "The Challenge of Peace: God's Promise and Our Response." I spoke on Christian nonviolence, with references to the Gospels and contemporary peacemakers, and concluded with my own "theology of peace."

It was my first time speaking publicly about war and peace. I've given thousands of lectures since, before hundreds of thousands of people. But that day, speaking in a circle of a dozen Jesuits about such thorny topics, my knees went weak and my stomach lurched. I began with a quote from Father Richard McSorley, a Jesuit who taught Peace Studies at Georgetown University:

> The taproot of violence in our society today is our intent to use nuclear weapons. Once we have agreed to that, all other evil is minor in comparison. Until we squarely face the question of our consent to use nuclear weapons, any hope of large-scale improvement of public morality is doomed to failure. The nuclear weapons of the Communists may destroy our bodies, but our intent to use nuclear weapons destroys our souls.

I spoke of Father McSorley's visit with Dorothy Day shortly before her death, when he asked her for a coherent theology of peace. She replied:

> All you have to do is compare what the Gospel asks and what war does. The Gospel asks that we feed the poor, give drink to the thirsty, clothe the naked, welcome the stranger, house the homeless, visit the prisoner, and perform works of mercy. War does the opposite. It makes my neighbor hungry, thirsty, homeless, a prisoner, and sick. It kills them by the millions. The Gospel asks us to take up our cross. War asks us to lay the cross on others.

Every Christian, she said, must perform works of mercy and peace in deliberate opposition to the culture's wars and injustices. "As you come to know the seriousness of our situation—the war, the racism, the poverty in the world—you come to realize it is not going to be changed just by words or demonstrations," she once wrote. "It's a question of risking your life. It's a question of living your life in drastically different ways." This, she believed, was the Gospels' theology of peace. To her it couldn't be clearer.

I went on to outline Gospel injunctions that seemed to pertain: "Love your neighbor," "Love your enemies," "Blessed are the peacemakers," "Be compassionate as God is compassionate," "Hunger and thirst for justice," "Put down the sword," "Take up the cross," and "Peace be with you." I concluded that Jesus practiced and taught radical nonviolence, and that if we are to follow him, we must do the same. We must, as Jesuits and Christians, speak out against war, poverty, injustice, nuclear weapons, and every form of violence, as well as adhere to creative nonviolence and disarming love, as Gandhi and King did.

I finished my presentation feeling relieved, but a hand went up and someone asked, "Does this mean you're a pacifist?"

The question caught me off guard; no one had ever asked me to label myself before. But with every eye trained on me, I couldn't duck it. "Yes," I responded, "because I think that Jesus rejects violence, that he's a peacemaker, and that he commands us to reject violence, too." With that, my confidence mushroomed. "My heroes are Dorothy Day, Martin Luther King Jr., Mahatma Gandhi, Daniel Berrigan, and Thomas Merton. Someday I, too, hope to engage in civil disobedience in opposition to war, as they did."

The class gaped at me. I felt a little like an exotic species in a zoo. They were at once bored with the topic and appalled by my boldness. But I was on fire. I had gone public. I was claiming my vocation.

回 回

One night after Christmas, I saw the new movie *Gandhi*, a biopic of Mahatma Gandhi starring Ben Kingsley and Martin Sheen. I left the theater bedazzled. This Hindu man provided the best example of radical discipleship to the nonviolent Jesus I'd ever seen. Gandhi challenged himself to go deep into truth, love, and nonviolence. He pursued community life, voluntary poverty, contemplative prayer, steadfast resistance to South African racism, and ongoing civil disobedience against British imperialism. He suffered imprisonment and ultimately assassination but emerged the greatest saint and peacemaker of the century.

"I have not the shadow of a doubt that any man or woman can achieve what I have, if he or she would make the same effort and cultivate the same hope and faith," Gandhi wrote. He said his optimism "rests on my belief in the infinite possibilities of the individual to develop nonviolence. The more you develop it in your own being, the more infectious it becomes till it overwhelms your surroundings and by and by might oversweep the world."

I decided then and there to learn everything I could about Gandhi and attempt to undertake the same steadfast commitment to creative nonviolence—as a Jesuit, a Christian—that he had. And it was the perfect time to do so, because in a few days I would begin the quintessential Ignatian experience: the thirty-day silent retreat of St. Ignatius of Loyola, the Spiritual Exercises.

Thirty Days
of Silence
(1983)

The retreat started on January 3, 1983. For thirty days we spoke to no one but our spiritual director. We didn't watch TV or listen to the radio. We didn't read books or open mail or talk on the phone. We gave all our attention to Jesus by attending daily Mass and practicing five one-hour meditations every day.

The Spiritual Exercises are divided into four "Weeks," each one bringing you deeper into the life of Jesus and the mystery of the living God. During the First Week, you pray over your personal sinfulness and that of the world. This experience heightens your awareness of being a sinner yet unconditionally loved by God.

The subsequent weeks guide you through the Gospel story of Jesus. The meditations of the Second Week focus on Jesus' birth, baptism, and temptations in the desert; his proclamation of God's reign; his Sermon on the Mount; his healings and miracles; and his conflict in Jerusalem. The Third Week's meditations focus on Jesus' action in the temple, his arrest and torture, his crucifixion, and his steadfast forgiveness. The Fourth Week's meditations concentrate on

Jesus' resurrection and what it means to live free from death and, on the other side of the coin, what it means to live devoted to the way, truth, and life of Jesus.

The Spiritual Exercises end with the Contemplation to Attain the Love of God, in which you beg to enter into perfect universal love. This is the point at which you ask to embody gospel love on behalf of those in need—anywhere, no matter what, and not just in words but in deeds. The Spiritual Exercises are a school of prayer and, more than that, a revolutionary training camp for nonviolent love, radical discipleship, boundless compassion, selfless service, and prophetic peacemaking.

How hard it is to write about that powerful month. The days were profound and ineffable. I took a long walk each day through the cold, snowy countryside. Trudging in no particular direction, I envisioned Jesus' life in as much detail as I could. I felt his presence and, as deliberately as I could, listened for his call to radical discipleship. Over and over again, I said yes to that call.

I pondered my identity as a white, male, well-educated, upper-class American and tried to embrace, instead, a more egalitarian identity—as, in biblical terms, the beloved son of God, a brother of Jesus. Being a beloved son of God, as the Beatitude explains, meant I would be a peacemaker, a companion of Jesus who works to disarm one and all through creative nonviolence. Just as Jesus learned, after his baptism in the Jordan and again on Mount Tabor, who he was in relationship with the loving God, I was discovering my true identity—in relationship to Jesus. That new self-understanding has enabled every step I have taken since. It puts my life in context, not as a citizen of the United States, but first and foremost as a citizen of the reign of God.

Quickly enough, though, I glimpsed my own violence and faithlessness. I began to see the little ways I rejected God and hurt family and friends and those around me—and still do. Whether through sinfulness or selfishness, I end up focusing on myself rather than the needs of others. Most days, I think of myself as God's gift to humanity, or, at least, to the Society of Jesus and the church. In reality, I wake up grouchy, mean, angry, and violent, a mere shell of a loving human being. Through the day, I might make a presentable Jesuit, but too often I carry within me violence, pride, and selfishness. So much of the time I am simply a reflection of the culture of greed, aggression, and domination.

It dawned on me, too, how very differently Jesus lived—he practiced perfect selfless love and embodied divine, creative nonviolence; he disobeyed the customs and ordinances of institutionalized injustice and imperialism; he forgave those who killed him and, even as he died, trusted that he would live on in God's realm of peace. Again inspiration swept over me. I acknowledged my own longing to engage in creative nonviolence and advocate it publicly.

This would put me in a lonesome spot. I would have to stand against the church's bulwark on matters of war—namely, its entrenched and sacrosanct just-war theory. Moreover, standing publicly against injustice would put me at risk of harassment, rejection, and imprisonment. But in the contest between hesitation and longing, my longing won out.

During the retreat, a quote from César Chávez, the United Farm Workers union organizer, appeared on the bulletin board. "The truest act of courage, the strongest act of being human, is to sacrifice ourselves for others in a totally nonviolent struggle for justice. To be human," he said at the end of his great fast in 1968, "is to suffer for others." This statement cut to the heart of things. His simple words moved me deeply, and they summed up what I was learning. I began to pray that they would be my words as well. I, too, wanted to spend my life in selfless service, to take part in the nonviolent struggle for justice. And here was another lens through which to look at things: I could gain my humanity by consciously suffering in love for others.

Years later, I was honored to become a friend of César Chávez. We stayed up late one night a few months before his sudden death, and I confessed how those words had inspired me. Did he still believe them? I asked. Yes, he said. He still believed that the greatest contribution one could make in the struggle for justice and peace was to offer one's life, even if it meant suffering and death.

I was allowed to read one book during my retreat, so I chose *The Nonviolent Cross*, by Jim Douglass, one of the world's leading theologians of nonviolence. "The logic of nonviolence is the logic of crucifixion and leads the person of nonviolence into the heart of the suffering Christ," Douglass writes.

> The purpose of nonviolence is to move the oppressors to perceive as human beings those whom they are oppressing. Nonviolent resistance seeks to persuade the aggressor to recognize in his victim the humanity they have in common, which when recognized fully makes violence impossible. The goal of human recognition is sought through the power of voluntary suffering, by which the victim becomes no longer a victim but instead an active opponent in loving resistance to the one who has refused to recognize him as a human being. The person of nonviolence acts through suffering love to move the unjust opponent to a perception of their common humanity, and thus to the cessation of violence in the

commencement of brotherhood and sisterhood. The greater the inhumanity, the greater the power of suffering love necessary to begin restoring the bonds of community. Suffering as such is powerless. Love transforms it into the kind of resistance capable of moving an opponent to the act of mutual recognition we have described.

With such insights, I finally began to understand the logic of the cross, Jesus' nonviolent resistance to imperial injustice, his perfect suffering love, his willingness to forgive and die, and his trust that this act of nonviolence would bear good fruit and transform the world. As his follower, I now understood even more that I was called to join his way of nonviolent, suffering love in order to disarm, redeem, and transform the world.

回　回

Sunday, January 30, 1983, was the thirty-fifth anniversary of Gandhi's martyrdom. It was the dead of winter, but according to the schedule of our retreat meditations, it was Easter Sunday. I had just finished meditating for seven days on the brutal death and nonviolent love of Jesus and now began to pray through the Resurrection accounts. But here I was stuck. What does the Resurrection mean? How does the resurrection of Jesus shed light on the cruel martyrdoms of my heroes: Mahatma Gandhi, Martin Luther King Jr., Bobby Kennedy, Archbishop Romero, and the four churchwomen of El Salvador? I wanted to believe in the Resurrection. I wanted to experience that joy and confidence—to "taste it," as Daniel Berrigan put it. But the savage deaths of those I admired knocked the wind out of me. The story of the Resurrection was pleasant enough, but the reality of the world seemed grim. The evidence shows that death does get the last word. We're all going to die. And if we stand up for peace and justice, we might be killed more quickly, and the struggle crushed. There seemed to be no hope. I could imagine no way out of this despair.

I sat in meditation, picturing myself in the tomb with Jesus' dead body. I grieved over his death. I grieved over death itself. I grieved once again for Dr. King and Bobby Kennedy, my cousin Mark and my grandfather. I grieved for Mahatma Gandhi. I grieved for innocent victims of global violence and greed.

Still, the eternal questions plagued me: Why would Jesus have to suffer and die? Was there any worth to his agony, even if he responded with perfect nonviolent love and forgiveness? What difference did it make? Is the cross the only way to peace and justice?

I heard no answers but stayed with the questions. And, oh, did they spring up from my turbulent insides like bubbles in boiling water. I thought of the four churchwomen in El Salvador and other just men and women who had been brutally killed. What is it in the fabric of the world that demands that saints suffer and die? What good does it achieve? Are their deaths related to Jesus? Do they somehow, through their suffering love and martyrdom, participate in his redemptive—even disarming—work? How realistic is it to hope for an end to crucifixion and all its analogies—executions, poverty, hunger, racism, sexism, environmental destruction, nuclear weapons, and war? Behind all these questions lurked another, more personal one: When I die, what will happen to me?

After a while, the hard questions subsided, and I turned my imagination back to Jesus' body, rising now, greeting me, offering me his gift of peace. Gandhi and King and all the saints and martyrs, he seemed to say, were alive and well in the paradise of peace. He, too, was alive and well, and I would also live on after spending my life in the nonviolent struggle for disarmament and justice.

Here was just the meditation I needed. It swept me beyond despair and into biblical hope, the hope of things unseen, the hope that leads to an abiding trust in the God of peace. I found myself able to trust the power of love and truth to withstand hatred and lies, the power of nonviolence and peace to withstand violence and war. I could trust that life overcomes death, that our survival is guaranteed. I had only to follow Jesus and, as he did, resist injustice in a spirit of nonviolence; then my life would bear good fruit, and my mission would be fulfilled. I would join the company of the martyrs and saints, the cloud of witnesses that surrounds me. I am called to enter the paschal mystery of dying and rising in the struggle for a new world of nonviolence, which God is bringing about. It is in God's hands, not mine, but I must do my part.

For the first time in a long time, I felt peace and joy. I recalled the passage from John's Gospel in which Jesus tells his disciples at the Last Supper: "I will see you again, and your hearts will rejoice, and no one will take your joy away from you. On that day you will not question me about anything" (John 16:22–23).

As I pondered my upcoming vows of poverty, chastity, and obedience, I recalled the many vows Gandhi professed at the beginning of his public work. Regarding his vow of nonviolence, he wrote in 1915:

> The active part of nonviolence is love. The law of love requires equal consideration for all life from the tiniest insect to the highest man. One who follows this law must not be angry even with the perpetrator of the greatest imaginable wrong, but must love him, wish him well, and serve him. Although

he must thus love the wrongdoer, he must never submit to his wrong or his injustice, but must oppose it with all his might, and must patiently and without resentment suffer all the hardships to which the wrongdoer may subject him in punishment for his opposition.

Years later, in a letter from prison to his ashram comrades about the vow, he added, "By concentration an acrobat can walk on a rope. But the concentration required to tread the path of truth and nonviolence is far greater. The slightest inattention brings one tumbling to the ground. One can realize truth and nonviolence only by ceaseless striving. We must strive day by day toward the ideal, with what strength we have in us."

Given my own violent times, my own inner violence, and that the Sermon on the Mount was still ringing in my ears, I considered professing a similar vow of nonviolence. I told Bill Sneck of my desire, and he encouraged me. So for the next year and a half, I prepared for my personal vow of nonviolence. I studied Gandhi's teachings and experimented with how to embody such a vow. More, I brooded over how to live it out publicly against the aspiring empire of the United States.

The Spiritual Exercises conclude with this prayer of St. Ignatius:

Take, Lord, receive all my liberty,
my memory, my understanding, my entire will,
all that I have and call my own.
You have given it all to me.
Now I return it, Lord, to you.
Everything is yours. Do with it what you will.
Give me only your love and your grace.
That's enough for me.

I repeated the prayer like a mantra until the retreat ended at seven on a cold February morning in 1983. I felt ready to face the world. I burned with zeal, as if I were St. Paul, St. Francis, and Martin Luther King Jr. all rolled into one. More and more, my vocation crystallized.

Much time has passed since that initial retreat. But those thirty days have buoyed me through the many years since. Life has been rich and varied beyond anything I could have imagined. I've enjoyed high moments, but I've also suffered depths, stumbled into detours, and taken falls—all of it part and parcel of my journey with Jesus.

I talk of my journey without claiming any special stature. It perseveres not because of my own faithfulness but because of Jesus'. I lapse into pride, patting myself on the back for my bold Christianity. But soon enough I become aware of some new blindness, some new depth of selfishness. I discern another level of sinfulness and slap palm to forehead. Once again I've turned away and tried to live the Christian life under my own steam. I know of my missteps, because once I make them, I head down the slippery slope of fear, anxiety, confusion, loneliness, and despair. Darkness descends. I flail about and can't find my way.

But Jesus continues the relationship he began. He seeks me out and leads me back. He still loves and encourages me. He never changes.

I am a work in progress. No matter how far I've wandered, Jesus extends again his invitation to share his life of nonviolent love. I've accepted it over and over, and in the process I have come to understand myself as a pilgrim, walking with Jesus as best I can. I can't judge my successes, only my desire. And my desire is to spend every moment in companionship with Jesus as he tends to the world by healing the sick, disarming the violent, expelling the demons of death, and announcing the good news of justice and peace. On my best days, I adopt the attitude of St. Francis of Assisi, who claimed that he was the most sinful, violent person on earth, not as a form of self-hatred, but as an awareness of my need for Christ's healing love and disarming peace, which then pushes me into the world of the broken and oppressed to share that gift of compassion and disarming love.

Companionship with Jesus is the essence of the matter. There's no denying the truth of John's Gospel: "Just as a branch cannot bear fruit on its own unless it remains on the vine, so neither can you unless you remain in me. . . . Without me you can do nothing. . . . It was not you who chose me, but I who chose you" (John 15:4, 5, 16). I take this to heart and try to keep it close through time-honored ways: daily meditation, Bible study, life in community, service, sacraments, and solidarity with the poor. My disciplines still teach me about Jesus and fortify my discipleship to him. And the greatest impetus of my discipleship was that period of those abundant thirty days. They guided me from the matrix of death into the spirit of life, off the accustomed path to war and onto the road to peace. From violence and indifference to compassion and service, out of a fog of confusion into grace and purpose. I breathed out despair and breathed in peace, gentleness, and hope. Those thirty days foreclosed my ever turning back. They found me ready to follow Jesus all the way—to the cross and into the new life of resurrection. From now on, there were fewer questions, just the beckoning hand of the Risen One inviting me to join him on the way.

The Experiment,
Phase One
(1983)

The night before our thirty-day retreat ended, the novice master summoned us to the chapel. Father Jim, clipboard in hand, announced the plans for us over the next six weeks. Each of us would be setting out on an "experiment"—in Jesuit parlance, a service mission whereby novices put into action their newfound gospel commitment. Before revealing our assignments, Jim delivered a pep talk about the times ahead: "Don't be afraid, do not worry, be strong in faith, trust in Jesus."

Five novices would go to Calvary Hospital in the Bronx to serve the terminally ill poor. Others would be sent to work at the Franciscan-run St. Francis Inn soup kitchen in the Kensington section of Philadelphia, one of the poorest neighborhoods in the nation. My assignment came last. I would be headed for the Trinity Retreat Center in Harrisburg.

I was devastated. I would be heading off alone. For the last thirty days, I had been imagining swashbuckling adventures by Jesus' side: proclaiming the gospel, serving on the front lines, going to the cross.

But a retreat center? I would be leading confirmation workshops for Catholic high school groups. How desperately I wanted to join the others, to care for the dying and serve the poor. How ironic, too. Thirty days of declaring to God my selfless willingness to go anywhere, and now Providence was putting my declaration to the test. I suppose I needed to learn something about Jesuit obedience, about letting go of my own desires. I needed to learn to go "where you would rather not go," as Jesus warned Peter he would have to do.

At the Trinity Retreat Center, I received a warm welcome from the directors, Sister Cathy Rebello and Jesuit Father Ed Sanders, whose good-heartedness told me everything would be all right. They showed me around and explained my job. Each morning at 8:30, a busload of forty students would arrive for a seven-hour workshop. I would have a different group each day. The kids would spend the day discussing faith, Jesus, the gospel, and the sacraments. The workshop was mine to design and lead—and it would begin in three days. I wanted to panic but didn't have time. As I prepared my talks, I realized why I was there. I had told the novice master that I had rarely spoken about my faith and wasn't sure I could. It made me feel ill at ease. In typical Jesuit fashion, he resolved to take care of that problem straightaway by throwing me to the lions.

The first day, standing before forty ninth graders, I launched into a catalog of exciting reasons we should follow Jesus. I talked of the many ways of living the gospel and what the sacrament of confirmation means. Confirmation is a celebration of our discipleship, I said. It's a sign of our life in the Holy Spirit and our pursuit of justice and peace.

I think back on those talks and suspect they were a little abstract. But the students were bright and curious, and they responded positively. Soon I was on a roll. I ended up speaking to more than a thousand young people during my time at Trinity. I have no idea what became of them, nor do I know the impact the workshops had on them. I know only the impact they had on me. They eroded my fear of sharing my heart and speaking publicly about my faith.

From one perspective, it never got easy. The kids bombarded me with those enduring hard questions: "Why do people suffer and die?" "What should we do when we grow up?" "How do you know Jesus existed?" "Why was he crucified?" "Why do most Catholics support killing?" "What happens when we die?" The questions were heartfelt and heartbreaking. Thoughtful kids can detect glib answers, so I answered carefully, often getting them to address their questions to one another so we could puzzle out together some semblance of light and truth. The daily interrogations were hard, but they prepared me for the thousands of audiences I would face in the decades to come.

When I wasn't with the students, I was reading the autobiography of Mahatma Gandhi. I was deeply impressed with his relentless efforts to change himself and train his heart in nonviolence. His story challenged me profoundly. Everything he was I wanted to be. Could I pursue gospel nonviolence with the same reckless abandon?

I peered again into my inner depths of violence and tried to figure out how to disarm my heart. I resolved never to hurt anyone again and to try to root out every trace of violence within me. Not only that, but I would join every peace-and-justice group I could find. I sought out peace demonstrations to attend and signed up with Pax Christi USA, the national Catholic peace movement, and the Fellowship of Reconciliation USA, the interfaith peace movement.

I tried my own experiments in truth and nonviolence. I visited a downtown soup kitchen and volunteered from time to time. I joined a local charismatic prayer group and a weekly peace vigil. And I accompanied Father Ed to the Camp Hill state prison for his monthly

Mass. The Camp Hill prison transported me back to Dachau with its spic-and-span white buildings, security towers, and dormitory cells all surrounded by pristine suburbs. During Mass, Father Ed told the prisoners that God loved them unconditionally and that they were forgiven and could live every day from now on in the mercy of God. Go, he said, and share that love and mercy with one another. The faces before me betrayed sorrow and despair. I could see in these prisoners the suffering Christ. I spoke with some and learned of their crimes, their suffering, and the abuse they had endured from the justice system. I saw how society's unwillingness to disarm had obstructed the healing of these broken men. If we modeled nonviolence, these poor men might have practiced nonviolence. If society taught kindness and compassion, these poor men might have practiced kindness and compassion. And still, in prison, they were learning oppression and aggression, not compassion and nonviolence.

I sensed a convergence in myself, mourning for these suffering men while becoming bolder in my confirmation workshops. I soon found myself speaking unflinchingly. I opened my mouth, and out they came: fluent words on behalf of the world's poor, on the Christian duty to disarm and live in peace with everyone. Those six weeks were a whirlwind—teaching the kids, mingling with the poor, studying the likes of Gandhi. It was another boot camp, one for which I was grateful.

On the bus ride back to Wernersville at the end of my six-week experiment, I resolved to go even deeper into Gandhian nonviolence and talk about it more with my fellow novices. My excitement mounted when I arrived home. We gathered that night in the basement lounge, feeling like the disciples back from their missionary expeditions, having exorcized demons and healed the sick. Late into the night we talked about our experiences. The guys assigned to the hospital in the Bronx told harrowing tales of accompanying the homeless and the poorest as they died. They fed them, sat with them, cleaned their sheets, and washed their pans. And after they died, they prepared them for burial.

But Peter Cicchino held us spellbound with his adventures at St. Francis Inn in Philadelphia. "The neighborhood is like a war zone," he said. "Block after block of trash, rubble, drug dealers, homeless people, and stray dogs." In Kensington, life was cheap; people died of gunshot wounds and drug overdoses. Peter stayed at the Inn, a Catholic Worker house, with the homeless and a handful of Franciscans. There he prepared food, counseled addicts, and helped people find jobs. The staff at the Inn fasted one day a week, he said, and every Saturday held a vigil against nuclear weapons in downtown Philly. The fasting left him thinner, but his enthusiasm spilled over. He told us he would hereafter work for the justice and dignity of the homeless. By evening's end, we all felt exhilarated, renewed, and ready for more.

The Experiment,
Phase Two
(1983)

The next day, we first-year novices, accompanied by our directors, headed for another "experiment": two months in inner-city
Philadelphia. We took over a decrepit Jesuit rectory attached to the
Gesu, an old church held up by outsize pillars and filled with ugly art.
With peeling paint and stained masonry, it was an architectural eye-
sore from every angle. The rectory, too, resembled most of the decay-
ing houses in the neighboring slums. Here we would try to create
community among ourselves and be of service to the poor outside our
doors. We would also reflect on the social, economic, and political
arrangements that made them poor.

We disembarked from the bus, settled into our rooms, and
received our assignments: visiting the elderly, teaching children,
repairing apartments, and taking the graveyard shift at a nearby
shelter. During the first few weeks, Mark and I visited neighborhood
shut-ins. Later, Michael and I painted a blighted apartment for a sweet
elderly woman.

While we were in Philly, the local church marked the twentieth anniversary of Pope John XXIII's encyclical *Pacem in Terris* ("Peace on Earth"), an occasion that in Philadelphia inspired a peace march through the streets to the Philadelphia Cathedral. Peter, Frank, and I joined in. At the cathedral, a bishop addressed the crowd, calling us to pray, fast, and work publicly for disarmament. "Peace," he said, "is held hostage by war, by the fear of nuclear holocaust, by poverty and the denial of human rights, and by the entire system of national sovereignty." His words struck us as utterly true. On the way home, the three of us agreed to meet every afternoon and discuss this call for peacemaking. We shared our questions and insights and worries. We read Gandhi, King, Merton, and Day. We organized our own weekly prayer service for nuclear disarmament and took up the ancient disciplines of fasting and yoga. We went on this way for a year and a half. Later, we realized that we had formed our own boot camp in gospel nonviolence, a novitiate within a novitiate for justice and peace.

I was more or less happy but suffered nagging doubts. Could I follow the radical Jesus within the Jesuit order, with its regimen and orderliness and hierarchy and law? Would I have more freedom if I joined the Catholic Worker movement or the Franciscans? By now, I had visited St. Francis Inn, where my fellow novice Peter Cicchino had labored, and had been duly inspired by the Franciscans and their hospitality to the homeless.

At the time, Congress was poised to vote for yet another military increase. The Sojourners community in Washington, D.C., issued an appeal to all Christians to come to Washington on Pentecost Sunday and join a prayer service for disarmament and civil disobedience at the U.S. Capitol. I knew I wouldn't be able to sneak away to participate. I went immediately to Father Jim to ask if I could attend, and perhaps risk arrest. He looked up from his desk and muttered a summary denial and returned to his work. He saw my deep disappointment, though, and his look softened. If it meant that much to me, he said, perhaps I might send a written request to the assistant provincial for formation, who was higher up in the chain of command.

I spent a week composing the letter. Participating in the Sojourners Peace Pentecost witness, and risking arrest, I wrote, would ground my Jesuit vocation in "the faith that does justice." Moreover, my participation would afford me the chance to register my protest against the U.S. nuclear weapons industry. I shared my experience of the Israeli-Lebanese war in the most passionate language I could muster and described my call to work for peace.

The response took another week to arrive: *Novices aren't allowed to do such things. You most certainly cannot get arrested—not now, not ever.*

Father Jim was no doubt apprised of the decision, and was obligated to uphold it. But once again, he relented when he saw how disappointed I was. I could go as long as I promised to steer clear of arrest. It was the best deal I could negotiate, so I tendered my pledge: I would not engage in any civil disobedience or get arrested. Joe Sands, living in Scranton on his six-month experiment, would be going as well, so Jim suggested we go together.

The night of Pentecost Sunday, more than a thousand people gathered in the Washington National Cathedral for stirring words and rousing music. The evening concluded with a moving rendition of "We Shall Overcome." The next morning, we marched, carrying peace signs, from a neighborhood church to the east side of the Capitol, where 242 people entered the rotunda singing hymns and sat down in peaceful protest. First to enter was my friend Father Richard McSorley. Methodically, the police carted off everyone in handcuffs to paddy wagons and then the D.C. jail, where they endured five grueling days.

Joe and I stood across the street with the other supporters, but my heart burned to be in the rotunda. I wanted to be in the procession, to oppose U.S. war-making, to disrupt business as usual as Jesus had when he turned over the money changers' tables in the temple. But I kept my promise, and my distance. Besides, Joe told me to stay put.

Never before had I experienced the Spirit moving through such a large Christian gathering. It was as if we were writing a new chapter in the Acts of the Apostles. For the weeks that followed, I was on a high. The songs we had sung repeated in my mind as a mantra. With Peter and Frank, I fasted and prayed for peace, ministered to Philadelphia's poor, studied nonviolence, and talked gospel politics into the wee hours.

But questions remained. If my superiors so opposed my taking part in a Christian witness for peace, perhaps I belonged elsewhere. Where had the old Jesuit apostolic fervor gone? What was the point of studying the Jesuit saints if I was forbidden to emulate them? Why should I have to beg to take part in a witness for peace while others could freely attend Broadway shows, endorse conservative causes, pursue prestigious careers, even support war?

To my mind, my vocation was indisputable. God wanted me to work for peace and justice, and I had good Jesuit role models at hand in Richard McSorley and Daniel Berrigan. Still, I felt somewhat on my own in this situation. All I had in terms of immediate support were a few sympathetic novices and the Franciscans at the St. Francis Inn. I fleetingly wondered if I belonged among the Franciscans, but I filed the thought for another day.

⧈ ⧈

We left Philly in late May and headed for Baltimore for the annual gathering of the Maryland Province Jesuits. I sat on the lawn of Loyola College with Richard McSorley and talked about the Peace Pentecost. It was exhilarating, he said, to kneel in the rotunda. His five days in jail had worn him out but made his spirits soar. The whole experience, he testified, was holy, Pentecostal, peace-filled.

I listened to him eagerly. Here was a Jesuit doing the things I wanted to do, while I suffered frustration and obstacles and doubt. I felt promise in my Jesuit life but also restriction. I asked Richard why he had joined the Jesuits. And why had he stayed? More to the point, how had he managed to balance his antiwar work with Jesuit life?

During World War II, Richard had been a prisoner of war in the Philippines. Soldiers brought him before a firing squad three times. Later, in the fifties, he joined Horace McKenna in southern Maryland in working to abolish segregation, which eventually led to friendships with Martin Luther King Jr. and the Kennedys. He decided along the way to spend the rest of his life speaking out against war. He said that no other work was more important for a U.S. Jesuit.

Richard, like Daniel Berrigan, was widely misunderstood within the Society of Jesus. I spoke to him of my disappointment in the institutional church and the Jesuit edifice, with its officers and hierarchy and chain of command. Richard listened patiently. "No matter what you do," he said, "keep your focus on God. Be committed to Christ's path. That's the most important thing, the only thing that counts." He spoke gently and from the heart, and my depression began to lift. It felt wonderful to be understood. "If you speak against war," he said, "you'll be doing it the rest of your life, saying the same things over and over for ten, twenty, thirty, or fifty years. People will oppose you, the culture will ignore you, the Jesuits will treat you dismissively. But go on speaking out and contributing to peace. You will be just like Jesus and the prophets. In the end, your life will bear good fruit."

He went on to tell me that Thomas Merton was the first Catholic priest to condemn the nuclear arms race. His superiors silenced him, forbidding him to write on certain subjects. Imperialism, nuclear weapons, racism, and the war in Vietnam were all off-limits. Astonishingly, Merton obeyed. He closed his mouth and chose to stay in the Trappist order—and his fidelity bore good fruit. I determined to stay the course as well, and trust that my witness for peace would be fruitful. "Don't worry," Richard said. "Don't be anxious. Use your time to prepare for your work ahead. And keep your eyes on Jesus. Somehow, someway, he will use your struggle and work to help transform the world."

I could have cried tears of relief. His affirmation would sustain me for years to come. I headed back to Wernersville filled with hope that somehow everything would work out.

When I returned, it was clear that things had been stirring. My interest in taking part in civil disobedience had been widely debated, and my superiors asked me to account for it. I fielded an array of questions and found myself constantly pulled into discussions on the topic. An essay on civil disobedience written by an older Jesuit scholastic made the rounds. It said that any public action for justice and peace had to come from a heart rooted in God's love, or it was just another expression of violence, egotism, and domination. That point became the focus of my continued soul-searching. Was I merely shadowboxing? Looking for love? Reaching for stardom? My destiny would include public witness—that much was clear. But would I do it in the right spirit? Amid the flurry, I felt I had better examine myself for ulterior motives. I spent the summer exploring the basement of my heart, searching out my personal violence and facing my own darkness. I resolved to try to root whatever I did in selfless love and compassion, and ultimately in the nonviolence and peace of Christ.

I knew that the other novices saw me as an eccentric who harangued incessantly about war, injustice, and nuclear weapons. But I was set on my course. I camped out in the library when I got the chance and continued my peace studies. On Saturdays, I walked the countryside with Peter and Frank and discussed with them the great questions. We brought along readings from our favorite peacemakers. We memorized speeches by Dr. King and then recited them to one another. Our days together were exhilarating.

In August, the twentieth anniversary of Dr. King's "I have a dream" speech would be marked by a national rally in Washington, D.C., featuring Jesse Jackson and Coretta Scott King. Peter, Frank, Ed, Mike, and I submitted a fervent request to attend. To our minds, the reasons for going were abundant. It would be an excellent way to prepare for work in justice and peace. We were denied permission but invited to do something on our own, there at Wernersville. So we planned an all-night vigil and a twenty-four-hour fast in solidarity with the marchers. We read aloud Dr. King's writings and held a special prayer service for racial justice and nuclear disarmament. We even sent Mrs. King a telegram offering our support. In some ways, it refined our focus and deepened our commitment.

The following year, I would stay up late one night in the sanctuary of a church talking with Coretta Scott King after her lecture on the meaning of nonviolence as unconditional love. She had spoken with authority and dignity, urging everyone present to practice universal love. I told her of my hopes and desires and thanked her for her influence and inspiration. I was amazed by her faithful spirit, and her kindness was a source of encouragement for many years.

▣ ▣

Back at the novitiate, I began to reconsider how to live my vocation. I still harbored memories of those radical Franciscans at the St. Francis Inn, of how they seemed content to live meekly and lowly in the interest of serving the meek and lowly. Bailing out of the Jesuits and hooking up with the Franciscans didn't seem like a bad idea. Perhaps it would allow me to move closer to Jesus.

I began praying about it and then asked to meet with Father Jim. I wondered if he would be open to discussing the idea of my joining the Franciscan community. I sat down in his office, and, after all the discouraging nos that had emanated from that place, he handed me a bouquet of yeses. He looked almost relieved. "You're much closer to St. Francis than St. Ignatius," he said. "You might as well deal with it before you profess perpetual vows." And so I was given leave to write to the Franciscan vocation director.

Off I drove to Philly to meet Father Kevin, a dynamic, charismatic young Franciscan priest. I approached the Inn and found him perched alone on its rickety tin roof. He was not at all the paragon of clerical primness: he wore a white T-shirt and faded blue jeans and was barefoot.

We talked for hours. He asked about my life, my interests, what I read, the things I wanted to do. He was wise and compassionate and, in the end, concerned only that I discover God's will and do it—whether as a Jesuit, a Franciscan, or a layman.

Father Kevin made a distinction I had never considered. "The point of the Franciscan vocation," he said, "is to be little, to hang around street corners with the people. The Jesuits, on the other hand, are high-profile people. They're the elite of the church, the ones who write books, speak out on the issues, point out the way for the rest of us." This brought me up short. He had named the very things I wanted to do—change the world, speak out on the issues, and announce God's reign of peace.

"John," he said finally, "you sound to me like a Jesuit. I don't think you would be happy hanging around street corners. Changing the world—that's a Jesuit's vocation, not a Franciscan's." I felt a great sense of relief. That fall, I wrote him and thanked him for his support and encouragement. I would be staying in the Society of Jesus after all—even the Franciscan vocation director said it was meant to be. Father Kevin wrote back with an offering of blessings. My doubts vanished, and I never considered another vocation again, but I would always be grateful to Kevin.

I was back in the fold, just in time to start the two-week walking pilgrimage reserved for second-year novices. Ignatius had wanted novices to learn how to beg, to know powerlessness, and thereby to discover a deeper trust in God. He ordered second-year novices to beg alone, usually in some far-off place, for up to a year. So all the second-year novices—Peter, Frank, Michael, and the others—set off, heading out on their own in all directions for a hundred miles. They carried no money, slept under trees, and begged for food. They returned purified and glowing, and brimming with amazing stories of generous people.

I had desperately wanted to go, too, and was required to go by custom. But a week before, Father Jim had called me into his office. "The last thing you need," he said, "is another pilgrimage." Apparently, my roaming through Israel and Palestine was pilgrimage enough. "What you need," he said, pointing his finger, "is to stay home, sit in silence, be quiet, and listen to God for a change." I felt disappointed, singled out, and unduly chastened, like a kid sent to the corner for a time-out. It was time for another eight-day retreat.

Here was Jesuit obedience all over again. Father Jim was testing me by making decisions on my behalf and thwarting my self-reliance. But maybe he was right. In an unexpected way, things worked out. I spent the eight days meditating on Christ's powerlessness. I prayed to let go ever more radically of my first-world bearings. I prayed to accept Jesus' gospel invitation ever more completely. When all was said and done, I felt more surely than ever that God wanted me to be both a Jesuit and a public advocate for justice and peace.

We second-year novices were supposed to begin our next experiment, working two days a week in Reading among the poor, but I was deeply interested in gospel nonviolence, so I asked Father Jim if I could spend my two days a week writing about it with the goal of publishing an article, in order to prepare for my vow of nonviolence. He granted me permission. Two months and a hundred pages later, I didn't have an article on my hands, but a burgeoning book. The nonviolence of Jesus, the nonviolence of the ages, the meaning of nonviolence today—the sheets of paper kept stacking up. I ended by urging readers to pledge themselves to gospel nonviolence, just as I was getting ready to do. *Disarming the Heart: Toward a Vow of Nonviolence*, my first book, would come out in 1987. As a result, and through the efforts of Pax Christi, tens of thousands of people around the world would profess a vow of nonviolence.

Maybe my life would bear good fruit after all.

◙ 12 ◙

First Blood
(1983–84)

Y ou most certainly cannot get arrested—not now, not ever." So the assistant provincial had warned me. Should I disobey, I'd be in for troubles unspecified—in other words, expulsion. But for me, the edict did not resolve the matter. More and more, my conscience bound me over against the weight and sway of institutional mandate. Even if most Jesuits and their institutions remained silent—or worse, supported the culture of war and injustice—I would not. At some point, I would take a stand, and stay there. For now, all I could do was take one step at a time and put the whole insoluble matter in better hands. As it turned out, the matter would resolve itself during the next eight months.

Things began happening during my five-day visit with family in December of 1983. During that Christmas week, following my heart, I joined the annual protest for the Feast of the Holy Innocents organized by Jonah House, the Baltimore community of nonviolent resisters founded by Philip Berrigan and his wife, Elizabeth McAlister. I figured that I didn't need permission; arrest wasn't in my immediate plans.

A hundred of us gathered in a church basement in Washington, D.C., to discuss war, nuclear weapons, and the demands of the gospel.

Philip Berrigan stood at the center of it all. Even at sixty, he was strapping and tall as a Roman patrician, with a face classical sculptors envisioned before they lifted chisel to marble. As an officer during World War II, he had set targets for bombing raids on Germany. Afterward, he joined the Josephite order and spent years serving the African-American poor in New Orleans and Newburgh, New York. In Newburgh, he spoke out against the Vietnam War and was soon removed from the semi-nary where he taught and ordered to a parish in Baltimore. Undaunted, he organized nonviolent raids on draft boards—most notoriously in Catonsville, a sleepy suburb outside the city. His actions landed him and his brother in prison and on front pages across the nation. After Philip's release from the federal prison in Danbury in 1972, he left the priesthood and, together with Elizabeth and the others at Jonah House, organized nonstop antiwar actions in Washington, D.C., and, later, the well-known Plowshares disarmament actions.

Meeting Phil felt like meeting the prophet Jeremiah. He did not indulge in small talk. In the 1990s, one judge called him "the con-science of his generation." With a trenchant mind, a sharp glance, and a thunderous tongue, he stood nearly alone in America, declaring by word and action, "'Peace, peace!' they say, though there is no peace."

Early the next morning, the protesters gathered at the Pentagon. After a brief prayer service, we entered the building, and, after some prayers and a song, a few resisters poured their own blood on the lino-leum floor. After they were arrested, the rest of us went outside on the lawn near the Potomac River and lay down in a "die-in" to demon-strate the effects of the Pentagon's war-making and nuclear weapons. We lay there for some fifteen minutes before a child walked among us and touched us, waking us up in a gesture of resurrection.

The blood on the gleaming floor—a primal, visceral sign—was meant to confront the Pentagon with the gut-wrenching reality of blood spilled all over the world from its wars. But I doubt anyone felt the shock as keenly as I did. I had never been to the Pentagon before or witnessed its self-proclaimed power and grandeur. I had never taken part in an event as dramatic and raw as this one. I had never seen blood like that before—huge puddles all over the floor. The blood, the police, my new friends under arrest, the fear that clenched my belly, the fearless proclamation of God's word—all of it shook me to the core and made me feel once again that I had stepped into the Acts of the Apostles.

The Pentagon mopped up and went about its business. The police descended, and the blood pourers served months in jail. As for me, I was never the same. I'd never find satisfaction in scripted life again. I had touched a deeper level of reality, and it had thrown me headlong into a kind of mystical concord with the early martyred Christians, who had enacted daring public witnesses of their own. They had shed their blood but refused to shed the blood of others. From now on, I would do the same.

Meanwhile, in January 1984, I returned to Wernersville to receive my six-month assignment, the last before I was to profess vows in August. Father Jim assigned me to go to Georgetown University and, under the direction of a Jesuit professor, start a program to help Salvadoran children, who were arriving from war zones at the rate of fifty per week.

All those Salvadoran children, suffering post-traumatic stress disorder and grieving their family members killed by death squads! Some had known the martyred Archbishop Óscar Romero, their shepherd. None of the kids could speak English, and they'd been abandoned for the most part by the abysmal D.C. public schools. The Jesuits knew about the crisis only because of an exposé in the *Washington Post*.

Our program, the D.C. Schools Project, recruited Georgetown students to befriend and tutor the Salvadoran kids. Many Georgetown students signed up, primarily because of the tireless efforts of my colleague on the project, a talented, precocious Georgetown senior named Dan Porterfield. Headed for Oxford on a Rhodes Scholarship, he knew everyone on campus and had the respect of the faculty. He talked up the program, recruited the tutors, and attracted widespread publicity. I took on the job of locating the children, building ties with the Salvadoran community, and meeting with D.C. school officials. Dan and I worked all day long, seven days a week

We commandeered university vans to bus Georgetown students to various D.C. public schools in the afternoons and the kids to their overcrowded apartments in the evenings. When we couldn't get the campus to the kids, we brought the kids to the campus. The Georgetown students, God bless them, lavished the kids with kindness. We threw picnics on the weekends, hosted sporting events, and screened movies. These were life-changing experiences for everyone involved, the student volunteers as well as the children. The program continues today, on a grander scale. It now embraces immigrant children who land in D.C. from all over the world.

I passed those days in a surreal aura, crisscrossing from Georgetown and the pristine suburbs of my youth to the crowded apartments of the Salvadorans, fresh from the killing fields. They occupied all my attention and were my only concern. During the 1980s and early '90s, some eighty thousand Salvadorans died from the repression funded by the administrations of Ronald Reagan and George H. W. Bush. The Salvadorans I befriended, the children and their parents, told me their harrowing stories, and I witnessed their new poverty firsthand. I tried to ease their transition, but it was they who changed me, by sharing their helplessness and fear. Spurred by their suffering, I began studying El Salvador—not just the infamous death squads but the heroic church and its outspoken fidelity to the God of justice and liberation. I also studied the histories of Guatemala and of Nicaragua, where Reagan's contras aimed to destroy the Sandinistas and anyone in their path.

The contrasts overwhelmed me. I lived on campus with a hundred indefatigable Jesuits, all put up smartly in a stately brick lodge right in the central square. At dinner, waiters in vests and ties moved among us, taking our dishes. It was as far from El Salvador as it could be. The posh life began to grate on my conscience. I felt as if I was back at Duke, facing the revelry of the frat house after a day of caring for the mentally ill. It didn't help that hardly any of my fellow Jesuits seemed aware of what to me were obvious conflicts.

But two Jesuits on campus lent me support. One was Richard McSorley, who taught a popular peace studies class. The other was Father Robert Drinan, the former congressman from Boston ordered by Pope John Paul II to step down from politics—the only reason given was that priests can't hold elective office. Father Drinan urged me to write books, give talks, and do everything possible for peace and justice. Richard included me in his projects and travels around town and regaled me with stories of the Kennedys, Dr. King, and Dorothy Day. I spent many hours in his tiny monastic cell of an office exploring the heaps of books that lay around and studying the memorabilia piled up from his years in the peace movement. He always had time for me.

I was so grateful to these two extraordinary Jesuits, and I would soon get to know the Jesuit I admired most, Father Daniel Berrigan, who would be appearing at the Kirkridge Retreat Center in Pennsylvania. With flyer in hand, I knocked on the door of the community superior, Father Jim Devereux, and asked if I could attend. I had known him since my days at Duke, when he was a professor at the University of North Carolina at Chapel Hill. We both had roots in that state, and for that reason he seemed to tolerate me. The moment I said Daniel Berrigan's name, though, he dropped his head into his hands.

"A hundred years from now," he said with a sigh, "the only Jesuit from this century that people will know will be Daniel Berrigan." He brought his fingers to his temples and closed his eyes. "He'll be revered as a hero and a saint, the one who spoke out against Vietnam, the one who took action against nuclear weapons. That's all people will ever say." He continued, as if I weren't there, "Another Daniel Berrigan—that's the last thing we need around here." Then he exhaled deeply, blinked, and looked at me.

"Okay, you can go," he said reluctantly, "but please don't come back another Daniel Berrigan."

▨ ▨

Daniel Berrigan was born in 1921, entered the Jesuits in 1939, and published his first book of poetry in 1957 to great acclaim. He has traveled the world for peace; has written more than fifty books; has taught at more than a dozen universities; befriended Thomas Merton, Dorothy Day, and Thich Nhat Hanh; marched in Selma; has led countless Scripture retreats; and has been nominated repeatedly for the Nobel Peace Prize. In 1965, his Jesuit superiors kicked him out of the United States for his antiwar stand and sent him to Latin America for several difficult months.

After burning draft files in Catonsville in 1968 and writing an award winning play about the trial in 1969, Dan went underground in 1970, only to appear regularly on the evening news and in the *New York Times*. Under J. Edgar Hoover's sinister obsession, hundreds of F.B.I. agents sought him out and finally captured Dan on Block Island, Rhode Island. Dan and his brother Philip made the cover of *Time* because they were the first priests in U.S. history to resist war and go to prison. For decades, Dan addressed audiences across the country on the meaning of war and peace. He remains to this day a faithful Jesuit, having lived for many years in New York's West Side Jesuit Community.

When he walked through the door of Kirkridge to start the retreat, he was wearing a black beret, a brightly colored shirt, and a large fish medallion around his neck. He seemed smaller and frailer than Phil, yet he was equally intense. His wit, spirit, sense of humor, and joy were contagious.

That night, I introduced myself—he knew my name because I had written him several times—and sought his wisdom on being a Jesuit for peace and nonviolence when there was so little support among the ranks. He stated simply that fear was at the root of this resistance. "But we're not supposed to live in fear. Jesus said, 'Do not be afraid.' We should not root our lives in fear." That was the first lesson Daniel Berrigan taught me: "Don't be afraid."

The next morning, Dan gave one of the most inspiring talks I've ever heard, and I copied down every word. He reflected on Paul's letter to the Philippians. "Jesus comes into this world of death," Dan taught, "and does the wrong things, in the wrong places, with the wrong people, at the wrong times. He does everything wrong."

> He says to us, "I will be your God no matter how wicked you are. My being God doesn't depend on your being godly." God is disarmed for all time in Christ, and that is the scandal. We

are being asked to live out the drama of the disarmed Christ in a world armed to the teeth. The disarmed human being, in today's world, like Christ, is a freak. We're not a disarmed church because we're not yet worshipers of a disarmed God. To confess Jesus these days, in this world of war and death, is to work for peace. If we're not capable of personal disarmament, we're no help to the peace movement. If we're not having a tough time over a long period of time because of our Christianity, maybe our discipleship—our humanity—is in question.

The weekend came to a close, and I recommitted myself to stand against the culture of war no matter the consequence or cost. I envisioned myself returning to the Pentagon and confronting it as Jesus confronted the unjust temple in Jerusalem. It was just a matter of time. I would take a stand, as Dan had, and let the chips fall where they may.

Such was my attitude when I returned to Georgetown, to life among the privileged students and Jesuits and the tyrannized Salvadoran children. Outside my window, ROTC cadets jerked their rifles, chanted war slogans, and pretended to fight. *Something must be done*, I thought. So I wrote to the Jesuit president of the university and asked him to put a stop to Georgetown's war-making.

"I write you with serious concerns about the university's financial, academic, and public support of the U.S. military and the structures of violence," I began.

Understanding the teachings and example of Jesus, who was totally nonviolent, I ask you, as a brother Jesuit, to end immediately all of Georgetown's support for the U.S. military by

(1) ending the ROTC program and providing academic scholarships for those students who are in it, (2) closing Georgetown's Center for Strategic and International Studies (and its research into nuclear weapons and post-nuclear laser-beam warfare), and (3) returning all financial contributions from the U.S. Department of Defense and ceasing any further cooperation with the Pentagon. I realize that these are difficult decisions to make, but I trust that God will give you the necessary courage to speak out and act on behalf of Georgetown for Christ's way of nonviolence. Such decisions will surely lead Georgetown University to become an even greater center for scholarship and service and to be regarded highly in centuries to come for its fidelity to the gospel of peace.

Two weeks passed in chilly silence. Every night I saw the president at dinner; every night, he refused to greet me. Finally, his secretary called with a message: Report to his office at once. The president's office was the size of a basketball court, with a vaulted ceiling and oak paneled walls. It took up most of the second floor of the main building on campus. Fine paintings and glass bookcases lined the walls. Antique furniture stood on beautiful oriental rugs. I entered the expanse and settled into a leather chair in front of his outsize oak desk.

In a few moments, a side door swung open, and he burst in, slamming the door behind him. "How dare you write me a letter like that!" he began. "What gives you the right to instruct me about the operations of this university? Do you realize that if we don't have Christians running the Pentagon, there will be even more wars, even worse atrocities? We need Jesuit-educated people

running the Pentagon, the military, and our nuclear arsenal. . . .
You're a disgrace to the Society."

"I stand by what I wrote," I answered. With a stomach full of
butterflies, I pressed right back. "I ask you in the name of Jesus," I
said arrogantly, "to end the ROTC program and close all research
into nuclear weapons." He left as abruptly as he had come in. Shaken,
I found my way out the main door.

Lenten Wednesdays
at the Pentagon
(1984)

My encounter with Georgetown's president, coming on the heels of my retreat with Daniel Berrigan, spurred me back to the Pentagon. I was determined to engage in my own Gandhian "experiment with the truth" of nonviolence. I called the other novices stationed nearby and asked them to join me at the Pentagon for a prayer vigil every Wednesday morning during Lent. Peter Cicchino was the only one to accept.

We met on Mardi Gras night and planned our first action, for Ash Wednesday morning. We decided to distribute a leaflet and stayed up most of the night composing. The leaflet talked of repentance and conversion—both Ash Wednesday themes—and of the coming reign of God. "All human beings, as children of God redeemed by Jesus, have the right to the goods of this earth and a life in which to enjoy them," it said. It ran rather long, but we liked it and brimmed with hope that the Pentagon employees would study it, perhaps over lunch. We thought that we might convert thousands to our cause, as St. Peter had with his bold first public speech. Peter and I believed deeply in what we had written:

> This building which commands the machinery of war is a symbol of the sin and disorder which presently afflicts us, a disorder which denies food to the poor while spending billions of dollars on instruments of mass destruction. The evil of this waste is compounded by the fact that it has placed so many Americans in a position where their livelihood depends upon threatening, planning, and ultimately implementing the deaths of millions of others. We urge you to reexamine your values and repent of the sin of war. Lay down your arms, relinquish your fears, and open yourselves to God and God's reign of love and peace.

We produced a thousand copies and took them to the Pentagon to distribute to employees as they arrived at work. It soon became apparent that they wouldn't be studying our leaflet over lunch. To a person, they declined to take it. Our hearts sank, but we didn't give up. We walked over to the nearby subway station, descended into the tunnel, and tried to distribute our leaflets there. But the police surrounded us in short order and threatened us with arrest if we continued, so we left.

That afternoon, Peter and I met over lunch and reflected on this our first public witness for disarmament. The employees had refused our leaflets, the police had shooed us off, and we had nine hundred leaflets left, but we glowed nonetheless with a sense of empowerment. Energized and excited, we planned the following Wednesday's action. We would proclaim the good news of peace for all to hear.

A week later we were back, standing atop the massive stone buttresses at the Pentagon's riverside entrance, taking turns reading aloud the Sermon on the Mount as employees streamed past. I began: "Blessed are the poor in spirit . . ." Peter took over at the antithetical teachings: "You have heard that it was said. . . . But I say to you . . ." And then we read the revolutionary commandments, "Love your enemies" and "Be compassionate as God is compassionate." After that, we started all over again. We read for exactly one hour.

Afterward, we talked of our disappointment with the uninterested crowds. No conversion was apparent—except, we confessed, our own. We realized that neither of us had heard the Sermon on the Mount read out loud before. As we read it over and over, facing the Potomac River and the government buildings, our backs to the Pentagon, the words touched us profoundly, summoning us to a deeper commitment. Perhaps we were being converted!

We returned the next week with a new leaflet. It questioned Pentagon employees about attaining eternal life in the context of their plotting for war. "What must I do to inherit eternal life?" it asked, quoting the rich official's question to Jesus. And it suggested Jesus' response: "You must not kill. Love your enemies."

Eternal life, we reminded them, isn't a private or an individualistic matter but involves the whole human community. Ethics are never abstract or vague but concrete and specific. "Personal virtue, love of God has no meaning unless it permeates every aspect of our lives, including government policies and laws." And so we called for an end to military aid to Central America and to the covert arming of Nicaraguan contras.

We reached out with our leaflets, and, much to our delight, the employees snatched them up. What a happy reception! we thought.

But then we noticed that the police had set up trash cans near the door. The leaflets went from our hands to their cans.

We needed a new plan. "Next week," Peter said, "let's march right up to them and let them have it. Let's yell at each one of them, 'For the love of God, go home, you heathen warmongers, and repent of the sin of war and nuclear weapons!'"

"No, we're people of nonviolence," I said sagely, then explained as gently as I could the mindfulness of peace and the methodology of nonviolence. "You and I are gentle, loving people of peace. We don't yell. We don't call anyone names. So get hold of yourself. Whatever we do, we must be as gentle and nonviolent as possible. How about this: Let's approach them calmly and say, 'Will you please not go to work today? Please go home and reflect on the gospel of Jesus and his way of nonviolence and consider quitting your job at the Pentagon.'"

Peter was embarrassed about his self-righteous anger and agreed. "Of course—you're right. That sounds much more non-violent. Let's do it."

The following week, we headed back to the riverside entrance, this time wearing our clerical black suits and white collars, which we thought would lower defenses and help us gain a listening ear. The sky was muted like gray wool, the air heavy and chill, and both of us were nervous. Here we were, two Jesuit novices—with no media backing, no celebrity support on hand, no throng carrying their signs—about to plunge defenselessly into the crowd and call people to conversion, as John the Baptist and St. Paul had. We imagined that the Pentagon had never seen the likes of what we were about to do.

As I approached the imposing building, I was unexpectedly over-come by the vastness of death and destruction orchestrated in this one sinister place. Thousands here had their bloody hands in dozens of wars and countless massacres around the world. There was no other place like it on earth—I saw that it was the center of death for the whole planet, its prime purpose to organize the empire's killing sprees at the behest of multinational corporations and politicians. The stories of my Salvadoran friends hit home in that moment, and I was hurt and angry that this building stood behind the deaths of thousands of innocent Salvadorans, including good nuns and priests. The place stood as a blasphemy against the God of peace. What in the world would Jesus have made of this place? If he had been so upset at the unjust temple and committed civil disobedience there, an act that led to his arrest and execution, what would he do at the Pentagon?

Near the entrance, my equanimity gave way, my focus crumbled, and I surged with anger. Just then, a long black limousine pulled up to the curb, and a general emerged—as fate would have it, a member of the Joint Chiefs of Staff—his shoes gleaming, the crease in his trousers crisp, the medals on his chest bright and shining. I exploded and charged him, flailing my arms, shouting for all to hear: "For the love of God, go home, you evil warmonger! Stop planning the destruction of the planet! Stop killing Christ in the poor!"

Peter watched in horror, realized that I had lost it, and ran up from behind and grabbed me. I had a few more things to say and tried to say them, but Peter pulled me away, telling me all the while, "I thought you said we were going to be peaceful, remember? Didn't you say we were going to be gentle and nonviolent? Get hold of yourself!" I regained my composure, and the general moved on smugly.

I breathed deeply and tried to stay calm. Someone yelled at us: "You ought to be ashamed of yourselves. Go home!" Soon the police arrived. Once again, they threatened to arrest us, so we called it a day.

That afternoon, Peter and I met for our usual reflection session. Now it was my turn to be embarrassed. "What was *that* all about?" he asked. Well, what was it all about? I cast about for an explanation. I told him how the Pentagon's countless innocent victims had flooded my mind, how I felt overwhelmed as I approached the mammoth gray building, how the pools of blood, from Vietnam to El Salvador, were soaking my memory and heart. But Peter was not satisfied. His steady gaze called me to account for my actions. I dug deeper and owned up to my anger, violence, and rage.

Now all I felt was shame. The debacle forced me to face a humbling truth about myself: I had nowhere near the inner strength of Gandhi or King. I simply didn't have the wherewithal to confront the general with disarming love. I, too, was full of violence. The roots of war lay deep within *me*. As Gandhian experiments went, this one had been a failure; I wasn't ready to practice gospel nonviolence. Then again, it succeeded in that I became aware of my lingering inner violence, the need to rid my heart of war.

"Next week," Peter said, "we ought to stand right there in front of the Pentagon in silence, to try to radiate peace from within."

So we returned the following week, stood by the entrance along the slate gray Potomac, amid the buzz and clatter of employees arriving for work, and prayed for an hour in silence. I didn't brandish my fists or yell; it was all quite simple. I blessed the employees and prayed for peace in Central America, and I importuned the God of heaven: "End these awful wars. Expel this demonic war-making spirit. Help us abolish nuclear weapons!" But more, I centered myself in peace and tried to radiate peace from within in the hope that my very presence would be disarming. It is a practice I'm still working on these many years later.

At our reflection session that afternoon, Peter and I both felt a deep sense of consolation. How good it was to stand for peace and actually feel at peace. Our plan for the final Lenten Wednesday was to write a message in the form of a memo—something every Washington bureaucrat could relate to—and pass it out. We created a one-page memo and managed to get most of the copies into people's hands. Then we quietly and gratefully went on our way.

Lent was drawing to a close. Peter and I had weathered our experiments and come out exhilarated and changed and itching for more. We wrote to our superiors for permission to join the Jonah House community in its Holy Week protest, held each year at the Pentagon. Might we risk arrest? we asked. We received a perfunctory no. So we joined the vigil but kept a safe distance from the trespass line.

I was galled by my superiors' refusal to let me take part in civil disobedience, and finally my frustration grew unbearable. I simply had to take a leap of faith and force the issue. On April 27, a Friday, I took the subway by myself to the Pentagon. I walked to the riverside entrance and sat down right in the doorway, just as thousands of people were coming to work. I pulled out my Bible and started to read from the Gospels about Jesus' crucifixion.

Six policemen descended on me in a hurry. "Excuse me, sir," said one. "I must ask you to move, or we're going to have to arrest you. You've got four minutes." We attracted the attention of a small crowd of employees, who gathered around and gawked. I bowed my head in prayer and stayed put during the four solemnest minutes of my life thus far. The time expired, and a policeman announced that I was under arrest. Several arms hauled me to my feet, several more stretched my hands behind me, and the cuffs clicked shut. It was my first arrest, and it inaugurated many more.

The policemen patted me down, emptied my pockets, and took me deep into the belly of the Pentagon to a holding cell. A couple of men in uniforms questioned me. Then they took my picture and inked my fingers. When I told them my address, the Jesuit community at Georgetown University, one of my keepers grew boiling mad. "A Jesuit?" he bellowed. "What kind of Jesuit are you? You're just a troublemaker."

"I love the church, the Jesuits, and the whole human race," I told him. "And I'm trying to follow the nonviolent Jesus. He got arrested, so I have to speak out against war and injustice and risk arrest, too. Jesus died in pursuit of God's reign of peace and justice. I have to give my life, too." The guard rolled his eyes and shook his head.

Hours later, they released me with a written order to appear in court the following month. I faced thirty days in jail. I went back to Georgetown, took a few moments to say a prayer of thanksgiving, and then called Daniel Berrigan. My story surprised him and raised his spirits.

Then I called Father Jim, my novice master. I told him the news, and he heard me out. Then he announced matter-of-factly that I was hereby dismissed from the Jesuits. He ordered me to come back to Wernersville at the end of my time at Georgetown and await the provincial's ratification of my expulsion.

I wasn't really surprised, but I was sure that what I had done was right. I felt in my bones that God had called me to two irreconcilable vocations: to be a Jesuit and to take action against war and nuclear weapons. I had disobeyed my superiors on the one hand; I had obeyed my conscience on the other. And now my goose was cooked. All I could say was that I had done my best and put the burden on God. I had done what I was supposed to do and now would be sent packing. All things considered, I felt scandalously at peace.

And then, out of the blue, Father Jim Devereux, the Georgetown superior, was named the new provincial. He knew me well by now and intervened to put a halt to my expulsion. He also ordered me never to open my mouth about the arrest—which is to say, along with my reprieve came a muzzle. In the parlance of religious orders, I had been silenced. What an uncanny, fragile outcome, everything touch and go. Thomas Merton had been subject to the same fate, and so my own silencing took shape in my mind as a kind of honor: I must be on the right track. At any rate, my arrest excited Richard McSorley, who seized on the episode and lickety-split wrote a long essay for the *National Catholic Reporter*. Whether for editorial or political reasons, the article was never published.

A month later, I left Wernersville and headed to northern Virginia to stand trial before Magistrate Grimsley, where I pleaded guilty to blocking the Pentagon entranceway. He asked if I had anything to say. Of course I had.

I went to the Pentagon in response to the direction our country is taking, with its billion-dollar defense system, its nuclear weapons, and its war against the world's poor. I have no desire to go to jail, but I acted in conscience. For months, I have been asking myself, when is it time for a person to put his body on the line, to say no to war? I concluded that now is the time for everyone, including myself, to act in faith for others.

I found myself no longer able to stand idly by while my government continues its wars. My sitting down was a definite no to violence and a resounding yes to peace, truth, and nonviolence. As a follower of Jesus, who was arrested and killed by the ruling authorities for speaking out against injustice and announcing God's reign of love and truth, I hope to share in his arrest and sufferings. I am trying to imitate him, to practice active nonviolent love for others, to serve people in love and truth, even to lay down my life for others, and I accept the consequences. My action symbolically shows my dissent with the direction our country is taking. I hope it will encourage others to work for peace through creative nonviolence, to serve the poor, and to stand up or sit down in opposition to violence and preparations for war. In the end, I am simply trying to be faithful to the God of peace and witness to the creative nonviolence and resurrection of Jesus.

The courtroom fell silent. At last, the judge spoke. "I respect you," he said. "You put great thought into this. Nonetheless, I sentence you to thirty days in jail." A pang of anxiety came first, then calm acceptance. He added, "However, I suspend the sentence." I was free to go.

My last two months at Wernersville before I professed final vows went by peacefully and uneventfully. On August 18, 1984, my family and friends gathered around me. The day brimmed with pomp and solemnity and rich ancient tradition. I knelt before the altar and professed perpetual vows of poverty, chastity, and obedience in the Society of Jesus. I stood up grateful for the journey and committed to the road ahead.

That July, Peter, Frank, Parke, and I had asked if we could add to our profession a vow of nonviolence. "Absolutely not" was the answer. "Don't do anything out of the ordinary. Don't do anything to upset the vow day feast."

Our request refused, the four of us had climbed a nearby hill the day before vow day, on August 17, and under a grove of pines held a private ceremony of our own. We confessed our sins of violence. We read from the Sermon on the Mount. Then we took turns professing to one another the vow we had written:

Loving God, Father of Jesus and Mother of all creation, you worked the salvation of the world through the life and death of Jesus and the outpouring of the Holy Spirit. In his perfect act of nonviolent suffering love, Jesus gave his life as a ransom for many and redeemed his lost sisters and brothers from sin. Trusting in your infinite goodness and mercy, before the cross of Jesus, I vow perpetual nonviolence in fulfillment of the command of Jesus and in imitation of his holy life and death. I seek the intercession of his mother Mary and all the saints and martyrs of nonviolent love. Loving God, I trust in your sustaining love and believe that just as you gave me the grace to desire and offer this vow, so you will also bestow abundant grace to fulfill it.

A palpable sense of peace settled on us. Our consolation seemed full and complete, a sign to us of the Spirit's affirmation. We were ready to set out into the culture of war with a steadfast faith in gospel nonviolence. We were going to change the world and ourselves—and, in the process, even the church.

Two days after vow day, we piled into cars for our next assignment—two years of graduate studies in philosophy. Our destination: Fordham University in New York City.

回 14 圓

Peacemaking in
New York City
(1984–85)

The maternal hills of eastern Pennsylvania vanished from view, and the boisterous streets of the Bronx received us indifferently. We inched through the clamor of Fordham Road, where a diverse crowd of thousands shop and eat, and took up residence at Murray-Weigel Hall, behind the tall black wrought-iron gates that marked the Fordham campus.

A hard path lay ahead. We faced four graduate philosophy courses each semester for two years—St. Ignatius's idea. He had ordered that all Jesuits study not only theology, but philosophy as well, so as to be grounded in the intellectual life. From the beginning, I couldn't muster any enthusiasm for the project. But off to class I went like a truant seized by the ear, slogging through assignments and surprisingly making good grades.

I found relief of sorts by throwing myself into the city. I paid visits to the Catholic Worker and joined Pax Christi groups, served at soup kitchens, and volunteered at shelters. And I attended every peace vigil that came along, making many friends in the process. For the two years that Fordham had me manacled to books, I offered the balance of my time to those struggling for justice and peace. It was a real education—a graduate program in peace studies of the earthiest kind.

A few days after we arrived, my Pentagon cohort Peter Cicchino and I met Jack Marth, a bright, engaging sophomore from Philadelphia. He had attended the trial of the Plowshares Eight and sat enthralled as the Berrigans leveled their vision at the hapless and exasperated judge. Inspired and emboldened, Jack formed the Fordham chapter of Pax Christi. Would Peter and I care to join? We eagerly agreed.

The Fordham chapter of Pax Christi served as our base of operations for the next two years. We composed antiwar leaflets and screened films. We organized vigils and arranged forums that brought in guest speakers, from Belfast's Nobel Peace Prize winner Mairead Corrigan Maguire to Eileen Egan, cofounder of Pax Christi USA. The place was a hive, with everyone going nonstop—exploring nonviolence, raising consciousness, forcing people to stake out a position.

We also had a soup kitchen—and a four-star one at that. Its founders, two unusual NYU professors of Russian literature—Lorraine Wynne and Andrej Kodjak—started out with modest aims. They secured the basement of a Jesuit church on the Lower East Side, invited a few students, and offered the down-and-out locals a free meal.

Other neighborhood programs opened their doors on weekdays and shunted people through. Lorry and Andrej filled the weekend hiatus with a Saturday meal. Their vision was charged with graciousness. They figured if they served one meal a week, it might as well be a feast. Instead of bologna sandwiches off the assembly line, they provided a full-blown bistro for the penniless. Checkered cloths and flowers dignified the tables. A waiter approached every party and announced the menu, returning with a tasty soup, then a salad and a bounty of meat, bread, vegetables, and fruit. The delectable meal was topped off with coffee and dessert, if one had room. "We wouldn't serve anything we wouldn't eat ourselves," Andrej told us that first day.

He and Lorry ran the place with precision: tables were cleared in a snap, dishes were rushed to the kitchen, and crumbs were wiped away with a whisk of a towel. A watchful host would see a table being cleared and assemble the next party for seating. Six hundred people lined up each week for this free gourmet feast.

Lorry and Andrej became our good friends, along with some of the volunteers and many of the homeless. "We're not holy, but the work is," Andrej told us. "We get nothing out of it—no money, no interest. It's hard work. But when it's over, we find it's been a great blessing." Peter and I agreed. Every Saturday we saw the gospel played out before our eyes—the homeless Christ offered food and drink.

▣ ▣

Father Daniel Berrigan lived in town with twenty other Jesuits in a run-down, sprawling pre-war building on West Ninety-eighth Street. They called themselves the West Side Jesuit Community. Not long before vow day, Dan had sent me a letter thanking me for my civil disobedience and my speech before the magistrate—the only thanks, the only encouragement I received from anyone, besides Richard McSorley.

"I was so moved by your statement to the worldly court," he wrote in the first of hundreds of letters he would send me over the next twenty-five years.

It deserves to be a footnote to the Acts of the Apostles, where the early sisters and brothers also faced things. And were shipped off and eventually disposed of. I've said this before (and much more often and with anguish to my soul over the years), that I cannot comprehend the attitude of provincials. They niggle over your "case," and see nothing of the huge tipped missiles (the "beam" of the Gospel) in the open eye of Georgetown. They dismiss you, saying you are "overworked." Well, they said Jesus was mad—his own relatives, we're told in the Gospel. So congratulations—you're in the best of companies, Company of Jesus. You've done something momentous though humiliating and lost on most, for that Society which exists like Christ, "a ragged figure flitting from tree to tree at the back of the mind" (as Flannery O'Connor wrote). For this I thank you with all my heart.

Once settled in New York, I called up Dan, and he invited me to dinner at the community. Peter came along as well. A few years earlier, Dan had moved into a small two-room apartment. One room was covered floor to ceiling in gorgeous, colorful artwork that he had received from friends over the years. The other room, housing his desk and bed, was covered floor to ceiling with photos of those friends and heroes—Merton, Gandhi, Dorothy Day, Dr. King, Nhat Hanh, Phil, and countless others. He called this his "non–wailing wall." The apartment was like a peace museum, the only one of its kind in New York City. We eased our way through dinner, and then I began to pose questions; he had agreed to a little interview for the Pax Christi journal. I asked about his current work, his recent trip to El Salvador and Nicaragua, his legal appeal for the Plowshares action. But I was grasping for the real question. I didn't know what I wanted to ask him, only that I needed to ask something. I was like the stuttering student before the master, the witless disciple before the guru. Finally, I blurted out, "So, Dan, what's the point of all this?"

"The point," he said with tender earnestness, "is to make our story fit into the story of Jesus, so our life makes sense in light of the life of Jesus."

"To make our story fit . . ." I spun the logic out in my mind. Follow Jesus, resemble Jesus, do what Jesus did. And so speak out against war and nuclear weapons, serve the poor, confront the powers, practice nonviolence, offer peace and compassion to all. Make our story fit with his—this answer explained Dan's life in a nutshell, and it offered a framework for everything I was trying to do, and everything I would try to do for the rest of my life.

During the course of the evening, Dan invited Peter and me to join his small peace group, the Kairos Community. The group met every other Tuesday night at a West Side church rectory. They prayed, reflected on issues, and took a public stand for peace and justice in the city, often through civil disobedience. At my first meeting, I reconnected with Sister Anne Montgomery and Elmer Maas, members of the Plowshares Eight whom I had heard speak in Reading two years before.

Peter, Jack, and I also agreed to join the group's weekly vigil at Forty-second Street and Times Square, in front of the Riverside Research Institute. The institute's purposes were dark, its talents and energies devoted to laser-beam warfare and post-nuclear Star Wars research. The place was staffed by the remnant of the Manhattan Project. For two years, Peter, Jack, and I spent every Friday morning with friends from Kairos and the Catholic Worker, keeping vigil for an hour and handing out leaflets that we took turns writing. We denounced the institute's work as inhuman and immoral. Employees coming to work threaded their way through our group, annoyed and embarrassed. Neighbors who had never been informed of what went on in the place grew concerned. On Good Friday, Pax Christi joined in, bringing one thousand Catholics to the institute's door demanding disarmament. On the anniversaries of Hiroshima and Martin Luther King Jr.'s birthday, solemn occasions marking violence in the one instance and nonviolence in the other, we blocked the entrance and faced arrest. During my time with the group, nothing happened, but we stayed our course. Finally, in the mid-1990s, the Riverside Research Institute quietly moved out of its Manhattan apartment building in Times Square.

Since the late 1970s, the Kairos Community has continued its work—faithfully, quietly, like a Thessalonian house church. It is my model of a grassroots community, much like the base communities I would encounter in El Salvador, Nicaragua, Haiti, Colombia, and the Philippines. Kairos stands on the front line of every issue, calling for justice through nonviolent resistance. It grows out of the soil of conscience, but also the soil of friendship.

回 回

My life in New York was full of contrasts. On the one hand, my time with Kairos and other groups energized and enlivened me. On the other hand, my academic studies in philosophy blunted my senses. Then I had an inspiration: Why not undertake a research project of my own on the philosophy of nonviolence? That might even things out. While at Georgetown, I had copied dozens of articles by Richard McSorley and stashed them away for future reference. I would begin with these. I set to work editing his writings for an anthology, published in 1991, titled *It's a Sin to Build a Nuclear Weapon: The Collected Works on War and Christian Peacemaking of Richard McSorley, SJ*. In the meantime, I plugged away at my own manuscript, on the vow of nonviolence.

Still dear to my heart were the Salvadoran children I had left behind in Washington. Those traumatized little ones had found a measure of safety and now had a modest chance to learn and play. I thought of their expansive happiness and my heart softened. At the same time, the Jesuits in the United States were beginning to receive impassioned letters from the famous Jesuits of Central America. The substance of their letters can be summed up in a few words: *Implore your government to stop military aid to El Salvador and Guatemala. Expose the U.S. contra war against the people of Nicaragua.*

Six months earlier, I had met Pat and Ray Donovan—parents of Jean, one of the churchwomen who had died so brutally in El Salvador. When I told them of my interest in their daughter and my work with Salvadoran children, they shocked me by saying, "You must go to El Salvador! You need to see the place for yourself."

The thought had never occurred to me. But Daniel Berrigan had just gone, and now the Central American Jesuits were pleading for solidarity. I knew that few U.S. Jesuits would do anything, but I could not ignore the plea. I tossed and turned at night and wrestled with trepidation during my waking hours. I prayed over the idea and pondered the lives of Romero and the four churchwomen. That fall, I put shaky pen to paper and wrote a request to my superiors. Would they consider letting me go to El Salvador? To my surprise, they granted me permission immediately. Some of my friends couldn't help but tease: "They want to get rid of you. How better than to ship you off to El Salvador?"

The trip was scheduled; I would leave in six months. Meanwhile, I kept busy with philosophy studies, writing projects, soup kitchen duties, Pax Christi meetings, and monthly overnight stints at the homeless shelter. And now I had Spanish to learn—and *rápido*. Peter and I carved out some time around Lent to do our experiments with nonviolence, this time at Riverside Research Institute, and with less drama than the last time.

We decided to undertake a new campaign, one aimed at the horror of South African apartheid. We petitioned our superiors to join the sit-in actions at the South African Embassy in Washington, D.C. to protest apartheid, but were denied. More, we were interrogated and ostracized for being nuisances. Why did we want to make such a scene? Who did we think we were? We were pushed to defend ourselves, even over such a clear-cut case of massive injustice that eventually the whole world condemned. I was never allowed to protest apartheid publicly, but I did what I could.

We were, however, allowed to take part in the Good Friday Pax Christi peace walk. Two thousand Catholics marched across Manhattan on a modern-day Way of the Cross. At the end, a hundred stalwarts blocked the entrance to the USS *Intrepid*, an aircraft carrier turned war museum docked at West Forty-sixth Street. Peter and I joined Dan Berrigan and other friends in that sit-in and spent the day in jail.

Easter arrived, and Pax Christi officials asked if I might write a vow of nonviolence. My partner in the effort would be Eileen Egan. Together we'd compose the vow and assemble a pamphlet. Pax Christi would promote it, hoping that Catholics would get the message, renounce the pagan just-war theory, and start emulating the nonviolence of Jesus.

In the early 1970s, Eileen Egan had cofounded Pax Christi USA with another Catholic writer, sociologist Gordon Zahn. For decades, she had worked for Catholic Relief Services, traveling to the world's poorest slums. Both Dorothy Day and Mother Teresa counted Eileen among their closest friends. She was a petite woman in her seventies when I met her—thin, with short white hair and dark glasses, and turned out smartly in an old tweed suit. She strove to affect an attitude of gentleness and kindliness, but as I grew to know her, I came to believe that her truest bearing was one of solemnity and sadness. We talked for hours the first night we met to work on the vow and read aloud from the Sermon on the Mount. Our vow began: "Recognizing the violence in my own heart, yet trusting in the goodness and mercy of God, I vow to practice the nonviolence of Jesus . . ."

Over the next five years, more than ten thousand American Catholics professed the vow. Eileen herself would take it to dizzying heights years later. One night when she was on her way home from Mass, a thief struck her in the head and snatched her purse. The assailant made tracks but was soon caught by a policeman. Eileen, her skull fractured, refused to press charges, preferring to forgive the man publicly, a happening as rare as roses in Manhattan. It made the news, including a story in the *New York Times*.

In the late 1990s, Eileen's health declined, but her steadfast spirit was strong as ever. She plodded on, writing and speaking as best she could. In 2000 she died quietly after a long faithful life. Her funeral brought together a small band of peacemakers and Catholic Workers. "She embodied the very nonviolence she vowed and taught," I eulogized.

As May 1985 approached, I looked forward to my second Peace Pentecost gathering in Washington organized by Sojourners. A thousand gathered for talks and prayer, and then the climax—six demonstrations set off simultaneously from Lafayette Park to key points around the city. I marched with a silent crowd to the U.S. State Department, where we held vigil for an end to U.S. wars in Central America.

More than a thousand streamed into The Catholic University of America gymnasium on Pentecost Sunday to hear the famous spiritual writer Henri Nouwen. He preached for an hour and a half with great passion and eloquence, his impromptu wisdom ringing through the rafters. One of his themes came from John's resurrection stories. "Jesus doesn't ask, 'What have you done for peace and justice?'" he suggested. "Jesus asks, 'Do you love me?' He asked it of Peter three times. He asks it of us, too. Jesus wants to know if we love him. That's the real question."

I felt both the weight and the glory of his words and have yet to hear a more powerful sermon. Everyone leaned forward in hushed anticipation. "We must love Jesus as we pursue justice and peace— and for the rest of our lives," he pronounced in his Dutch accent. "Only then can we be sure that our work will bear fruit."

Then came the weightiest words of all: an admonition to steer clear of cheap grace. He reminded us of Jesus' words to Peter—not a congratulations for a job well done, but, for the first time in John's Gospel, a call to discipleship. Just when you think the journey is over, it has hardly begun. That's when the great call comes. "When you were young," Jesus said to Peter, "you put on your own belt and walked where you liked; but when you grow old, you will stretch out your hands, and somebody else will put a belt round you and take you where you would rather not go. . . . Follow me" (John 21:18–19, JB). In other words, take the road that I take, the road of resistance to injustice, the road that ends on the empire's cross. And that's just the point, Henri said. If our work springs out of love for Jesus, we'll be able to complete the Gospel journey, to give our lives for justice and peace, to endure anything—arrest, death, the cross. I swallowed his words whole, bittersweet sustenance. In two days, I would be on my way to El Salvador.

回 15 回

In the Land
of the Savior
(1985)

I went to El Salvador at the height of the U.S.-backed war there. The violence was brutal, the poverty wretched, the law in the hands of puppets. Pulling the strings and supplying the bullets was the Reagan administration, suffering its imperial delusions. I would live in El Salvador and then travel to Guatemala for several weeks and Nicaragua for several more. I offered myself to the Jesuit Refugee Service (JRS), which arranged for me to help the Archdiocese of San Salvador build a refugee camp deep in the woods of Calle Real, on the road north of San Salvador to Chalatenango.

Fifteen miles away stood the towering, ominous Guazapa volcano, its slopes home to countless civilians and sanctuary to rebels of the Farabundo Martí National Liberation Front (FMLN). U.S. aircraft bombed the region on the hour. I saw them with my own eyes—apocalyptic horsemen of the air, beyond the restraints of law, outside the contours of what we name human. The refugee camp had yet to open officially, yet hundreds of women, children, and elderly men converged there and made it their makeshift home. They had all survived massacres in their villages. Many had taken flight out the back door as the death squads stormed in the front. Loved ones left behind had been shot dead. Others were never seen again.

The death squads, supplied and trained by the United States (many at Fort Benning's notorious School of the Americas*), stalked the countryside. Often, these "soldiers" were terrorized, brainwashed, drug-fueled teenagers armed to the teeth, filled with fear, and ready to shoot on sight. They hovered like some harassing specter, sidearms on their hips, M16s slung over their shoulders, and wearing drab olive clothes and helmets and dusty boots.

I had the dubious job of greeting them when they arrived at the camp. I would steel my spine and try to take peaceful strides in their direction. "Hola," I would say. "Hello. I'm an American citizen, un ciudadano de los Estados Unidos. Ustedes va por favor." Please leave. The idea was that they wouldn't go so far as to gun down a U.S. citizen—or campesinos in the presence of one.

I had set foot on another planet, and my every sense was assaulted. The Jesuits threw their JRS people right into the thick of things. They knew what they were doing—immediately we became part of the struggle.

回 回

That first week, the four other scholastics and I were kept busy, touring the capital, San Salvador, and meeting dozens of community organizers and thousands of displaced people in various church-run refugee camps in the city. We prayed at Archbishop Romero's tomb, stood reverently outside his hermitage, and gazed silently at the altar where he was shot. Jesuit communities welcomed us for dinner.

---

*The School of the Americas was renamed Western Hemisphere Institute of Security Cooperation.

The highlight of our week was a visit to the Jesuit University of Central America, a graceful campus of palm trees, preened lawns, stucco buildings crowned with red-tile roofs, and vast clusters of flowers—a plot of Southern California dropped from heaven. There we met the renowned philosopher and theologian Father Ignacio Ellacuría, the university president.

He was in his fifties and had a hairline in recess, piercing dark eyes, and a brow that bespoke intelligence. It was a good face, but stern, serious, and urgent. He welcomed us into his office and started the introductions. Then he settled into his chair and stated his manifesto: "The purpose of the Jesuit university in San Salvador is to promote the reign of God." Every course, he said, every paper and department, was aimed at liberating the poor and oppressed. Education here was geared toward a new, peaceful El Salvador, with justice and human rights for all its people. If a course or course work didn't confront what he called "the national reality," if it didn't promote political, social, and economic transformation, it wasn't education, he said. I marveled at his compelling vision and couldn't help noting the contrast between this university and the ones back in the States.

"We have learned in El Salvador," Ellacuría said, "that to be for the reign of God means we have to be against the anti-reign." The world has changed so much, he said, that we can no longer promote peace unless we actively and publicly resist war. We can no longer do good without taking pains to resist systemic, institutionalized evil. We can no longer stand abstractly for justice. We must concretely and conspicuously fight injustice. His was a new take on Gandhi's maxim, "Noncooperation with evil is as much a duty as cooperation with good."

And so, he said, we oppose the war—the death squads, the ruling junta, U.S. military aid, and bombing raids, poverty, disease, and every form of systemic violence that plows Salvadorans under. We oppose the violence of the rebels. This work brings danger, but it's what Jesuits are supposed to do, he said flatly. This is what it means to follow Jesus: to defend the poor, "to accompany Jesus as he carries his cross in the world," to practice "the faith that does justice," to offer God's reign in the midst of the anti-reign.

Ellacuría's moral authority rang like a tower bell. His vision both inspired and frightened me. Fearless, outspoken, daring, and challenging—I'd never met his like, except perhaps in Philip Berrigan. Everywhere Ellacuría went, he spoke the truth. He was constantly in the papers and on TV. He denounced government honchos, military brass, and cosseted landlords. In the late 1970s, he had written speeches and pastoral letters for Romero. Now, he seemed the heir apparent. The poor knew and respected him, and, in turn, respected all the Jesuits. Ellacuría was a modern-day prophet, and like every prophet before him, he flouted the makers of war, raised the hope of the despairing, and took little account of personal danger. He would give his life as Romero had, as Jesus had, if necessary, for God's reign of justice, not in some far-off heaven, but here and now, in the "land of the Savior." Being with him challenged me to take a strong public stand for peace.

After the meeting with Ellacuría, we had enough to take home and reflect on for years. But come afternoon, we were granted an audience with liberation theologian Father Jon Sobrino, SJ. He was a mirror image of Ellacuría—gentle, charming, and quietly inspiring—but equally prophetic. He urged us to give ourselves for justice and to reflect on the meaning of our Christianity—our humanity—while in El Salvador. Life in the camps, he said, will teach you how to be human.

"The Jesuit task is to risk our lives, to be on the frontiers of history," he told us. That's what God wants of us. God wants the poor to be liberated from poverty and death. That's the work we're given to do—to liberate the poor from poverty and death.

"You'll be in the refugee camps," he said, "and feel profound shame. You'll say to yourself, 'I am ashamed to be a human being.' But you'll experience profound joy as well. You'll think, *Life makes sense if I share in their suffering. At last, I'm part of the human race!*" My throat tightened. "For the rest of your lives," he added, "you'll have a basic reference point." How right he was.

Properly oriented and shown the ropes, I headed off to the camp at Calle Real, along with a Jesuit scholastic named Tom Forsthoefel. The camp had no plumbing, no electricity, and no phones. Together with the displaced people, we cooked around a fire and for a while slept under the stars. We awoke at four in the morning, stretched our aching sacroiliacs, and trudged two miles to a creek for water, bringing it back in jugs on sore shoulders. After coffee and little else for breakfast, off we went, machetes in hand, to clear the fields of low-lying weeds. The day wore on, the sun beat down, and the war raged around us.

After weeks of clearing, we were ready to loosen the soil and plant corn—backbreaking work, the work of the campesino. We scratched the soil as U.S. jets bombed the volcano and military aircraft criss-crossed the sky. Now and then, death squads paid us a visit. "Hola," I would say, my passport in hand. They would throw me a grudging look and turn on their heels. I looked calm and self-assured, but my belly churned with fear.

For good measure, we rid ourselves of "subversive materials"— biblical literature and photos of Óscar Romero. We made our byword *vigilance.* Remember, the Jesuits had cautioned us on our first day, you are in a war zone.

In the evening after working the fields, we sat under the mango trees—at the beginning of my stay there were about a hundred of us—quietly eating our dinner prepared by a few of the women with contributions from Catholic Relief Services. During the day, the campesinos told us their stories, and this continued into the night, as we sat in hammocks around a fire, singing songs.

One hot day, after a month of arduous work and quiet accompaniment, Tom and I took a walk after lunch, strolling in the shade of a grove of trees, talking about the Christian response to war as bombs rumbled in the distance. Salvadorans store their machetes high up in tree branches, out of the reach of children—but not quite high enough for me. Tom and I were deep in conversation, reflecting on the life of St. Francis, the meaning of nonviolence, and the connections between poverty and war, when I walked right into the handle of a three-foot machete hanging from a branch. I knocked it loose, bringing it down in one swift slice on my outstretched right hand. Pain seared through me, and I looked down to see a gaping wound, the skin ripped off. An anatomy lesson for both of us—bleached metacarpals bared and visible to anyone with stomach to look. Then the blood flowed heavily, and panic set in. We were in the wilderness with no vehicle, no phone, no way to get help. Would I lose my hand?

The nuns who worked with us came to my rescue. Sister Margaret-Jane produced a first-aid kit, poured some torturous alcoholic cleanser over the wound, scrubbed it with something like steel wool, applied pressure and a bandage, and sent me off with Tom through the woods to the road, where a bus eventually came along to carry us to the hospital. I clutched my bloody hand and arrived at nightfall at the ER—the very emergency room to which Óscar Romero had been brought. The medical staff brought me in, cleaned the wound again, and stitched up my hand.

Days later, I returned to the camp. The men rushed over to see my wound. "Now you are one of us!" they exclaimed. They showed me their own collection of scars—one or two on every limb of every man; some even had missing fingers. But unlike me, they never had access to an emergency room. They mended their bodies as best they could and bore ever after the marks of their wounds. An old man took my arm and said, "Someday, when you raise your hands in the air with the bread and wine, you will look up and see El Salvador."

What jaw-dropping, heartbreaking poetry. He was so childlike as he said this, his eyes sparkling with wonder. He'd summed up everything: the Eucharist, the scarred Savior present in the bread and wine, and my own scar, a road map of El Salvador across my right hand. To this day, the scar reminds me of those suffering, faith-filled Salvadorans. As the old man prophesied, I remember them every time I offer the Eucharist.

回 回

Before I left the country, my father arranged for me to meet a prominent news correspondent in San Salvador. Like most of the U.S. press, she made her base of operations in the classy Camino Real hotel downtown. She reported on the war, U.S. military aid, the deaths of Romero and the four churchwomen—but I quickly concluded that she was not so much a reporter as a supporter of the Pentagon, the junta, and the death squads.

She greeted me with professional detachment. How were things going for me? What were my impressions of the country? I gave her an earful—the suffering I had seen, the bombing raids, the poor under distress. I told her with some heat that U.S. military aid to El Salvador must stop.

Contempt shone in her eyes. She sized me up and wrote me off. "You Jesuits are all the same, always dredging up the same damn lies. Why, just the other day, one of the generals took me up in his plane. We flew all over the country, and he showed me the great progress being made. I saw no bombing raids, no death squads, no bomber planes flying over fields. I'll never understand you people. You'll say anything to embarrass your country."

I gaped at her. Here was a professional journalist dismissing my testimony out of hand, yet embracing on blind faith every word the general said. Apparently, it hadn't occurred to her that the bombings might stop at the general's order, so that a major U.S. newspaper might see how the junta was bringing peace. It seemed that she wrote only what the Pentagon authorities told her.

It was a wrenching civics lesson to see the media's uncritical support of U.S. war-making. Even now, most mainstream newspapers and news networks practice the same shoddy, biased reporting. Embedded in war and funded by weapons manufacturers, they have become an essential part of the war machine. For the most part, they do limited investigative reporting but trust the reports that Washington and the Pentagon give them.

But I testify to what my own eyes have seen—and I took pains to see for myself the consequences of El Salvador's dark politics. One day, Tom and I caught a bus north to the village of Aguilares, where the Jesuit martyr Rutilio Grande worked. On Saturday, March 12, 1977, he had concluded Mass there and started by jeep down a dirt road, fields of sugarcane all around, toward his home village of El Paisnal, a short distance from the Guazapa volcano. Assassins from the army pulled up behind him and opened fire. Father Grande died, along with a seventy-two-year-old and a fifteen-year-old.

That night, Archbishop Romero stood over their dead bodies. Later he confessed that at that moment scales fell from his eyes, and for the first time he understood the gospel of Jesus, the call to lay down our lives in love for one another. From that day forward, he faced down the oligarchy, scolding them, denouncing their torturing and killing, and demanding justice. A line had been crossed, and Romero saw to it that another was drawn.

Then the repression of the church began. "Be a patriot, kill a priest," read posters in the city. The age of the Salvadoran martyrs had dawned. With Rutilio Grande and Óscar Romero, the world would witness an authentic church after Jesus' own heart.

Aguilares was typical of small Salvadoran villages: hovels, a bus stop, tiny shops containing the barest inventories, and a church in the middle of it all. Soldiers prowled about; they had occupied the town since Grande's death, for some eight years. They had commandeered the church and turned it into a makeshift camp: a barracks, an arsenal, and, in the back, cluttered with provisions, the altar to the Prince of Peace. No admittance.

The temperature hovered around one hundred degrees the day Tom and I arrived. We had determined to travel the same lonely road to El Paisnal that Father Grande had taken—to walk it, making holy pilgrimage, to find our bearings on the way to peace. We set off with desolate countryside stretching out in every direction. Helicopters thumped along the horizon. Sharp booms reached our ears from the volcano—ordinance exploding on the slopes, dead ahead. Calm settled on me despite the din, and I glimpsed in my mind's eye a different stream of history, the history of the poor, the disappeared, the assassinated, the plowed under. A mile into our walk, we came upon a small white cross—the spot where Grande had died. We bowed our heads and offered a prayer.

El Paisnal's little church is where Grande is buried; it was our first stop when we arrived. We lingered there in prayer and then searched out the one-room house where he'd lived. Our praying done and the sights meager, we entered a shop for a cool drink before the walk back to Aguilares. Dawdling inside were five gun-toting young men, filthy and sweating, looking as if they had just emerged from the jungle. We nodded a greeting and started on our way. Two of them followed not far behind.

We realized then that we had FMLN rebels on our trail. Like Father Grande, we had crossed the line between two warring sides, having come from a town occupied by death squads and arrived in the underground world of the guerillas. We attracted sinister looks from both and prayed in both places for peace. The rebels didn't scare us much, but the soldiers, in their U.S. army uniforms, did. Like the vultures we saw hovering everywhere, they lurked about the countryside and systematically visited death on poor villages, on the prowl "to destroy the people to set them free," to kill them to give them "democracy," to risk "collateral damage" on behalf of manifest destiny.

Once, while being interrogated by a soldier, I looked down at the machine gun he'd aimed at my heart and saw a sticker that read, "Smile, Jesus loves you."

Later, I traveled alone to Chalatenango to visit the graves of Ita Ford and Maura Clarke, the two martyred Maryknoll sisters, who had been buried among the poor. It was a bleak, remote region, and the fighting raged more fiercely there than anywhere. I took the bus north and bounced along, gazing at the distant mountains. A sudden stop threw us forward in our seats. Soldiers stood in the road, their palms in the air. One of them boarded and barked, "Off the bus!" We filed out and lined up along the center yellow line—no other vehicles were in sight. There we stood, forty campesinos and me, the sole gringo. We all remained silent. I did not know what to do, so I took my cue from the others and kept my eyes riveted to the ground.

One by one, we were questioned and searched and made to produce our papers, which were unceremoniously snatched and examined. The soldiers rummaged through our possessions while an agony of anxiety settled in. I worked to stay calm. Before long, one of the soldiers came to me holding my passport in his hand. "And what are *you* doing here?" I said nothing; he looked me over and tossed back the passport. The process went on and on. Only when we were back on the bus and on our way did everyone exhale, almost as one.

We arrived at Chalatenango finally, and I proceeded directly to the church, only to find it occupied by soldiers. It was a scene out of the movies, the plaza full of soldiers, sandbags, and machine guns. Soldiers filled the church sanctuary as others crowded in the church steeple, aiming their machine guns in every direction. A few nuns appeared and introduced themselves. I explained who I was and asked directions to the cemetery. I told them I wanted to pray at the graves of the Maryknoll sisters.

"Absolutely not!" It was a shout within a whisper. They showed me their two-room dwelling attached to the back of the house where Ita and Maura once lived. Then they urged me to get back on the bus. "Go near the cemetery," they told me, "and they'll arrest you, interrogate you, and deport you." I was still shaking as the bus departed but grateful to have met such stalwart Salvadoran nuns.

回　回

As my time in El Salvador drew to a close, the people of the camp threw a going-away party for Tom and me. They hung a piñata, blindfolded us, and placed a stick in our hands. They made me go first. I took swings at it, missing every time. The sight of the dopey gringo was too much, and everyone convulsed with laughter. The children took turns, giggling with each swing and then racing after the falling candy when the piñata was finally broken open. The adults milled about, sipping coffee, telling stories, and wishing us well. It broke our hearts to leave these lovely people.

Later, we said good-bye to the families at the Jesuit Refugee Service compound in San Salvador. They, too, held a party for us. The father of the largest family approached me, smiling bashfully. He presented me with a gift—a belt he had made from yellow and blue hemp. Suddenly, the thick Dutch accent of Henri Nouwen flooded my ears: "When you grow old, you will stretch out your hands, and somebody else will put a belt round you and take you where you would rather not go." I put on the belt and the people applauded, so proud of their gift. I blinked back tears, feeling that a cross had been laid across my shoulders, an unspoken invitation arising from their gratitude. I was being led where I'd rather not go: back to the States, to resist its wars for the rest of my life, on behalf of beautiful sisters and brothers like these.

The work done, the Jesuits took the five of us scholastics to a mountain lake to reflect on our experience. To a man, we talked of the pain we had seen, our frustration at having little to offer, and the helplessness we experienced before such overwhelming evil. "Our plan worked!" the Jesuits said. Then their tone grew more serious. "Our hope was that you would experience something of the powerlessness of the poor. That was the most important lesson to be gained this summer, to taste their utter powerlessness. That was the best teaching we could offer you. This is what they deal with their entire, short lives: hunger and labor, planting crops, carrying water, disease, injury. Then, of course, arrest, torture, brutal death. You've tasted their pain. Never forget it."

The day I left, the Jesuits drove me to the barren road where the four churchwomen had been driven five years earlier to be raped, murdered, and disposed of in shallow graves. A stone marker with a plaque read: "Ita Ford, Maura Clarke, Dorothy Kazel, and Jean

Donovan gave their lives here on December 2, 1980. Receive them, Lord, into your kingdom." We stood in silent prayer. Hours later I was on a bus, crossing the Guatemalan border.

El Salvador was for me a land of firsts. My first encounter with death squads. My first look at a persecuted and crucified Christian community that was rising from the dead. The poor there had lost homes and loved ones, lived hand to mouth, or not at all. But their faith, hope, and joy never completely went under—a doggedness all but unheard of in the United States, except among the African-Americans of the faith-based civil rights movement. When you have seen that kind of faith, you never forget it.

In the midst of suffering, a great gift is given—a spirit of hope, loving-kindness, and courage. When people share in the paschal mystery, when they suffer and die but remain faithful like Romero, they rise. El Salvador is truly the "land of the Savior," dying and rising. It shines a bright light on North and South America, inviting all to enter that same transforming dynamic, the mystery of nonviolent love.

Taking a Stand in Nicaragua, at the Pentagon, and at West Point (1985)

Tom and I bounced by bus along a rutted road to the capital of Guatemala, Guatemala City, exhausted but spellbound by the glorious countryside. We passed lush jungles and slumbering green volcanoes towering in the distance, the thick forests at their tops lining the horizon.

We found in Guatemala City a metropolis filled with skyscrapers, glitzy banks, a McDonald's every few blocks, and hectic streets. It could have been Chicago, even New York. We then ventured further into the countryside, which was primal and secluded, exotic in its beauty. The areas were sparsely settled, with a poor village here and there fitted with the barest necessities. On early mornings in those hills, the clouds drifted mere yards above the green fields—it seemed magical. The indigenous people in their brightly colored, handmade clothes struck us as gentle, salt of the earth.

Yet everywhere the Guatemalan death squads patrolled in tanks and jeeps. One morning, I watched hundreds of soldiers tromp through Antigua, a colonial town under the shadow of three tall volcanoes. The soldiers' presence raised a cloud of fear among the townspeople, and for good reason. During that era, nearly two hundred thousand people died at the hands of death squads supported by the United States. In Guatemala—as today in Colombia and Haiti—military and corporate interests overrode the needs of the poor and voiceless. The telltale signs were everywhere: government corruption, grinding poverty, internally displaced people, brutal armed forces, multinational corporations monopolizing local lands and industries, and civilians turning up dead by the thousands—or not turning up at all.

That August, I caught a plane to Nicaragua for a two-week vigil with Witness for Peace, a Christian solidarity organization. Their cause was to bring U.S. citizens to the borders between Nicaragua and Honduras and between Nicaragua and Costa Rica, where they would shield Nicaraguan peasants from the contras, who launched attacks from the edges of nations where the United States held sway. I arrived in Managua and reported to the Witness for Peace officials, but to my great disappointment, they turned me away.

"We're sorry," they said. "You didn't participate in the orientation back in New York." I explained that I'd been in El Salvador for months—where I had faced down death squads, lived among refugees, invested sweat and blood. I was more a veteran than any new arrival they could name. Plus, I had already been approved by Witness for Peace in the U.S. But the officials held firm: "Policy." They shut the door on me, so I took a bus across town to the Jesuit house. Two days later, the news flashed around the world that the contras had kidnapped twenty-nine North American activists near the San Juan

River and fired shots. For days, I worried. Then suddenly they were released unharmed.

Miguel D'Escoto, the Maryknoll priest who served as foreign minister for the Sandinista government, had begun an open-ended fast for an end to the war and was now on his twentieth day. Every night, he held a Mass and a rally at a Managua church. His fast was followed with great interest throughout Latin America. I attended the daily Masses, met D'Escoto and other visitors, and joined in the prayers for peace. Once while I was standing in a crowd of five hundred Nicaraguans outside a church, President Daniel Ortega came by, unannounced. He saw me standing in the back of the crowd, head and shoulders above everyone else, and walked toward me. The crowd parted; he approached and asked who I was. "I'm a visiting Jesuit working to end the contra war." He smiled and thanked me. Another day, while hitchhiking, I was picked up by a silver limousine carrying Adolfo Pérez Esquivel, the Nobel Peace Prize winner from Buenos Aires who had spoken out on behalf of Argentina's disappeared during the brutal junta of the 1970s. He had become Latin America's voice for peace.

Still, the Honduran border was where I wanted to go. And the Jesuits graciously offered to take me. We drove along a road that would give my chiropractor bad dreams and visited churches in the border towns of Ocotal and Jalapa. The people there recited to me the litany of assassinations and massacres committed by the contra army. Periodic gunshots sounded in the distance. But again I saw the kind of faith, hope, and love that we only read about in the Acts of the Apostles.

A day later, I was struck with a fever, complete with aches and chills. The Jesuits took me in a worn-out pickup truck back to Managua, where I worsened. My temperature was near 104 degrees, and people told me later that I'd been delirious. Eventually, a doctor peered into my eyes and down my throat and diagnosed dengue fever, a mosquito-borne viral infection. It was rampant throughout Southeast Asia but new to Central America. "This is serious," he said, and fed me antipyretics and ordered me to bed. I tumbled in and remained there until my flight home. I spent my twenty-sixth birthday in the Jesuit house bundled in damp blankets and convulsing with chills.

I later found out that my friend Kathy Kelly, who founded "Voices in the Wilderness" in the 90s, had been in Nicaragua that same month and had also contracted the fever. Two years after my visit, the *New York Times* reported that the CIA had practiced germ warfare in Nicaragua. The very summer I was there, it had unleashed a swarm of mosquitoes carrying the dengue virus. Thousands of people fell ill within days. When I read this report, my mind began to turn. The dengue fever link to Southeast Asia raised a dark and chilling inference: the CIA had employed techniques in Central America that it had honed in Vietnam.

Riding out the disease was hard, but I think back on it now, oddly, as a measure of grace. I didn't get to join Witness for Peace, yet I assumed a share of the sufferings that the United States had inflicted on the people of Nicaragua. I tried to love my country's "enemies" and paid the price by enduring their pain. I felt a profound sense of solidarity. As César Chávez said, "To be human is to suffer for others."

回 回

In the fall of 1985, I was home from Central America and busy again at Fordham. Jack, Peter, and I threw ourselves into one demonstration after another. In October, we organized a teach-in on Central

America that lasted seven days. We showed films, met with faculty and student groups, held vigil on campus, and hosted a number of guest speakers, including the Donovans, who gave a spellbinding lecture to a packed auditorium, and Bill Ford, a Wall Street lawyer and brother of martyred Maryknoll sister Ita Ford. I resumed work at the soup kitchen, rejoined the weekly vigils at the Riverside Research Institute, paid visits to the sick in the Fordham infirmary, and got back into the rhythm of Pax Christi and Kairos meetings, all in the course of studying philosophy. But I was underweight and listless, and a doctor diagnosed me with parasites from the jungle water and put me on a yearlong treatment.

That fall, my father arranged for me to meet the secretary of the army, John Marsh. I doubt he relished the idea of a peacenik Jesuit invading his sanctum, but he agreed out of respect for my father. Aides ushered me through the Pentagon's endless dark corridors, the walls decorated with enormous bloody murals of famous revolutionary battles. I arrived finally at Marsh's office overlooking the Potomac—right above where Peter and I had kept vigil two years before. The aides withdrew and Marsh appeared, brimming with cordiality. How was El Salvador? he asked. Tell me about your time in Managua.

Genteel chitchat was the furthest thing from my mind. Cut all military aid to the death squads, I urged him. Stop propping up the juntas in El Salvador and Guatemala. Put an end to the U.S. contra war against Nicaragua. Send food and medicine. These people want to be allies. They're dying needlessly, unjustly, immorally. I relayed a message from the displaced of Calle Real: "We don't want weapons or bombs, but food, medicine, and homes."

Marsh sat impassively, rocking gently in his chair. "I can't do that."

"As a servant of the gospel and in the name of peace, I ask you to reconsider."

He scarcely stirred. I could see that my intrusion was a blip in his day, a courtesy visit, a nuisance to ride out, part of the job. He was simply employing the tools of his trade, a perfected pleasantness and rehearsed affability.

"No, I wish *you'd* reconsider," he said. "The military needs good Catholics like you. Would you consider joining the chaplaincy program and working for me?" A full five seconds passed as I tried to come up with a suitable rejoinder. I had been prepared for an argument, even to be tossed out on my ear. But a recruiting pitch?

I managed a polite no and, as I stood to leave, presented him with a few gifts: a book outlining humane policies toward Central America and a piece of art from the Solentiname community in Nicaragua. It portrayed a Nicaraguan Jesus, his campesino friends standing around his cross being shot at by contras. Marsh took them politely, and I left trembling.

There was a lesson in all this. This man—sociable, pleasant, engaging, self-possessed, a true-blue American—embodied patriotic militarism. Yet, in one way or another, that militarism stood behind the deaths of hundreds of thousands of Latin Americans, millions of Vietnamese, and how many countless, nameless others, in the past and to come? On the train back to New York, I recalled Thomas Merton's reflections on Adolf Eichmann, head of the Jewish office of the Gestapo: "It is precisely the *sane* ones who are the most dangerous."

The encounter left me shaken for weeks, and I searched for a way to respond. Then news came of a demonstration at West Point at the cadets' open house. Jack and I drove up along the Hudson River to the academy. Thousands poured in, friends and relatives and nearly a hundred demonstrators. We placed signs at Thayer Gate and lined the road holding banners demanding an end to the U.S. wars in Central America. Cadets shouted obscenities. For the time being, the police let us be.

A few hours later, Jack and I and ten others slipped onto the campus and made our way to the middle of the barracks complex, a grove of towering dormitories. We planted ourselves and handed out leaflets. Then we dramatically unfurled our banner: "U.S. out of Central America, Stop the War against the Poor!" That set things into action. The police converged on us in no time, reinforced by German shepherds. Urged on by cadets cheering from the windows high above, the police handled the matter with Rambo-like bravado, throwing us against the hoods of their cruisers and slapping cuffs on tight, the dogs all the while snarling and baring their incisors.

We landed in the campus police station, where the police booked us, inked our fingers, and left us on the floor chained to a wall to stew for a few hours. Eventually, they released us with a document banning us for life from the academy's hallowed grounds. If we were supposed to feel shame, it escaped our notice.

▣ ▣

Adolfo Pérez Esquivel, the Nobel laureate who had stopped to give me a ride in Managua, was in New York for a meeting at the United Nations. His office contacted me and asked if he could stay with me at Fordham. It was an honor to host this humble, simple man of peace—a living saint, as far as I was concerned—an outspoken voice for the disappeared. In 1977, he, too, had been arrested, disappeared, and tortured; international pressure saved his life.

At the end of his stay, he made time to speak to a large group of Fordham students and then stayed up late so that I could interview him for a Catholic magazine. He affirmed my vision and spirituality and encouraged me to press on in the work for justice, nonviolence, and liberation of the poor.

As November settled in, my routine trudged on: classes, vigils, writing, volunteer work, and speaking engagements. Studies would end in the spring, and then I would enter regency, the next phase of Jesuit formation, a two- or three-year stint of service, more often than not a teaching job in a Jesuit high school. The last thing I wanted was to teach. After months in Central America and hearing about other Jesuits from my province who worked in South America, I very much wanted to go to Chile and work among the poor. I wrote for permission and was quickly approved.

Then came December and a visit by the provincial assistant for secondary education. He requested a one-on-one meeting with each scholastic, his purpose being to size up the next crop of teachers. I sat down, chatted amiably with him, and made sure he understood my plans for Chile. The idea was fine with him.

Was there anything else I would like to discuss? "Well, yes, one more thing," I said. I had prayed over this conversation and proceeded in good conscience, but gingerly. Having been educated in a Jesuit high school, I felt qualified to say that such schools mollycoddled over-privileged, upper-class boys. To my mind, we were not fulfilling the Jesuit mission, much less the gospel. The five Maryland Province high schools should stop serving the rich and should enroll the poor— and teach social justice and gospel values.

"Well," he said. "I don't think you'll be going to Chile after all." With that, I was assigned to teach in a Jesuit high school in Scranton, Pennsylvania. I was hurt and angry, but years later I realized that if I had gone to Chile, I might have stayed, might never have become more involved in the peace movement, and might never have undertaken a Plowshares disarmament action. Perhaps obedience even in the face of what appears to be personal injustice can be used providentially for some greater purpose. I am still pondering these turns in my journey.

🔲 17 🔲

Disturbing the Peace
in Scranton
(1986–87)

During my last few months at Fordham, I learned that the dean of students had invited a CIA recruiter to campus. Although the date of the visit wasn't made known, Pax Christi kicked into high gear. On a Monday in March, we learned that the recruiter would be coming to campus the next day. We called an emergency meeting, organized until the wee hours, made signs and banners, and produced a thousand copies of a leaflet we composed.

Forty of us from Pax Christi arrived to greet him the next day, lining the hallway outside the dean's office. We urged every student who walked by not to apply to the CIA and told them how the the agency trained the contras to assassinate Nicaraguans. When the recruiter arrived, Jack Marth and eight other undergraduates sat down in the doorway and blocked the entrance. (I was told that if I joined the sit-in, I would be dismissed from the Jesuits, so I held back.) The recruiter stopped and announced loudly that the CIA would never again set foot on Fordham's campus. And—*poof*—he was gone.

A cheer went up, and we rejoiced for weeks afterward. The Fordham Nine faced expulsion and ended up on probation, but the experience emboldened us all. We had learned that steadfast, organized nonviolence does work, that it bears good fruit and leads to new avenues of justice, peace, and hope. For years to come, that episode would inspire me to organize other, more daring, public actions.

We then drafted a thirty-page proposal for the president and his staff requesting the abolishment of ROTC, the creation of a peace studies program, and the designation of one dormitory for students who would be required to work fifteen hours a week among the neighborhood poor. Of the three suggestions, they implemented the last two.

As Good Friday approached, Jack, Peter, and I kept busy. We helped organize the annual Pax Christi peace walk through Manhattan, setting up stations of the cross throughout the city and creating liturgy and signs at each to remind ourselves of Christ's passion in the world today, as manifested in homelessness, poverty, the sick, the imprisoned, and those targeted by bombs.

I strummed a guitar and led the singing from the back of a truck as two thousand proceeded behind. We ended at the Riverside Research Institute—the fifteenth station, the Resurrection—where a hundred of us placed handmade stoles on one another's shoulders before entering the lobby. Then we sat down and demanded nuclear disarmament. The police swept in and arrested us, releasing us a few hours later.

The next day, Peter and I attended the Catholic Worker Easter Vigil Mass, then joined some forty homeless people who, throughout Lent, had camped out by day at various churches and slept at night on the steps of St. Patrick's Cathedral, as a nonviolent demand for housing. That night, Peter and I slept on the steps of the cathedral.

As the sun set, temperatures dropped and a cold wind blew. The concrete steps were hard as ice; lying on them set the most youthful spines aching. The homeless taught us to search the streets for cardboard for makeshift shelters. A bend here, a flap there, a square or two to plug a gap, and you crawled inside, or at least found partial cover. It was my first time seeing Manhattan from the underside, with the famous church towering above. Passersby would scarcely look at us, and the few who did cast looks of shame.

At five the next morning, Easter, Peter and I hauled up our aching bones, thanked our new friends, and headed back to Fordham. The Jesuit liturgy would soon begin, and afterward the community dinner. We headed down Fifth Avenue and into the subway, unlit but for a small lightbulb in the distance. We plodded ahead into the dark bowels of the city, exhausted from lack of sleep, still freezing cold, our footsteps echoing down the passageway. Our growing apprehension forced us to pick up the pace. The light grew closer. Soon it illuminated a man on the ground, homeless and reeking, swaddled in blankets and rags. He jumped to his feet, stretched out his hands, his filthy blanket flying off his arms like a castoff shroud, and shouted, "Christ is risen! Happy Easter!"

What a word of blessing! What good news! Peter and I should have rejoiced, but we were in no frame of mind to receive it. We took off like Olympic sprinters. Neither of us slowed until we were in the subway car and on our way back to Fordham. It was only later that I realized we had had an Easter encounter of sorts. Like frightened disciples, we had met the risen Christ in a homeless man. And, true to form, we ran for our lives. We failed to respond with gratitude and joy but instead took to our heels to save our skins. I've pondered the mystery of that moment for years: the presence of Christ in the homeless man, my fear, being reminded of the Resurrection not by the rich and powerful but the poor and powerless.

◫ ◫

When summer came, I bought a one-way ticket to Washington, D.C., where I prepared lessons for my teaching assignment at Scranton Prep. My base was St. Aloysius Church, a parish near the Capitol. While in Washington, I volunteered at the Witness for Peace national office and continued my opposition to the contra war.

Over the previous six months, a few friends and I had been busy planning a three-day gathering of Jesuits that we called Jesuits for Peace. In June, to my delight, fifty Jesuits arrived, along with fifty friends. We spent a day at the Pentagon, calling for an end to the contra war; a day focusing on the suffering of the homeless; and a day at the White House, calling for an end to nuclear weapons. Daniel Berrigan spoke to a packed crowd at St. Al's on a Friday night. Mike Wallace of *60 Minutes* brought a crew to film the events. The next day, twenty of us held a sit-in in front of the White House entrance as the news crew filmed.

We sat for hours. The police kept their distance; clearly the TV crew inhibited the White House response. There was no need to arrest these church people, they probably figured, before a national audience. Finally, someone inside turned on the sprinkler system, dousing us with presidential water. We stood after a time, our shirts clinging to our skin, and concluded with a prayer. A decade later, Mike Wallace remembered that powerful weekend and asked to join my trip to Iraq, but CBS executives decided there had been enough coverage, which disappointed us both.

In September, I headed to Scranton, a small, predominantly Catholic city nestled in the Lackawanna Valley, the Pocono Mountains guarding it like sentries. Bleak and poor, Scranton seemed to have advanced little since the 1920s. I didn't appreciate it at first, because I felt like an exile and harbored some resentment. I even considered quitting the Society. After all, it seemed to take perverse delight in undermining my interests, blocking every project I proposed, and had assigned me to a place to which I felt the least calling—Scranton Prep, the Jesuit high school.

But my sense of God's presence had by no means failed. I retraced my steps, reflecting with wonder on the conversions that had set me going—at Duke and in Galilee. God had taken such trouble with me that I figured I'd stay the course out of respect. I surrendered myself and vowed to make the best of things. And there was one consolation: my classmate and friend Ed DeBerri was assigned to Scranton, too.

I was to teach five freshman classes of world history and a religion class to thirty or so sophomores. A hundred and eighty students passed through my classroom each day. I decided to toss out the bloody yardstick by which history measures progress and refused to clock history by the horrors of war. On the first day of history class, I explained how we would proceed. We would study history from the perspective of the poor, the oppressed, and the peacemakers. There would be no memorizing battle dates; instead, we'd study the lives of Jesus, Buddha, and Muhammad. We'd explore the lives of saints like Francis and Clare. We'd look at Karl Marx and the ideas of democratic socialism. We wouldn't study Hitler but those who resisted him—Franz Jägerstätter, the students of the White Rose, and the Norwegian, Danish, and Bulgarian resistance movements. We'd spend weeks examining Gandhi, Martin Luther King Jr. and the civil rights movement, Benigno Aquino and the People Power movement in Manila, Desmond Tutu and Nelson Mandela and their struggles to abolish apartheid, and the Berrigans and the global antiwar movement. At one point, I asked the students to write letters of support to Winnie Mandela, Mandela's wife at the time and one of the leading anti-apartheid spokespersons. She sent a beautiful letter in return.

Within a few days, the office phone began to ring. Parents were furious with my syllabus and urged administrators to transfer their children out of my class. Some called me a Communist; others said I should be fired, that I had no place in the Jesuit order. By now, I was getting used to negative reactions. Despite everything, I couldn't help but grow fond of my students and our lively classes. Many memorable debates arose. Some students vehemently opposed me, others lagged behind in bewilderment, while still others came alive with new awareness. In any case, my classes were unlike any others in the school. Our debates spread from my tiny classroom into every other classroom, even into homes and churches, "like a Jesuit virus," as some parents put it.

I quickly made new friends in Scranton, and together we started a Pax Christi group there. At our first meeting, we planned a peace vigil against the contra war. The last time a peace vigil had been held in Scranton was some twenty years prior, during the Vietnam War, and it was all but a musty memory. The Saturday after our first meeting, we gathered in the center of town in a quaint little park and stood for an hour holding banners and signs. The next morning, our picture appeared on the front page of the Scranton newspaper. The town broke out in a heated buzz, in barbershops, at luncheonette counters, under hair dryers at the beauty salon. The faculty of Scranton Prep and the Jesuits took notice, too. But in true small-town fashion, no one spoke of it to me. They gave the cold shoulder instead.

But I refused to let up. In October, a recruiter for the armed forces arrived at school. Jesuit administrators encouraged our teenage boys and girls to consider a career in the military. Some thirty seniors filled the room to hear the recruiter speak. I sat in the back row in my clerical garb. The recruiter described in glowing terms all the benefits he had to offer: world travel, a free college degree, a career. "Any questions?" he asked. I raised my hand. "You didn't mention that they'd have to learn how to kill. What guns would they use? Will they operate weapons of mass destruction? Will you train them to massacre villages, like in Vietnam and Nicaragua? Do they know they may be killed in your wars?"

The recruiter narrowed his eyes. "Yes, they have to handle guns and learn to kill people. Yes, they have to follow orders and do what they are told, even if they don't like it. Yes, they may be killed. Yes, they may have to work with weapons of mass destruction." Then he started packing up to go. The faculty adviser was livid, but so was I. I went to the office of the superior of the Jesuit community. "How can this so-called Christian school encourage its students to make a career in the business of killing?" I asked. "How can we allow the military to recruit here?"

He looked at me and asked me frankly if I wanted to become a Jesuit priest. He reminded me that the Society of Jesus was not pacifist and that I would never change that.

For the next several months, I lived in this atmosphere, suffering ridicule from students, parents, and fellow Jesuits. One bright moment came when Ed DeBerri tapped on the door of my religion class and stepped into the mayhem (a group of disruptive students had been assigned to me) with a box of copies of my first book, *Disarming the Heart: Toward a Vow of Nonviolence*. The kids seemed mildly impressed. At any rate, it put their rowdiness in check for a day or two.

But a week later, I caught Jamie Hailstone, my best student, chatting in the back of class. It was the last straw; I ordered him to detention. Sit there, I growled, and write me an essay on why you shouldn't talk during a class on Christianity. He turned it in the next day: "Disarming the Mouth: Toward a Vow to be Silent in Mr. Dear's Class." I laughed and laughed and kept that paper for years. It went a long way toward dispelling my melancholy.

In March 1987, I was ordered to do an eight-day retreat so that I could discern further if my calling was with the Society of Jesus. I headed off to the Trappist monastery in Berryville, Virginia. For several days, I awakened with the monks at three in the morning to join in prayers and prayed the other offices with them throughout the day. I read the Gospels, contemplated Jesus, and strolled the peaceful banks of the Shenandoah River. Soon my depression lifted and my energy returned. My sense of vocation, buried for a time, emerged with gusto. Yes, I was sent to work for justice and disarmament. Yes, I would follow the troublemaking Jesus, come what may.

For the first time, I imagined life after Scranton, a good life. In the meantime, I would stay in touch with my friends in the peace movement, write more about nonviolence, keep teaching the history of peace, consider taking part in a Plowshares action, say my prayers. And bide my time.

Like it or not, the Jesuits had me for life.

Community and Jail in New York (1987–88)

M y first year in Scranton ended amid heavy sighs of relief from all sides. I packed for New York and moved into the West Side Jesuit Community on West Ninety-eighth Street. Some twenty gracious and welcoming Jesuits lived there, among them Daniel Berrigan.

The summer was one of the hottest on record, but for me it was a breath of fresh air. I enjoyed the rush and vibrancy of the city after living among the somnolent hills of Scranton. I rejoined the world of the homeless and the company of resisters. And I began a new book, *Our God Is Nonviolent*, a collection of profiles of modern-day peacemakers.

The West Side Jesuits were scattered among small apartments in an immense pre-World War II–era building. During the 1970s, more than a hundred people had lived there, most of them from nearby Woodstock College. The streets at that time were mean. Crack users harassed people, and drug dealers reigned. By 1987, the Jesuit community in the building had dwindled—but what a lively and dedicated bunch they were, most of them working on the margins, as I was, each bearing the scars of conflict with communities who did not fully condone what they were trying to do. I fit right in.

It was a wondrous place to tend a tattered soul. We came and went as we pleased. There was no undue pressure to attend community functions, and precisely for that reason, everyone arrived— freely, happily, delightedly. We prepared daily dinners and celebrated monthly liturgies, created weekend getaways every spring and fall, and did an eight-day retreat in the Poconos every August.

Our spiritual director was Fred O'Connor, a man of immense dignity. His deportment and charisma were much like Gandalf's in *The Lord of the Rings*. He had a gleaming bald head, a flowing gray beard, and wise eyes. He was sparse with words and could signal agreement and welcome, unity and belonging with a mere opening of his arms.

We had a wonderful mix in our community. Lew Cox traveled the country leading journal retreats. Don Moore, a professor of theology at Fordham University, now spends six months every year in Jerusalem promoting dialogue between the faiths. Bob Keck, a massage therapist in constant demand, steeped his workouts in the ambience of meditation and prayer. Dave Toolan was an amateur scientist and cosmologist and, until his death in 2002, a book review editor. Al Briceland and Bob Springer were hospital chaplains. Ed Zogby offered guidance to parishes on ways to deepen community life. Gerry Huyett taught English as a second language to newly arrived immigrants. And Bill McNichols, a chaplain at St. Vincent's hospice, was the first New York priest to minister to people dying of AIDS and accompanied more than 150 people to their deaths.

Community was important to me, which is why the West Side Jesuit Community was such a healing place. I had searched up and down the Atlantic seaboard for community, visiting Catholic Worker houses, the Sojourners community, Jonah House, L'Arche communities, and the Community for Creative Nonviolence. Needless to say, I never came across any glittering New Jerusalem. Communities are made up of sinful, broken people; the key is to embrace our brokenness, be quick with forgiveness, and reflect the compassion of Christ.

The communities that touch me most practice the ancient virtues: forgiveness, kindliness, humility, compassion, prayer measured in hours. Somehow, the West Side Jesuits endured in these virtues, even forged a new way to practice contemporary religious life. They made a place of uncommon peace. There was no shadow of competition among these simple men, no anger, jealousy, meanness, or fear.

For the first time in ages, I felt happy. I wrote, took long walks through Central Park with Dan, and enjoyed the lazy evenings in the community dining room. I also helped Kairos prepare direct actions against the Riverside Research Institute for the August 6 anniversary of the bombing of Hiroshima. The solemn day arrived, and scores of us converged on the lobby, leafleting the apartment dwellers, singing hymns, and holding aloft signs. Twenty-five people blocked the doorway to the building and landed in a police van. A few hours later, as we left, the authorities handed each of us a summons to appear in court. Everything seemed choreographed: we protesters carried ourselves as model citizens, respectful and deferential, even as we broke the law, while the police officers comported themselves with professional joviality, with near-chummy warmth, regarding us as an innocuous, perhaps virtuous, breed of criminal.

Afterward, the group headed out for a late-afternoon lunch— the traditional reward for a job well done. Then Jack Marth and I turned right around and did it again. And this time things turned out differently.

"You'll regret this!" the precinct commander exploded as we stood at his desk for the second time that day. "This time, I'm putting you through the system."

Jack and I had been discussing risking two arrests on Hiroshima Day; we had wanted to push the envelope. We had gotten what we wanted—twenty-four hours of being routed through precincts, holding cells, and jails. We moved among dozens of police officers, mostly white, and suffered with the prisoners, mostly black.

The once-genial officers now shoved us along and poured out contempt on us. I asked the one taking my prints, "How do you manage to maintain your self-respect while treating us so harshly?" "Those dogs aren't human," he spat, referring to prisoners in general.

To drive home the point, they had us sit with our hands cuffed behind us in a steaming van for hours. The heat was unbearable. Folks told stories to pass the time, tales of a minor drug infraction here, a petty theft there. Then they looked at Jack and me.

We told them what we had been up to. And they *thanked* us. Here, at last, was a sympathetic audience. But their thanks were mixed with doubt. They held out little hope. To a person, they expected no justice, at least not in their lifetimes. "We're just trying to survive the streets," one said, and the others nodded.

After the sun had set, the police chained us together and crammed us into a much smaller van, and we took off for nowhere. Apparently, all the holding cells in the city were full. Nor was there room in any of the jails, so we cruised the streets. Finally, around midnight, space was found at the Harlem jail. We were divided into pairs and thrown into an underground prison—the jail's original pit, built ages before. Each pair was put in a cell made for one person: a four-by-eight-foot space with concrete walls, a bench, and a toilet. The walls and floors were covered with a wretched slime and splashed with urine. My cellmate collapsed on the bench and fell asleep. And I began a solitary vigil. My first night in jail.

It was a horrible night spent in a reeking, slimy hole with no place to sleep, yet in another sense it was an uplifting experience. In such a world as ours—wars raging by the dozens, nukes beyond counting, millions starving—I had landed, it seemed, where I belonged, like Jesus: in a dungeon.

"Under a government which imprisons any unjustly, the true place for a just man is also in prison," Thoreau wrote in *On the Duty of Civil Disobedience*. That night, I repeated his words like a mantra.

I pondered Henry David Thoreau's night in jail and the many nights for Dr. King. I thought of Dorothy Day's imprisonment in this very city for flouting air-raid drills and of the thousands arrested regularly for protesting war and injustice, corporate greed, and nuclear weapons. I meditated upon Jesus' long night in a Jerusalem jail, the minutes lurching toward his trial, torture, and execution. And I thought of the two hundred thousand people vaporized forty-two years earlier in Japan.

Earlier, in the van, using the chains that bound us together, I had prayed the rosary, link by link. Now, in the cramped cell, I slipped into deep contemplative peace and felt God's presence. I was surprised with a sense of how free I was. Chains, heat, abuse, dungeons, slime— whatever might happen, I was free.

Jack and I were released the next morning. Unrehabilitated, we decided on a further step. We called together some friends—Daniel Berrigan, Sister Anne Montgomery, Sister Chris Mulready, Sister Kathy Maier, Elmer Maas, and Peter Cicchino, among others—to gauge interest in a Plowshares disarmament action at the Trident submarine base in Groton, Connecticut. The idea was to undertake a dramatic gesture to spark new energy in the peace movement. We agreed to meet monthly over the next year to plan our action, share our stories, read the Scriptures, and celebrate the Eucharist. For the next year at Scranton, I quietly stole back to the city once a month to help organize.

That summer, I met the actor Martin Sheen, who was in town filming *Wall Street*. Known for his great performances in *Apocalypse Now*, *Gandhi*, and *Badlands*, he would later appear as President Bartlet on TV's *West Wing*. Friend to Daniel and Philip Berrigan, Martin played Judge Salus to villainous perfection in the film *In the King of Prussia*—a chronicle of the first Plowshares action. Jack had met Martin earlier at a protest and had arranged for me to meet him after a Mass for peace.

We shook hands, and he invited us for a walk. We rambled along the streets of Manhattan into the night, discussing our life journeys, our families, the peace movement, the Berrigans, civil disobedience, and the elusiveness of peace. He brimmed with energy, exciting ideas, and hilarious tales. His devotion to the peaceful Jesus was clear, and his recent involvement in the peace movement was a matter of enormous satisfaction to him.

Martin and I hit it off right away, and in the twenty-plus years since, he has proved to be a bona fide hero, a lively font of encouragement, and one of my closest friends. We share the same hopes, perspectives, and enthusiasms.

回 回

As summer was drawing to a close, my imminent return to Scranton inspired dread, all the more because Ed DeBerri, a gifted teacher, had had it up to here and called it quits. The long, hot summer had wrung him dry of any remaining desire to work in first-world high schools. "I can't take it anymore," he told the superior: "spoiled wealthy families, contempt for the Jesuit mission, scorn for the gospel—the whole enterprise is about prestige. I'm sorry, Father, but I'm finished with Scranton Prep." He ended up working as an editor for the *National Jesuit News* and then as a teacher at Gonzaga University, in Spokane, Washington, before leaving the order in 1993.

I packed to return to Scranton, and my parents arrived in New York for a rare visit. Over dinner, they told me that my father had colon cancer that would require radical surgery. I managed a week away to tend to him in the hospital. His suffering placed my Scranton woes in a new light. I set aside my worries about classes, other obligations, and my own plans. Dad was alive, and so was I. I was grateful for the moment, grateful just to be.

Then more foul news arrived. On September 1, in Concord, California, a train struck my friend Brian Willson. A lawyer, former air force officer, and Vietnam vet who had seen his share of carnage, Brian had become a dedicated antiwar activist. He and a few friends had begun a fast and then sat on the train tracks to oppose the shipments of a military train freighted with weapons for Central America. It was the first time anyone had tried such an action, and it would not be the last. But on this occasion, the train accelerated, as FBI documents later revealed, because the FBI knew he was "a man of his word." Brian lost both legs and part of his skull but somehow survived.

In previous years, Brian had spent time in Nicaragua, witnessing the funerals of peasants and meeting children who had lost legs to U.S. land mines. He said, "I've grieved so many Nicaraguans who have lost their legs [that] I found I'd already grieved the loss of mine." Papers all over the world reported the action, and now the jig was up, the cover blown. The government had been denying this business, but now the world knew of the bombs and mines going to the contras down south.

I had met Brian in the summer of 1986 at the Witness for Peace office in Washington, D.C. One day as we walked along Connecticut Avenue, he admonished me to make waves in Scranton. "You should stir up the whole town until they finally run you out." Now he had sacrificed his legs out of love for our country's "enemies."

I returned to Scranton, more determined than ever to teach peace. Once again, my lot was to drum world history into the heads of 150 freshmen and the Gospels into the heads of 30 obstreperous sophomores. I kept them busy with weekly reports, a term paper every month, and, for the freshmen, oral reports every Friday on a current event. In the course of all those ordinary assignments, I shepherded the kids from party line to alternative view. I inched them from the culture of war to the wisdom of nonviolence.

"Did you really go to jail in Harlem?" a student asked out of the blue. Apparently, the news had reached Scranton. It soon spread through town, and by spring my notoriety had crested. Junior and senior classes began inviting me to speak. The faculty had little recourse to say otherwise. I accepted with pleasure and started rollicking debates. These talks were a great exercise for the kids; it got them forging new neural grooves. The talks also were a great exercise for me, a good opportunity to hone my public speaking skills.

For the most part, classes proceeded apace. Weekends came and went. Every month I'd slip off to New York to meet about the Plowshares action. I wrote the assistant provincial of formation about my plans, telling him point-blank that I hoped to fulfill Isaiah's prophecy of beating swords into plowshares. Would he kindly grant me permission? His call came on Good Friday: "Absolutely not."

An hour or so later, my mother called with urgency in her voice. The cancer had moved to Dad's liver. Experimental surgery was called for—and soon. I flew home and sat with Dad as he recovered from a successful surgery. Half of his liver was removed, but enough was left behind to keep the system going. It was nothing short of a miracle. I thought about the Plowshares action in light of my father's health troubles and decided to wait. Now was the time to celebrate the gift of life and support my parents.

Classes came to an end that June, and my time at Scranton Prep was over. I bade my students farewell and headed back to Washington, D.C.

19

With the Homeless
in Washington, D.C.
(1988–89)

The next step in Jesuit formation lay ahead, four years of the-ology studies. But I thought myself in need of a more primary experience—I wanted time among the poor. On one hand, I could be of service. On the other, as the liberation theologians say, the poor are of service in return—and in much greater measure. One learns from them, even receives from them, an invitation into the reign of God, the only thing they have at their disposal, and something the rest of us know little about. I wanted to learn from them, examine life's underbelly, make a new kind of friend.

The Jesuits granted me permission to take a position at both the McKenna Center and St. Aloysius Church, in Washington, D.C. I would have to travel no great distance between the two jobs: the McKenna Center is located in the basement of St. Al's. It was a good location in other respects as well—not only twenty-eight steps below the mother church, but only eight blocks from the U.S. Capitol and twenty miles or so from my parents.

I worked at the Center with its extraordinary director, Lisa Goode. Lisa had grown up in the nearby housing projects built by Father Horace McKenna himself. A few months before Bobby Kennedy died, he visited the projects. He held baby Lisa and kissed her, as candidates will do, and surveyed the place and delivered an address with Lisa bundled in his arms. Seventeen years later, St. Al's raised funds for Lisa's college tuition. She graduated from college, and then announced her intent to spend her life advocating for the collapsing neighborhood, uplifting the people, and keeping blight at bay. Lisa was an expert on housing rights, legal justice, and the needs of the African-American community. Fortunately, the Jesuits recognized her talent and commitment and rewarded her with the directorship.

We worked together on a variety of projects: helping the local food bank, finding jobs for the homeless, chasing down housing and health care. The shelter and the kitchen needed supervision, and local agencies needed to be continually reminded of the people's needs. The homeless in Washington that year numbered more than fifteen thousand. Many slept at the gates of buildings where succor is supposed to be found—the White House, the U.S. Department of Justice, the U.S. Department of Housing and Human Services.

I dispensed food and clothing, provided rental assistance, answered phones, attended advocacy meetings, edited the center's newsletter, picked up and delivered donated furniture—and made many friends. My job, above all, was to listen, to hear the people's harrowing stories, to remember them. Someone needed to help them see that their stories were significant, and in doing so help them reclaim some dignity.

"Do you know of any jobs, John?" "Know where I can stay?" "Got an extra blanket?" We were overwhelmed with requests. The poor arrived every day. "Any coats to spare?" "I need boots." I thought of

Horace McKenna's famous maxim: "The poor can't lift themselves up by their own bootstraps because they have no boots." Often we offered nothing but a listening ear and then an apology. And back they went to the streets, none the wealthier but with spirits lifted.

One busy day, I received a call from the nearby hospital. Mathias Tucker had died. Eighty-two years old and homeless for fifteen years, he had been a dear friend of the late Father McKenna. Would I claim the body? We arranged a beautiful Mass and sent him off in style and love. Afterward, I drove with the undertaker to the pauper cemetery. While he waited in the hearse, I stood at the graveside, offered prayers, and reflected on the Scripture: "Precious in God's sight is the death of the poor."

That was my first liturgical act, alone at the grave of Mathias Tucker. I trembled at the honor of blessing his worn-out body and praying him to the bosom of Abraham. All around me business went on as usual: Wall Street climbing, resources flowing, and not far away in the halls of power, plans for war constantly in progress. Standing there in the graveyard, I realized that all such powers were an abomination in God's eyes, but Mathias and all the homeless were precious indeed.

The stories I heard and witnessed in those years formed me profoundly. A woman who slept on the steps of the National Archives Building came by the center one day asking for help. I gave her a new tote bag and started to empty her old grocery bags. "Why all the handkerchiefs?" I asked, having counted more than twenty. "You need them," she said, "when you cry all the time."

Later that summer, Mary, a single mother of a small child, dropped by the center. She pulled out of her bag an eviction notice. She brought home $260 a month; her rent was $210. She suffered from cancer and had endured many rounds of chemotherapy. A friend had given her an air conditioner, providing relief from the one-hundred-degree days, but the utility bills had gotten out of hand. She had paid most of them but had come up short on rent. And now she was in arrears beyond recovery. The center paid the difference and forestalled eviction. But we had only two thousand dollars a month for rental assistance, and scores of mothers came to our door, all facing the grim prospect of landing on the streets. Mary didn't, but many others did.

The city enforced fifty evictions per day. And to keep the machine running, it hired the homeless to carry belongings to the streets—the homeless hired to make others homeless. Each eviction earned them $10 to $20. My friends and I began to discuss what to do in the face of this latest injustice.

Meanwhile, I helped Father George Anderson at St. Aloysius parish. George was quiet and gentle, a doctor of English literature, a latecomer to the Jesuits, a man who wore a rabble of black and a heavy chain of keys, his pockets bulging with French and Spanish literature so he could keep up his language skills. He had spent a dozen years serving prisoners on Rikers Island, in the Bronx. Now he was here with this small community of African-American Catholics.

George penned invectives against poverty and prisons for *America*, the Jesuit magazine. He'd later become one of *America*'s finest editors. He embodied compassion for the vulnerable and forgotten and went about his business quietly, never inviting notice. Rather he came upon the lost and lonely and tendered compassion, making room for them in the community of the exhausted, the helpless, the near dead.

I accompanied him on his rounds and built pastoral bonds with the shut-ins. The work required entering the high-rise projects, violent warrens marked by graffiti, befouled by urine, patrolled by police day and night. There I met beautiful gospel people: Ruth Payne, a faithful singer in our choir, trying to raise her great-grandnephew single-handedly; Mr. Taylor, an elderly blind man who had no family and no income; Hester Brady, confined to bed in a squalid apartment, a woman with a heart so loving that it stopped you in your tracks—when I entered her room, she raised her hands to the sky and shouted, "My baby!"—and David, a homeless man with AIDS, his life drawn out thin, the conclusion foregone. Father George and I accompanied him to Gift of Peace, Mother Teresa's home for the dying. There, after mere days, he slipped away, surrounded by love.

These were extraordinary people—the greatest in the great city, if you saw them through God's eyes. They were powerless, helpless, and insignificant, but nonetheless possessed of a profound faith in God, an inner peace confounding to those in power, the grace and light to dispel any demon. They bore out the words of our foremost beatitude: the blessing of God's reign belongs first of all to the poor in spirit.

My home during that time was the K Street Jesuit community, a row house blue as the Caribbean on a deteriorating block of the city known for its crack wars. It was also but a leisurely stroll from the U.S. Capitol, a zip code where crack claimed lives by the dozen. A crowd of amazing Jesuits called the house home. They were the "A-Team" in my mind, all-star advocates of "the faith that does justice." Dean Brackley had directed a community-organizing agency for ten years and would go on to teach at the University of Central America, in El Salvador. Peter Henriot directed the Center of Concern, a think tank that promoted Catholic social teaching and global justice. He later moved to Zambia to spend the rest of his life serving African villagers and promoting Catholic social teaching to priests and bishops all over the continent.

Joe Hacala had spent years among the Appalachian poor and now served as director of the National Office of Jesuit Social Ministries. Later, he would become director of the Catholic Campaign for Human Development of the U.S. Conference of Catholic Bishops, which distributed more than twenty million dollars annually to grassroots service centers, and still later the special assistant to the secretary of Housing and Urban Development in the Clinton administration. Frank Moan founded and served as director of Refugee Voices, a small nonprofit that advocated for refugees around the world, while Si Smith coordinated the U.S. office of Jesuit Refugee Services. Fred Kammer, a lawyer from New Orleans who had attended Yale with Bill Clinton, directed Catholic Charities, the largest Catholic charitable organization in the United States.

Next to this Who's Who group, I was a water boy. I raced home every night for dinner to hear their astonishing stories. Together, we all lived as conscientiously as we could. We prayed together, gathered our surplus and gave it away, took our turns with mop and ladle, and tried to bring to the tormented neighborhood a modest measure of peace. For me, the community fostered hope—for the world and for the Society of Jesus.

In August, I had the opportunity to make another trip to El Salvador, this time with the legendary Detroit bishop Thomas Gumbleton, to visit religious leaders and grassroots communities. More than anything else, it was a visit of solidarity, a chance to hear the people's stories of woe and in turn to issue a hot denunciation: No more assassinations of priests, catechists, and organizers! Our press conference was a small gesture but widely covered and by no means futile. In our limited way, we put the death squads on notice. Our renunciation could at least throw their atrocities into the light of day.

Once again, I entered the hinterlands and met the wrenching contrast between first-world power and third-world poverty. This was a different species of poverty from even that surrounding St. Al's. Here was extreme poverty and early death and systematic killing. Bishop Gumbleton and I arrived one day at a remote village of twenty families living in mud huts just as ten U.S. army helicopters landed in a field a few yards away. The helicopters disgorged dozens of soldiers—Salvadorans in U.S. army fatigues—who moved in close and raised their weapons. The villagers were ordered to turn over their sacks of grain. Before our eyes, the soldiers stole food from the poorest of the poor and, their mission accomplished, lifted off and flew away, leaving the villagers to starve. The villagers, in turn, begged us to leave, terror glistening in their dark eyes. They feared we might intervene—that we might utter a strong word or upbraid the soldierly machismo and thus break the dam of the soldier's wrath. After we returned home to the safety of our beds, those soldiers could return at any time and retaliate.

My one consolation on that particular journey was a new friend, the bishop. I had gotten to know Tom Gumbleton through Pax Christi. He was the first U.S. Catholic bishop to speak out against the Vietnam War. In 1979, he flew to Tehran to help secure the release of the U.S. hostages. He also coauthored the U.S. bishops' pastoral letter "The Challenge of Peace." To this day, he travels every week to some corner of the world, usually a war zone, advocating for peace. No matter what despair clutches the world, or how the church responds or doesn't, my friends and I take heart knowing that Tom is witnessing anew to the gospel of Jesus. Over the years, I have begun to introduce him at various church events as our own Óscar Romero.

When I returned to Washington, I went back to work among the homeless. The day after I arrived, I was in a van with Lisa, distributing bags of fresh bread to the *Sursum Corda* housing project, as dozens of police cars raided the place in search of drug dealings. We were prevented from distributing the bread, and left depressed and appalled. I had witnessed in First and Third Worlds the hostility against the poor, the government violence that leaves people hungry.

◫ ◫

Inspired by my trip, I managed in 1988 to finagle some time to join my Catholic Worker and Jonah House friends who were busy with protests. The "Arms Bazaar," also known as the Air & Space Conference and Technology Expo, came to town every September. The Air Force Association hosted this invitation-only showcase of the latest instruments of mass murder at the Sheraton hotel. Thousands of buyers from all over the nation trolled the displays. GE, TRW, Martin Marietta, McDonnell Douglas—they all had wares on display and were eager to land a lucrative deal. If you wanted tools of massacre, this was the place to be.

Pax Christi, Jonah House, and the Dorothy Day Catholic Worker House were on hand. A friend and I put on coats and ties and pinned badges to our lapels. Accoutred like ambassadors, we walked into the hotel lobby and, in the midst of two thousand people, unfurled a banner and called out the good news of peace.

"Excuse me! May we have your attention?" The milling crowd grew quiet and turned to look. "We call upon everyone here to stop producing, buying, and selling weapons." Despite some furious gazes, we went on. "These weapons kill people, especially the poor, our brothers and sisters. They're an offense against God. Jesus calls us to love our enemies, not kill them. For the love of God, stop killing the world's poor, close down this arms bazaar, and go home."

Within seconds, a handful of undercover guards drew near and ordered us to stop the protest. "Officer," I replied, "these people are buying and selling weapons. They are preparing to kill people. Please stop them. Arrest them. If you don't, we'll do what we can." The guards arrested us instead. We ended up in central booking and thrown into a cell similar to the one back at Harlem Jail. Later that morning, they let us go.

A few weeks later, I attended a hearing on homelessness at city hall. Also there was Mitch Snyder, leader of the Community for Creative Nonviolence (CCNV). Here was an angry and outspoken advocate for the poor—with his trademark army jacket and disheveled hair. Years before, Mitch was doing time at the Danbury prison for auto theft when the Berrigans arrived after the Catonsville action. They inspired him to dedicate his life to justice and peace. Mitch later joined the CCNV, lived among the homeless, and embarked on long fasts that attracted media attention. His anger at the government's apathy was absolutely combustible. He lined the shelves in his office with urns containing the ashes of dozens of homeless people who had frozen to death in the city, bodies he personally had salvaged.

On this day, Mitch attended the hearing at city hall, but in a different capacity from mine. His group staged a sit-in outside the council chambers. I watched the sit-in proceed from far down the hall as I fielded a reporter's questions. A policeman spied me in the distance and traversed the long corridor. To my surprise, he arrested me as one of the ringleaders.

This was a wide dragnet indeed; I had been arrested because of proximity. Back I went to central booking and rode out twenty-four hours with Mitch and his friends. I later regarded the arrest as a blessing, because it gave me time to acquaint myself with them and learn more of the CCNV, the largest shelter in the nation. Mitch and I would become friends and travel the East Coast together, organizing and speaking. We came up with the idea of a national march for the homeless, called Housing Now! which would eventually attract more than one hundred thousand participants.

As I sat in my jail cell, time came to a halt. I reached into my coat pocket and came upon Henri Nouwen's latest book, *In the Name of Jesus*, sent to me by Brother Patrick Hart, a Trappist monk at Gethsemani Abbey and at one time Thomas Merton's secretary. He had asked me to review the book for a Cistercian journal, but I'd been too busy. I had forgotten that I'd slipped it into my pocket. Now I opened its pages and read it in one sitting, electrified by Nouwen's vision of the weak minister, vulnerable and compassionate, dedicated first and foremost to the vulnerable and compassionate. I wrote a review there in jail and sent a copy to Henri himself, which started a correspondence between us. All in all, it was a fruitful day in jail.

After my release, I took part in daily civil disobedience actions that Mitch proposed and supervised. This was the time leading up to the election of George H. W. Bush, and Mitch's actions at the U.S. Capitol were designed to throw light on the plight of the poor. One group dropped a banner that read "Housing Now for the Homeless" from the public balcony in the Senate. A group from North Carolina let chickens loose on the Capitol lawn and unfurled a banner that said, "Money for Housing is Chicken Feed." Another group evicted the furniture from the office of Senator Jesse Helms.

One October day in 1988, seven of us unloaded a truck full of battered furniture in a busy D.C. intersection at the height of lunch hour. Couches, chairs, lamps, and toys, all laid out in the street between the U.S. Capitol and the Supreme Court. There we sat, a mock family subjected to a theatrical eviction. And I went back again to central booking, my home away from home.

Months later, the seven of us came to court. We faced a year in prison. During the three-day trial, we testified of our work among the homeless, the need for low-income housing, and the injustices that went on in the nation's capital every day. Witnesses came forward to tell how the homeless suffered. Most notable among these witnesses was Dr. Janelle Goetchus, who moved her entire family into a medical facility for the homeless called Christ House. Our combined testimony moved even the judge. Finally, the jury handed in a verdict of not guilty. Judge Mildred Edwards thanked us for our witness, and the *Washington Post* reported our action as a rare example of the power of nonviolence.

In August 1989, it came time for me to say good-bye to family and friends. I was off to Seattle, to attend the Pax Christi National Assembly. In Seattle, I took my time and caught my breath, climbed Mount Rainier, and sat in on speeches by Father Jon Sobrino of El Salvador, and Reverend William Sloane Coffin, who had served at New York's Riverside Church. The time in Seattle renewed my strength, refreshed my perspective, and got me in a good frame of mind for my next stage of Jesuit formation—four years of theology studies at the Jesuit School of Theology at Berkeley.

Theology and Vision
at Berkeley
(1989)

I arrived at "Holy Hill," just north of the University of California, Berkeley, in late August 1989. Given its name by playful locals, Holy Hill is known officially as the Graduate Theological Union, a consortium of seminaries and graduate schools established by thirteen denominations and religious orders that welcome one another's students. I was now one of them.

Berkeley was a paradise, a haven for first-world progressives with shops and salons, bistros and boutiques, wine festivals and farmers' markets, eucalyptus trees and a marina, all drenched in sunshine. It was a world apart from the K Street war zone.

At the pinnacle of Holy Hill sits the Jesuit School of Theology (JSTB), a stately manor the color of frosted mint. There I joined a hundred Jesuit scholastics and another hundred laypeople, most of them women, from all over the world. I enjoyed my classes from the start—especially those on the Scriptures. I had never formally studied the Bible before, but here I had the best professors to teach me, Jesuits such as John Donahue, John Boyle, and Don Gelpi, plus brilliant feminist theologians, such as Sandra Schneiders and Anne Brotherton.

As far as I was concerned, Anne was the heart and soul of JSTB. She directed the service program, which required each student to volunteer fifteen hours a week. We put in our hours and then met with her weekly to discuss our work. It was an appointment I eagerly awaited. I enjoyed her charming southern accent, her wit and humor. Over the years, she supervised my work forming peace groups and organizing protests—off the usual map as far as service projects go, but not a matter of consternation for Anne. She had spent the 1970s as Coretta Scott King's personal assistant, organizing nonviolence trainings at the King Center, in Atlanta, Georgia. I think she was glad to have my troublemaking spirit disturbing the Berkeley peace.

I spent three years on a master of divinity and a fourth on a master of spiritual theology. The psalms, the prophets, St. Paul, the Gospels, Christology, the sacraments, the church, anthropology, the Wisdom Literature, spiritual direction, and the Second Vatican Council—a smorgasbord of absorbing subjects, which I determined to study while also incorporating them into my life. I would eat, breathe, and live theology in the midst of all my peacemaking activities.

Still, I found theology studies far too comfortable and not engaged in the work for justice. By now, I was corresponding regularly with Henri Nouwen, and he pointed a way forward for me in this new culture. "Live as if you're in exile," he wrote me that fall, a maxim by which he himself had survived university life and, for that matter, life in the United States. "Once you understand that, like our Hebrew ancestors in the desert, you're in exile, you can wait patiently, make do, get by." I knew this was sage advice that a person didn't get every day. I was fortunate, too, to find such a like-minded friend. If exile was to be my choice, I wouldn't choose it alone.

My first day at the JSTB, Steve Kelly—a California Jesuit, lean and taut, with intense eyes and the coiled-spring look of a young Clint Eastwood—sought me out. He had grown up an adopted son in a military family and had bounced around the world. The 1960s were his heyday, and he was as wild as the times. But along the way, he experienced a dramatic conversion and entered the Jesuits. Before long, he itched for adventures in the gospel. He worked awhile in Sudan and El Salvador and in the end cast his sights on the thorny business of nuclear disarmament. Steve is one of the most radical people I know; he has spent six years in prison, three of them in solitary confinement. Daniel Berrigan would later call Steve his mentor.

Steve had come by to ask me to join a gathering at the Concord Naval Weapons Station to mark the second year since Brian Willson had been crippled. The next day, September 1, hundreds gathered at the tracks to hear Brian's talk, a fiery oration delivered at full height on artificial legs. This day by the tracks also marked the beginning of long friendships with Father Bill O'Donnell and Dr. Davida Coady, whom I had first met in 1988 in a small parish in El Salvador.

Davida is a woman of gigantic vision. She helped end the Biafra famine of the early 1970s and has spent the past thirty-five years working to ease the plight of tortured communities in El Salvador, Guatemala, Nicaragua, Cuba, Colombia, Korea, Palestine, the Philippines, and Sudan. She counts Martin Sheen a close friend, as does Bill, and in the years after I reconnected with them, we all would travel together on various missions. Eventually, Davida would found and direct Options, a groundbreaking treatment program for Berkeley's homeless, developing a model to be used around the country to eradicate the addictions that push so many souls onto the streets.

A big man who always wore a black leather jacket and sunglasses, Bill O'Donnell grew up in California, entered the seminary in his twenties, and was assigned to three different parishes—and promptly kicked out of each one after preaching about social justice. Full of Irish wit and wisdom, this reformed class bully ended up spending twenty-two years as the pastor of St. Joseph the Worker Church in Berkeley and became the quintessence of the city itself: he was arrested some 250 times by his own count and attended two to three protests a week for decades. He and I would often travel together to various protests, including down to Southern California and Nevada, where we repeatedly crossed the line at the Nevada Test Site in a call to end nuclear testing.

Like Bishop Gumbleton, Bill will one day be recognized as a giant in the church. He was of great support when I landed in prison years after we became reacquainted and decided that he would risk prison as well. In November 2001, in his seventies, he crossed the line at the School of the Americas and spent six difficult months in a California prison for it. In the late 1990s, he had suffered heart problems and a stroke, and while we thought he was doing well, prison surely hastened his end. Up early for morning Mass on Monday, December 8, 2003, he had a cup of coffee, read the sports page, went to his desk to write his weekly bulletin announcement, and had apparently written three sentences about the Gospel and the meaning of Advent when he fell over, dead from a massive heart attack. He was seventy-three years old.

Once, while driving through the Nevada desert with him, I asked, "Why in the world, Bill, are you a priest? You are the most irreverent, most provocative, most disruptive person in the whole church." I expected a wisecrack so was surprised when he took my question seriously. "I am a priest," he said, "because it is the best way for me to become a human being." I'll never forget that powerful answer. I think he had been pondering that question for decades. Bill learned early on to dismiss the pomp and privilege of the priesthood and spend his days in loving service, as Jesus did. In the process, he became whole, holy, the human being he was meant to become. That is the goal of the spiritual life, to become fully human. Bill challenged me through his holy irreverence and holy reverence of every human being to become the person I am meant to be.

Bill was also a model for me of "holy resistance." He was irrepressible. He never stopped protesting every form of violence, injustice, and war. He understood that following Jesus in the empire our country has become requires steadfast, public, nonviolent resistance to war, the death penalty, the oppression of the poor and workers, and our nuclear arsenal. Bill's "holy resistance" was a model not only for church leaders, but for all Christians. Bill showed us how to live in dark times.

Finally, Bill taught me "holy humor." He was constantly laughing and making others laugh. As Daniel Berrigan says, if we are going to spend our lives resisting death, we better learn to live life well along the way. Laughter is a key element in the life of Christian resistance to imperial violence. Bill knew this well and did not take himself too seriously.

Another friend I made by way of Steve was Cindy Pile, a beautiful, smart woman who was passionate about the church and the Scriptures, justice, and peace. She was doggedly pursuing a master of divinity—in preparation, she said, without a smidgen of irony, for ordination as a Catholic priest. She knew her Testaments and history; she could cite chapter and verse of the great women who ran entire Christian communities and became deacons, priests, and bishops during those early centuries. She operated from deep certainty of her call and went on to prove her talent for preaching. Today she's a much sought-after speaker and continues to work for justice and peace.

▣   ▣

Over the next four years, these friends and I made our way together, taking on the world of war and injustice. I can't speak for them, but I was full of myself. I was overconfident and knew the answer to every question. I also had a chip on both shoulders. But I didn't know at the time how much I needed help. Fortunately, help was on the way, in the person of Sister Jane Ferdon.

A Dominican nun and spiritual director, Sister Jane was I'm sure the most influential person on Holy Hill. She moved among us Jesuits, saving our souls, cocky and jaded as we were. She listened and prodded day after day, from dawn to dusk, and taught me more about prayer than anyone since Bill Sneck at the novitiate.

Jane didn't look or act like a nun, or at least not how I expected a nun to look or act. Fashionable, dignified, and professional, she brimmed with good cheer and interest, humor and common sense, and hid from view the immense store of wisdom she had accumulated. Each Jesuit scholastic met with her for an hour every month and faced her questions aimed like darts: "Where is God in your life?" "When have you felt God's presence?" "What is God saying to you personally?" She subscribed to the theory that the more you talk about the specifics of God's presence in your day-to-day life, the more you become aware of God's action in your life. For instance, I would say, "I felt blessed by . . ." or "This consoled me . . ." and she would skewer my obtuseness: "Don't you see how God came close to you and you turned and ran?" Each time, it was a revelation. She was more coach than guru, a referee between lovers, One faithful as intimacy nears, and the other running off in a flash. Jane's God was the Hound of Heaven, and her challenge was to let God find me and to help me realize what a blessing that would be.

"Above all," she taught, "prayer is intimacy—a loving relationship between you and God." I didn't know what she was talking about. So in my defense I tried to explain to her my high level of prayer: thirty minutes every morning for going on ten years. It was special, I assured her. Every day, I told God in no uncertain terms to get the world in order: Stop the contra war, disband the Salvadoran death squads, put an end to Reagan's oppression of the poor, and, while you're at it, for crying out loud, abolish nuclear weapons, too. "Get busy, God!" That was my sincere holy prayer. Very intimate indeed—angry, belligerent, mean, bossy, and strident, every day for ten years.

She listened attentively for a long time, and then one day she let me have it. "John," she said, a hint of alarm in her eyes, "is this how you talk to someone you love?" I stiffened in my chair and looked down at my shoes. I had never thought of it this way. "Think of the person who loved you the most, John. The one always there for you, who always affirmed you, supported you no matter what, gave you pure unconditional love. How would that person feel if you yelled at her every day for thirty minutes for ten years? If you never once allowed her a word in edgewise? You've been yelling at God for ten years and never once have you stopped long enough to hear what God is saying to you."

My prayer changed from that day forward. I stopped badgering and started listening. I knew God loved me—Joe Markwordt told me so long ago, and I had experienced it during my long retreat— but now, I would see my prayer as time to be with the One I loved, the One who loved me, time to sit in that loving presence, to be the beloved, to listen and to enjoy the silence of pure love and gentle peace. I began to savor the serenity, the sense of God's presence.

Jane guided me deeper into life with God than any other teacher had. She taught me how to know Jesus, listen to him, be his friend, and attend to his problems and needs, hopes and pains. The focus, she explained over the years, was not me, but him, not so much how I felt about what was happening in my life and in the world, but how Jesus felt. That subtle distinction makes all the difference. By losing myself in his thoughts, his feelings, his vision, I am entirely transformed for the better. Jane told me: By all means beg God for peace and act for justice, but know that your prayer is above all time for intimacy with God. She led me into the contemplative, mystical depths of peace as the foundation for all my future work for peace. In the process, as Bill O'Donnell would say, she helped me become a better human being.

回 回

Those first days at Berkeley were thrilling; I was surrounded by lively people, good friends, and much wisdom. But some dark cloud appeared on the horizon, an ominous sense that tumultuous events were at hand. This feeling was palpable, and I wasn't the only one who experienced it. Steve, Cindy, and another Jesuit, John Savard, expressed the same unsettling feeling. We needed to prepare, but we did not know for what. Steve would visit my room and pace back and forth. Something must be done, he would insist. We have to start meeting and talking about the world and what we can do with this precious time here in Berkeley. But how, and for what exactly?

It was a Friday night in October, over dinner in a Berkeley café, when conversation turned to Ched Myers, a young biblical scholar whose book, *Binding the Strong Man: A Political Reading of Mark's Story of Jesus*, was causing a stir. Ched was holding a retreat in Las Vegas the next day, to be followed by civil disobedience at the Nevada Test Site. Steve, John, Cindy, and I decided on impulse to go. We piled into Cindy's Honda and headed for Vegas, drove all night under the stars, arriving early, sleepy but exhilarated, as the retreat was just beginning. Ched talked of Mark's Gospel in new and exciting ways, as a manifesto of nonviolent resistance against the empire. Jesus had taught his disciples to nonviolently resist imperial culture and had exemplified resistance himself in the Temple, had embodied suffering love on the cross, and had emerged from the tomb. We were summoned to enter the story, to take up where Jesus had left off.

We debated the Gospel and pondered Ched's radical reading. The next day, we drove to the Nevada Test Site, larger than Rhode Island, where the United States has detonated more than a thousand nuclear weapons. We took part in a beautiful prayer service and a simple Eucharist, then crossed the line onto the test site. Arrests followed swiftly. It was my first nonviolent assault on the site. More than ten thousand Christians have crossed that line since the early 1980s, and the campaign continues today.

On Sunday night we headed back, our spirits light and our minds racing with ideas of how better to turn our lives over to Gospel nonviolence. We wanted to ready ourselves for the violence toward which the world seemed to be careering. We wanted to get moving, to make Mark's story come alive here and now, so that when the worst happened, we would be ready.

This may sound ridiculous, our sense of global collapse, but sure enough, the world dropped out from underneath us just a few days later, on Tuesday, October 17, 1989, just after 5:00 p.m. I was at the main Jesuit residence in Berkeley, discussing with five other Jesuits in my class study group the meaning of baptism. A distant rumble sounded. Then oscillations set the room in motion. Everything not bolted down began to shake. Pictures fell from walls; dishes crashed to the floor. We learned later that the earthquake had measured 7.1 on the Richter scale.

When the earth began to roll, I turned to the other Jesuits in the room and only then noticed that they were all native Californians. At the height of the earthquake, they sat there, moving with the earth yet perfectly calm. There was scarcely a hiccup in the conversation. For me, on the other hand, each second lasted an hour; the Richter scale didn't go high enough for my mounting panic. It was all I could do to keep it from showing. I endured it for seven, eight, nine seconds, then stood up and said coolly, "I think I'm going outside for a minute."

No one was fooled. "It will end soon," someone said. "You should just stand in the doorway."

I started the journey across the room—a large one, big enough for three hundred—and before my eyes, the floor rose several feet and fell. I staggered a few steps and then plunged to the ground. It was like walking through a fun house. I hauled myself to my feet and tried again. Another wave rolled through; it felt as big as the ones the Atlantic tosses on the Outer Banks. Not being a Californian, I didn't know how to surf the floor. Instead, I bolted for the door, giving way to total panic. Any minute, I presumed, the whole building would come down on us. After it was all over, I stood outside and caught my breath, then returned to find the others inside, still engrossed in their debate over the meaning of the sacraments.

My colleagues' calm notwithstanding, more than sixty people died that night. Part of the Bay Bridge and the upper tier of the Cypress Street Viaduct section of the Nimitz Freeway in Oakland collapsed. Fires erupted in parts of San Francisco. I climbed the Berkeley hills at sunset and watched the city burn. Life is hard enough, I thought— disasters of all sorts, epidemics, tsunamis, hurricanes, earthquakes. Why squander our precious time and talent on war? Why design weapons? Why dissipate money acquiring useless possessions? Why risk bringing harm to others when the very ground beneath us can turn to Jell-O at any moment? We should spend every moment help- ing one another survive in peace.

November 16, the Kairos Moment (1989)

O n Thursday, November 16, 1989, the kairos moment arrived.
At around nine o'clock in the morning, I was in my room at my desk when someone knocked on the door. Steve Kelly walked in looking stricken. Had I heard the news? he asked, then began to cry. Only a few hours earlier, around one o'clock, twenty-eight soldiers of the Salvadoran army, nineteen of them trained at the School of the Americas, had raided the University of Central America in El Salvador, seized the sleeping Jesuits in the community there, dragged them outside, and shot them dead. Ignacio Ellacuría, Segundo Montes, Ignacio Martín-Baró, Joaquín López y López, Amando López, and Juan Ramón Moreno. Murdured along with them were Julia Elba Ramos and Celina Ramos, a mother and daughter who worked at a nearby Jesuit community and had come to take shelter at the university.

Later in the morning, the Jesuits' bodies were found lying on the lawn. Their brains had been removed and laid beside them, a macabre sign and an implicit threat: Some things we will not permit you to ponder. This is what you get if you *think* about war and peace. (Father

Jon Sobrino, who also lived in the community, would have been killed as well had he not been speaking at a conference in Bangkok.)

My heart stopped. The ground beneath me gave way, but this was an earthquake of a different order. Great men I had known and admired had been murdered by soldiers trained by the United States—and some within our borders, as the world would later learn. It instantly became clear why we had been preparing.

"We have to do something," I said.

"A group of Jesuits and Catholic Workers are heading into San Francisco for a vigil outside the Salvadoran consulate," he answered. "Let's go."

But first we went to see our superior, Father George Murphy. We broke the news to him and begged him to join us. Of course he would, he said, much to our astonishment. This was a seismic change in its own right—a Jesuit superior not only not condemning our protest but also joining us. Later he would face arrest with us and vigorously urge other Jesuits to confront the war. In the weeks that followed, he would ask each Jesuit what he was doing to stop U.S. military aid to El Salvador. If the Jesuit in question was not committing civil disobedience, George wanted a good reason why. Suddenly I felt a new level of support.

Two dozen of us lined the street outside the Salvadoran consulate, an office building in downtown San Francisco. Several of us went upstairs and asked to meet with the consul general. After an hour, he agreed to meet with two of us. George and I went into the consulate, introduced ourselves, and told him of our outrage at the assassination. "We want an explanation," I demanded. "We want you to put a stop to these killings."

He leaped out of his chair. "You don't know what you're talking about. You're stirring up lies just like Ellacuría."

"Ellacuría is dead," I said, "and you're complicit in his murder."
We stood facing each other across his desk. "You're partially to blame,"
I continued, "not only for the deaths of the Jesuits, but for the deaths
of thousands of the poor, for Romero and the four churchwomen. You
have blood on your hands."

He pulled back and threw a punch that would have landed on
my nose had George not yanked me back by the clerical collar a split
second before. He pulled me backward to the door as I shouted, "We
demand you put a stop to your death squads and end this war!"

Back at school, I was still shaking. The daily 5:00 p.m. Mass was
packed. I sat in the corner, trying to let the news settle in. Memories
of Ellacuría and my time in El Salvador rose in me like a tide. The
responsorial psalm began, "The Lord hears the cry of the poor,"
and tears began to flow. I was sobbing and had to sit outside for ten
minutes.

Steve and I had asked George to host a public meeting that evening
to discuss a response. We invited all our friends, and by seven o'clock,
hundreds had arrived at the Jesuit residence. As I walked into the
large hall, George took me aside and said, "You're the one who knows
most about this—you facilitate this meeting." After George's opening
prayer, I took several deep breaths and wobbled to the podium.

I thanked everyone for coming, recounted my time in El Salvador,
and shared my love and admiration for the murdered Jesuits. Then I
suggested that we organize a large-scale public response, an action
that would force an immediate end to all U.S. military aid to El
Salvador—letter-writing and lobbying campaigns, public prayer,
media outreach. Moreover, we needed to renew our solidarity with
the Salvadorans in the Bay Area. And most of all, we needed to stage
a massive public protest, perhaps on Monday morning in front of
the federal building in downtown San Francisco. I suggested that we

break into groups to plan each facet of the campaign and report back in forty-five minutes to the whole group.

As the groups chattered away, I stood alone at the podium, trying to figure out how to coordinate the whole thing. Father Bill O'Donnell sidled up to me and whispered in my ear: "John, this is all fine and good. But I just want you to know that when the Monday morning protest ends, some of us will sit down and block the entrance to the Federal Building. I thought you should know." He walked away, leaving me stunned. Bill had pushed the protest in a far more radical direction, and though I agreed with his action and was pleased—I would join the sit-in myself—I felt a shadow of concern about the other Jesuits. How would they respond to the blockade? Never before in U.S. history had a Jesuit institution organized civil disobedience. From the outset, things bode ill.

For the next few days, I worked nonstop on the campaign, calling every Jesuit in the area and urging each to bring fifty people to the protest. On Sunday night we had a moving prayer service. When Monday morning came, I drove to the Federal Building. The streets were blocked off, and more than a thousand people—including Jesuit high school students who had been bused in for the occasion—gathered in front of the building. The media jockeyed for position. Halfway through a beautiful prayer service, with Scripture readings, songs, and pleas for peace, Father Jon Sobrino himself arrived, just off the plane from Bangkok, shaken and pale, grief in his eyes. He stood on the sidelines, watching in disbelief yet slightly consoled by our effort.

I addressed the crowd and explained the scenario for the civil disobedience. A handful of us would engage in a sit-in; I asked that everyone else please continue with a legal support vigil. Six Jesuits would be participating in the sit-in—Harry Geib, Frank McAloon, John Savard, Steve Kelly, Jim Flaherty, and me—plus two women dressed in black, one of them Cindy Pile. The eight of us would stand for the eight martyrs. Father Bill, Davida, and a few others were expected to follow behind.

The crowd sang hymns as the eight of us ascended the steps to the door, where the police waited, and knelt and bowed our heads in prayer. I heard a shuffling behind me and turned to look. More than 120 people had followed and knelt behind us. The police hauled in 150 of us—priests, nuns, theology students, and eighteen Jesuits—to this day the largest number of Jesuits ever arrested in a single protest in the United States. Crowded into cells beneath the Federal Building that day, we sang and told stories, our hopes growing that one day it would be the norm for the church to disrupt the government business of killing.

That was just the beginning. Every day brought some new protest, some new chance to lobby a government official, speak to a reporter, or address an audience. I was tired but forced myself forward.

Then, during Christmas break, I accepted an invitation to retreat for a while at the Trappist monastery where Thomas Merton had lived, about an hour outside of Louisville, Kentucky. Once there, I placed myself in the rhythm of the prayers, the meals, and Mass, and roamed the grounds every day thinking about the deaths of the Jesuits in El Salvador, as well as the United States' invasion of Panama, and entering into prayerful silence. During those ten days, I gained a better understanding of Merton but also perspective, a deeper peace, and a stronger faith to carry on the campaign for El Salvador. When I waved good-bye, I felt ready to take on the next challenge.

And lo and behold, one awaited me. My friend David Hartsough, a longtime peace activist, suggested I undertake a long fast. He wanted Jesuits and Salvadorans to fast for peace in El Salvador. I immediately understood his vision, took a deep breath, and agreed.

回 22 回

The Fast
(1990)

In early January 1990, I began a twenty-one-day fast with Steve Kelly, Bill O'Donnell, a Jesuit friend named John Arthur, and two Salvadoran women, Gloria and Adela. We met every evening at five for a public prayer service at a San Francisco church, where we repented of the sin of war and begged God for an end to military aid to El Salvador. We invited everyone everywhere to join the fast for a day or two.

After three days, my internal plumbing shut down, and pangs of hunger fled. No longer living off the fat of the land, I drew from the fat of the waistline—and for a time felt exhilarated and energized, as if fed solely hot-fudge sundaes. I had no idea I could feel such extraordinary adrenaline, unlimited energy, and good feelings. Not only that, but fasting gave me three extra hours each day to work.

Classes weren't held during January, so I threw myself into activism. It kept my mind off food as the fat dwindled and the pangs returned. My activism resulted in arrests in Los Angeles, San Francisco, and Washington, D.C., and each arrest resulted in the traditional celebratory lunch—the first, in L.A., with Martin Sheen and the singer Jackson Browne. Steaming plates were set before them, while Steve, Bill, and I waved off the waiter—"Nothing for us, thank you"—doing our best to ignore the sumptuous aromas.

Later in the month, in D.C., Martin and I joined a protest at the U.S. Capitol, where we staged a sit-in and landed in central booking. Afterward, the K Street Jesuits hosted a pizza party. I gazed longingly at the best pizza in the nation's capital. Flying back to California, I nearly swooned from the savory smells of the in-flight meal. By the fourteenth day, pizzas swirled in my head as I slept. I was supposed to be fasting, but I lived and breathed pizza. Nonetheless, I stayed on course.

On the fifteenth day of the fast, my strength draining, I allowed myself juice. I also allowed myself more sleep. I required several hours a day to stay calm and rested. It was hard going, but the fast carried me into a deep peace where elemental things came into focus: breezes and birds and sunshine. It was a kind of Zen world, or like the bottom of the ocean, where life moves at quarter time. The weight fell off my frame—thirty pounds altogether—and at every twinge of hunger I called on God afresh and recited my mantra: *Please end all U.S. military aid to El Salvador immediately!* It was about all I could do.

That month, Bill, Davida, Steve, and I had joined the Wednesday Morning Coalition against Military Aid to El Salvador in Los Angeles. Every week, we would gather with a thousand others at a downtown church to prepare for the protest and pray. Several Salvadorans would offer their reflections on the war, and the organizers would outline the action. Then off we went in solemn, almost funereal, procession to the Los Angeles federal building.

At the first protest, in mid-January, several priests, actors, and local politicians spoke, and then Jackson Browne sang his antiwar song "Lives in the Balance." The melancholy chords were our cue to surround the building and sit down. Some 125 of us were hauled off to the L.A. jail and divided by gender into two holding cells. We spent the whole day on the floor, waiting to be booked and released. But the organizers had no intention of spending the day idly. Why not get acquainted and organize future acts? For the next few hours, we all took turns speaking about what had brought us to jail. It was an assembly of amazing people—priests and ministers; a dozen city council members; state representatives; entertainers, such as Martin Sheen, Ed Asner, and Mike Farrell; and Reverend Jim Lawson, the Methodist minister and civil rights leader whom Dr. King had called "the greatest teacher of nonviolence in the world." Jim had organized the Nashville student sit-in movement in 1960 and then moved to Memphis, where he supported the garbage workers' strike. Here in jail, I got to meet him for the first time.

I also got to meet Jackson Browne. I noticed him sitting off by himself and motioned for him to come over. He settled next to me, and I asked what brought him to this group. "This is my church," he answered. "These are the people I want to be with. This is what religion means for me." I thanked him and told him about my work and the plans for a big rally in San Francisco in March to mark the tenth anniversary of Óscar Romero's assassination. Would he join us? He said he'd come, gave me his number, and told me to call with details.

Steve, Bill, John, Gloria, Adela, and I had settled on a twenty-one-day fast based on the example of César Chávez and Gandhi. Now the twenty-one days were drawing to a close. On a Monday morning, after a quietly moving seven o'clock Mass at Bill O'Donnell's Berkeley parish, we broke our fast, sharing a simple breakfast. Then Adela, the Salvadoran mother who had fasted with us, called her family in El Salvador to say she was all right. I helped her place the call in Bill's rectory and heard her speaking through tears. She could hear bombs exploding in the background. Her children cried, "Mommy, we're afraid!"—and she was powerless to console them. She hung up, turned her damp eyes my way, and said, "Please, please, do what you can to end this war." During the fast I had wondered if it would count for anything. Would it inspire people to act? Garner support? Drive the momentum? The questions were all but unanswerable, the answers known to God but beyond my scope. But Adela gave me an answer: Plod on, keep at it until military aid ends.

Momentum against the war in El Salvador was growing. Amid my classes, I worked like a fiend to prepare for the rally. Jackson Browne called and asked if he could bring a few friends. On March 24, he arrived at the event with Kris Kristofferson and Bonnie Raitt, who had recently waltzed off the stage at the Grammys with an armful of awards. Bonnie was overwhelming—blazing red hair, radical politics, and flirtatious spirit, part Emma Goldman and part Mae West. Jackson, Bonnie, and Kris arrived early, ran a sound check on the stage in front of city hall, and then sat with me for a few hours in the mayor's private conference room awaiting their cue. They talked of the Grammys and strummed a few songs, and we brainstormed ways to energize the peace movement. After the Salvadoran women who had fasted with us gave stirring speeches, Jackson, Bonnie, and Kris took the stage and sang brilliantly. The crowd roared its approval.

As their music rose into the air, I remembered a dream from the night before I'd ended the fast. It was one of those once-in-a-lifetime dreams, crackling with energy and more vivid than most of my waking moments. I stood in the foyer of a large church, alone, standing before the closed doors to the sanctuary. I peered through the crack between them and saw billions upon billions of people, all of them happy and glowing, suffusing the sanctuary with an eerie, peaceful light. They were on their feet and singing, all gazing at an altar I couldn't see. For some reason I couldn't enter, so I paced the foyer, my eyes fixed on the tiled floor. Soon someone else entered the foyer—a man with a Spanish accent, black-rimmed glasses, and a crosier in his hand, wearing the colorful robes and tall pointed white hat of a bishop. He approached the sanctuary doors, appearing ready to enter, perhaps even to process up the aisle. But he turned, looked me straight in the eye, and said, "Thank you." Then he disappeared into the sanctuary, the massive doors shutting behind him. When I awoke, I realized that I had just met Archbishop Óscar Romero.

As Bonnie and Jackson sang, I looked out over the scene. Twelve thousand people were spread out before me, all of them on their feet and singing, thrilled and energized, gazing up at the stage, remembering Romero, giving thanks to Romero, reclaiming Romero. That same day, a rally took place in Washington, D.C, and news of both spread through the country. We had turned a corner. Shortly after, Congress cut military aid to El Salvador, and in 1992 a peace accord was signed. The bombing of villages was put to a stop. The Jesuits, the four churchwomen, the countless martyrs, dear Romero—they had not died in vain.

23

Zones of Peace
(1990)

My first year of theology studies came to an end, and I went to the Philippines, traveling under the auspices of Pax Christi, by invitation of heroic bishop Antonio Fortich. The bishop had inquired whether friends might journey to the faraway island of Negros to offer solidarity. There the rural poor suffered death inflicted by left and right—Communist rebels and the Philippine Army. Fortich inspired the people of Negros to declare their villages "Zones of Peace." I tried to imagine what a peace zone in a war zone might look like.

"Our village is open to everyone whose intentions are good," announced the people of Cantomanyog, the first to declare peace zone status. "Whoever enters this zone of peace should not bring any guns with them."

Fortich, like Romero before him, delivered sermons against both the military and the rebels and suffered constant death threats. For three weeks, I toured the remote villages of the island and could scarcely contain my astonishment at the people's steadfast nonviolence in the face of such ruthlessness. I grew to admire them deeply, Bishop Fortich most of all.

Shortly after that trip, I was invited by the Bay Area Salvadoran community to go as their guest to the site where the Jesuits were slain in 1989. When I arrived, I prayed at the Jesuits' tomb, asking that I, too, might be faithful to the gospel of peace and justice. From San Salvador, I traveled north, at 4:00 a.m. one morning, to Chalatenango, in first-class accommodations: under a load of cloth in the bed of a pickup truck to avoid detection at government checkpoints. I found myself a guest at a special Mass to celebrate the renaming of a little northern village in honor of Ellacuría—Ignacio Ellacuría Comunidad. Jon Sobrino delivered a moving homily as FMLN rebel leaders stood about in respectful silence.

The gorgeous countryside shimmered green in the slanted sunlight, but the beauty couldn't efface the scars of brutality and poverty on the people and the land. Blood and bone were in the soil, bereavement and trauma in the air. Still, the Mass felt like a resurrection. At the benediction, it was easy to believe that Ellacuría and the others were alive and well—they had risen in the people. Mass was followed by feasting and dancing, against all reason. It was an astonishing thing to see—dispensable lives celebrating life, the crucified poor confounding death. Resurrection—as Dan Berrigan defined it—is the slight edge of life over death. The people knew that one day they would live in peace.

Upon my arrival home, I received news that my friend Mitch Snyder, advocate for the homeless, was dead. I had spoken to him only a few weeks earlier and knew that he was despondent over a broken relationship. He had told me that he had no hope, that his work seemed futile. Drugs and alcohol had entered the picture as well. But he had begun to devise a path out of the misery; perhaps he would spend time at the Trappist monastery in Virginia. I encouraged him to go, saying that time for prayer would do him good. Instead, he hanged himself in his room by an electrical cord. His suicide devastated many, including Dan and Phil Berrigan and Martin Sheen, who had portrayed him in *Samaritan*, a TV movie of Mitch's life. Beyond being devastated at the loss of this friend, I also became concerned about my own frantic pace. Mitch's death summoned me back to prayer and reflection, especially as another risky trip to El Salvador was planned for November. Indeed, Mitch's death goaded many in the movement to reflect on the mindless activism—the push for results, the neglect of contemplative prayer—that leads to violence.

As mid-November neared, I flew back to El Salvador for the first anniversary of the massacre of the Jesuits. On the sixteenth, thousands of campesinos from around El Salvador and church people from around the world gathered at the university. Obdulio Ramos, husband of Julia Elba and father of Celina—the two murdered women—planted a spectacular rose garden on the murder site. Jon Sobrino preached. He urged us not to focus on the murderers but to recommit ourselves to ending the injustice and U.S. military aid that kills people in El Salvador and elsewhere.

The martyrs' relatives brought forth glass bowls of blood-soaked soil from where the bodies had lain and set them before the altar, and someone produced a bloodstained copy of Jürgen Moltmann's book *The Crucified God*. As the soldiers had dragged Father Moreno's body inside, the book had toppled from a bookcase and landed on his chest. At the anniversary gathering, the bloody book was held aloft, a gripping symbol of the abiding crucifixion of God in the people of Latin America and in the martyrs who dared insist on justice and peace.

The next morning, some forty North Americans joined seventy-five campesinos in a caravan into the countryside. These campesinos were determined to repopulate the village they had fled seven years before to escape U.S. bombing raids. In the town of San Vicente, not far from the village, Salvadoran soldiers awaited us, wielding U.S. weapons. They ordered us out of the trucks and quickly surrounded us, then seized a truck hauling materials and arrested the driver. We were being detained, the commander told us. The risks we had feared were now being realized: the North Americans would face rough handling, deprivation, and, in the end, deportation. The campesinos faced far graver punishment.

Within an hour or so, about forty of us were led to the police station and the soldiers' barracks, and there kept vigil through song and prayer. Dozens of armed soldiers hovered, watching our every move. As we prayed, we noticed several U.S. military advisers entering and leaving the barracks, so we started to pray out loud for them, that they "be converted from war to the peace of Christ." One overheard and came storming out. "I've been serving my country for twenty-one years," he thundered. "Went to Catholic schools for sixteen years. Pray on my knees every day, go to church on Sundays. My work for the Salvadoran army is my patriotic duty."

"How can you support these human rights violations?" we asked.

"Name one!" he shouted back. "Name a day when there was even one!"

Our voices rose in unison: "November 16, 1989!" He rolled his eyes and stomped back inside.

Everything seemed to hinge on the soldiers' whims. One of them tried to seize a campesino in our company, and a woman from our delegation threw her arms around him and held him close. The rest of us gathered around them, forming a protective shield. The soldier backed off.

Four hours passed with no word. Finally, an officer emerged and asked which campesino would be willing to take "full responsibility" for the attempt to reoccupy the village.

A young Salvadoran mother stepped forward. "I'll take full responsibility," she said. She signed her name while the rest of us watched in awe. She bore the very spirit of Romero, exemplified the best of the four churchwomen, the Jesuit martyrs, and all the martyrs of Central America. By signing her name, she risked her life for the villagers, and her courage led to our release. We got back into the trucks and headed off into the jungle.

I found myself next to the young man the soldier had tried to seize. "What's your name?" I asked.

"Jesus," he said.

That night, sitting in the formerly abandoned village during the prayer service and celebration, I gave thanks for the gift of meeting Jesus in El Salvador. I counted it an honor to serve him in his time of need.

24

Death Row and
Mother Teresa
(1990)

The summer of 1990 threw me into the tragic world of death row—or, more specifically, into the tragic world of Robert Harris and Billy Neal Moore.

I had always been against the death penalty—Jesus himself was a victim of it. Execution clearly violated every principle of the gospel, in no way squaring with Jesus' commandment to forgive without keeping score. It conveniently ignored his challenge to let the one who is without sin be the first to throw a stone.

I had first heard about Billy in 1984. The Catholic Worker folks who had taken up his cause told me extraordinary things about him. After being sentenced to death row for a robbery gone terribly awry, he underwent a religious conversion and resolved to devote himself to the care of others. Upon hearing his story, I followed in the footsteps of his Catholic Worker supporters, penning him letters of support every month and, in 1989, traveling to Jackson, Georgia, to visit him. He was being held at the Georgia Diagnostic and Classification Center, a shabby, unconvincing euphemism for death row. I spent several hours sitting quietly with Billy, listening to his story and sharing my own. His calm demeanor impressed me.

Billy's troubles had begun in 1974. He and a friend had drunk themselves reckless and decided to rob an old man, who happened to be the uncle of Billy's friend. The friend backed out of the plan at the last minute, but Billy went ahead. He entered the house, and the old man fired his shotgun; he missed, and Billy fired back. "The minute the man died, part of me did, too," Billy said. He didn't run. When the man's family showed up, Billy broke down sobbing and begged for forgiveness.

He was sentenced to death later that year, and by the summer of 1990 he had been on death row for years. The specter of execution drew close on more than one occasion. Billy told me that he'd attempted the robbery because he needed twenty bucks. Since his admission to death row, he said, the government had spent over a million dollars in pursuit of his death. He proposed that if he'd been able to get financial aid when he was younger, to get an education and a job, he wouldn't have stumbled into such dire straits. Everyone would have been spared the pain and trouble, not to mention the expense.

Not long after beginning his sentence, he was baptized in a prison bathtub and felt God's love for the first time. He became a devout Christian and spent his days in prayer and his efforts on behalf of other death-row inmates. He wrote epistles of peace to hundreds of people around the country.

"Your letter was appreciated and I do thank you, but know that the Lord Jesus Christ is in full control of my life," Billy had written in response to my first letter to him, in 1984. In what way, he asked, could he be of help to me? I had imagined myself at his service, but he turned the tables with a stroke of the pen. As the body of our correspondence grew, the nature of the man emerged. He wore the vow of nonviolence like a stole and bore the finality of his days with the detachment of Buddha. When I met him finally, I felt that I was in the presence of the converted Paul, once a pursuer and killer but now a bearer of the grace and wisdom of gospel nonviolence. Billy, like the Salvadorans I knew, confounded death. The peace and grace he radiated were off-kilter with his plight.

One Thursday morning back in California, I received an urgent call. The following Wednesday, Billy was scheduled to die. Friends urged me to fly to Georgia and organize protests and vigils, but I was broke as a Jesuit. How would I get there? That very morning, I found in the mail, for the first and only time, a coupon for a frequent-flier free round-trip ticket. I brought this bit of providence to George Murphy's attention, secured his permission, and that afternoon took off for Atlanta, ready to do what I could. I finagled a visit with Billy on Tuesday, the day before he was to die. When they threw the switch, he asked, would I please be there? I said I would.

But a last recourse remained. State law provided that the Board of Pardons and Paroles could hear pleas and consider clemency within twenty-four hours of an execution. Everyone knew the chances were minuscule—the board hadn't commuted a death sentence in many years, and Billy had pleaded guilty. But we had nothing else to work with. The hearing was scheduled for that Tuesday afternoon, so a group of us set about organizing press conferences, prayer vigils, and a lobbying campaign. On Friday night, we held a prayer vigil in Atlanta, begging God for a miracle of clemency. Then we were off to Macon, where we led a service Saturday night at St. Peter Claver Church. On Tuesday, an hour before the hearing was to commence, the Supreme Court issued a thirty-day stay of execution.

My work to help secure clemency for Billy wasn't my first assault against capital punishment. That had been at Berkeley, not long after the Óscar Romero rally in San Francisco. Shortly before the rally, I had read that George Deukmejian, governor of California, was preparing to execute Robert Harris in nearby San Quentin. Harris had murdered two teenage boys in San Diego in 1978. I condemned his brutality, but condemning him to death solved nothing and carried no didactic value whatsoever.

I felt energized to do something and knew I had one advantage: Mother Teresa's phone number. I had gotten it from Monsignor John Esseff in Scranton. I'd commented to him, upon hearing of an upcoming execution there, that the only person who could prevent it was someone like Mother Teresa. I didn't know that the monsignor directed her private retreats. "Would you like her private number?" he asked.

It turned out I didn't need it then, as that execution was stayed, but I kept her number. Perhaps now was the time to put it to use. She had never intervened on behalf of someone on death row; what if she refused? Should I bother her? But what did I have to lose? I dialed the number and heard that famous Albanian-Indian-English accent on the other end: "Hello?"

"Hello, Mother," I said. "I'm John Dear, a Jesuit scholastic calling from California, in the United States. I would like to ask if you would be willing to speak to the governor of California on behalf of a prisoner named Robert Harris who is about to be executed near San Francisco. Would you ask the governor not to execute the man?"

"What did he do?" she asked.

"He brutally murdered two young boys, and while we pray for the victims' families, we don't want the killing to continue. I would like to arrange for the governor's office to call you so you can speak to him, and then I'll call you back, and you can give me a statement that I can release to the press. Would you be willing to do that?"

"Of course I would," she said. "And I will ask all the sisters here to pray nonstop for the governor and for Robert Harris and the victims' families, and the people of California. Please try to get the whole United States to pray that this execution will not happen. God bless you."

I thanked her and called the governor, who agreed to speak with Mother Teresa. The call happened around six on a Monday evening. I waited awhile and then called Calcutta and asked her anxiously, "What did you say?" I imagined her sternly reprimanding the poor governor, heaping upon his soul chapter and verse. I could all but hear her calling California to repent.

"I said to him, 'Do what Jesus would do.'"

What? A confused moment passed. "Didn't you say anything else?"

"No, I just twice told him, 'Do what Jesus would do if he were in your position.'" She didn't yell, castigate, or guilt-trip. Instead, she appealed to the governor's conscience, pointed him toward Jesus, and left it at that. Surprised and bemused, I thanked her. She asked that I call back with news.

I stepped outside the Jesuit house. Twenty reporters milled around the stoop, waiting. Local stations would deliver my statement live; CNN would broadcast a lengthy report. The reporters rushed forward and thrust a nosegay of microphones at my chin. "What did she say?" they shouted over one another. "She said, 'Do what Jesus would do.'" And in case it needed clarification, I explained: Jesus wouldn't execute anyone; he would grant mercy to everyone and abolish the death penalty. He calls us to practice compassion and nonviolence. "Jesus," I said, "was clear in his opposition to injustice. He gave his life to stop the killing, was willing to die as a victim of the death penalty without a trace of retaliation." By now I had picked up steam. "If the governor executes Robert Harris," I said, "he will be siding with Pontius Pilate and all the executioners of history. He will crucify Christ all over again."

The story made the news across the country, most prominently in the *Los Angeles Times*. Paul Conrad, the political cartoonist, ran a scathing cartoon. It featured Mother Teresa in the upper left-hand corner, a phone in her hand, saying, "Do what Jesus would do." The governor held a phone on the bottom right of the panel, the bubble over his head reading, "But what would Pilate do?" Conrad later sent me the original.

Word was that Governor Deukmejian was furious, but we never got a chance to find out what his decree would have been. A San Francisco judge preempted him two days later and stayed the execution. I called Mother Teresa to tell her the news. "Thank God," she said.

But a year later, Pete Wilson won the governorship on a campaign to "get tough on crime," meaning "put more prisoners to death." Almost immediately, the state rescheduled Harris for execution. I imposed on Mother Teresa again, and she agreed to speak with Governor Wilson. He received her call politely but parroted the party line: "The law is the law, and I have to uphold the law." Days later, I called her back to say the execution would go on, and she asked me to get a message to Harris before he died: "Tell him to make peace with God." And: "Thank you, John, and everyone, for all you have done for those on death row. You must be discouraged, but don't be. Remember, God sees only love."

I asked San Quentin prison officials if I could visit Robert Harris, but the warden issued a perfunctory no. My only recourse was to write Harris a letter. I received his response the day he died—he thanked me for trying to save his life. The night of his execution, some five hundred people gathered outside the infamous San Quentin prison, overlooking the beautiful bay, as the moon lit up the water— a night for friendship and romance, not vengeance and death. Bill O'Donnell and I had put our heads together to devise some gesture of civil disobedience, but no befitting action came to mind. So we held aloft candles and prayed—for Robert Harris, for the abolition of the death penalty, and for a new culture of nonviolence.

"I know how disappointed you must have felt," Mother Teresa wrote me after Harris's execution. "But God sees only the love you have put into your efforts to save the life of one who was condemned to die. He has already blessed your efforts, and I am sure for all the concern you have shown and the love you have shared, Harris must have died a different man. Let us pray."

And now, here I was in Georgia, keeping vigil and praying for a miracle from the Board of Pardons and Paroles as it delibrated the fate of Billy Neal Moore.

At the hearing that Tuesday afternoon, Billy's family testified, followed by local clergy and, finally, the victim's family. The members of the board—five stodgy white men—sat impassively, careful not to betray their leanings. Several board members had spoken with Mother Teresa, Jesse Jackson had issued a statement, and hundreds of others had written or called. Toward the end of the hearing, Sarah Farmer, a niece of Billy's victim, gave her testimony, speaking on behalf of the family. She spoke of Billy's tears sixteen years earlier when he realized what he had done, and she described the relationship she had since formed with him. She concluded, tears brimming in her eyes: "This is our brother Billy, and you can't kill him. We've lost one family member and we're not going to lose another. We don't want you to execute him."

Thirty minutes later, the board returned with a historic, unanimous verdict of clemency. For the first time in years, a death sentence was commuted. A few years later, Billy was quietly released. Today, he serves as a prison chaplain and remains a good friend.

Mother Teresa rejoiced at the news. "I am so glad to hear how God has heard and answered our prayers for Billy," she wrote. "It is so wonderful to know he has been granted pardon and will be out of jail."

The only contrary sentiment in the whole episode came from Billy himself. Shortly before the start of the prayer vigil in Macon the Saturday night before Billy's hearing, I received a surprising letter from him. He thanked those of us who had come to his aid but took us to task. He had learned a thing or two about clemency, having received it from his victim's family. Clemency was for him a secondary issue. "Thank you for all you are doing for me," he wrote. But how can God take your prayer seriously, he asked, when none of you grant clemency to those who have hurt you? If you want to do something for me, he said, forgive those who have offended you. Your prayers for me will have no authenticity until you offer clemency yourselves. So do not bother God until you are serious about practicing clemency in your own lives. As for him? He planned a prayer service of his own—for a peaceful solution to the crisis in Iraq.

His letter pierced us, and the weight of conviction settled into our bones. Immediately we devised an entirely new prayer service. I read Billy's letter to the congregation, along with a passage from the Gospels. After some silence, I invited everyone to recall those who had hurt them, to forgive them and grant them clemency. Then we raised chastened hands to the altar and said, "Dear God, we grant clemency to everyone who ever hurt us. Now please grant us the miracle of clemency for our brother Billy. Abolish the death penalty and grant clemency everywhere."

I've never overcome my astonishment over Billy's letter, or forgotten its lesson. My clemency skills had grown rusty. I took Billy's words to heart: If we want to receive clemency, we had better practice it. So I began to practice it—me, an apprentice, emulating Billy, the master.

As for Mother Teresa, she wrote me regularly with words to see me through:

It is a great grace for you to be chosen to be a priest of God. You are like the door key to open the hearts of people to Jesus. It is such a great privilege and also a great responsibility, as you know. There will be times in your life when you will feel lonely, helpless, and hopeless. But remember always that he wants you to be his priest. At those times, cling to our Blessed Mother. She will help you to be the presence and love of Jesus in the lives of the poor and prisoners you work for. I pray for you that you grow in holiness through prayer that comes from a humble heart, for a humble heart is a pure heart. A pure heart can see the face of God in the distressing disguise of the poor and love and serve God in them with great love. My prayer is with you that you will become a holy priest of God, his presence, his living love, and his mercy to all entrusted to you.

回 25 回

War in Iraq,
Resistance in the Streets
(1991–92)

January 15, 1991, Martin Luther King Jr.'s birthday, was the date
the United States had set for commencing war on Iraq if it did
not withdraw from Kuwait. Thousands took to the streets of San
Francisco. Some blocked the Bay Bridge and others the federal building. The next day, bombs tumbled relentlessly from the Iraqi sky, and
the President George H. W. Bush appeared on TV glowing like a
groom. A day after that, we took to the streets again and circled the
federal building.

Hundreds of police, dressed head to toe in protective gear, heaved
toward us. It crossed my mind that we might be in for beatings or tear
gas. To the contrary. For me things proceeded in a nearly agreeable
manner. One cop seemed drawn to my clerical outfit and ran up to the
sergeant in charge and pointed my way. The sergeant nodded, and the
cop threaded his way through the crowd toward me. "Who are you?"
he asked. A Jesuit at the theology school in Berkeley, I told him.

"Really?" He grinned. "I graduated from Bellarmine Jesuit high
school! This is a great moment for me—I get to arrest a Jesuit!" Off I

210

went in the clutches of a product of Jesuit education—just doing his job and now with a story to tell over dinner that night. The police arrested 1,087 of us, the largest mass arrest in San Francisco history.

The time in jail was awful, but our collective spirit was high. We gained satisfaction in knowing that we had done what we could. We sang songs, told stories, strategized, and prayed for the suffering people of Iraq and the U.S. soldiers, pawns of the Pentagon. We knew that the war would plod on.

But so would we. I felt permanently nauseated by the slaughter of Iraqis but grateful for friends who joined me in resisting war. For the next six weeks, I spent every day in the streets, in jail, or in a church—most days in all three. It was almost routine—mornings spent marching, afternoons in jail, and evenings talking to local congregations. I kept my talks simple, expounding on Jesus' commandment: Love your enemies; don't bomb them.

Friends and I had decided that as soon as the bombs began to fall, we would gather at Bill O'Donnell's rectory and plan a response. Our deliberations produced the Interfaith Coalition Against the War, a sprightly group that organized weekly protests, recruited religious leaders to lead interfaith prayer services, and trudged through the dark days lending one another support.

Our maiden event was a funeral procession through the San Francisco streets. I had pulled it together with my friend the long-time activist Ken Butigan. In 1984, Ken had organized the Pledge of Resistance against the contra war. Tens of thousands pledged that if Reagan's war did not end soon, they would stage a sit-in at congressional offices across the country. Eventually we did, and the campaign may have prevented Reagan from undertaking a full-scale invasion. Now some three hundred people—Christians, Jews, and Muslims—gathered in procession to mourn the Iraqi and American dead. We walked silently, carrying coffins covered with Iraqi and American flags to the Presidio, the army post near the Golden Gate Bridge. We knelt in prayer every fifteen minutes to stay centered, to remain nonviolent, and to beg for peace. When we arrived at the Presidio gate, a wall of marines awaited us, their batons at the ready. We surged toward them and knelt down. An interfaith prayer service got under way.

Meanwhile, about fifty of us stole away along an old stone wall and clambered over it onto the base, where we knelt in "illegal" prayer. In due time, the marines found us out and hauled us away along to our sweet strains of "We Shall Overcome."

We spent the day in jail, and later that night we watched as Pentagon generals announced with considerable pride on the evening news that during the previous forty-eight hours, the United States had dropped eighteen thousand tons of bombs on Iraq, the largest bombing campaign since World War II.

All told, the United States would drop more than eighty thousand tons during the six weeks of slaughter. The destructive force each week was the same as that of an atomic bomb. Our nation's leaders crowed and exulted. The Pentagon had cast its spell. It was an ancient story all too sinister: the manufacture of patriotic insanity, the periodic inciting of violent frenzies, and the bountiful harvest—this time, their oil in our hands.

Where was the church throughout this festival of death? At that time, the U.S. Catholic bishops were hotly debating, nearly ten years late, the arrival of AIDS—and what the Catholic Church must do about it. They were adamant about not condoning the free distribution of condoms to those in need to stop the epidemic. One friend noted that if the United States had dropped eighty thousand tons of condoms on Iraq, the bishops would have denounced it and done civil disobedience at the White House. Evidently, bombs did not hold the same priority.

On Saturday, January 26, a massive demonstration took place, with more than two hundred thousand people marching through the streets of San Francisco. The day began with multifaith prayers for peace and ended with a rally in front of city hall. In the afternoon, Mickey Hart of the Grateful Dead took the stage and pounded out an explosive percussion performance. As I stood alone behind the stage, who should appear but Joan Baez. She began to dance and beckoned me to join her.

Here was a world-renowned folksinger, a champion of nonviolence, a hero of the peace movement—she had marched in Selma with Dr. King, read poetry with Thomas Merton in his hermitage, sung for Dorothy Day in prison, and introduced the world to Bob Dylan—and she had deigned to dance with me, a dopey scholastic. That was the beginning of our friendship; over the years, Joan has helped me with several peace projects. She welcomes me to her concerts, and afterward we talk about life, peace, spirituality, and nonviolence. One day, I received a package from her in the mail, a picture that she had drawn of me speaking out for peace.

Hart concluded his drum solo, Joan and I ended our dance, and she bounded on stage and closed the rally with her rendition of "Amazing Grace" and by inviting everyone to embrace the lessons of nonviolence from Gandhi and Dr. King. In a few weeks, we would confront one of the obscenest episodes of the war, the Ash Wednesday bombing of civilians, mostly women and children, at the Ameriyah shelter in Baghdad, and we would somehow have to cope with it. But in the meantime, Joan's joyful gesture, her soaring voice, and her parting advice lifted my spirits. During the dark weeks ahead, I would return to that moment over and over and feel consoled.

On Ash Wednesday, February 13, a hundred people gathered in a circle outside the San Francisco Federal Building, this time to appear in court for our demonstration at the Presidio. Before we entered, we prayed for peace, read from Jonah, and repented of the sin of war. As we concluded, dozens of police materialized and made quick with the handcuffs. I ran over to the officer in charge. "You can't arrest us," I told him. "You haven't given us a warning. This is illegal!"

He realized his mistake and had the cuffs removed, then announced through a bullhorn, "You're all under arrest." But by then it was too late: we had scrambled into the building. Emerging some hours later, we heard the horrible news: the United States had bombed the shelter in the suburbs of Baghdad. The media had obscured the facts about Iraqi deaths, but news of the attack had leaked out. More than seven hundred people had died, mostly women and children. All that remained of them was a pile of ashes. We were struck numb with grief. We wept, unable to comprehend the horror, formed a circle, and held another prayer service—this time to mourn the innocent dead.

Day upon day, grief upon grief. When the ground war began in late February, the United States Army mowed down Iraqi troops, burying tens of thousands alive on the road to Basra. At this point, some Bay Area antiwar protesters turned violent. Cars were burned and police threatened. People tore through the streets screaming in anger. The interfaith coalition had to do something. We decided to attend the more raucous protests, stand amid the melee, and sing hymns of peace. We hoped that our songs and prayers and steady nonviolence might disarm the crowd and soothe some of the more hot-tempered protesters. Things did settle down, and the rioters sheepishly moved on. People on all sides thanked us, including the police.

Finally, with great fanfare, Bush declared Kuwait "liberated" and the papers declared victory. I didn't believe the "liberated" part; still,

I cried at the news—cried in mourning and in relief. I cried in gratitude that it had ended. I cried out of emotional exhaustion.

After months of hard work, I found sustenance where I could. I had
founded fifteen Pax Christi groups around the Bay Area, as a network of Latin American-type base communities, and I began attending the one in nearby Oakland, where I forged lasting friendships.
A key member was the young photojournalist Mev Puleo, who had
recently moved to Oakland with her husband, Mark Chmiel. Mev
was deeply involved in solidarity movements from Haiti to Brazil,
and her pictures of third-world poverty regularly appeared in journals
and newspapers.

Mev and Mark practiced mindfulness according to the teachings
of Thich Nhat Hanh, the Zen Buddhist master, and they urged everyone in the group to take it up. A group of us met every week to ponder
nonviolence and mindfulness and then practice it by easing ourselves
into silence and lingering over the rhythms of our breathing. After the
tumult of war, this peaceful practice helped us heal.

War's tumult, as one would expect, had battered people all
over the peace movement. Most felt shell-shocked and burned out.
Everyone wondered where to find healing, and many found it in the
desert. A thousand people gathered in Las Vegas that March 1991 for
prayer and reflection and to support the Nevada Desert Experience's
relentless witness against nuclear weapons testing. Those in my circle
included Bill O'Donnell, Davida Coady, Martin Sheen, and Daniel
Berrigan.

On opening night, the throng filled a sanctuary, sang hymns,
and silently prayed. Then we were invited to turn to those nearest us

and discuss the question, where do we go from here? I sat in the back corner with Daniel Berrigan and Jim Wallis of Sojourners, and both of them turned to me. I took up the challenge with a good amount of gusto. "Here's where we go from here," I began. "First, we have to mobilize the nation against war-making. We need to build a strong movement, one that will lead thousands against the Washington establishment, even to jail if necessary—and there demand an end to our nuclear arsenal and to this culture of war." A grand discourse was in the making, one peppered with shiny references to a new culture of peace. But the more I talked, the more their eyes glazed over. After a long pause, Dan stepped in with a smile. "I just think we need to unleash the contemplative springs within."

This was typical of my friend and teacher—an apt word at an apt moment. I pondered Dan's wisdom for months and years. I took it to mean something along these lines: Let justice and peace happen. Don't get entangled in concerns for results or success. Do good and seek the truth because they are good and truthful, and let them bear fruit in their own time. Focus rather on the Source of peace, who offers peace as a gift. We are not in charge; God is.

My faux pas aside, the time with this ragtag band of peacemakers was heartening. We came looking for a word of hope and found it—in one another, in our prayers, in Dan's presentations on Isaiah, and in the vastness of the wilderness. On the last day, we drove deep into the desert, to the Nevada Test Site. There, a thousand peacemakers formed a circle under clear skies, a caressing breeze in the air, the featureless desert all around, misty mountains looming in the distance.

We began the Eucharist service with the reciting of Scripture. Then a frail old man, short and rotund in a brown cassock, stepped forward to preach, his black beret at a jaunty pitch and his English creaking under a heavy Portuguese accent. He bore a vague resemblance to Yoda from the movie *Star Wars*.

The man was Dom Hélder Câmara, the legendary archbishop of Olinda and Recife, Brazil; father of liberation theology; poet and thinker; author of several books, including *The Desert Is Fertile, Spiral of Violence, Hoping against All Hope,* and *A Thousand Reasons for Living*; and nominee, a number of times, for the Nobel Peace Prize and, on several occasions, for pope.

Born in Fortaleza, Brazil, on February 7, 1909, and named archbishop in 1964, he learned nonviolence from the International Fellowship of Reconciliation ambassador Hildegarde Goss-Mayr and helped form Brazil's grassroots base community movement, which today comprises more than a hundred thousand communities. As the primary organizer of the 1968 Latin American bishops' conference in Medellín, Colombia, he was one of the first in the Latin American church to promote the notion of "the preferential option for the poor."

For twenty years, he campaigned tirelessly against Brazil's military dictatorship, often under death threats, now and then surviving attempts on his life. The regime banned him from public speaking for thirteen years, and newspapers suffered sanctions if they dared print his name. In 1984, the Vatican forced him to retire. But until his death in 1999, he remained an apostle of Gospel nonviolence.

"When I feed the poor, they call me a saint," he said famously. "But when I ask why there are poor, they call me a Communist."

"My dear brothers and sisters," he preached as we strained to hear, "let us make every possible effort to help love grow among humanity. . . . Let us be an example to create strong families of love that help each other, so that we can love one another. Let us live without war and be peacemakers, the true children of God, that we may never have opulent riches or degrading misery. Let us all be sisters and brothers, children of the same loving God, sisters and brothers of Jesus our brother."

Then he laid aside his page of notes, took off his glasses, raised both arms to heaven, and called out: "My brothers and sisters, please, no more war! No more war!" He lifted his face to the sky and cried: "Dear God, we want peace. We really want peace." Then he raised his right hand and waved—to the sky, to God! He had unabashedly given voice to our deepest yearnings. Then he turned away quietly, his head down, crying. The crowd gasped. His actions illustrated our roller coaster of emotions.

There was nothing left to do after that but cross the line onto the nuclear weapons testing ground. The police met us on the other side, arrested seventy-five of us, and led us to an outdoor pen made of chain-link fence, a corral that has held thousands of demonstrators over the years.

A few days later, back in Berkeley, Dom Hélder spoke at a crowded church. He offered a brief reflection and then fielded questions. A student rose and said: "Dom Hélder, you've survived an assassination attempt, faced soldiers at your door, endured death threats, been ridiculed throughout South America, and been ostracized by the hierarchical church. From all your experiences, what would you say has been your greatest obstacle to peace?"

Dom Hélder let a long silence pass, then pointed his finger toward the sky. With all the showmanship of a circus ringmaster, he slowly turned his finger downward, back toward his heart. "I am my own greatest obstacle to peace!" he replied. A reverent hush fell over the crowd.

回 回

That year was a time for mourning not only the loss of innocent lives through war, but also the loss of loved ones. Within six weeks, in early 1992, both of my beloved grandmothers died. Besta, my father's mother, died suddenly on March 1. My parents and aunt and uncle were with me in Berkeley to celebrate my ordination to the diaconate. My brother called with the news. Besta had been involved with the family newspaper business all her life, and had traveled the world and lived into her nineties. We flew home the next day and took part in a joyous service at her Georgetown Presbyterian Church. I offered a eulogy: "When I was a teenager, she took me aside, looked me in the eye, and said, 'I believe in you!'" I spoke of her love of life, her enduring hope, and her interest in everyone.

A few weeks later, my mother called to say that Grandma, her mother, had taken a turn for the worse. Grandma had spent most of her life in Brooklyn until moving to Bethesda to be near our family. I had just visited her after Besta's funeral. In Oakland, I bought a stack of beautiful cards and mailed her one each day, offering my encouragement, prayers, and love. At the news of her downturn, I returned home and sat with her overnight. Early the next morning, she simply stopped breathing. My friends George Anderson and Richard McSorley presided at her funeral Mass. We know that because of the risen Jesus, death doesn't get the last word. Grandma was so sweet and good that she must have been ushered right into heaven.

Still, a few things about my grandmothers' deaths left me unsettled. Their attitudes had shifted with the passing years. Grandma had always oozed lightness of spirit, had evoked such laughter that I could barely get down her famous grilled cheese sandwiches topped with everything in the fridge. But during her later years, she rarely set foot across her threshold. She grew testy and angry and carped at my parents over the most trivial slights. Though she had lived a life of faith, the terror of death seemed to grip her, and she fought back like a caged animal. We tried our best to help her, but we felt helpless.

Besta, on the other hand, focused on her work and notorious for her bigotry, had softened over the years. Her light and joy advanced with age. She even gave away her possessions, throwing caution to the wind. Near giddiness came over her. On my arm one afternoon as we headed into a Georgetown restaurant, she threw open her hands and announced, "I love you all!" The other patrons in the stuffy place tried to smile despite themselves. And when she died, the occasion was peaceful, even joyful.

I loved them both, but the contrast made me ponder. How would I face *my* death? Does it have anything to do with how I live today? Can I reach the selfless love, the downright Easter joy that Besta manifested daily? Can I trust resurrection by practicing it here and now?

Answers would begin to emerge, in part because Daniel and Philip Berrigan paid me a visit. Dan came to lead a weekend Bay Area Pax Christi retreat. He spoke on the nonviolent resistance embodied in Revelation and of "the slight edge of life over death"—an image that struck me as true to experience. More than four hundred people crowded the UC Berkeley Newman Center for his talks that spring weekend. In the days that followed, I was able to spend more time with him, talking and relaxing by the sea.

Phil joined me that year on Good Friday for the annual march to the Lawrence Livermore National Laboratory, where technicians assemble nuclear weapons. He took the podium and gave a stirring lecture to one thousand of us before joining in our trespass and arrest. The next day, he participated in our vigil at San Quentin for the abolition of the death penalty, and on Easter morning we arranged a sunrise service at the Concord Naval Weapons Station, where we celebrated

Christ's resurrection over the culture of death. Dan's words—"the slight edge of life over death"—crossed my mind, making me shiver and rejoice at once.

That night, I pressed Phil about the Plowshares movement. How do you prepare for the possibility of being shot? How do you survive a long stint in prison? How might destroying government property, albeit a nuclear weapon, be construed as nonviolence? How could I undertake such an action and cope with rejection by family, friends, and Jesuits? He listened patiently, gave measured answers, and issued a challenge. Put aside your anxieties, he said. Trust in the God of peace. Take the next step in faith and in discipleship to the nonviolent Jesus on the way of the cross. Let's try to fulfill the prophet Isaiah's vision of swords hammered into plowshares and leave the rest to the God of peace.

Phil's visit, coming on the heels of Dan's, would change my life.

26

Ordained to Make Peace (1992–93)

Upon completing my master of divinity degree, I headed to Guatemala. There I toured the country and studied Spanish. I toyed with the idea of relocating to Central America, perhaps finishing my fourth year of Jesuit studies at the University of Central America in San Salvador. It had occurred to me once or twice to just abandon the rich world for the poor and be of service there. But the words of UCA's Jesuit martyrs haunted me. They had said heatedly that I was needed more in the U.S. My place and heritage well suited me for confronting U.S. imperialism, the bane of the world's poor. I credited their words and trusted their insight. And I hesitated to transplant myself on a pricklier point: I didn't wish to further the colonial legacy of the white priest descending on the poor world, an eminent benefactor doling out from his trove of answers. I briefly considered taking a job at Pax Christi USA, but mostly my thoughts revolved around Dan and Phil Berrigan. Their actions inspired me, their humanity drew me, and their biblical witness challenged me.

People's Campaign for Nonviolence to protest U.S. sanctions on Iraq: Bishop Thomas Gumbleton and Rev. Jim Lawson—Washington, D.C. July 3, 2000.

Photo courtesy of Jay Solmonson

Top: About to be arrested with five Jesuits and two women friends, a few days after the massacre of six Salvadoran Jesuits and two women. Another hundred church people knelt behind us and were also arrested—Federal Building, San Francisco, November 20, 1989. I am fifth from right.

Bottom: Under arrest at the gates of Livermore Lab—Livermore, Ca., 1993.

Top: Sitting in sackcloth and ashes with Kathy Kelly at Los Alamos, N. Mex, Hiroshima day, August 6, 2006.

Bottom: Marching with Daniel Berrigan, before our arrest at the USS *Intrepid*—New York City, Good Friday, 2001.

Top: Visiting with a dying child and her mother—Baghdad, Iraq, March, 1999.

Bottom: With the displaced peoples in the jungle of El Salvador—summer, 1985.

Top: At the altar, one of my first Masses, St. Al's church—Washington, D.C., summer, 1993.

Bottom: The Chapel of the Beatitudes, at the Sea of Galilee, Israel, on the day I saw the jets—July, 1982.

Top: Standing outside the School of the Americas: Dr. Davida Coady, Pete Seeger, Martin Sheen, Daniel Berrigan, me—Fort Benning, Ga., November 21, 1999. Bottom r.: Richard Deats and I visit with Buddist leader Thich Nhat Hanh—Vermont, summer, 1998. Bottom l.: Discussing negotiations leading up to the Good Friday peace agreement: Gerry Adams, Martin Sheen, me, Janet Sheen—December, 1997.

Top: A visitor smuggles a camera into the
prison visiting room: me, Bruce Friedrich,
Philip Berrigan—Edenton County Jail,
Edenton, N.C., June, 1994. Right: With
Dom Hélder Câmara and Friends—
August, 1992. Bottom: Kneeling in prayer
before our arrest at Livermore Lab, with
Philip Berrigan on the left—Good Friday,
Livermore, Ca., 1992.

With Fr. Bill O'Donnell at the School of the Americas, just before his arrest and imprisionment and one year before his death—Fort Benning, Ga., November 2002.

Perhaps I should engage in a Plowshares action. Perhaps it was time I took the risk.

With all of this swirling in my mind, I arrived in Antigua, moved in with a family, and spent seven hours a day studying Spanish with a tutor. Alas, I quickly learned that my Irish gift of gab failed to translate to another tongue. After weeks of study, it became apparent that the language and I had come to an impasse. Finally there came a reprieve. My friends arrived from the north—Martin Sheen, Bill O'Donnell, Davida Coady, and human rights lawyer Joe Cosgrove. For two weeks we toured the countryside, learning of the repressive regimes that would kill two hundred thousand Guatemalans, and visiting the rectory in Santiago Atitlán of Oklahoman Father Stanley Rother, who had been murdered there for opposing the death squads. In 1990, some fifteen indigenous people had been massacred in the plaza by those same death squads.

After trudging through the squalor of the massive garbage dump on the outskirts of the capital where tens of thousands of children and their families live, we left for El Salvador to pray at the university where the Jesuits had died, and from there traveled to villages and cooperatives throughout the country.

Heading for remote regions, Martin and I spent the better part of one day jouncing our kidneys silly in the back of a pickup truck. We had endured our fill of tales of death squads and murder. And each looked to the other to lift his spirits. We talked about Jesus' nonviolence and then drifted on to the movie *Gandhi* and Martin's experience in the making of the film. I pressed him for details, and he was happy to regale me. Then a twinkle came into his eyes. "Do you know why Gandhi was so popular in Hollywood?" "No," I said. "Because he's everything Hollywood aspires to be—thin, tan, and moral."

On my way back to the Jesuit house in Oakland, I spent a few warm New York evenings with Daniel Berrigan. My ordination was still a year off, but my mind churned with questions. Once orders are conferred and the blessing is bestowed, what then? What does it mean to be a priest and a Jesuit? Was there an essence, a core, to life as a Jesuit? I longed to get to the heart of the matter. Dan pondered my questions and offered reflective responses. He said that the essence would unfold if I became a priest in the vein of the Jesuit martyrs. Standing in defense of the suffering and continuing to work for justice and peace was the best we could offer, and still a great need in our poor world. I gave the matter some thought and took Dan at his word.

Dan and I parted ways one morning after coffee. My next stop was St. Patrick's Cathedral, to attend a special Mass with Mother Teresa, who spoke to a packed church on Matthew 25 ("Whatever you do to the least of these, you do to me"). I enjoyed a brief chat with her afterward and then drove to the Newark airport to pick up Dom Hélder Câmara, arriving all the way from Brazil to attend the Pax Christi convention at Seton Hall University. I helped him get settled and rushed over to Seton Hall for the keynote address by César Chávez. Afterward, I interviewed him for the Pax Christi journal.

It was, by any measure, a day among saints, and one of the most blessed days of my life. I recall it now with wonder and gratitude.

▣ ▣

Martin Sheen had introduced me to César in 1989 at a United Farm Workers rally outside Safeway's national headquarters in Oakland. The next morning I heard César give a stirring speech to a small crowd, urging us to organize a boycott of Safeway. At issue were the carcinogenic pesticides on grapes sold by the company—migrant farmworkers were constantly exposed to these toxins. Steve Kelly and I spent a day going door-to-door in San Francisco explaining matters and promoting the boycott. In the evening we joined a celebratory social.

When I interviewed César at the Seton Hall convention, I asked him why he never wrote about nonviolence.

We have a rule not to write or preach about nonviolence. I've never written a word about nonviolence. There are many people, including you, who have written all about it. We don't have to write about it, interpret it, or dissect it. It's very simple. Just do it. Nonviolence has to go beyond rhetoric. There's no real trick to being nonviolent if you're locked up in your room and praying the rosary. Anybody can do that. But how about being nonviolent in the face of violence? That's where it really happens.

In the early days of the struggle, I talked a lot about nonviolence, more than I should have. And so we had many people, grown men, running around like saints with their hands folded together, looking like angels. So I said, "No, no, no. You don't have to go around like you're in another world to be nonviolent. You don't have to go around like you're walking on eggshells. That's not the idea. Be yourselves and do things, just don't use violence." Nonviolence, you see, can go the other way, too. You can become passive, and that's not going to change anything.

Primarily, there has to be action. Without action, you're kidding yourself. In the struggle here in the United States, you have to be part of real action. You have to get beyond the talking, writing, and planning stage and get into real action if you want to change anything. Things do not change by writing or reading about them, but they do change when you actually confront other people—in our case, the grape industry.

I asked him where he found God in the midst of the struggle for justice.

God is manifested through God's people. It's always me and God and you and all people, never just me and God. If it's just me and God, then we get into trouble. It's me and God and you and everyone—always. You've got to have faith in God and in God's people, too. That faith in God has to transcend also to God's people. If you have faith, you can withstand the things that shouldn't happen, the injustices, the setbacks. We need people who are committed to the struggle; otherwise, nothing will happen. Jesus never gave up. He didn't say, "Well, I'm going to be here just for a little while, and then I'm going to forget you." He said, "I'm going to be with you all the time, forever."

I don't know how much I've accomplished, but I know I've been there for people. When the poor and the destitute needed love and attention and caring, I was there for them. I don't know how much I helped, but I was there for them. That's what counts. There's a difference between being of service and being a servant. If you are of service, you serve at your convenience. You will say, "Oh, I can't do this today at five, but perhaps next week." If you are a servant, you are at their convenience. You have no escape. You are at their service all the time. You are there to serve. That's faith and commitment.

I took the opportunity and slipped in a request for advice. "Don't ever give up," he said, "on public action for justice and peace."

I saw César twice just weeks before his death, once at the funeral of a mutual friend, the legendary Los Angeles priest Luis Olivares, and again at an awards ceremony in Los Angeles. On each occasion, he spoke optimistically about the boycott. He seemed sure in his pursuit of justice, in his ability to rally others to the cause, and that the boycott would succeed.

"I'm always hopeful," he said during my interview with him at Seton Hall.

In April 1993, César was in Arizona to stand trial in a lawsuit against a grape-growing company. He had been on a private fast for six days. On the evening of April 22, he retired early to read. The next morning he was found dead, a book in his hands.

Many thousands journeyed to Delano, California, for his wake and funeral, held at Forty Acres, the former United Farm Workers headquarters, in the heart of California's Central Valley. Fifteen thousand farmworkers viewed his body, resting in an open pine coffin, and then gathered for a rosary service under a huge tent, a banner of César's visage fluttering overhead. The people prayed, sang, read Scriptures, and told stories all night long, until the sun rose. On April 29, I joined fifty thousand marchers through Delano to the funeral Mass. Dignitaries, church people, and farmworkers alike compared César to Gandhi and King. They declared him "a prophet of justice and nonviolence" and together pledged to continue his struggle for justice. In a rose garden at the foot of a hill at La Paz, the United Farm Workers headquarters, they laid him to rest. It was where he had prayed every morning at sunrise.

回 回

The fall of 1992 marked the five hundredth anniversary of Columbus's "discovery" of America. Bill O'Donnell and I wanted to mark the occasion not with a celebration but an act of repentance. We had read that Columbus had planted a large cross on the beach before embarking on the steady genocide of indigenous peoples, so we decided to go to the Concord Naval Weapons Station and plant a cross near a nuclear bunker—a sign of protest against genocidal weapons. The action wouldn't be easy and would certainly be risky. We would have to climb two ten-foot chain-link fences topped with barbed wire. Bill figured we could tie the ends of two ladders together with stout rope, lean them against the fence, and throw the outer one up and over.

A dozen of us set off before dawn on Columbus Day. A friend dropped us off at the remote edge of the base with our ladders and our four-foot cross. The rising sun illumined miles of rolling green hills. A sign on the fence tendered typical government words of welcome: "Trespassers will be shot on sight." We leaned the ladders against the fence, threw the outer ladder over the top, and went over. Ladders and cross in hand, we headed over the hills. A mile in, we came upon another fence and employed Bill's technique to get over that one, too. On we went, not quite sure where the bunkers were or what lay ahead. Then a small concrete building came into view—an entrance to a bunker, we figured. Our goal was to plant the cross as near to it as possible.

When we were some fifty yards away, we heard a thunderous voice, as if from on high. "Stop what you are doing, stand still, and do not move—or you will be shot." We scanned the distance and spied a dozen soldiers on the ground ahead, peering back at us through the sights of their machine guns, all of them frozen and silent. I turned and said, "Don't move." We put the cross down and our hands up. Seconds later, police cars came roaring over the hill. They hadn't fully come to a halt before officers scrambled out. They grabbed us and cuffed us while we recited the Lord's Prayer. As they none too gently took us away, we felt gratitude. The soldiers presented a hitch in our plans, to be sure, but we had managed to bring the cross of nonviolence to the very heart of our country's nuclear intent—a sacramental gesture we prayed would cultivate gentleness in the world.

A few weeks later, I flew to Haiti, the poorest country in the Western Hemisphere. I had met exiled president Jean-Bertrand Aristide a month earlier at Father Bill's rectory. In September 1991, Aristide had been overthrown in a U.S.-backed military coup that left more than four thousand dead. As far as I was concerned, he was the real leader of Haiti, a hero of justice and peace. I admired his message of nonviolence and his work for democracy.

I had come to Haiti with Mev Puleo to lead a delegation of other Pax Christi friends. Together we toured sprawling Port-au-Prince and one of Haiti's poorest slums, the teeming Cité-Soleil. That was one of the hardest encounters of my life—half a million people living in shacks, with little food, no running water, and the stagnant ooze of sewage. The shaggy crowds regarded us as rock stars; they trailed us joyously and pressed to catch a glimpse. I offered a warm and sunny countenance, but not without effort. Underneath I was crushed and overwhelmed.

From Cité-Soleil we headed north for Cap-Haïtien, where we gathered in darkness with eighteen priests and nuns in fear for their lives. Dark murmurs passed among us—of treachery by the military regime, of the Catholic hierarchy's refusal to stand up against the death squads.

Before we left the country, I testified on behalf of the delegation before the Organization of American States, which was keeping tabs on the crisis. I spoke of the death squads who threatened Aristide supporters and kept them in fear. I cataloged some of the human rights abuses and laid out how poverty was deliberately woven into the ragged social fabric of Haiti, making it so that the destitute suffered at the bottom while a handful lived like kings. I concluded with a petition to restore Aristide to office. A leap toward justice would follow from that deed alone. This plea was met with mild interest.

回 回

In January 1993, I was asked to coordinate the annual Good Friday protest at Livermore Lab. I agreed and got started. I had heard that William Sloane Coffin, the esteemed preacher and former Yale chaplain, would be teaching at the Graduate Theological Union that semester, and I wondered if he would agree to address the crowd at the Livermore rally.

Big in stature and balding on top, with streamers of white hair on the sides, Bill Coffin was a man of rare eloquence and stentorian voice, an authority in the biblical sense. He was distinguished by his civil rights work, his resistance to the Vietnam War, and his pastorship of Riverside Church in New York. *Time* magazine named him one of the ten greatest preachers in the nation. He welcomed me into his spartan office and accepted my invitation to speak at the protest.

Something came over me, and I launched into a lengthy and animated proposal about what he might say in his address. "I think you need to pick a great text, denounce nuclear weapons, and call for the disarmament of Livermore Labs and then urge everyone to engage in civil disobedience at the lab gates," I said as the great man eyed me. "Here's how you should do it. Combine two Gospel passages, the story of Jesus' nonviolent civil disobedience in the temple and the commandment from the Sermon on the Mount to love your enemies.

That would combine the vision of nonviolent love and nonviolent action. It's never been done before. Doesn't that sound perfect?"

Coffin's face bore a distinct look of amusement. "I'm thinking more along the lines of Matthew 27:39–40."

I was in over my head; I didn't know Scriptures by chapter and verse. "Those passing by reviled him, shaking their heads and saying . . . 'If you are the Son of God . . . come down from the cross!'" Coffin quoted by heart. "I think this is the general attitude among Californians as they drive past Livermore thinking, *If only something could be done* to stop the planned crucifixion of humanity. Little do they realize they're repeating the same words as the bystanders at Jesus' crucifixion. Would that be okay?"

Of course. There was a clear connection between Jesus' crucifixion and Livermore's intent for nuclear crucifixion, but the further link between the Jerusalem bystanders and the Californian bystanders was genius. I mumbled words of agreement and then slunk off, pledging never again to advise him or any other great preacher.

Good Friday arrived, and about a thousand people gathered for the rally. Bill Coffin preached, his baritone drawing us in, that those first disciples should have protested the crucifixion of Jesus. Similarly, we should protest Livermore's planned nuclear crucifixion of humanity. He then painted a breathtaking picture of a new world without war, poverty, and nuclear weapons.

Bill O'Donnell had crafted some five hundred wooden crosses. Carrying them, the protesters marched the mile to the lab's main gates, where Bill Coffin, Martin Sheen, and I knelt along with a hundred others and obstructed the entrance. After our arrest and release that afternoon, we gathered at Davida's house, in the Berkeley hills, to share food and listen to Bill's stories. He told about one night, in 1966, when he was at a gathering of activists against the Vietnam War in the home of Rabbi Abraham Heschel. They despaired together, what could be done?

"There's one voice," said the noble Heschel, "who could denounce this war and get a hearing—Dr. King. But I don't know how to reach him."

"Why, I have his number right here in my pocket," Bill said. So they called Dr. King at home. Bill and Heschel both got on the phone and vehemently urged Dr. King to speak out against the war. Dr. King kept his thoughts close to his vest. All he said was "Uh-huh" over and over again. "Martin," said Bill, "was a great 'uh-huh' guy." Of course, he agreed to speak, and his address at Riverside Church on April 4, 1967, shocked the nation with its clarion call to end the war. It also marked him for death one year later to the day.

回 回

As I began my final year of theology studies, I set a weekend aside for a retreat at Kirkridge with Dan and Phil Berrigan. Afterward, Phil and I took to the Pennsylvania woods. The leaves were tinged in gold and red, and sunlight dappled the ground. As we heaved ourselves along steep hills and paths, I talked about my summer in Guatemala. Then I looked at him sidelong and said, "I spent the summer, too, thinking about the Plowshares movement." Phil returned my glance, and I took a deep breath. "I've decided to take part. I'm ready." He stopped in his tracks, looked me in the eye, and said, "Okay." We agreed to hold meetings the following summer, after my ordination. He would make the arrangements; all I had to do was show up.

On the night before my ordination, the Jesuit provincial threw a party for those who would be ordained the next day. There, I was loudly upbraided by a certain cardinal for my support of Aristide and

Pax Christi. I managed to stand up for myself with grace, but the encounter put a damper on the evening. It helped that hundreds of letters had poured in all week from across the country. Bill Coffin congratulated me on my "coronation." Mother Teresa offered a laundry list of suggestions—their sum and substance how to be a good priest. And just as I was getting ready to depart for Baltimore on the morning of my ordination, a UPS truck squealed to a halt out front. It was a package from Toronto, a large poster of Rembrandt's painting *The Return of the Prodigal Son*, a gift from Henri Nouwen. Maybe I still riled some people in the church, but the support I did have was rich indeed.

On June 12, 1993, I arrived at last at the Baltimore Basilica, a ponderous monument—with its immense portico lined with brown marble columns, its dome like a planetarium, and its two rapier spires piercing the sky. The place was packed with candidates, relatives, Jesuits, and friends. My family was there, and a handful of friends.

At the prescribed moment, I lay prostrate with the other candidates, and the cardinal prayed: "Hear us, Lord our God, and pour out on these servants of yours the blessing of the Holy Spirit and the grace and power of the priesthood. In your sight we offer these men for ordination. Support them with your unfailing love." Then one by one we knelt before him, and he laid his hands over us in silence.

It was our privilege then to honor a Jesuit to vest us. Daniel Berrigan came forward for me. He placed on me the stole and chasuble, and there I stood looking to all the world like a priest. It was at Dan's touch that I truly felt ordained; his was the blessing I counted most meaningful. His was the example that moved me to pursue disarmament and peace in the name of Jesus.

The next day, hundreds packed St. Al's chapel for the first Mass I would preside over. The gospel choir launched into a rousing, joyful hymn. I stood before the people, Bishop Walter Sullivan behind me, and made the sign of the cross—the last orthodox thing I would do. I had resolved to uphold the gospel's witness for humility and risk, justice and peace, and so I discarded centuries of patriarchal language. "In the name of the God of peace," I intoned, "the nonviolent Jesus, and the Holy Spirit of love." My words were met with smiles all over the room.

The homily became my opening statement for a life aimed at following Jesus in nonviolent, healing love. The response was a standing ovation—an encouraging start. During intercessory prayers, Miss Ruth, a much-loved African-American elder, prayed from the choir, boldly and with passion: "Dear Lord, we pray for Father John and ask you to raise him up, to take him up higher and higher, to keep taking him up until he never comes down and just goes right on up to you!" Then Communion, the people clustered about the altar, and to round out the service, a poem read by Daniel Berrigan. The party that followed celebrated a great day, the culmination of years, and a new beginning.

27

Down by
the Riverside
(1993)

Not long after my ordination, my friend Art Laffin of the Dorothy
Day Catholic Worker House, approached me with news that
the United States was about to launch a Trident submarine, the USS
Rhode Island, the fifteenth in a fleet that could blow up the planet
several times over. Art was headed to Groton, Connecticut, with our
friends George Ostenson and Jim Reale. They had hatched a plan:
we would take a leisurely summer ride down the Thames River—in a
canoe—and, at the right moment, unfurl our banner in protest. How
could I say no?

The launch was scheduled for a Saturday morning in July. Hundreds
gathered outside the U.S. Naval Submarine Base with antiwar posters
and banners as Art, George, Jim, and I stumbled like clowns down
a side street with a canoe under our arms. The launching of the sub
had prompted the closing of the river, and cops jetted around in small
boats. Ignoring them, we got into the canoe and heaved starboard,
keeping a weather eye out for the speed of the river. It moved at a brisk

pace, and I entertained a fleeting worry that the river would outmatch our puny paddles and we would float out to sea.

"The river is closed today," a cop yelled. He motored up close and set us rocking. "You'll have to return to shore."

"But it's such a beautiful day," I yelled back with a smile. "We're just out for a canoe ride!" He zoomed off, and we paddled onward. The USS *Rhode Island* loomed ahead on our left. It was massive, a sea monster half out of the water, poised for the ceremonial moment when it would set off into the river to prowl the world's oceans. To its left sat another sub, the USS *Maine*, still under construction.

To the right of both stood a reviewing stand, all scaffolding and beams, its red, white, and blue festoonery snapping in the wind. By the look of things from the river, thousands were in attendance—it was a sea of starched U.S. Navy whites. A navy band played one Sousa march after another, and long-winded officials made addresses. Before we knew it, the current had delivered us to the right spot. We bobbed right up in front of the Trident itself, within a hundred yards of the crowd.

A coast guard boat caught sight of us and neared. A voice boomed from the bridge: "Okay, fellas, you can't be in the river. The river is closed. We're going to escort you back."

"Thanks, officer," I yelled, "but we're fine. We're just out for a canoe ride."

Three police boats joined the fray, drew in close, and circled about, a maneuver to force us around. Jim and Art paddled in their direction, all but conceding the end of our escapade. But the wake and the current nudged us ever closer to the crowd. We seized the moment. Jim and I leapt to our feet and unfurled the banner: "Trident Is a Crime!" A police boat pulled alongside us. "Okay, fellas, that's enough," said one of the officers. "You're coming with us."

He lunged, the canoe rocked wildly, and Jim and I, still standing, reared back at his reach. All at once, we capsized, and the four of us fell into the river.

I kicked around for a moment and then saw the Trident sub towering over me. The current was moving me toward it, and I swam hard with it. Soon the reviewing stand came into view, too, the throng looking on in disbelief. I figured that now was as good a time as any for a speech. "I'm a Jesuit," I yelled, bobbing, "a Catholic priest. I work with the homeless in Washington, D.C., and this submarine is a sin and a crime against God and humanity. It robs the world's poor. This money should be spent on food and housing, not nuclear weapons. Trident is nothing to celebrate. It's Auschwitz all over again. It threatens us all. For God's sake, dismantle it!"

Everyone in the crowd was leaning forward, trying to hear. They all seemed stunned. I punched the air with my fist to punctuate my speech, just the opportunity the cop was waiting for. He gunned the engine of his one-man speedboat, came up next to me, grabbed my arm, and plucked me from the river, hurling me on board. He buzzed us back to the riverbank and tossed me ashore like a fish. Art and Jim made a similar landfall a few moments later. Like a good skipper, poor George stayed with the canoe, trying his hardest to keep it from sinking to the bottom of the river.

As we were handcuffed, I resumed the script, having practiced it many times. "Officer, we mean you no harm. We're just trying to speak out against this evil nuclear submarine."

"I understand," he said. "We respect you—but we have to take you in."

At the station we went through the drill: fingerprints, photos, questioning. Then the solemn escort to the jail cell. There seventeen others awaited us, the ones who had blocked the entrance to the reviewing stand. As we entered, they greeted us with applause. A hymn began, and we all joined in.

We were in for a long wait, so I sat there and pondered the day—the sheer adventure, the improvisation, the cops' respect, the joyous welcome to jail. Later, my thoughts drifted toward the future, toward the Plowshares action I would soon undertake. Phil had told me that plans were well under way—was I still interested? I had said yes. But the Plowshares action would not involve slapstick and farce, and would probably result in no applause whatsoever.

Art, George, Jim, and I returned to Connecticut a few weeks later to stand before a judge. It was within his discretion to hand us a year in prison. Instead, he sentenced us to time served and ordered us never to come around again.

They Shall Beat Their Swords into Plowshares (1993–94)

Having been assigned after ordination to work at St. Al's, I returned to the parish, immensely happy to be among friends and pleased to be back at K Street and with the dedicated Jesuits there. Masses, baptisms, and confessions occupied my time. But the imminence of the Plowshares action tinctured things, a red sock in a load of whites. I was really going to do this. It kept me up nights. I began to have nightmares.

Caution was the name of the game. When it came to anti-nuclear activism, the government behaved immoderately, dropping a wide net and snaring fish of every stripe, often dragging in as co-conspirators people who had only a passing knowledge of the action. Our goal was that only the actors themselves get arrested. Consequently, we did not discuss plans by phone, by mail, or in church gatherings. Surveillance techniques were well established even in those days. The only citadel in such occasions was silence; they can't hear what you don't say.

So for the next six months, I surfaced here and there along the East Coast for weekend retreats with Phil and Bruce Friedrich, of the Catholic Worker, who would also be taking part in the action. We prayed, read the Gospels, studied nuclear weapons, rehearsed our action, reflected on nonviolence, prepared ourselves for the ordeal of court and prison, and tried to build ourselves into a community of trust. We were later joined by Lynn Fredriksson, a brilliant young activist who had graduated at the top of her class at Brown, traveled through the Soviet Union to protest the cold war, and directed Women Strike for Peace, a leading women's peace group. The team for the Plowshares action would consist of Lynn, Phil, Bruce, and me.

We considered several military bases, but I had a target firmly in mind: North Carolina. It was my home state, and many friends there could lend support, including my brother Steve. We set the date tentatively for early December. Phil, Bruce, and Lynn made plans to go down and case our chosen spot: the Seymour Johnson Air Force Base, in Goldsboro. I would arrange to meet my provincial and ask, yet again, for permission to break the law. I knew I had a slim chance of receiving it, given my history. But what did I have to lose?

In a hidden corner of my soul, I detected a measure of comfort in my dismal chances. I could look the team in the eye and say, "Sorry, friends. I tried. I sure would love to go to prison with you, but I guess it's not God's will." My soul thus divided, I drove to Baltimore to see Father Ed Glynn.

"Ed," I began, "I would like your permission to walk onto an air force base in North Carolina, hammer on a nuclear weapon, in keeping with the prophet Isaiah's commandment that we beat our swords into plowshares, and go off to spend time, perhaps even years, in prison."

"What?" he responded. "Are you crazy? Why do you want to do a fool thing like that? What if they open fire and kill you? What am I going to tell your mother?"

"Well, like you, I'm just trying to follow Jesus. And the way I see it, he was killed for turning over the tables in the temple, for confronting the structures of injustice, and I'm supposed to do what he did, so—"

"Yes, I know, but—"

"So as his follower, whether I like it or not, I have to confront the structures of injustice that oppress the world's poor, risk arrest, and offer my life for God's reign of justice and peace."

"Well, there are certainly other ways to—"

"For years, I've been trying to figure out what it means to take up the cross. And for me, it means engaging in nonviolent resistance against our country's wars and nuclear weapons—despite the consequences to myself. It means I really have to break the law that legalizes mass murder. I have to confront the nation, even if everyone thinks I'm crazy."

"Well," he said. He stroked his chin, and the look of alarm faded from his eyes. He leaned back in his chair. "Who will you be doing this with?"

I told him about our group, our weekend retreats, and, in broad terms, our plan of action. "You know," I mentioned, "you could be indicted if you know the details ahead of time." He waved his hand and insisted on hearing everything, so I divulged the whole plan.

Finally, he said, "You know, I spent many years teaching college. And at the end of every semester, I always made the same speech."

Out of courtesy I settled in, expecting some yarn and bracing myself for his refusal.

"I would invite the students to imagine themselves after their death, standing before God at the gates of heaven."

I nodded.

"I told them that God would invariably ask them what they had done with the gift of life, so I put the question to them, what will be your answer? What will you say to God? 'Reflect now,' I would say. 'Prepare now to account for your life.'"

A pause passed between us.

"Now I get it." He exhaled. "You want to be able to say to God that you stood up against war and nuclear weapons and gave your life for God's reign of justice and peace."

Suddenly he smiled, his grin as big as a crescent moon. "This is wonderful!" he crowed. "Just wonderful! Absolutely! Not only do you have my permission, but you have my blessing. May God bless you." He reached across his desk to grab my hand. "And if anything happens to you, I'll preach that you were a faithful Jesuit, a great Jesuit, because you were trying to follow Jesus. I'll tell them all, even your mother."

This was a turnabout I couldn't have imagined. All those years of being stonewalled and ridiculed and reprimanded dissolved in an instant. Here was a superior who not only was tolerant of my interests but also understood them, pushed them, affirmed them, blessed them.

I left his office exhilarated—and in a state of primal fear. Permission was decidedly *not* denied. And I immediately had a sense, to borrow a phrase, of my hour approaching. I was headed for prison.

It was time now to take that proverbial leap of faith, to rile the powers and throw my future to the wind. Life was out of my control. The team plunged ahead. I spent a lovely Thanksgiving with my family, then drove off for a friendly visit to the good state of North Carolina.

回　回

It is dark—early in the morning, December 7, 1993. We will hike through woods, over fields, and onto a tarmac. On the runway, we'll approach an F-15E bomber and swing hammer against steel; then, in the spirit of nonviolence, and with whatever courage we can muster, we will await our arrest. Instead of waiting for the government to begin nuclear disarmament, we will start it ourselves.

We expect, in the mood of Christmas, a silent night. But as we near our destination, we notice a flurry of traffic. A car approaches, its headlights pointed our way. We throw ourselves behind bushes. Another car comes, then another. Do they know we're here? Should we call things off? We take stock of the situation and press on, trusting God's grace to get us through. As we reach the woods, a caravan of trucks comes near. We lie on the ground and watch it pass. We look into one another's faces, wondering what to do. "Let's go on," Phil says.

We get to our feet and stumble through the dark woods under a moonless sky. Before long, we hear the burbling of a creek; we have no choice, it seems, but to wade across. The cold water reaches our knees, and we battle to make it to the other side. A hill rises along the opposite bank. Bruce climbs it to reconnoiter. He reports that a car, its lights on, sits not too far off. We sit, collect our wits, pray in silence.

I finger the hammer in my coat pocket. I have engraved it with words dear to my heart: "Swords into plowshares," "Seek the unarmed Christ," and "Love your enemies." I wonder what it will be like when we're caught. Will we be shot at? I feel the chill of fear. I've had it all day and it won't let up. I try to console myself with memories of the great peacemakers and martyrs—Gandhi, King, Romero, Ellacuría, Donovan, Ford.

We decide to keep moving. Lynn proceeds first, then Bruce, then Phil, then me—over the hill, along the forest's edge. The tarmac appears in the distance. Another caravan approaches, and we lie motionless until it passes. Then we scurry over to a grove of pines. We peer about, and there it is, sprawled before us—the vast complex of the Seymour Johnson Air Force Base, its lights glaring, trucks going every which way, airmen darting about.

No silent night at all. We have marched right into the middle of full-scale war games. My eyes widen. I want time to think this through, but there is no time. Bruce and Lynn take the lead, and Phil and I follow. We steal along until we realize that no one is taking notice of us. Thereafter, we walk plainly.

Before long, we spy a lone F-15E—no airmen attending it, no lights illuminating it. The God of peace has set this one aside. Lynn and Bruce reach it first and begin hammering the pylons. Then they take aim at a guidance light and the flight pod and sprinkle blood on the fuselage and in the air intakes.

When Phil and I arrive, the enormity of the plane surprises me. I locate the radar tracking device—a narrow fin beneath the plane. At long last, by the grace of God, I will strike a blow for nuclear disarmament. I swing. *Clang!* The vibrations travel through my bones. I expect damage, but there's neither dent nor chipped paint. I glance at Phil and see instead soldiers racing toward us, raising their weapons—just time enough for one more swing. *Clang!*

"Put your hammers down and come to the other side," a soldier orders. The four of us emerge, and several soldiers surround us. "Put down your hammers," he repeats.

"We are unarmed, nonviolent people," I say loudly and calmly. "We mean you no harm. We're here to dismantle this weapon of death." The soldiers gape at us and freeze.

But they soon recover, bellowing orders and manhandling us to the ground. "Faces on the ground!" they shout. A soldier yells into his walkie-talkie: "This is the real world! DefCon Charlie. This is the real world! Exercises canceled!" Another soldier tears the Salvadoran cross from around my neck and sends it through the air toward the plane. It pings off the aircraft. The cross, too, wants to enact the prophecy of Isaiah, I think to myself.

Our noses face down on a green lawn, we reach out for one another's hands and offer a prayer of thanksgiving, despite the weapons aimed at our heads. Minutes later, we are hauled to our feet, cuffed, and shoved into separate squad cars.

回 回

Hours later, a new day begun, I was ushered to a building and into a room with a window. I lay on the floor in a swath of sunshine. Some hours later, the door's rattling roused me. A man in a green sport coat walked in. "Al Koehler, FBI." He ordered me to remove my clothes, then searched me. I respectfully declined to answer questions. He, on the other hand, was talkative. "Can't believe I'm questioning another Berrigan and his friends," he said. "I'm the agent who arrested Daniel Berrigan on Block Island twenty-three years ago."

Around two in the afternoon, we departed by van, chained to one another, for the Vance County Jail, in Henderson. I gazed out the window at the passing pines along the highway. For the moment, the consolation of creation seemed the realest thing in the world.

Vance wasn't our home for long. After two days, we were taken to the Robeson County Jail in Lumberton, one of the worst in the nation, where twenty-five men had died mysteriously during the previous decade. At first, we were in different cells; then Bruce, Phil, and

I were reunited just before Christmas. I will never forget listening to Phil for hours each day that Christmas week, telling us his entire life's story. Then one morning well before dawn, guards raided our cell, saying we had five minutes to prepare to leave. While we did, they overturned our mattresses, swept our things onto the floor, and patted us down. Then they shackled us together, and we trudged clumsily to a waiting van and piled in. After a brief stay at the Smithfield jail, we made the long trip to Edenton, along the coast, not far from my birthplace. We passed through Elizabeth City, to drop off Lynn at the women's jail, and I saw my elementary school and the parish where my brother David and I had served as altar boys. My heart filled with melancholy and wistfulness as pleasant memories crowded my mind. My life had come full circle: from peaceful childhood to peacemaking adulthood.

Then we stopped abruptly, and guards flung open the doors. We were at the Chowan County Jail in Edenton. As we shuffled inside, a guard sidled up close and whispered in my ear: "I know you. I watched you grow up as a boy, even babysat for you a few times. I know your father, the newspaper publisher." Before I had time to thank him for his greeting, I was thrown into a cold holding cell.

In Jail,
on Trial
(1994)

The atmosphere at the Edenton jail seemed more relaxed, and the guards friendlier, than at Lumberton. After days of sleeping on the floor of the main common cell with twenty-two others, Phil, Bruce, and I found ourselves in somewhat of a private "suite"—Phil and I in one cell, and Bruce and another prisoner in the adjoining one. We had all the amenities one would expect: an open steel toilet in each cell, and between the cells a shower stall that probably hadn't seen a mop or a sponge in decades. I didn't know mold could come in so many different colors. Food was delivered through a slot in the door; our entertainment was a television hung from the ceiling. The cell, at least, was a repose—a repose with a vengeance. Not once in seven months did we leave it, except to appear in court or to have a few minutes with the occasional visitor. We tried to make the wretched place our home.

We had been placed together in our cells by the warden, a genuine good old boy, head gleaming and belly protruding, who had latched onto the three of us for some reason. He came by more often and earlier than we would have liked to chew the fat. At seven in the morning, he would let himself in and rattle on and on about his troubles: unruly inmates, slack guards, petty rules by which he had to abide. "The job is just trouble waitin' to happen," he told us.

His life story emerged gradually, an installment every day or two—stories of his family, his illustrious career, his involvement with the Ku Klux Klan. And we were compelled to listen; our cell was his confessional, and he held the keys.

One morning he arrived bright and early and, to our surprise, inquired about our well-being. Were we managing all right? Then he asked, "So where you boys from?"

His taking an interest in us signaled a change in the air. He had divined that something was up. The *New York Times* and the *Washington Post* had written stories about our action. ABC's *20/20* had submitted a request for interviews. What exactly, he asked, did we do? For weeks afterward, we held him rapt with *our* stories. "It don't make a lick of sense," he objected. "You can do so much more good on the outside." "This is where we need to be," I returned. He shook his head, puzzling over that. Later he asked how he might get books we had written. Against all odds, a friendship developed.

Over time, he began to handle our press arrangements. "I got someone comin' at one," he would announce, a reporter from the Associated Press or the *Toronto Star*. And he made exceptions for visitors and allowed us to clutter our cells with piles of mail. I decorated the dingy walls with photos and cards I received, sticking them to the cinder block with toothpaste. The dungeon bloomed into an art museum of sorts—everywhere icons, portraits of the saints, pictures of friends, postcards of the Grand Canyon and Nags Head—a glimpse of heaven, my non-wailing wall.

Gradually, the warden manifested a kind of solicitude. One day, he put his nose to Phil's. "Plead guilty," he urged. "You're too old. You shouldn't be here. Let the young Turks go to prison." His gestures of concern were sincere and helped ease the tension of our impending trial. Now and again he unleashed gales of laughter. "When they make the movie about you," he said, "be sure you get some good-lookin' Bubba to play me—some worked-out, good-lookin' guy with a head a hair."

The trial date, February 15, 1994, arrived at last. At four in the morning, marshals loaded us into a van. They took care to move along a circuitous route so that we couldn't consort with our supporters outside the courthouse.

Among those supporters were two attorneys, Joe Cosgrove and former U. S. attorney general Ramsey Clark, who offered to defend us. We were grateful for their guidance and help but insisted on defending ourselves, in keeping with St. Mark's admonishment: "Do not prepare a defense, but let the Holy Spirit speak through you."

Our strategy was simple: we would tell our story. And to the extent the court permitted us to explain ourselves, we would do it in terms of international law and the "necessity defense"—that is, setting aside a minor law in order to honor one much higher, such as when an ambulance runs a red light to save a life, or civilians break through the door of a burning house to save those inside. They break laws or destroy private property for a higher good, a higher law—to protect human life. We had acted in good faith to spare humanity the cataclysms and horrors of nuclear war.

Actually, we were obeying international law, which requires citizens to violate and stop their government's preparations for genocide. Unfortunately, it was likely that the court would deny us this line of argument. We pledged among ourselves that if that happened, we would disrupt proceedings.

Phil, Bruce, Lynn, and I were left to cool our heels in a cell behind the courtroom. It was the first time in a month that the three of us had seen Lynn, and we quickly discovered that her incarceration had been tougher than ours. She had no companions with which to share the ordeal; her first three weeks were spent in solitary confinement; and now she was in a cell shoulder-to-shoulder with a dozen other women. She offered them kindness and friendship; she managed, but it was rough.

Soon it was time for jury selection. In our stylish orange jump-suits and orange sandals, we lined ourselves along the defendants' table. The judge entered and grumbled a greeting. Catholics make up a small percentage of North Carolina, but Judge Terrence Boyle was one—and a prominent one at that. A Reagan appointee, he had a reputation for right-wing and anti–civil rights verdicts. On top of that, he harbored resentment against my father, who years earlier had led a newspaper campaign against his judicial appointment.

Boyle prodded us through selection of the jurors. The four of us accepted the first twelve on principle—that we're all citizens able to discern the truth—but the prosecutor had particular jurors in mind, and before long we stood face-to-face with our jury—each member having some connection with Seymour Johnson Air Force Base. Most were in the air force; one was a specialist in F-15Es. Here was a jury of our peers.

It was a great joy to see our families and friends sitting in the court-room. In one row sat a group of Jesuits, among them Bishop Walter Sullivan, of Richmond, president of Pax Christi USA. They greeted us with smiles. And near them sat Martin Sheen, loyal friend. A hundred or so others stood outside with banners and leaflets, unable to get in.

Judge Boyle read a motion in limine—a list of requested excluded evidence. And what a list it was, full of banned topics and forbidden lines of argument. Judge and prosecutor had composed the list together, so of course the request was granted. Boyle warned that, to avoid contempt charges, we should stay clear of the following topics:

- All the "military activities" of the United States
- International law
- The necessity defense
- The activities of the United States military and government relating to any person other than the defendants
- The Nuremberg defense
- Crime prevention as a reason for entering the military facility at Seymour Johnson Air Force Base
- Alleged crimes committed by the United States government, its officials or agencies
- The United States government's foreign or domestic policies
- The military or other use of the aircraft alleged to have been damaged by the defendants
- Divine or natural law or other religious teachings
- Alleged crimes committed in the past or presently by the United States military and/or other federal officials at Seymour Johnson Air Force Base

Phil, Bruce, Lynn, and I exchanged a knowing look. We would undertake civil disobedience—or better, we would bring the civil disobedience from the air force base into the courtroom, where weapons and wars were legalized.

Lynn spoke first, on our behalf, reading our opening statement to set the tone.

"Good afternoon, jurors, friends and supporters, members of the press, Judge Boyle. On December 7, 1993, the four of us walked onto the Seymour Johnson Air Force Base, in Goldsboro, North Carolina, to nonviolently disarm one F-15E Strike Eagle, a nuclear-capable fighter bomber which has already been used notably in the massacre of Iraqis during the Gulf War."

"Objection," the prosecutor said.

"This court indicts peace activists," she said, "while ignoring those who make nuclear hostages of us all."

The prosecutor again, louder: "Objection!"

"Sustained," growled the judge. "You're impugning the integrity of this court."

"The criminal justice system—" Lynn continued.

"Stop right there," ordered the judge.

"—and the nuclear strike force are two sides of the same coin."

"I'm admonishing you that you're in contempt," Boyle said, pounding his gavel as though he were driving in a nail.

"This court, like all others, protects the interests of the national security state—"

"Take the jury out," the judged yelled. "She's in contempt."

"—and uses its illegitimate power to suppress the truth—"

"She's in contempt. The jury is excused," he roared.

Marshals snatched the statement from Lynn's hands and led her away.

Without delay, I stood up and declared my intention to complete the statement. All necks craned in my direction as I continued: "The four of us have been denied our basic rights."

"If you continue," the judge said, "you'll be in contempt."

"We've been denied the chance to meet together to prepare a mutual defense—"

"No, no!" the judged yelled.

"The trial's date and location have been manipulated—"

A marshal lunged at me and tore away my statement.

Bruce stood up and continued: "This court has made a fair trial impossible . . ."

One by one, we broke the injunction, getting every banned item on the record.

"You're in contempt," shouted the judge, his face florid.

"From this point," Bruce said, "we shall remain silent and non-violently non-cooperate with these proceedings."

I was the last seized and hauled away. It was an ungainly and graceless departure, but I managed a parting invitation before the courtroom doors slammed shut behind me: "We invite all our friends here in the courtroom to join us by standing and turning your backs to the court." With that, I was hustled out of the courtroom and thrown into the holding cell.

A muted commotion followed, then a loud recitation of the Lord's Prayer. About twenty minutes later, we heard the news: twenty-one people, including Martin Sheen and Daniel Berrigan, had stood up and shown their backs to the honorable judge. In retaliation, the judge unleashed his pack of marshals. They waded into the gallery and made arrests for disorderly conduct.

Matters by now had gone from bad to ruin; the proceedings in shambles, the judge declared a mistrial. He ordered us back to the Edenton jail to sit on ice and once again face the prospect of blank time until another trial was scheduled.

That first trial was perhaps the most difficult performance of my life. Yet we had demonstrated our point: Nuclear weapons are the new idols, and as such enjoy legal status, legitimacy, even honor. They, not God, are revered as our true security.

Long ago, Thomas Merton had written Daniel Berrigan to that effect: "When they finally succeed in blowing up the world, it will be perfectly legal." In the same way, the powers that be upheld the crucifixion of Christ as legal. Likewise, the work of disarmament, the experience of resurrection, is totally illegal. All things are upside down. And so it was for us—modern-day witnesses to the Resurrection, reclaimers of an old tradition, strict followers of the nonviolent Jesus—now back in jail, marked as criminal troublemakers, just as the early Christians, the abolitionists, the suffragists, and the civil rights heroes had been.

Our Plowshares action was the fiftieth, as best we knew. Many other people, including several priests and nuns, had committed similar actions and spent years in prison. Phil considered our chances and figured on five years. Still, in the long run, the prospect of years in prison did nothing to erase my sense of calling, peculiar as it was in the eyes of many. I had resolved to keep the word of God in the tradition of the nonviolent, troublemaking Jesus, which meant that I, with all audacity and temerity, had to love my enemies. My Bible's translation of that verse meant stopping my government's plans to kill my enemies, which meant beginning the process of disarmament myself, without waiting for the government's permission.

As I would later tell audiences around the country, "The church doesn't take me seriously; the media doesn't take me seriously; the Jesuits don't take me seriously; my family doesn't take me seriously—but the government takes me very seriously!"

Others in recent times have undertaken far greater actions and suffered far greater consequences. I drew strength, first of all, from the Jesuit martyrs and the four churchwomen of El Salvador. During my arrest, with boots on my back and weapons at my head, images of Ellacuría and the others flooded my mind—they too had lain facedown beneath soldiers, just before being killed. I knew them, and, for a moment, I knew the faith and shared the terror that must have been theirs. As I lay there, I recalled, too, the daily bombings at the Salvadoran refugee camp, and I evoked the suffering and fear that millions of Latin Americans lived with every day. I was doing what the poor of the world hoped someone would do: trying to stop the killing, dismantle the weapons, and begin the conversion from violence to nonviolence.

▣ 30 ▣

Waiting
in My Cell
(1994)

I can write about the trial now with some bravado. But back in the
cell, truth be known, the walls began to close in. Phil, Bruce, and
I resumed our routine: studying Mark's Gospel, praying daily, and
passing the Wonder Bread and plastic cup of grape juice, plus con-
ducting press interviews and answering thousands of letters. Still, we
all felt by now the pinch of confinement. Our nerves were shot. I
surveyed the future and felt a measure of anxiety. Would we spend
years in prison? I was desperate to breathe fresh air, walk on the beach,
enjoy a pasta dish and the company of friends.

I quickly abandoned the motto "One day at a time." Weeks were
born, and weeks died—like ice ages, one after another. "One hour at
a time" better served my purposes, and then, as the hours came to a
stop, "One minute at a time." The only image I can summon is that
of lying alone on a hospital bed, where the world and time come to a
crashing halt.

We tried to settle down, but soon enough Phil, Bruce, and I got on
one another's nerves, or, at least, I got on theirs. They were extroverts,

but I'm really an introvert, and I turned inward, not opening up even for my friends. Given the severe pressures, we worked extra hard at being nonviolent. We had begun our ordeal with saving practices in place—daily Bible study and Eucharist and a formal check-in time to air grievances and share feelings, every morning at six. Even though we had been together for the previous twenty-four hours, we asked one another innocently, "So, how was your day yesterday?"

There's an undisputable efficacy to it—you ask for help, share your problems, and offer suggestions. This practice offers a safe space to let out steam and work out grievances. But I spent twenty-four hours a day with Phil and Bruce, never left their presence. I knew every detail of their lives, each indistinguishable day after another. We had exhausted all topics of discussion; I had nothing left to say. Increasingly, my attention fixated on time. Each day lasted a hundred hours. Years passed between April and June. Nothing lay at hand to eat or drink—nowhere to go, nothing to do. We took turns falling into frustration and despair, and we also took turns trying to pull one another out.

We needed more help to get through the days, so we instituted a short prayer time after lunch to offer intercessions for peace. We would formally beg God for every miracle of peace and justice we could think of for the whole human race. And to keep our minds supple and fit, we set about writing for one solid hour afterward. Following writing teacher Natalie Goldberg's advice, we kept our two-inch pencil stubs moving over the paper. We churned out dozens of articles within a month, many of which later made their way into print in church and peace-and-justice journals all over the country. Years later, Natalie and I became friends; she probably had no idea that her classic work, *Writing Down the Bones*, could be so useful to prisoners of conscience and troublemaking priests. For the time being, our writing practice sustained our sense of bearing: we had important work to do; we would write, and people would read us. We had a message for the world: The time for nuclear disarmament has come. Repent and believe the Good News!

I had a few good days and occasionally laid claim to a sense of profound peace—like Jesus on Mount Tabor, transfigured, radiating light, God declaring to my soul, "You are my beloved." But most days I felt like the crucified Jesus on Mount Calvary, my heart echoing his rock-bottom prayer: "My God, my God, why have you forsaken me?"

I prayed often for the strength to go on in a good spirit. But at a primal level, I struggled like a trapped wolf—and began even to look like one, with an untamed beard taking over my boyish face. I woke up often in the middle of the night gripped by fear: "Where am I? . . . Oh my God, I'm in jail! Get me out of here!"

The occasional visitor was a lifeline to those of us treading water at sea. My family came, as did Patrick O'Neill of the local Catholic Worker community. He would arrive in coat and tie, pretending to be our lawyer, the requisite briefcase in hand. Once we all were ensconced in a secluded room, he would open up his treasure chest and offer us a variety of illegal goods: fruit, candy, toothpaste, letters, and even, on occasion, gourmet coffee. We would smuggle our contraband back to our cells and rejoice for days after.

One day I was escorted to the glass visiting booth, and there on the other side sat Father Jim Devereux, the former superior of the Georgetown community who had told me as a novice not to become another Daniel Berrigan. He who had spared me from dismissal in the early years laid eyes on me now, a wolverine in orange, and immediately broke down. He spent most of that ten-minute visit crying. Between sobs, he tendered apologies for past hostilities. And then he offered congratulations on my gospel witness. "You," he said, "are not only like Daniel Berrigan; you're like Jesus."

Another day, I found Father Ed Glynn, the Maryland provincial, sitting in the visitor's booth. He had traveled six hours for a ten-minute visit. A decided awkwardness prevailed between us, as both of us tried to ignore my fashionable attire and the guards behind me with sidearms on display.

We made small talk until, finally, in the last minute, I leaned close and asked, "Ed, I really need to know. Do you still support me?"

He leaned back, put his hands in the shape of a box, and said, "John, you're right where we want you!"

A quintessential Jesuit punch line that resulted in a great incongruity—the stony guards moving in to haul me away as Ed and I shared a hearty laugh.

Martin Sheen visited, too, his coming a big occasion for the warden. It caused great stirrings and a relaxing of inflexible policies. In defiance of his own rules, the warden welcomed Phil, Bruce, and I into his office, where we lounged on leather couches and enjoyed thirty fabulous, companionable minutes with Martin. He told us finally that this illicit visit came with a catch: he must meet the warden's family. When our visit was over, Martin stepped out of the prison and came face-to-face with twenty-eight of the warden's immediate kin, standing in single file and waiting for individual greetings. Martin spent over an hour signing cards, smiling for photos, and offering friendly words to each as they stepped forward with starstruck eyes.

Such visits tempered the pangs of an unexpected development, that of losing friends. I knew little of the fragility of fidelity. Our action left no one neutral; we had drawn a line in the sand, one that forced everyone to size things up and make a choice. How difficult it was to receive red-hot missives from friends, many of them peaceniks like me, claiming, in some cases, that I had single-handedly derailed the U.S. peace movement.

Phil, a crusty veteran and an emotional citadel, tried to explain matters, saying that these responses were par for the course. Those who best understood nuclear weapons took our action as a threat. It shone a harsh light and nudged them in directions they would rather not go. We reminded them that followers of Jesus must bear a cross, and who wants to do that? We lay on their shoulders a considerable crisis of conscience, one that demanded resolution. Some people coped by keeping distance, Phil said, others by cutting us off entirely. In either case, they realized that the gospel demands more of us than we dare admit.

On the other hand, conservative church people, including many Jesuits, surprised me with their charity. Many showed themselves to be pastoral, even kind. New friends emerged, some from the unlikeliest places.

Constancy of friendships kept me afloat as the second trial loomed. Each kind word empowered me for this next ordeal. The cards and letters lifted my sagging spirits and brought some cheer into the dungeon. Henri Nouwen, in particular, kept busy at lifting my spirits. He wrote nearly weekly, sent manuscripts and books, and read my letters during Masses at L'Arche, urging his community to stand for peace.

Mother Teresa wrote with an offer to visit should she get back soon to the United States. She was right with me. Almost everyone else's letters expressed the hope that I would soon be released, a pleasing enough sentiment. But saint that she was, Mother encouraged me to *embrace* the suffering, to take it in, to hold it as a lover—to unite my suffering to Jesus' very own for the sake of the world. "Be glad," she wrote, "you are to proclaim the love of Jesus even to the poor in prison." No one before—not in one letter out of five thousand—had exhorted me to gladness. "Give Jesus your pain and limitations and trust in him," she wrote. "In your weakness, his power will be a protection and a strength. Be assured of my prayers."

Sister Joan Chittister, the voice of churchwomen around the world, wrote along similar lines, adding that my action was leading her to the difficult conclusion that "perhaps the only way change will come about is through our participation in the paschal mystery of Jesus." I found her insight a beacon for my increasingly addled thoughts. I still ponder her wisdom after all these years. Yes, Sister Joan, the paschal mystery is the way forward. Once again, you are right.

From House Arrest to Rome (1994–95)

Phil, Bruce, Lynn, and I were to be retried. And shrewd Judge Boyle set four dates—a trial for each of us. One by one, we came before judge and jury. The motion in limine remained in force, a muzzle. And at such disadvantage, each of us went under quickly.

Phil went to trial first, on April 11, 1994. "Phil, please don't call me as a witness," I begged him that morning in our cell. How I longed to be alone, to have a few hours to myself in peace and quiet—what a luxury. And here, for the first time in ages, was my chance.

Phil made no promises, and a few hours later, the marshals came for me with their shackles. On the witness stand, I raised my right hand and took an oath to tell the truth—the very thing the judge wished to suppress. I looked around; the courtroom was packed. Ramsey Clark sat next to Phil at the defense table. Phil asked me quietly, "What happened on December 7, 1993?"

In keeping with my oath, I said, "I saw Philip Berrigan and our friends take a stand for peace by trying to stand up for humanity, to stop this so-called willful destruction of property and human life.

1994-95   🔲   263

I saw Philip Berrigan unfurl a banner that read, 'Disarm and Live!' Our intent was to offer a symbol to the country of the way out of the madness of violence, to say, 'We need to disarm.' Our intent was to stop the killing, to offer a symbol of disarmament. We were trying to do something noble for society, for the world, in our own humble, human way."

"Objection, your honor!" said the prosecutor. And the judge ordered me to stop. Silenced again.

"Objection, your honor" became a brusque refrain to my poetics of truth. I would utter a sentence or two—or a paragraph or two, if I picked up the pace—and the gavel would fall and the judge would stop me. This wasn't a trial but a travesty. A verdict of guilty was the foregone conclusion.

The next day brought my trial, a shorter affair than Phil's. Joe Cosgrove guided me through it, and Bruce took the stand. My guilty verdict came down in thirty minutes.

Bruce's trial was still briefer—pronounced guilty in a mere six minutes. Had we known the race was on, we would have started a pool: whose guilt would be declared the quickest? Lynn changed the rules of the game; she marched into court and refused to open her mouth. The whole charade went on under her accusing silence—like Jesus before Pilate. She was pronounced guilty in minutes also. Reports came to Phil, Bruce, and me about her beautiful witness. It left us awestruck. In recent times, scarcely has there been a more courageous act against such a kangaroo court.

The prosecutor—African-American, Republican, sycophant of the war machine, presumably a proponent of the policies of Jesse Helms himself—was quite a character. During the cross-examination at Phil's trial, the prosecutor set fiery eyes on me, rose up from his seat and pointed a finger at me. "Who *dro-ove* the car?" he bellowed.

"Who drove you and Philip Berrigan to Seymour Johnson Air Force Base on December 7, 1993?"

Who else, he was hot to know, was in on the conspiracy? I suspect he held a few people under suspicion already—some of our friends sitting in the first row of the gallery.

I pondered a moment before offering my response: "I take responsibility for my own actions." The judge pounded his gavel and ordered the jury out. Then he turned to me and said sternly, "If you do not answer the question, you'll again be charged with contempt of court. You'll face several more years in prison. This is not an option. You have to answer the question, or you are breaking the law."

"Okay," I sighed. "I'll tell."

The jury shuffled back in, and the prosecutor resumed his histrionics. "Who dro-o-ove the car?"

A hush fell over the room and everyone leaned forward. I looked out at my friends in the peace movement, watching me with dismay in their eyes and probably thinking, Poor John; he's lost it. He's going to betray us all.

"Thank you," I said, "for pushing me to tell the truth. We've spoken a lot here about truth, and I want to speak it." I exhaled a big sigh, no stranger to melodramatics myself. "The truth is we were driven to the Seymour Johnson Air Force Base by the Holy Spirit!"

"What?!" the prosecutor cried. A gasp arose from the spectators; the judge pounded his gavel; the jury jumped in surprise.

"Who drove the automobile?" yelled the judge, taking over.

"The Holy Spirit," I repeated. "You think it's easy to drive to Seymour Johnson early in the morning and hammer on a nuclear weapon? It could only have been an act of God!"

"Are you going to tell us who drove the car?" he shouted.

"I'm telling you honestly." I smiled.

Again the jury was shuttled out, and the judge turned to me. "I order you. One last time. Divulge the driver's name."

"I insist," I returned in measured tones, "it was the Holy Spirit."

"Strike his testimony from the record," he ordered, "and handcuff him." Marshals hustled me back to the cell, much to my relief. At last, peace and quiet!

▣ ▣

Sentencing was scheduled for July. After two interminable months, Phil, Bruce, Lynn, and I were sent back to court to pay another visit to Judge Boyle, again one at a time. I arrived to a packed courtroom. Friends and relatives were on hand, along with the North Carolina media, which had widely reported our escapades and statements. I was allowed to make a final one before my sentencing:

> I've often wondered what I would have done if I had lived in Nazi Germany. Would I have been a good, law-abiding, obedient German citizen? Or would I have been a good, gospel-abiding Christian, obedient and faithful to the God of nonviolent love—and thus necessarily disobedient to the state's murderous policies? I hope I would have had the grace and the strength and the spiritual fortitude to walk into those German death camps and begin to take apart the gas chambers and cremation ovens, to literally and symbolically start dismantling those legal instruments of mass destruction. I suppose if I were not shot then and there, I would have been arrested, jailed, and quickly tried in court for breaking the law, perhaps for "willfully destroying government property."

I believe we're faced with a similar situation today. As I ponder the United States—the most violent nation in the history of the world; the inventor of the atomic bomb, the hydrogen bomb, and the F-15E; the nation that possesses a nuclear arsenal of unimaginable proportion—I conclude that what the Nazis tried to do to Jews and others, our country threatens to do and is preparing to do to the whole human race. All of us have a responsibility to do what we can to stop the killing, to dismantle our nuclear arsenal, to renounce war, as well as to promote peace and life for all.

And then I appealed to the judge to join us: "Let's not support or defend the F-15E or other weapons of mass destruction. Let's not support mass murder any longer, you and me. Let's not be instruments or puppets of the war-making nuclear establishment. Let's not be servants of death. Instead, let's be people of peace. Let's obey God's law of nonviolence. Let's be servants of life."

The judge let none of this pass unchallenged. He sang his praises of America and the troops. Then he passed sentence: I would be released the following month. Had I heard right? Next month? But once home at the K Street Jesuit Community, in D.C., I must stay put, for nine months of house arrest. I let out a sigh of relief. Phil would be released shortly after I was, but Bruce and Lynn would not fare as well. They each received a sentence of a year more in prison in West Virginia—Bruce in Morgantown and Lynn in Alderson. No rationale was offered, no rhyme or reason.

At midnight on July 22, 1994, the warden drove from his home to the jail to release me personally. He delivered me to my waiting parents and our friend Patrick O'Neill, then bubbling with small talk, delayed us a half hour next to the car. Finally, we extricated ourselves, and my parents dashed me to a hotel, where I dropped on the bed, like a sack of flour from the back of a truck.

My exhaustion, however, was flavored with exhilaration. Fragrances and colors and beauty and space—new freedom overwhelmed my senses. The first day of the rest of my life. Like that Ash Wednesday back at Duke, long ago, in a previous lifetime. Peace, joy, hope and resurrection all rolled into one.

回 回

I uttered the joke more than once: Nine months of house arrest in a Jesuit community is cruel and unusual punishment. But compared to jail, it was like a vacation. Finally, the peace and quiet I craved. I had long quiet days alone. I reconnected with family and friends, took longs walks on the Mall, and enjoyed the company of my Jesuit brothers.

But darkness dogged me. Early on, I would be sitting alone among my papers, reviewing those days in the dungeon, typing and sorting them to publish my journal, *Peace Behind Bars*, and a storm would descend, all fury and surprise, causing tears to flow. A bout of sobbing might last an hour—at my cluttered desk, in an empty house, for no discernible reason.

Monthly I paid a visit to my parole officer, who admitted me into his cubicle, flung questions of an officious sort, scribbled in a file, and, satisfied with my meek compliance, dismissed me. I did not have to wear an ankle bracelet, but the police were authorized to show up at my door at any time, day or night, to check on my whereabouts. They put in an appearance three times, once during the community dinner. Would you care to join us? I asked. They declined. "Just checking to see if you're here, Father John." The truth of the matter is that I wasn't always there. On three occasions, I flew out of town to give a lecture or a retreat, but nothing notorious or conspicuous.

Still, the first few months under house arrest proved stony, with nightmares, depression, and bouts of anxiety. After the long loneliness of jail and the deprivation of senses, life on the outside felt overwhelming. The loneliness continued now, in a different way. The war machine barreled on, our action against it dismissed as old news. My family had been wounded by my action and continued to be baffled. My church, too, seemed unable to make heads or tails of a lawbreaking, gospel-abiding priest. It was impossible to explain to anyone how bad jail had been, and no one really wanted to know.

During those months, as I studied the movements for social change—from the abolitionists, the suffragists, and the labor movement, to the civil rights and anti-war movements—I concluded that the arrival of dawn comes at a high price. It requires good people to break bad laws, to risk their lives, and, afterward, to stand there and accept the consequences. It has been the way of justice and peace since the foundation of the world—that mysterious paschal mystery, the way of the cross, the way of Jesus, which eventually leads to the new life of resurrection.

In 1995, with my house arrest about to expire, I planned a trip to Italy for the fiftieth anniversary of Pax Christi International. A gala and conference would take place in Assisi, the birthplace of St. Francis. Might I go? I petitioned my parole officer. He acceded, on one condition: I must place myself in the custody of Bishop Walter Sullivan. Evidently, the bishop could serve as the state's surrogate.

In the spring of 1995, with my custodian Walter Sullivan, I boarded the plane for Italy. I lugged along a pile of biographies of St. Francis in case I got bored. But I never had the chance. Assisi was another world—a far remove from the rigors of jail, the scorched terrain of El Salvador, and the shabbiness of inner-city Washington. Assisi portended heaven—picturesque and spacious, with red tile roofs, cobblestone streets, ancient stone arches, and in the distance, the vast plains and timeless mountains. The beauty tempted me to skip the lectures and workshops and panel discussions and head out into the fields, a true Franciscan at last. I gave in and rambled through the countryside, explored the hills, and poked about in all the churches. I spent an entire afternoon sitting in the fields below Assisi, gazing up at the town and imbibing Francis's spirit of peace. I breathed it in and out like a man deprived for years. Gradually, almost imperceptibly, the healing began. As I searched his churches, fields, and caves, I felt consoled. I was not alone or crazy but part of a tradition. I was learning from St. Francis the wisdom of peace, the way of peace, and the life of peace. For days, I pondered his conversion from the brutality of the Crusades to the nonviolence of Christ, from the lure of his father's wealth to the freedom of Lady Poverty.

Francis's determination to fulfill the Sermon on the Mount and love his enemies led him to march into the camp of the hated sultan of Egypt and, risking everything, offer his hand in friendship. At least the sultan listened respectfully and allowed Francis to return across battle lines. But when Francis made his way back over the line into the murderous Catholic crusaders, he barely escaped their wrath over his having tried to broker peace through such a meeting with the enemy.

Finally, his own friars rejected him; home and institutions were foremost in their desires. He resigned and retreated to La Verna and died before his time. In all this, he demonstrated profound suffering love and experienced the mystical depths of peace.

I could learn a lot from this saint. By now, I knew a thing or two about being rejected; it's a core experience for any disciple of the rejected Jesus. But Francis's response marked him for greatness. He set aside revenge and resentment. He offered instead forgiveness, love, and compassion. I spent hours in San Damiano, the chapel where he heard the crucifix speak, directing him to rebuild his church, and in the Portiuncula, the little stone chapel he rebuilt by hand. Each morning, I descended to the basement of Basilica San Francesco to pray at his tomb.

Before leaving Italy, I joined a Pax Christi delegation for an audience with Pope John Paul II. Our time with him would be brief; we were told he could spare us only twenty minutes. I regarded him with equal measures of respect and misgiving. His passion for people moved me, and his good social teachings inspired me. Yet I looked askance at his subordination of women, his appointments of conservative bishops and cardinals, and, in particular, his misunderstanding of the Central American church, especially the holy martyr Romero. In a storm of ambivalence, I waited with the others.

Shortly, we were admitted. We clambered flights of stairs to a chamber of the pope's private quarters with ornate columns, a lofty gilded ceiling, and a parquet floor. An array of chairs filled the room, all facing his majestic gold throne. Presently, he entered, hunched, shuffling, and trembling slightly but in command of his faculties. He eased himself into the chair and offered a warm and lengthy speech of welcome.

His words surprised us all. He thanked us for our works of peace and declared Pax Christi "precious" to the universal church. He seemed genuinely pleased to be among us. I fleetingly regretted that all Catholics couldn't be on hand to hear this. Maybe if they could hear what we were hearing, they would no longer dismiss Pax Christi but would join the campaign to abolish war in the name of Christ.

Pope John Paul II grew more animated, and as our time expired he sought out his courtiers. Cancel my afternoon plans, he ordered.

Then he heaved himself to his feet and moved into our group, taking time to meet each one of us.

I lingered at the rear of the crowd, but the pope, with a squint of his eyes, saw me—I was obviously a cleric, the only one in the audience besides Bishop Sullivan wearing the uniform. Still, I made no move, so he set out toward me. Before long, he stood before me, extended a hand, and asked my name. Prepared for such an emergency, I produced a copy of my new book, *The God of Peace*, and placed it in his palm. A gift with my compliments, I said.

"Ah, peace!" he shouted out to everyone around him in that Polish accent thick as gravy. "Peace! The God of peace! Yes, John Dear!" It seemed that my name had preceded me. His wizened face lit up; perhaps the idea of a young priest working for peace pleased him. A smile escaped my lips. The pope had won me over.

The next morning, I arrived at the Jesuit curia to be met graciously by Father Peter-Hans Kolvenbach, superior general of the Society of Jesus. The top Jesuit, he couldn't have been sweeter. How was it in jail? he asked, true concern glowing in his eyes. And how is Daniel Berrigan? He laughed heartily when I explained how glad my Jesuit community was to have me under house arrest, because it meant I finally would do my chores and clean out the basement.

Then his smile faded. He thanked me for enduring the malice, for bearing up under the slights and scorn of those who did not understand the mission for justice and peace. My breath caught short. Here was a benediction that salved the bruised places of my heart. "Don't stop," he added. "Don't be discouraged. You're doing just what St. Ignatius wants—and I'll always be grateful." My embattled heart healed on the instant. With a few words, he had rendered my sufferings tolerable. His blessing heartened me to face a lifetime of ordeals.

That same day, Mother Teresa was in town, visiting the head-quarters of the Missionaries of Charity to preside at vow day for an assembly of novices. My friend Sister Roni Daniels, Mother Teresa's personal nurse, arranged an introduction. "This is the Jesuit you've spoken to so many times about the death penalty," Sister Roni said to her.

Mother Teresa was a diminutive woman, her back bowed down. She looked up at me, then reached up and, like an Italian grand-mother, gave my cheeks a slap. Then she pulled my face low. Her eyes met mine, her smile warm as the Assisi sunshine. She gazed at me for a long while, not saying a word. In her look I sensed an extraordinary unconditional love.

She turned me loose at length and, in a sudden change of mood, crossed her arms over her chest and said with a frown, "And what did I tell those governors to do?"

I offered a halting answer: "You told them . . . to do what Jesus would do."

"And what did they do for your friend in Georgia?"

"They granted him clemency."

Then she tossed up her arms, slapped her hands together, shook them back and forth and exclaimed, "Isn't it wonderful?"—an ancient woman engaging as best she could in a merry jig. Then she took my hands and said she would pray for me for the rest of her life. And with a glorious smile, she said, "Thank you."

Trouble at the Smithsonian (1994–95)

My involvement with the Enola Gay—the plane used to drop the bomb on Hiroshima—began innocently enough. In the fall of 1994, I read in the *Washington Post* about the upcoming Enola Gay exhibit at the Smithsonian, so I walked over to the National Mall, entered the National Air and Space Museum, introduced myself, and asked if I could meet the curator of the exhibit. I was shown to the office of Tom Crouch, a widely respected aviation historian. I found him immensely likeable. He sat amid stacks of papers like a true academic.

I offered a brief overview of my credentials in the peace movement and then lobbed a series of questions at him: What is the purpose of the exhibit? Why spend resources on a plane that killed so many and gave birth to the nuclear arms race? Would the exhibit imply that vaporizing over a hundred thousand human beings was somehow valorous or efficacious? Or would it urge that such a horror must never happen again? And had he read the historical research concluding that the Japanese were on the verge of surrender before the bomb was dropped? According to these theories, the United States had dropped the bomb and incinerated thousands of people to gain the upper hand in the brewing cold war, to show the Soviets who was more powerful.

Crouch glanced about nervously as I talked. He issued his replies in hoarse whispers, arching forward in his chair. "You have no idea of the forces within the government opposing this exhibit, not in your wildest dreams," he said, then surveyed the room. "I've spent the better part of my life working on it—spent years in Hiroshima, met with the Japanese government and many Hibakasha, the atomic survivors."

He looked around again and went on. "Americans have never dealt with Hiroshima. We've never admitted what we did there. I want this exhibit to change all that, to get the nation to take a long, hard look at Hiroshima. However," he continued, his tone hushed, "this exhibit could bring down the entire Smithsonian. The Pentagon and the military are watching everything we do. We are under enormous pressure. Jobs are at stake. The Smithsonian is at stake!"

I leaned forward, keeping my own voice low. "Would you be willing to meet with leaders of the peace movement at least, to hear our views?" Yes, he said. "And could I have a look at the exhibit's script?" I asked. Yes again. Script in hand, I emerged on the Mall. Heading home at a brisk pace, I tossed glances over my shoulder.

The script was all that I had feared. The story crowed about the making of the plane, about Los Alamos's wizardry in manufacturing the bomb. It portrayed in the breathless prose of Hollywood the tense flight to Japan, presenting the crew members as dashing and brave.

But it made not one mention of the terrors of the atomic blasts—of children's flesh consumed, of untold numbers turned to smoke. The Smithsonian had elevated the war myth—namely, that the fortunes of war had tied U.S. hands. The bombing was necessary "to save the lives of thousands of Americans." It followed naturally that the bombing was right, patriotic, even moral, that killing people saved people.

A few weeks later, about twenty of us from the peace movement, including Bishop Thomas Gumbleton, Elizabeth McAlister, and Daniel Ellsberg, had a formal visit with Martin Harwit, director of the Air and Space Museum, in its main committee chambers. I spoke of the Holocaust Museum, less than a mile down the Mall. It takes a stand, I said, and states in no uncertain terms that gas chambers and cremation ovens are wrong, unjust, and immoral. The Smithsonian should take a similar stand on the Enola Gay. Its exhibit should lead people to the conclusion that the bombings of Hiroshima and Nagasaki were wrong, unnecessary, unjust, and immoral—two of the gravest mistakes in history. And if those bombings were unjust and immoral, then the United States should dismantle its nuclear weapons and ensure that the likes of Hiroshima and Nagasaki never happen again. Please, we urged, rewrite the script. Present a true account of history so that history will not be repeated.

Harwit sat impatiently throughout this preamble. After a pause, he nearly exploded. "This is exactly what we've been trying to do! But we've been under enormous pressure from the Pentagon, the Air Force Association, the American Legion, even Congress. Where have you been? Why didn't you show up earlier? Why haven't you gone to the media and supported us?" His pointed remarks surprised me. Here was a decent man who had been battered by the powers that be, academic freedom all but snatched from his hands.

Of course he was right. Peace groups should have encouraged the Smithsonian's pursuit of truth much earlier. If they had, Tom Crouch's original vision might have been realized, and the nation might have taken its first forbidden look at the horrors of the bomb and begun the long turn toward repentance, conversion, and disarmament.

When the meeting ended, the twenty of us determined to do what we could. The following week, we held a press conference at the National Press Club featuring leading historians—including Kai Bird, Robert Jay Lifton, and Barton Bernstein, chair of the History Department at Stanford—who countered the Pentagon's version of events.

But the Pentagon snooped out the conference and quickly unleashed the full force of its PR staff—some seventy-five employees whose sole task was to compel the media to support war. They in turn mobilized the Air Force Association and the American Legion. And thus the Smithsonian, who dared admit a few doubts about our past, fell under heated denunciations from all quarters.

Suddenly the exhibit was news everywhere, thanks to an avalanche of Pentagon-issued press releases. The media ate them up, and the resulting stories bore the Pentagonal marks, such phrases as poor history, revisionist, misguided, liberal views, and ax to grind. Leaving nothing to chance, the Air Force Association dispatched its lobbyists to Congress, which in turn threatened to pull the museum's funding should it add one drop of "revisionist history" to the exhibit. The mouthpiece of Congress, Rush Limbaugh, even composed a few choice words for yours truly.

The debate raged for nearly a year, the hapless Smithsonian holding its own longer than anyone thought possible. But the outcome was all but assured. The Pentagon prevailed. The Enola Gay went on display with but one line framed to explain: "The bomber that saved American lives." Martin Harwit was forced to resign as director of the Smithsonian Air and Space Museum.

This turn of events set me thinking. Why not commemorate the horrid blast on our own terms? We could do so through vigils and acts of civil disobedience—at the White House, the Congress, the

Pentagon—and prayer services featuring prominent speakers such as Jim Wallis, Philip Berrigan, Lisa Goode, Howard Zinn, Jim and Shelley Douglass, Martin Sheen, bishops Thomas Gumbleton and Walter Sullivan.

I convened a cadre of friends, and together we organized. "Remembering the Pain, Repenting the Sin, Reclaiming the Future" was our theme. Every day for three weeks, we held a peace vigil and undertook an action of civil disobedience and offered a prayer service with a speaker; each day's events were organized by a different delegation from across the country. On the fiftieth anniversary of the bombing, August 6, 1995, we would hold a service at the Washington National Cathedral.

The speakers were brilliant, the prayers were inspirational, and scores were jailed in the tradition of Dr. King for saying no to nuclear weapons. On August 6, more than two thousand people streamed into the cathedral. Those of us speaking gathered in the sanctuary, along with various Episcopal bishops and canons. The organ sounded, and our group began its processional toward the altar. I had walked only a few steps when the dean of the cathedral took hold of my sleeve and whispered in my ear that the head of the Episcopal Church had called just a few days earlier and forbidden us, while in her jurisdiction, to urge nuclear disarmament. I froze and stared. Behind this ban was, as there so often is, a wealthy donor. If we took a stand in the cathedral, he would withdraw his pledge of millions.

The procession was under way, and in moments I would stand before a sea of supporters. My mind raced. Soon the speakers were in place, and the dean welcomed the assembly. He then launched into a litany of historic events that had taken place on the hallowed premises—such as when Martin Luther King Jr., Desmond Tutu, Nelson Mandela, and the Dalai Lama had each graced the pulpit.

Unfortunately, he continued, the National Cathedral and the Episcopal Church "take no stand on nuclear weapons or on nuclear disarmament." Jaws dropped. Then he introduced me.

I rose to face the dispirited crowd. My assignment had been to outline the liturgy and to urge everyone to attend our witness and civil disobedience the following morning at the Pentagon—a gesture concerning the little matter, now quite stifled, of nuclear disarmament.

This would have been the moment, had I the presence of mind, to say that it is precisely the vocation of the church in times such as these to uphold the gospel vision of nonviolence and peace, to pursue nuclear disarmament and announce a new world, one without war or nuclear weapons. But I stood before the microphone, mumbled a brief explanation of the meeting to follow, and mentioned the location of our meeting the next morning at the Pentagon, the whys and wherefores left to fertile imaginations. Defeated, I took my seat.

Daniel Berrigan, the keynote speaker, had been told by the cathedral staff to read a lengthy and tame quote and return to his seat. He approached the podium after I left it and took a deep breath. I sat behind him and noticed his hands shaking.

"Imagine," he began. "Imagine Dr. King standing in this pulpit taking no stand on racism. Imagine Archbishop Tutu standing in this pulpit taking no stand on apartheid. Imagine—"

He got little further before the place erupted. Two thousand people jumped to their feet and issued thunderous applause. Even the law-abiding dean and the cathedral canons eventually stood and joined in. Yes, a stand would be taken after all, thanks to Daniel Berrigan.

The next morning, I joined the crowds in vigil at the Pentagon. Dan, Elizabeth McAlister, and fifty-six others blocked the building's doorways. Days later, on the anniversary of the Nagasaki bombing, we concluded our three-week campaign. A hundred of us gathered in a circle in front of the Pentagon on the riverside lawn, bowed our heads, and prayed for nuclear disarmament—a modest but noble effort.

The *Washington Post* reported our actions, our gatherings, and the service at the cathedral. In the end, the cathedral paid a high price for our stand. Its benefactor made good on his threat and withdrew his pledge of two million dollars.

回 33 回

In Richmond,
at the Sacred
Heart Center
(1995–96)

My house arrest over and the basement cleaned, I needed to be put to some good use. My new provincial asked what I had in mind. I want to work among the poor, I said. What positions are open? He had just the place—an extraordinary community center in Richmond, Virginia, that serves hundreds of African-American women and children. A young Jesuit had founded the center in 1990. He had arrived one day at an abandoned elementary school owned by the Catholic Diocese of Richmond on the south side of town, a place of great poverty and deprivation, with a grant of $10,000 in his pocket. He began painting the front door and attracted the neighbors' attention; he asked them to join in, and in months they had the massive building renovated and open for business under the banner of the Sacred Heart Center. He had sparked the imagination not only of the neighborhood but also of Richmond's politicians, corporate leaders, churches, and social groups, such as the Junior League, which donated hundreds of thousands of dollars to the effort.

Before long, I was headed to Richmond to serve as the center's new executive director. Richmond embodies the U.S. version of apartheid. The James River divides the former capital of the Confederacy straight down class and race lines, with wealth to the north and privation to the south. The Sacred Heart Center tries to bridge the two worlds.

On the south side, financial stability was beyond reach, education a forbidden mystery, and achievement a mere dream. Most people were constantly going under in the struggle for bare survival. My first day there, I attended the funeral of Melvin, a thirty-five-year-old father of six who had died instantly of a heart attack. The center was in the midst of helping him and his wife, Nita, rebuild their lives. The whole family had benefited from what the center had to offer— sports, day care, after-school programs, parenting classes. Nita wailed at Melvin's grave. She had six hurting children—Lateshia, Rodney, DeAngelo, DeAndre, Tevon, and Melina—and not a penny to her name. I couldn't imagine the burdens she bore.

With her husband's death, Nita fell headlong into the ranks of single-parent households, which made up 65 percent of the neighborhood. Her family had always lived on the edge, but now she faced an overwhelming disadvantage in the struggle to keep her children properly fed. To earn enough to even meet the poverty level would have been a boon. Sixty percent of the households in the community scrabbled for far less than that.

This was Nita's desolate world, made all the worse now that she was alone: acres of misery and hopelessness, junk cars, broken pavement, gritty streets, idle days, with violence and aggression always close to the surface. At the time, Richmond had one of the highest crime rates in the country, and most of the brutality and killings occurred within ten blocks of the Sacred Heart Center. And many from our bleak neighborhood ended up on the state's death row.

The center had risen out of this wretchedness. The charismatic young director before me had raised money, made the place presentable, hired a staff from among the neighborhood women, and started a variety of programs. I inherited it all and, in time, built it up even more, with a licensed day-care center and after-school and summer programs for hundreds of children; a family literacy program that offered academic training and parenting classes for neighborhood women; an adolescent program for twenty-five teenagers; kindergarten, first- and second-grade classes; a neighborhood parents association; basketball and aerobics programs; Boy Scouts and Girl Scouts programs; emergency fuel and food assistance; an evening sports program for men; parents' support groups; and other services. The center's mission, cast in bronze, was "to be a sign of hope."

In terms of the physical building, a few odds and ends remained. I expanded the school and put in a beautiful playground, made the old building handicapped accessible, and turned the prehistoric kitchen into a state-of-the-art galley. Eventually, it served more than a hundred well-balanced meals per day.

On Thanksgiving Day 1995, we staff, along with other volunteers, served turkey with all the fixings to the entire neighborhood. The children, dressed as pilgrims, put on a pageant and made us all smile. These distressed boys and girls and their embattled families had survived drug addiction, violence, murder, starvation, and rock-bottom despair. For an afternoon, they were able to experience laughter, feasting, and real thanksgiving.

A few weeks later, a battalion of volunteers roamed the grim streets bearing turkeys and gifts for Christmas. The neighborhood came alive with delight. A Christmas pageant followed, replete with carols and processions. The first graders amazed us with a performance of a ballet to the Nutcracker Suite. And Kendrick, a severely disabled boy with a personality beyond his years, recited Luke's Nativity story with vim and drama. Everyone in the audience was moved to tears, God's preferential love for the poor in plain view.

▣ ▣

Most mornings, I arrived at the center at six to outline the day, but soon I found myself saying, "So much for the best-laid plans of mice and Jesuits." The only certainty was a lurking catastrophe ready to disrupt the schedule. The toilet would overflow or the power go out, the bus break down, a car get set on fire.

My charges looked upon me as chief problem solver, although I was theologically trained and therefore feckless in most practical matters. It fell to me to dirty my hands and resolve all thorny issues, whether lofty or menial. One day I'd be running a board meeting, another day wooing some banker or business owner over lunch, hot for a $25,000 gift. Our $2 million budget kept me on the move. In between, I responded to the cries: "Father John, we can't start the bus . . . can't find the forms . . . can't turn on the lights." And the one sure to make me blanch: "Father John, the boy's toilet is backed up again."

The hot water heater failed, exploding in a hiss of steam, turning the basement into a sauna. On another day came the cry: "Father John, there's a bird down there." And not just any bird, but a hawk, with a wingspan half as big as mine. Addressing that situation required a whole afternoon. Later, I couldn't help but think how fitting it was: me facing off with a hawk, a symbol of war-making.

On top of everything, I found myself the ex officio principal and president of a grade school. Allegedly, I was in charge. But the towering figure behind the school was Mrs. Walker, the first-grade teacher.

Part Oprah, part Maya Angelou, part Tina Turner, she turned out each day in taste and style, ever ready for a fashion show, arriving for work in a classy gold Mercedes. A woman of high and imposing standards, of stern eye and firm convictions, she served as advocate, judge, teacher, and shaper of young minds, a welcome presence and impressive spirit among us.

The students' good manners didn't satisfy Mrs. Walker. She put them in sharp uniforms, compliments of the Junior League, and led them each morning through their mantra: "We are scholars." You are the smartest kids in the nation, she insisted, and they began to act as if they were.

Not only that, Mrs. Walker didn't suffer fools gladly. Nonsense withered in her presence. At every disruption there would be hell to pay. Serious misbehavior would provoke her stentorian cry: "Father John!" It carried to distant corners of the immense building and invariably made me, and others, jump. I would come running to the scene, the idea being that my elevated ecclesiastical self would over-awe the diminutive miscreant. But one holler out of Mrs. Walker was more effective, and there was no telling who was more awestruck— the student or me.

The place was a major enterprise, and growing. It exuded warmth and love on a scale I've experienced nowhere else in the United States. I came to believe that its name was well chosen. But we needed funds to keep the free programs running, to keep the school doors open, and, most critically, to sustain dozens of families on the brink of star-vation. It would require largesse on a grand scale. We came to the inevitable conclusion: Our survival depended on our wealthy white neighbors across the river.

We sent out a regular newsletter, along with thousands of appeals every few months. We applied for countless foundation grants. Nearly every weekend I presided at a Mass in some Virginia church, where I introduced the center, shared stories, tugged heartstrings, took up a special collection, and returned with enough donations to see us through a few more weeks.

I approached local businesspeople, too, hat in hand, and pressed them for donations—doubling my request on occasion from $10,000 to $20,000, and getting it. But the constant scramble for money wore me down. My sleep soon became a luxury the center couldn't afford. I had scarcely a need to make my bed. I unburdened my woes on my buoyant friend Martin Sheen, who gallantly came through with a proffer of help. How about a celebrity basketball exhibition? A while later, players from all over Virginia gathered and put on a show of athletic prowess, with Martin acting as jester and charmer and master of ceremonies. The Spring Family Picnic, as we dubbed it, drew four hundred people.

Jackson Browne came to the rescue, too. He would perform with local rock star Bruce Hornsby at Richmond's Landmark Theater. I planned the concert for months, stumping around the state and alerting the media, arranging the site, taking care of hotel arrangements, providing a dinner before the concert, and handling the security and cleanup. It seems I was destined for showbiz after all.

The legendary theater, we soon learned, had sold out, and on Friday night, some forty-five hundred people arrived. The two artists put on a spectacular four-and-a-half-hour show. Afterward, Jackson presented the center with nearly $100,000 from the receipts. As if this enormous gift weren't enough, he had also put the center in a favorable light. Everyone in Richmond knew about us now.

Peace in
Northern Ireland
(1997–98)

In the autumn of 1997, I was to begin tertianship, a word found only in Jesuit dictionaries. St. Ignatius required newly ordained Jesuits to be removed to some peaceful corner of the world to undertake the Spiritual Exercises again and be renewed. I would be going to Belfast, Northern Ireland.

I set out a month early and made a wide sweep of Europe—Paris, Barcelona, and Assisi, and a solemn stopover at Auschwitz. On the appointed day, October 1, 1997, I arrived at the Jesuit house in Belfast. Six tertian priests—four from the States and two from Ireland—and our two directors, Father Senan Timoney, a gentle Irishman, and Father Ron Darwen, a witty Brit who had spent years in inner-city parishes and came to Belfast from Soweto, South Africa, gathered in the community living room and got acquainted. Father Ron outlined the year ahead—classes three days a week and pastoral work the rest of the time. Come January, we would embark on the month-long Spiritual Exercises.

We would live in small groups scattered across the country. Off I went to Derry, the town famous for the Bloody Sunday massacre, on the northern border of Ireland, near County Donegal. My fellow tertians Terry Howard, a high school teacher from Galway, and Leo Leise, a missionary in Paraguay, and I took up residence on Barry Street, a narrow road of skinny brick row houses not far from the River Foyle and the ancient wall surrounding the city. We quickly befriended our neighbors, most of whom had lived in Derry all their lives and suffered under the British.

Each weekend, Terry and I set off to explore the glorious coastline. We first drove west, along the Donegal coast, where we discovered mountaintop shrines to our Lady. We walked beaches as spectacular as any the Caribbean has to offer and enjoyed pints in tucked-away pubs. One numinous day as we drove along the Giants Causeway, fifteen vivid rainbows appeared one after another before our unbelieving eyes. They arched in the sky, end to end, a veritable mountain range of rainbows. By year's end, we had visited every centimeter of coastline from Dublin north to Belfast, and westward as far as Galway. The landscape appeared not only magical but mystical.

But by no means does Northern Ireland qualify as all magic and mysticism. It's also a land of pain and enduring crisis. Since the Troubles began in the late 1960s, more than three thousand have died in the violence. The British have imposed dominion since the 1920s, and Unionists and many Protestants still proclaim allegiance to Britain and derive their economic and political advantage from that fidelity. Nationalists and many Catholics, on the other hand, demand an end to repression, discrimination, and the notorious "emergency laws" and the withdrawal of the British military presence. Some Nationalists want reunification with the Republic of Ireland; all want equality, human rights, and power sharing as a means to build trust between divided communities.

Shortly before my arrival, the Irish Republican Army announced a cease-fire. The eye of the storm seemed to have settled over the place. For the first time, sustained peace talks proceeded, with the British, Irish, and U.S. governments lending support.

Thanks to the cease-fire, I didn't witness the ominous barricades that once lined the streets of Belfast. Still, the atmosphere hummed with menace. Twenty people had been killed in the few months before my arrival, and the memories of past violence remained fresh. The infamous Royal Ulster Constabulary's Land Rovers patrolled the streets. British army barracks, a dark presence, stood every few miles—one around the corner from our house in Derry—with machine guns sticking out of their towers. Still a frail hope lingered on the overcharged air.

Many fractures of that brittle peace, that fragile hope, occurred during my stay. Mayhem broke out in Derry one fevered weekend that December, cars and stores going up in flames in a matter of minutes. This was small potatoes by Northern Ireland standards—a marginal eruption, troubles with a little t. When I talked about it with our neighbors, two elderly sisters, they just shrugged. If the riots and fires were still going after two weeks, then they might grow concerned.

The Nationalists called for the disbanding of the Royal Ulster Constabulary (RUC), the British police force; the demilitarization of the country; a new and fair judicial system; equal housing and job opportunities for Catholics; and the release of all political prisoners. Complicating matters, fringe paramilitary groups on both sides wanted nothing to do with peace talks. Ask an average person why, and the response was a shrug and slight shake of the head. They're inured to violence and war, the people said. They know nothing else.

Indeed. Terror hardens into a way of life. Each generation learns its own peculiar method of participating in the bigotry, oppression, poverty, and violence: how to mix a Molotov cocktail, how to punish your own people by shooting off their kneecaps, how to raise money for murder under the myth of revolution, how to hide mounds of weapons, how to dispose of the bodies. I heard people dispassionately explain such behavior as if it were the noble thing to do.

People rarely mentioned nonviolence, and those who dared uphold a vision of real peace were scoffed at and dismissed.

Belfast, the capital, was particularly wounded and quite literally divided. Walls had been erected decades before, intended to "keep peace" by dividing the city, with the Catholics on one side and the Protestants on the other. Should Catholics and Protestants ever find themselves together on one side, the walls prevailed in spirit, and they took to opposite sides of the street.

This way of life is baffling and impenetrable to the outsider. It has grown out of centuries of hatred and bitterness, anger and resentment, long memories residing in the genes. Few can let go of the past; people see bloodstains everywhere and remember.

Despite this abiding hatred, human exchanges between sides carry on, albeit with great risk. During my time there, two young men were gunned down in a pub in the village of Poyntzpass. The two— Damien Trainor, a Catholic, and Phillip Allen, a Protestant—were lifelong friends. They died over a pint as they planned Phillip's upcoming wedding. The squandering of their youth shocked the nation and hustled slack and dilatory politicians back to the bargaining table.

回 回

By and large, our neighbors in Derry received us graciously. Not so the bishops of Derry and Northern Ireland. They cared little for Jesuits and forbade us to work in the parishes or preside at Mass. They had allowed Jesuits to return to Northern Ireland only in the late 1980s, on the condition that we keep a low profile and never speak of the Troubles.

Nevertheless, I was drawn to join the work at a human rights center in Belfast, along with two priests, Des Wilson and Joe McVeigh, who had given their lives to serving the beleaguered Catholics of the Falls Road (the focal point for the Troubles). I was asked to put together a monthly journal, which I named the *Irish Witness* and filled with articles and statistics about outrages against Catholics and the road to peace through active nonviolence.

I wrote about Pat Finucane, the Catholic lawyer who was assassinated in Belfast by a loyalist paramilitary group for defending Republican prisoners. I listed acts of repression and harassment by British soldiers and the RUC. I outlined the reasons for reunification. I discussed the human rights violations by the British government and defined the biblical reasons for justice.

The first issue took aim at the Catholic Church itself. I urged the church to speak up for human rights for Catholics: "The Irish Catholic Bishops Conference must ask itself now at this important moment in our history if it has spoken out as clearly and as loudly as it should about the violation of the rights of Irish nationalists and Catholics living within the northern state, not just over the past thirty years, but for all the years of the state's existence. The Irish Bishops Conference has failed to speak out. Is it any wonder that so many [people] are disillusioned with the leadership of the Catholic Church?"

When that first issue came out in November, my priest friends and I celebrated at a nearby pub with fish-and-chips and a pint or two. By the next day, the weather had changed. The *Irish Times* got wind of the publication and put together a lengthy story, widely read. Featured prominently my choice words against the bishops—words all the more scandalous because they had come from a priest. And the priest named for orchestrating the attack, for stirring up trouble for the poor Irish church, was that notorious Jesuit Father John Dear.

This did not sit well with a number of concerned Catholics. I wasn't present at the meeting that convened between the bishop and my Jesuit superiors, but evidently parishioners in Down & Connor had been calling the bishop's office. The bishop in turn required that my superiors reign me in. I was told to cease and desist, and my name was never again to appear in the newsletter—or, for that matter, in the Irish media.

The following week, I was back at Falls Road working on the next issue. I gathered articles denouncing crimes against Catholics and the silence of the bishops. I composed essays on the vision of nonviolence. And in all this I tendered the bishop my full obedience, writing under a pseudonym, Sean Achara, my name in Gaelic. On the masthead, under the title of editor, I listed Daniel Berrigan. Under this arrangement, I published the next eleven issues without trouble.

Dan Berrigan was the first to connect me with Father Des and Father Joe. My first day at the center, Father Joe introduced me to Gerry Adams, president of the nationalist political party Sinn Féin ("We Ourselves"), whom many considered the head of the Irish Republican Army. He bore an air of charm, intelligence, and wit that I've rarely encountered, and he seemed genuinely interested in a peaceable future.

I later crossed paths with a great hero of nonviolence, John Hume, leader of the Social Democratic and Labour Party. We first met at a

restaurant in Fanad Head, on the Donegal peninsula. He had helped
form the Northern Ireland Civil Rights Association and had helped
develop their campaign of 1968, in which Nationalists and Catholics
marched from Belfast to Derry for civil rights, following the nonviolent example of Martin Luther King Jr. But Unionists lurking in
alleys and in the countryside laid siege to the marchers, swinging their
clubs and counting on the RUC to look the other way. They also
mocked the marchers in the media. Over time, veterans of the march
grew angry and bitter and decided to fight back. In 1969, when violent
conflict broke out in Derry and Belfast, nationalist politicians invited
the British army into Northern Ireland to protect the Catholic community. Eventually, the British army became part of the problem as
the IRA and loyalist paramilitary organizations waged battle against
each other, plunging the nation into a downward spiral of death and
destruction. Violence and counterviolence brought the two sides to
the brink of civil war.

But since the late 1980s, John Hume had been secretly meeting
with both sides to negotiate a future of peace. At one point, he told
me, he was poisoned and nearly died. After the success of the Good
Friday Agreement, the 1998 peace accord that ended the Troubles, he
invited me to his house along the ocean in Greencastle. I remember
in particular his insistence that I befriend the media: if you persist, he
suggested, you can teach them the vision of peace and reach a wider
audience. The following year, he won the 1988 Nobel Peace Prize.

Inspired by such meetings and eager to hear more of the land's
travails, I visited family members of the victims of Bloody Sunday,
January 30, 1972, when streams of families with their children
marched through Derry for civil rights, holding banners and chanting
for peace. The British Parachute Regiment, a unit of the British army,
stood above the group, high atop the old city wall, and on orders,

opened fire. Twenty-eight protesters took bullets. Fourteen of them died, six of them under the age of seventeen.

As I made my rounds through Derry, it became apparent that the pain still gnawed after twenty-five years. People arched forward in their chairs as they spoke, voices quavering and eyes filling with tears. They had been doubly wounded, by state and Church. The state had put their loved ones in their graves, while many priests and bishops looked the other way, not wanting to get involved, sometimes even denouncing the innocent dead as if they deserved what they got.

Years after the fact, the sense of betrayal had not dimmed. How could it be, they asked me, that the church abandoned us? I sat before them, grief-stricken. From their indication, I was apparently the first cleric ever to lend them a sympathetic ear. The best I could do was offer an apology, tardy condolences, and a blessing for healing and peace. I spoke of my own work for peace, my respect for their relatives, and my hope in the nonviolence of Christ, who understood well their pain. They welcomed these words.

On another day, a high school friend I hadn't laid eyes on in twenty years appeared out of the blue. I had lunch with him and his two Derry friends, who didn't seem eager to open up much at first. But as my buddy and I talked and relaxed, they decided I could be trusted and finally revealed their identities. One was a member of the Irish Republican Army, the other a fifteen-year veteran of prison— five of those years spent "on the blanket."

The "blanket protest" was staged by IRA prisoners locked down at Long Kesh, near Belfast. They considered themselves political prisoners, but in 1976 the British authorities cracked down on paramilitary inmates, denying their status as prisoners of war and categorizing them as common criminals. As such, the authorities said, they must hereafter don prison uniforms and submit to perform prison work. The prisoners refused. Some went about clothed only in prison blankets.

The British government refused to budge. In short order, repressive measures came down hard. The worst one: anyone refusing to wear the uniform would be refused toilet privileges. The prisoners responded by turning the "blanket protest" into the "dirty protest." They smeared their cells with urine and feces and refused to wash or to cut their hair, for years. Many stopped eating. My new acquaintance leaned forward and confided that his cellmate in the notorious H-Blocks had been Bobby Sands, who died in prison in 1981 from starvation, at age twenty-seven.

Just before he died, Sands was asked if there was anything he wanted. He replied, "A visit from Father Daniel Berrigan." Dan was summoned, but the British refused to allow him in. While Bobby died, Dan kept vigil outside the prison, speaking of peace and ministering to the families of prisoners.

On another occasion, a friend asked me to visit Enniskillen, where the IRA had blown up an old church building some nine years earlier. The army had loaded it with explosives and waited for an opportune moment. They set off the blast at the height of the annual parade on Remembrance Day 1987. Eleven people died, including one Marie Wilson. Her father, Gordon Wilson, suffered injuries. Then he did the unthinkable: he publicly forgave his daughter's murderers. He pleaded with loyalists not to take revenge.

In an instant, his name rose to prominence, but of an ambivalent sort. In hawkish quarters, his remarks elicited denunciations. In others, they provoked genuine reflection on the meaning of forgiveness. He toured Europe for years advocating peace, until his death, in 1995.

After touring the town, I was invited to tea with Marie's mother and Gordon's widow, Joan. My friend and I arrived at her house and spent an hour or so talking of Gordon's remarkable career, his extraordinary gesture, and their beautiful daughter. Then I posed the million-dollar question: In this land, of all places, plagued as it was by resentment, how had they found the wherewithal to forgive?

She told me that every night since the day they were married, decades earlier, she and Gordon had knelt down before going to bed and prayed the Lord's Prayer aloud together. After Marie died, Gordon said that, now more than ever, the custom must persist. But there was that sticking point: "Forgive us our trespasses as we forgive those who trespass against us." Joan told us, "Gordon said to me in the hospital that afternoon that he still wanted to pray the Lord's Prayer together that night, so we had better get on with the business of forgiveness."

Joan reminded me of another great Christian widow, whom I met in Austria while on my way to Northern Ireland. There, in the remote village of St. Radegund, I met the saintly Franziska Jägerstätter, age eighty-five. She was the widow of Franz Jägerstätter, a devout young Catholic farmer who had refused to fight for the Nazis—over and against pleas from priests and bishops—and for his refusal was beheaded on August 9, 1943. My arrival was met with warm welcome. The family sat me down, produced refreshments on the spot, told me their story, hauled out family albums, and showed me Franz's grave. Next morning we held a Mass in a little chapel nearby.

Franz's cause for canonization has begun, and years after this visit, I would concelebrate at his beatification Mass. But it occurred to me that Franziska should one day be canonized too. She bore the same beautiful smile, the same great love, and the same sparkling eyes that I found in Mother Teresa. And not a trace of bitterness. She had inspired Franz's stand for peace, and once he died, she carried on in a spirit of forgiveness and love, leaving the imponderables to God. She expected to die without anyone but a few friends knowing Franz's story, until an American sociologist, Gordon Zahn, came along in 1960 and wrote Franz's story, proposing him as the epitome of Christian nonviolent resistance to Nazi fascism.

Finally, I began spending time with one of the world's towering apostles of nonviolence, Mairead Corrigan Maguire. On August 10, 1976, two IRA gunmen opened fire on a British army foot patrol in Belfast. Missing their target, they attempted to flee the area in their car. An army mobile patrol returned fire, and the IRA driver was killed. His car plunged out of control and onto the sidewalk, hitting Mairead's sister Anne and killing three of Anne's children. Anne barely survived her horrific injuries. Days later, Mairead called upon the country to march for an end to war. Tens of thousands turned out in Northern Ireland, Ireland, and Britain. She showed the world that not everyone in Northern Ireland loved bombs and guns. Then, along with Betty Williams and Ciaran McKeown, Mairead founded the Community of the Peace People. The following year, she and Betty were awarded the Nobel Peace Prize.

Soon after that, media interest in Mairead died down. But the war continued, as did the peacemaking. Mairead stepped up the work, traveled the world preaching nonviolence, and met the pope and other great figures, from Dorothy Day to the Dalai Lama. More than anyone else in Northern Ireland, she denounced violence of every species—that of the paramilitaries and their guerilla tactics and the British government and its emergency laws, interrogation centers, and human rights abuses.

And every faction came to shun her, in part for her rebuke, but also in part because she dared operate boldly in a man's world. She met the fate of peacemakers everywhere—ridiculed, discounted, ignored, despised—while starry-eyed audiences swarmed to those who upheld vengeance. Nevertheless, she remained faithful to the nonviolent Jesus.

I first met Mairead in the mid-1980s, at Fordham. We maintained a correspondence and met again when she returned to New York to address Pax Christi. Now that I abided in her corner of the world, I visited her regularly at the Peace House in Belfast. "I used to want to save the world," she told me quietly one rainy afternoon. "Then I had to learn to let it all go and trust in God to lead me. That's what you need to do, John. Let it all go, even your desire to do good, and trust in God and do your wee bit for peace."

Mairead had taken her message to the four points of the compass, prodding and pleading and conferring deep wisdom, but she had never published a word, a small matter I proposed to rectify. Would she be amenable to my compiling her writings into a book? She reluctantly agreed, and I set myself to the task. Her great love and wisdom were ultimately published under the title *The Vision of Peace*. In it, she writes:

> If we want to reap the harvest of peace and justice in the future, we will have to sow seeds of nonviolence, here and now, in the present. . . . I believe that hope for the future depends on each of us taking nonviolence into our hearts and minds and developing new and imaginative structures which are nonviolent and life-giving for all. Some people will argue that this is too idealistic. I believe it is very realistic.

After the tragedy that started it all, Mairead had settled in for the long haul to care for her injured sister. But the pain was too deep for Anne and the loss of her precious children too heavy. She took her own life. Once the caregiver, Mairead suddenly found herself the consoler, trying gracefully to heal her broken family. Over time, she fell in love with Anne's widower, Jackie, the quintessential witty Irishman. They married, and Anne's surviving children gained a loving stepmother. Mairead and Jackie had two children of their own, John and Luke, who would later visit me in the States.

回 回

The pinnacle of the tertian year finally arrived: the Ignatian retreat. Into this retreat I brought the impressions gathered during the previous months. I longed to penetrate the mystery of grace, to enter the presence of Jesus, to receive his resurrection gift of peace, to reclaim the spirit of those initial holy days long ago in the novitiate. So for thirty days, from January to February 1998, I laid the Gospel in my lap, along with St. Ignatius's meditations on sin, grace, the cross, and resurrection, and plunged once again into the world of the spirit.

Time stood still as I met with Jesus to ponder his words and study his cross and resurrection. I read the stories again, putting myself in each scene. This exercise was much harder than it had been the first time, in the novitiate, and took me much deeper; now I had some fifteen years of labor in the vineyard to reflect on. Here I was, thinking all was well, when in fact I needed much more than renewal—I needed a transformation.

During those beautiful days, sitting by the cliffs near Larne on the grounds of an old convent, looking out at Scotland in the distance, I discovered something of Jesus' perfect nonviolence, his willingness to forgive. It was as if a dawn had broken. I was struck by our failure to comprehend his last words to the church, words tossed over his shoulder as security forces hauled him in chains from the garden: "Put down the sword."

How did he maintain such perfect nonviolence before the Roman cohort—six hundred soldiers, guardians of the Roman procurator during Jewish holy days, all of them pitiless by training and raring for a brawl? How had he withstood the mocking, the insults, the slaps, the taunts, the purple robe, the thorns while being so peaceful himself?

I meditated further on the scene, and watched in wonder as Jesus chose not retaliation or flight, but perfect nonviolent love. They led him away, a bloodied deterrent, and yet his perfect peace held. Jesus never once lifted a finger. He blew up at no one. He showed not a trace of anger. He was way beyond retaliation, vengeance, or violence of any kind. He died trusting completely in his beloved God. He surrendered his life in faith and love. And as his breathing grew more difficult during the slow death of suffocation, he devoted one last breath to an intercession for clemency: "Forgive them, they know not what they do." Here was the most perfect act of nonviolence in history. Here was God revealed in astonishing compassion.

My soul saw all this vividly and nodded assent. These spiritual heights were held out to all! My heart yearned for them—to die without fear, anger, hatred, bitterness, resentment or retaliation. And I wanted to live every moment in surrender to my beloved God, radiating perfect peace as Jesus had. Was such a life possible, or was I fooling myself with such dreams?

Then I remembered Billy Neal Moore on death row, years ago. He had challenged me to search my own heart and grant clemency to everyone who had caused me pain. Now, on this retreat, having encountered the peaceful hearts of Joan Wilson, Franziska Jägerstätter, and Mairead Maguire, I understood again that my own heart was the only place to start if I truly wanted a nonviolent world.

So one day, on the cliffs of the Antrim coast, I gritted my teeth and took up Billy's challenge.

I would make a list of the few people I felt hurt by, those I resented. I understood from the start the danger of this sort of exercise. I might, in the naming, let everything go and freely grant clemency. Or I might dredge up every slight I'd ever suffered. Nevertheless, I began putting down names. Then a few more. And more. And more. And more. When I came to seventy-five, I stopped, realizing for the first time the lifetime of resentment I carried within me. More names were on the tip of my tongue, but shame got the best of me; I couldn't bear to add another. It seemed that I felt hurt by everyone—family, friends, Jesuits, presidents, professors, and popes. I peered at the list, which had spilled onto a second page, and shook my head.

Then, in the spirit of Jesus, and in the spirit of Billy, I uttered a prayer: "God of clemency, I hereby grant general amnesty and clemency to the following people." I respectfully said each name aloud. And ten minutes later: "I forgive them for the many ways they have hurt me, and I let go of my resentments, anger, bitterness, hatred, and hurts. I ask you now to forgive me as well and grant me clemency, just as I have forgiven and granted clemency." This would become my spiritual discipline for the next few years, and it broadened my path to inner peace. It was one of the great spiritual lessons of my life— learned in, of all places, Northern Ireland.

Living in Derry, working in Belfast, I held my breath with the rest of the country in the days leading up to the Good Friday peace agreement, on April 10, 1998. Both sides agreed to a new government, to a sharing of power, and to the establishment of a new police force. Everyone knew it was only a beginning. Tensions and violence continued, but not on the same scale as before. The spirit of reconciliation had erupted; the improbable had come about. By and large, the Troubles were over. It would be a rocky road, and still is, but the people of Northern Ireland had turned a corner.

By June my time in Ireland had ended. Before I had embarked on my tertianship year, my provincial had said that he had the perfect assignment for me after Northern Ireland: Rwanda. But during my sojourn, another opening presented itself. The Fellowship of Reconciliation, the largest interfaith peace group in the United States, needed a new executive director. I applied and was accepted.

After a good visit from my parents, I left Ireland with a heavy heart, as if leaving home, and headed stateside to begin a new chapter—as director of FOR USA.

The Fellowship of Reconciliation (1998–2000)

The years to come in my tenure as director of the Fellowship of Reconciliation would be filled with unusual events and inspiring gatherings. As an interfaith organization, FOR helped connect concerned people of peace and nonviolence within each religion and religious denomination. One of the first steps I took was to collect representatives from all the various peace fellowships. Many came, and for days we shared our stories, exchanged our visions of peace, and aired our thoughts on how to disarm the world. We were Buddhists and Muslims and Jews, Hindus and Baptists and Bahai, Lutherans and Catholics, women and men. We were Mennonites and Presbyterians and Episcopalians. And Native Americans. This was by no means just another conference; our wide circle of diversity and authentic belief lifted us to another plane. The spirit of unity surprised us and drew us in. We became respected friends, and each peace journey, exotic and unfamiliar at first, came to seem apt and inspired. We walked a common ground after all—the hidden ground of nonviolence. To everyone's delight, nonviolence was at the heart of each tradition. I had suspected it before, but now I knew it.

Muslims among us reminded us that "Islam" means peace. Hindus upheld Gandhi's legacy of satyagraha, that is, "soul force," as the power of peace. Buddhists shared their compassion and respect for all sentient beings. Jews spoke of the vision of shalom, of Isaiah's poetic oracle that we "study war no more." Christians confessed Jesus as one who blessed peacemakers and commanded us to "love your enemies" and "put down the sword."

On the other hand, each went on to share how people in their tradition had failed to grasp the full weight of its teachings and the implications of those teachings for actions and lifestyle. Mainstream followers of each tradition had by and large rejected nonviolence long ago. Today most of the faithful—from Hindus to Catholics—blink vacantly before the message of nonviolence. Even the Buddhists lamented the killings committed by Buddhist upon Buddhist in Sri Lanka's tragic civil war.

As we exchanged knowing nods, a sense of unity grew palpable. Here was our common ground: We were all called to return to that higher ground of nonviolence.

It was for just this purpose I had leaped at the job—to be on hand for miracles of reconciliation. When I returned from Ireland in June 1998, I moved back into the West Side Jesuit Community and eagerly arrived at FOR headquarters, a forty-room mansion on the banks of the Hudson in Nyack, New York. My first call was from Reverend Jim Lawson, hero of the civil rights movement. Formal, serious, and full of hope, Jim was the current chairperson of FOR's National Council, and now my boss. He called that morning with words of welcome and instructions about my assignment.

"John," he said, "your job is to organize nonviolent revolution in the United States."

"Okay," I said in amazement, exhilaration, and sheer terror. Organize nonviolent revolution. My heart burned to rouse the country, vitalize FOR, invigorate the peace movement, and teach nonviolence far and wide. "I'm your man, Jim," I said.

"Get to it, and stay in touch."

FOR was legendary. A branch of the International Fellowship of Reconciliation (IFOR), FOR USA had promoted justice and peace through creative nonviolence for more than eighty years. Founded in 1914 by two Christians at the outbreak of World War I, FOR set out to teach peace around the world as never before. It attracted Christians, Jews, Muslims, Buddhists, Hindus, and those with no formal religious affiliation at all.

The organization supported conscientious objectors, organized the National Civil Liberties Bureau (later known as the ACLU), met with world leaders, and opposed Nazism, World War II, the internment of Japanese Americans, and the atomic bombings of Hiroshima and Nagasaki. European members of IFOR rescued Jews and other political refugees from the Nazis. Others met with Hitler and Roosevelt to call for nonviolent solutions. Many of IFOR's members died heroically in the act of nonviolently resisting Hitler.

A number of the big names in the peace movement had at one time been associated with FOR. Gandhi wrote articles for *Fellowship*, FOR's magazine, in the 1920s, and a young woman named Dorothy Day worked for the organization before founding the Catholic Worker. In the 1950s, FOR worked closely with Martin Luther King Jr. during the Montgomery bus boycott. The staff encouraged King to practice nonviolence in every area of his life and led workshops on nonviolence for him throughout the South.

FOR's executive director during the 1940s and 1950s, A. J. Muste, broke new ground with his countless protests against U.S. war-making. Admired by Gandhi, mentor to Dr. King, friend of Thomas Merton and Dorothy Day, Muste was the driving force behind every peace protest until his death, in 1967. During the height of World War II, he debated the leading advocate for the war at a packed Carnegie Hall and notoriously advocated Jesus' commandment to love your enemies.

"If I can't love Hitler," he famously said, "I can't love at all." Only on account of a considerable national blind spot is he not recognized today as an American hero.

In the sixties and seventies, FOR focused on the Vietnam War and formed the International Committee of Conscience on Vietnam. People from forty countries joined. The committee raised money for medical aid for both sides of the struggle and sponsored a world tour with Vietnamese Buddhist monk Thich Nhat Hanh, which led to the foundation of the Buddhist Peace Fellowship and the dramatic growth of Buddhism in the United States.

In the early 1980s, FOR led more than a hundred nonviolence training sessions for thousands of priests and nuns in the Philippines. A few years after Benigno Aquino was assassinated, they all took to the streets, and in three days the "People Power" movement brought an end to the Marcos dictatorship.

When I became FOR's director, it had forty people on staff, twenty-five on its National Council, and some seventy local groups meeting regularly across the country. The International Fellowship of Reconciliation had upwards of half a million members. The U.S. branch had about twelve thousand. To be part of such a heritage warmed my heart.

During my first month, I heard that the venerable Vietnamese Buddhist master Thich Nhat Hanh was in Vermont, visiting his new

Buddhist monastery. Thay, or "Teacher," as he is known, is the world's best-known Buddhist teacher after the Dalai Lama. Author of more than one hundred books, Thay was the only person Dr. King nominated for the Nobel Peace Prize. FOR counts him among its friends and sponsored his first U.S. speaking tour, in the mid-1960s. And when Vietnam blocked his return, FOR helped him set up exile in France. I placed a call. Would Thay be willing to let me come up to Vermont for a visit? Come ahead, I was told.

With Richard Deats, editor of *Fellowship*, and Virginia Baron from the magazine staff, I hit the road early, the stars still out, and pulled up to the Vermont monastery around noon. Thay was resting. He had just returned that morning from a demanding speaking engagement before thousands, we were told, and was exhausted. We set off for a stroll along the verdant Vermont hills and shortly came upon a pine grove peaceful as could be. We sat down; I nestled in a bed of pine needles and promptly fell sound asleep. Some hours later, I woke up. And there, two feet behind me, in the lotus position, with a meager head of hair and a smile like the Buddha himself, sat the great Nhat Hanh. He had been praying over me for quite a while. I scrambled to sit up and introduced myself. His intense gaze gathered me in. After a long stretch of silence, he declared he liked me, my youth, my smile, my peaceableness. A few words from him, and all my troubles dissolved.

A second chance to visit him came a year later. I shared my ongoing struggles working for peace and justice and was amazed to learn of his—with community members, with lawyers and publishers, with Buddhists of a decidedly hawkish bent. This put everything into perspective. No one is immune to division and hostility. The Buddhist community, like the peace movement and the Catholic Church, is full of problems and divisions. Thay invited me to join him and some of the monks for dinner. We sat in a circle on the floor as trays of gourmet vegetarian pizza appeared, and ate in silence. Some forty-five minutes later, Thay parted the silence with a few gentle words. "I feel sorry for poor Father John. Someone should sing him a song."

One of the monks took up the task. He stood up, sipped some water, and began. His song had all the flavor of a Gregorian chant. "Poor Father John, who worked for peace, will one day die . . ." The serenade pressed on, deviating little from the opening theme. Finally, he rounded things off with a melancholy conclusion: "He worked for peace . . . and now he's dead." Death anticipated to death consummated. He sat down; everyone nodded in gentle agreement and took a bite of pizza, while I swallowed hard. But then the wisdom of the message emerged to my sluggish mind; like a good Zen student, I had solved the koan. The song was about perspective, proportion, littleness, humility, letting go, a reality far vaster than my own, and something of that great Buddhist teaching about impermanence. With Nhat Hanh by my side, I breathed in and breathed out, more mindful than ever.

My greatest consolation at FOR was Richard Deats, friend and colleague, former executive director and now editor of FOR's *Fellowship* magazine. As a seminarian in 1956 he heard of the Montgomery bus boycott and wrote Dr. King a letter of support, mentioning in the process his plans to drive with a friend from Boston to attend Dr. King's Sunday service during their semester break. Some weeks later they arrived and took in King's usual homiletic extravaganza and, after the benediction, stood in line with the others to shake the young preacher's hand. The two shuffled along, the only white people in the congregation. King sized them up and would not let them take their leave. Where were they going? he demanded to know. Coretta, he said, had spent the morning cooking a feast in their honor.

Thus a rare friendship was born, Richard and the Kings. Richard spent the 1960s as a missionary in the Philippines, raising his family. By the early 1970s, he joined the FOR staff and made his mark leading interfaith delegations to the Soviet Union to break down Cold War barriers. Nationally known in the movement for his dedication to nonviolence, Richard has been a friend for years.

Each day I heard from activists, religious leaders, and peace-and-justice groups around the country. I spoke to university audiences and celebrities and Nobel laureates. I made a hundred calls a day and received hundreds of e-mails a day. The job never lacked excitement. During my tenure, FOR increased its opposition to U.S. militarism in Iraq, especially to the draconian economic sanctions that led to the deaths of hundreds of thousands of children. We continued our Bosnian Reconciliation Work Camps, which brought together Muslims and Christians to rebuild their shattered villages. The staff of the Peacemaker Training Program took to the road and presented conflict-resolution workshops for youth. We dispatched peace delegations to Israel, Mexico, Puerto Rico, and Panama; sponsored forums on racial and economic justice; supported the various religious peace fellowships; and distributed our magazine and literature on nonviolence around the nation.

Twenty-seven thousand Covenants of Peace with the People of Serbia and Kosovo were collected from every corner of the country, signed by individuals and congregations. I crisscrossed the nation on weekends, speaking to audiences. *USA Today* asked me to write editorials. NPR's *All Things Considered* asked if I would offer a commentary. I agreed and provided a five-minute piece on violence not having the power to end violence—not in Bosnia or anywhere else. Why is it we don't know that yet? I asked. Dr. King's nonviolence, I concluded, was the answer to our prayers.

After Matthew Shephard died in Laramie, Wyoming—a victim of antigay violence—FOR organized an interfaith prayer vigil against hate crimes. The following year, on the anniversary of his death, we joined with Interfaith Alliance to organize some 350 vigils around the country.

I'm grateful for that interfaith gathering of peacemakers. I had pushed hard for it. Such a meeting hadn't occurred in decades. There we invoked the legacy of Mahatma Gandhi, our North Star. Gandhi saw early on the equality of the world's religions and understood that nonviolence undergirded them all. Thus he put them on equal footing and professed a vow of tolerance. The truth of nonviolence of each—Christian, Hindu, Jewish, Muslim—would thereafter guide his steps. There was something in his approach of the notion of one God who loves creation and beseeches us not to kill but to love our enemies.

In India during his time, Hindus and Muslims raged at each other. So interfaith nonviolence became the heart of his daily worship. His community read Hindu and Muslim scriptures as well as from the Sermon on the Mount and the Hebrew Bible. But to many, his interfaith nonviolence was a scandal. He was denounced. He received death threats and narrowly escaped an assassin's bomb. Then, on January 30, 1948, as he walked to his daily service—mindfully, peacefully, in possession of his soul—a Hindu fundamentalist approached and shot him dead. He had been preparing to host later that year the annual gathering of the International Fellowship of Reconciliation.

FOR, I believe, still calls us to fulfill Gandhi's vision of interfaith nonviolence.

"Religions are different roads converging to the same point," Gandhi wrote. "What does it matter that we take different roads, so long as we reach the same goal? I believe that, if only we could all read the scriptures of different faiths, we should find that they are at bottom all one and all helpful to one another. There will be no lasting peace on earth unless we learn not merely to tolerate but even to respect other faiths as our own."

In that spirit, Gandhi had some strong words to say about organized Christianity. Christianity, he said, has come to reject the nonviolence of Jesus. Since the earliest days, it has thrown its lot in with the empire. "I like your Christ, but not your Christians," he once remarked, "because they are so unlike your Christ." His words, of course, unleashed a grumble of consternation. But they also set minds free. Innumerable Christians since have taken them to heart. Thanks to the Hindu Gandhi, many have shaken dust from their Bibles and peered again at the core teachings of Jesus. More than anyone, the Hindu Gandhi inspired the Baptist Martin Luther King Jr. to follow Christ.

The glorious vision of FOR remains a guiding light. Its mission is my own—namely, to explore the religious roots of nonviolence, to listen for God, to allow God to disarm us, to create interfaith grassroots movements for justice and disarmament, and to embrace others as sisters and brothers. After that, there is just one thing left—to welcome the gift of peace given long ago.

回 36 回

Peace Mission
to Iraq
(1999)

In the late 1990s, FOR focused its energies on ending the brutal
and unjust sanctions on Iraq imposed by a United Nations that
had been flogged into acquiescence by the United States.

More than half a million Iraqis, mostly children, died during the
1990s, according to UNICEF and the World Health Organization,
because of these sanctions, which choked off the country's ability to
produce clean water and dispense simple medicines. Each day, nearly
two hundred children perished, their cries unheard. More than a million children under the age of five suffered chronic malnourishment.

Of course, FOR opposed the tyranny of Saddam Hussein. His
nonviolent fall from power would be an occasion for celebration, but
the United States was never sincerely interested in that. Indeed, our
government had set up Saddam and supported him for years. FOR
did not support the first Gulf War, either. Instead, we called American
citizens to stand in solidarity with their sisters and brothers in Iraq.
Tyrants can go under without a single shot fired, we said. Regime
change should happen nonviolently, whether at home or abroad.

But the United States proceeded with a heavy hand. It destroyed Iraq's sanitation and sewage systems, contaminated the water, dropped projectiles that released poisonous depleted uranium, and cut off all supplies to the country. FOR's call for solidarity stood—now no longer because of Saddam, but because of the United States.

Had the United States cared about democracy in Iraq, we would have funded its nonviolent, democratic movements; we would have gone to the Iraqi people, asked them how we could help, listened deeply, and done what they asked. But instead we chose to bomb and starve—a course that by its nature forestalls freedom and peace. And, far worse, it breeds the opposite: it sows the seeds of war and spills the blood of children.

Interviewing President Clinton's secretary of state Madeleine Albright on *60 Minutes*, Lesley Stahl said: "We have heard that half a million children have died in Iraq. I mean, that is more children than died in Hiroshima. Is the price worth it?" Albright stared coldly into the camera and said, "We think the price is worth it." Her words bore that demonic line of reason, by no means unique to her—that sprang from the fire-and-brimstone days of Vietnam, the same illogic embodied in the words of a celebrated general of the time: We must destroy the village to set it free.

We had forgotten that this country was the cradle of civilization, the birthplace of writing, the wheel, irrigation, and the first published legal code; the birthplace of Abraham. It was the destination of Jonah, the departure point of the Magi, and the burial place of the evangelist Matthew. We had forgotten our roots. Iraq is not just a beautiful land of noble, well-educated people; it is holy ground. By destroying its land and people, we were destroying our history as well. We must reverence it, protect it, and serve its people. We must learn from our Iraqi sisters and brothers about our common heritage.

FOR would take a stand. The National Council directed us to set up a Campaign of Conscience that would make a way for ordinary people to provide Iraq with medical equipment and water-purification systems. In doing so, they would violate the sanctions and risk arrest and trial. We distributed organizing packets. I took to the road and made speeches around the country. We arranged a press conference of religious leaders at the National Press Club, and I wrote editorials for *USA Today*. Plus, we composed a Covenant of Peace with the People of Iraq. Copies went to congregations around the country, and tens of thousands came back signed.

I dialed Belfast and got Mairead on the line. It seemed good to me that she and I sojourn to Iraq ourselves, talk to whoever might grant us an audience, and see the reality of the situation. We could even invite other Nobel laureates as well—FOR would foot the bill. If we were to love our enemies, as Jesus commanded, we would have to meet them, listen to them, and befriend them. St. Francis modeled this when he journeyed to meet the legendary and hated Sultan. If we put a human face on those declared to be inhuman—and expendable—we could help stop the bombings and the unjust sanctions.

Mairead agreed immediately. We wrote and cosigned a letter that we mailed to other Nobel Peace laureates. Over the next few months, I called them to see if they were interested. Five of them agreed to go, but in the end only Mairead and Adolfo Pérez Esquivel, my old friend from Argentina, were able to make the trip.

Mairead, Adolfo, and I met in Amman, Jordan. Akadim Chikandamina, an activist from Zimbabwe who had been imprisoned for four years for his work for justice and now served as the president of the International Fellowship of Reconciliation, joined us. Kathy Kelly, Rick McDowell, and Mike Bremer of Voices in the Wilderness, a grassroots organization that led delegations to Iraq, facilitated our journey. Few North Americans had been to Iraq in the 1990s, and since 1990, only one U.S. politician had; we were the highest-level delegation to enter Iraq in ten years.

What a boon it was to have Kathy Kelly among us. She'd been imprisoned for planting wheat seeds on the grounds of a nuclear base, and then imprisoned again, for a lengthier stretch, for trespassing at the School of the Americas. Nominated three times for the Nobel Peace Prize, she is a speaker in constant demand and a legend in the peace movement.

But in Iraq, Kathy took on a stature of stratospheric proportions. Wherever she went, she attracted massive crowds; it was like walking down the street with Madonna or Julia Roberts. To the Iraqi people, she was a blazing sign of hope. The entire Middle East followed her movements. More than anyone, she exemplified the fine skill of loving one's enemies.

In March 1999, we set off in a van from Amman, Jordan, in the wee hours, the sky dotted with stars. A sixteen-hour journey through the Iraqi desert lay ahead. It was hours until sunrise; the moon illuminated the ocean of sand. As we proceeded, I grew more aware of the tautness of my nerves. We were hurtling toward the war, the privations, the stage of the world's focus. The previous week, the United States had bombed Iraq every day. The previous night, U.S. bombs had killed several civilians in the north.

Finally, the sun peeped over the desert's edge, the beginnings of a spectacular ball of orange painting the sky pink and blue. It lit up the distance and brought into view the poignant scene of Bedouin people beginning their day. Their ancestors had wandered this desert for thousands of years.

We entered Baghdad and drove directly to the Ameriyah shelter, which the United States had bombed during the Gulf War. The first bomb had entered a ventilation shaft at four in the morning. It blew open the ceiling, forced the exits closed, killed seventeen people, and trapped the rest inside. Two minutes later, a second bomb roared through the hole in the ceiling and incinerated everyone else, some seven hundred women and children.

One woman resident of the shelter, Umm Greyda, had just stepped outside to do the family laundry in a nearby river. One of the only survivors, she could only watch the flames burn for hours. Years later, she took up residence in the bombed-out shelter and created a memorial to the victims, including her own two children and eleven relatives.

Umm Greyda shyly welcomed us and led us through the remains of the building. The walls of the massive concrete structure were charred black and adorned with flowers, prayers, and hundreds of pictures of the children who had died there. We walked through the shelter at a solemn pace and in stunned silence. In one area, children had been sleeping on triple-tiered bunks; the handprints of those who were sleeping on top were left in the melting concrete of the ceiling. In another area was the inverse shadow of an incinerated woman, her white silhouette against a black backdrop, her arm outstretched as if pointing. "I've seen this before," Adolfo said quietly, "in Hiroshima." We came upon another inverse shadow—the outline of a mother holding up a child.

At the end of this grim tour, we gathered beneath the gaping hole in the ceiling, stood in silence, and joined hands in prayer. Then we looked Umm Greyda full in the face, apologized, asked for her forgiveness, and pledged to do everything in our power to end the war on her people. I presented her with piles of signed Covenants of Peace with the People of Iraq to show that the sanctions were by no means unanimous. Then Adolfo led us in a prayer that God would forgive us, end the war and the sanctions, and heal the suffering people of Iraq.

Next we visited the Dijla School in downtown Baghdad. When we stepped out of the van on the edge of the campus, hundreds of teenage girls approached. One emerged to welcome us. Then they began to sing, in Arabic, the great civil rights anthem "We Shall Overcome." *Deep in my heart, we do believe, that we shall live in peace one day. We'll walk hand in hand. We are not afraid. We shall overcome someday.* After a moment, the girls rushed forward and flowed around us like a tide, animated and clamoring. One girl's voice rose above the others. "Why are you trying to kill us? What have we done to you?" she demanded. "We want to be friends with the kids in America!"

How empty-handed we were in this land of prodigious pain. Our only offering was a willingness to listen. And the girls, eyes ablaze, gave us an earful. They told us of having to scramble for cover, of their constant fear, and of the loved ones they had lost. "Your sanctions are killing our people!" I offered an apology and assured them that my friends and I were doing all we could to put a stop to the war. We love you, I said, and we want you to live in peace. We, too, want to be friends. Such would prove to be a pattern on our sojourn—facing those tearful, expectant eyes and having little to offer but compassionate love. The girls showed us around; we sat in on their classes and listened to their stories.

Our next stop was the al-Mansour Pediatric Hospital. From the outside, it looked like any clinic in small-town America. But inside, the consequences of the economic sanctions were clear: scarce medicine, intermittent power, equipment in disrepair, and contaminated water. Before 1990, there had been ample supplies. Now the doctors lost children to simple, relievable illnesses. Here, an average of seven children died every day.

We walked from bed to bed, held the children's hands, embraced weeping mothers, and listened to doctors' pleas. Few of the mothers said a word. They sat by their children's beds, weeping silently, and regarded us from behind dark hijabs. Mairead cradled a crying child dying of kidney cancer and suffering severe abnormalities.

We tried to dispense a kind word or two, to spend some time listening to the outpouring of the grief-stricken. It was our lot to absorb the people's anger as well. "These children are innocent," the director stated, pointing a finger our way. "They are not hurting anyone. They pose no threat to the United States. They are not violating your airspace. They have a right to food, medicine, and clean water. They have the right to live. They should not die because you want more oil. They ask only to live in peace. Please let them live." Another doctor joined in, eyes flashing: "Even if we had supplies, these children will eventually die from the water you contaminated."

Wherever we went, we were confronted by the reality of shortages. We viewed Saddam City, one of the poorest areas on the outskirts of Baghdad, a desolate expanse that was home to some two million. Its houses badly needed repair, raw sewage filled the streets, and the people scarcely had an opportunity to earn any sort of living.

We regarded the vast poverty around us and decided on a gesture. We approached a row of rickety tables in a shabby bazaar and bought a few items—clothes and gifts for family and friends back home. In doing so, we broke the law, exchanging American money for Iraqi goods, the sanctions for a brief moment set aside, rendered null and void.

Our education continued. We made the rounds of several humanitarian agencies stubbornly hanging on. We dined with workers from Enfants du Monde, the Middle East Council of Churches, Bridges to Baghdad, the International Federation of the Red Cross, Life for Relief and Development, and CARE. Margaret Hassan, CARE's saintly director of operations in Iraq, welcomed us as host. Five years hence, she would fall victim to kidnapping and be seen around the world on a video before being brutally assassinated.

Our new friends strained to convey the scope of devastation the sanctions had caused. The word genocide was cautiously put forth, and heads nodded in agreement. One friend summed things up: "A whole generation has been destroyed."

We met other people heroically staying on to monitor the crumbling of the society and making various attempts to stave off further disaster. At the United Nations headquarters, the deputy director, Farid Zarif, received us in the Office of the Humanitarian Coordinator in Iraq. Others—staff members of the Food and Agriculture Organization, the World Health Organization, the World Food Program, UNICEF, and UNESCO—converged there with stories on their lips. (In 2003, the UN headquarters would be destroyed in the second Gulf War.)

"Besides the children," said the papal nuncio, Giuseppe Lazarotto, "the main problem is the lack of hope." The people are well aware, he said, of their role as international scapegoat, their image tarnished in order to prop up American imperialism. "We invite others to come and visit us, to help save the children and to give us hope."

By now, despair as thick as a heavy fog began to settle on my mind. I tried to process and absorb it all, resorting most evenings and early mornings to scribbling in a journal, taking time for quiet meditation, rereading the story of Jesus, and begging for light and grace and strength.

Later in the trip, we made our way to the Umm 'Amarik Research Center, where researchers studied the lingering effects of the first Gulf War and documented the ravages of the current sanctions. Foremost on their minds was depleted uranium, the stuff of American projectiles, a substance pulsating with radioactive energy. It could be found throughout the country in massive quantities, poisoning rivers and land, cattle and children yet unborn.

"We would like to wish you a happy visit to Iraq," one of the researchers said, looking me in the eye. "But we are a suffering and dying people, and if you come to Baghdad, you will suffer with us. You cannot be happy visiting us. But please help us. Tell the world how we've been suffocated."

▣ ▣

We determined that a visit to Iraq's highest echelon was in order. Like St. Francis, we would try to approach the hated sultan—in this instance, Saddam Hussein.

While someone looked into it for us, we walked about sobered, in possession of a grim truth. First of all, the Iraqi people wrongly suffered the calumny of the world. If not for this slander against them, the world would not stomach the sanctions. We saw for ourselves the openness and hospitality of these people, and their long-suffering. Moreover, Iraq needed billions of dollars to restore its infrastructure. Until it did so, the cycle of disease would remain "vicious and ubiquitous," in the phrase of Zarif. His stark tone had impressed on us a sense of doom. The first world must give abundantly to rebuild Iraq, or the decimation of children would stretch into the distant future. We needed a whole new Marshall Plan to rebuild the country. Actually, we needed a global Marshall Plan.

Our meeting with Saddam almost came off. We were brought to his infamous palace and then, at the last minute, ushered into an evening with Deputy Prime Minister Tariq Aziz, Saddam's right-hand man. He was polite, cordial, and decent. For a long while we listened; then we entered into a give-and-take. "The United States must demonize us," he said, "if it hopes to destroy us and take our oil—as it's determined to do. But these sanctions are murdering our children."

We offered our observations. Yes, we opposed the unjust sanctions, but we also opposed Iraqi violations of human rights. We demanded they stop sending dissenters to their graves and the innocent to prison. "The Iraqi government," Mairead said firmly, "should uphold the human rights of all its citizens, regardless of race, religion, ethnicity, or politics."

"We agree that our goal should be to preserve life and create dialogue," he answered. He asked us to invite members of the U.S. Congress and other religious leaders to visit Iraq to pursue these goals. We pledged to do what we could and told him of our plans to agitate for an end to the sanctions and bombardments. I felt uneasy throughout, but I recalled that everyone from the pope to the president insisted that peacemaking begins with dialogue.

As we said good-bye, Aziz pulled me aside to announce that he had studied at Georgetown. "When you return to New York," he said, "please pass along my greetings to Cardinal O'Connor—he's an old friend of mine." He smiled at the surprise in my eyes. I managed a promise to convey his good wishes. How I would ever gain an audience with Cardinal O'Connor was another matter entirely.

Our sojourn winding down, we had a final task: the all-important press conference, an opportunity to impart the fruits of our scrutiny. That Nobel laureates would be speaking provoked a great degree of interest. We held the conference back in Amman, and journalists from Europe and the Middle East—plus CNN and the Associated Press—filled the hall.

I approached the podium to make an opening statement. "We call for the immediate lifting of the economic sanctions, an end to the U.S. bombings of Iraq, and a nonviolent resolution to this crisis."

"This is genocide, plain and simple," Adolfo Pérez Esquivel said more sternly. "Children are dying slowly and painfully. If we want democracy and human rights in Iraq, we have to stop the economic sanctions, which kill innocent people and destroy all educational and social services. The people cannot create democracy if they are suffering and dying from U.S. sanctions and bombs."

"I have seen children dying with their mothers sitting next to them, not able to do anything," Mairead Maguire said. Then she spoke about reconciliation between warring Catholics and Protestants in Northern Ireland:

> The president of the United States should seek peace with Iraq, just as he helped forge a peace deal in Northern Ireland. In Ireland, we are grateful to the United States for helping us accomplish the recent Good Friday peace agreement. But the U.S. president should be consistent in his call for dialogue and disarmament as the only way to make peace. Just as he told us that Northern Ireland should pursue dialogue and disarmament, so too the United States should pursue dialogue and disarmament. The United States should stop the economic sanctions and bombings of Iraq and begin to dialogue with Iraq.

"In fifty years," she concluded, "the next generation will ask us, 'Where were you when the children of Iraq were dying?' The United Nations is about to declare the first decade of the new millennium a Decade for a Culture of Peace and Nonviolence for the Children of the World," Mairead concluded. "We believe the United Nations should begin the new decade by lifting the economic sanctions, ending the U.S. bombings, and ending the death of Iraqi children. Then, they should give massive aid to rebuild the country, clean up the environment, and build a new, peaceful Middle East."

Around the same time, President Clinton made a fanfare of his tour of El Salvador and Guatemala, an occasion for a shallow display of remorse. He expressed regret for U.S. wars in the region during the 1970s and 1980s, which I regarded as a pale acknowledgment of the misery the United States had unleashed there. The gesture was rendered nearly ludicrous by our own tour—the United States apologizing for genocide in Central America while practicing it in Iraq.

Once home, I marched in protest and spoke at press conferences. I flew around the country and lectured to thousands; I met with directors of nonprofits and urged them to organize against the sanctions. But how to get our message into the mainstream? I lamented the roadblock one day to Sister Helen Prejean, who returned, "Oh, that's easy. Susan Sarandon can help you."

We concocted a plan. Susan and I cosigned a letter to every well-known figure we could think of. Lend your name to our struggle, we asked, and put a thousand dollars in the kitty. With names in hand and coffers bulging, we placed a large ad in the *New York Times* demanding an immediate end to the U.S. economic sanctions on Iraq and confronting readers with a photo of a hundred Iraqi children, captioned, in big, boldfaced letters, "Are the Children of Iraq Our Enemies?"

Underneath the photo was a list of recognizable names: Jackson Browne, Bonnie Raitt, Joan Baez, Pete Seeger, Richard Dreyfuss, Rosie O'Donnell, Liam Neeson, Martin Sheen, Richard Gere, Noam Chomsky, Joan Chittister, Arun Gandhi, Ramsey Clark, Howard Zinn. And on and on. "Lift the economic sanctions on Iraq now!" they demanded.

Then one day, the phone rang in my FOR office, the secretary to Cardinal O'Connor on the line. Would I come to his office and relate the details of my trip? At worst, I figured, I faced another dressing-down from a lofty personage; at best, a perfunctory meeting. I went to his office overlooking the United Nations. Surrounded by his entire senior staff and various key priests, the cardinal offered a few words of welcome and then said, "Tell me everything you want me to know about Iraq."

I heaped upon him everything I could conjure from memory—the effects of the sanctions in bitter detail, the conclusions of the laureates, the laments of the papal nuncio, and, perhaps audaciously, my take on Pope John Paul II's stand against U.S. war-making in Iraq. I spoke for nearly an hour, then rested my case.

The cardinal bore a poker face, but his entourage appeared as if they were being held there against their will. After a few seconds in silence, he spoke: "What would you like me to do about it?" I was dumbfounded. I blurted out, "You should go to Iraq!" He raised his eyebrows. I continued: "If you went, the media would cover your visit, and the whole country would learn about Iraq. People would listen to you. You could support the pope's work for peace in Iraq and maybe help stop the killing."

He looked left, then right, at those gathered around. "Okay," he replied. "I'll go." He spoke of making the trip later that fall. Let me facilitate it, I offered. "My staff will be in touch with you," he said. I passed on the greetings from Tarik Aziz and left. The trip, however, never came to pass. Weeks after my visit, the cardinal was diagnosed with terminal cancer.

I've pondered what might have happened had he gone to Iraq. To be sure, he would have loved his enemies, and started teaching others to do so as well. His visit certainly would have roused an earthquake under the feet of complacent church officials everywhere. It was delicious to think of it—the dream that nearly came true. Next year in Jerusalem.

回 37 回

Return to
Palestine
(1999)

Before plans for the Campaign of Conscience had proceeded very far, I was asked to join an FOR interfaith delegation to the Middle East. That November I set off with a rabbi, a Muslim activist, a Mennonite, a diocesan priest friend from Scranton named Bill Pickard, and my friend Bob Keck from the West Side Jesuit Community. It was my first time visiting Israel and Palestine since 1982.

Bill, Bob, and I were able to make a little side trip to the Sea of Galilee so I could visit the Chapel of the Beatitudes. It was a dark, bleak day, and after visiting the chapel we decided to take a boat ride on the sea. We bought the last three tickets for a tourist ride on a vessel designed like a first-century fishing boat. Twenty-five American tourists were already aboard. We set off on rough waters under a black sky.

These were the very waters I had swum in seventeen years before, the very waters on which Jesus had walked some two thousand years before that. The three of us stood in silence as the lively wind struck the sails and propelled us forward. We gazed at the shore, the trees, and the fretful sky in astonishment: it was the same scene taken in by Jesus and his disciples, beautiful but tempestuous.

But there were grumblings on board, the sound of the other tourists coming to life. "Thank God we don't live in this dreadful place," one woman shouted to the approval of the others. "Thank God for America," she added, "the home of the free!" An American flag was produced, and four or five men bustled about the mast, affixing the flag to it with tacks. We were surrounded by fundamentalist Christians from Texas! And they had claimed the Sea of Galilee for America.

We stood in speechless disbelief and watched as the twenty-five Texans formed a circle around the flag, placed their hands over their hearts, and began to sing "God Bless America." On the Sea of Galilee. As the last note faded, many burst into tears. "Thank you, Jesus, for the U.S. of A."

I was dumbfounded by their blind nationalism, by their blatant disrespect for the poor, itinerant rabbi, Jesus of Nazareth. America's ideals had supplanted Jesus' ministry of bringing God's reign to life right here. The Beatitudes and the Sermon on the Mount (offered just a hundred yards away on shore), not to mention Jesus' own love for the land of his people and his tireless work of healing and reconciliation right here—all of that seemed to me, in those moments, to be shown utter contempt. The tourists sang a hymn of praise to a nation hell-bent on war. They had just articulated their hatred of the land and the people Jesus loved. He would say, "They know not what they do," but I was grief-stricken and out of sorts. In an hour, we were back at the dock. I went ashore under the dark, turbulent sky, telling myself, "They know not what they do." Then the skies opened and the rain poured down.

As a delegation, we set out to see for ourselves what was happening in the Holy Land. We would witness not only the results of

America's misguided policies but rancor and disquiet in every corner. A rabbi, a Muslim, a Mennonite, a handful of Catholics—we were all in it together. When an angry Israeli confronted us in Hebrew, our rabbi friend explained matters on our behalf. When a displeased Palestinian challenged us in Arabic, our Muslim friend spoke words of peace. When Christians questioned us, the rest of us cited gospel nonviolence.

Our first week, we stayed outside Bethlehem in Beit Shahur, site of massive nonviolent resistance during the first Intifada, in the late 1980s. "The situation remains difficult," said Zoughbi Zoughbi, director of the Wi'am Center for Nonviolent Conflict Resolution, whom I had met long before in Santa Cruz while visiting the Italian social activist Danilo Dolci. "Settlements continue to be built, the innocent are locked up, our people can't travel freely, and we have no control over water or land. New Israeli military checkpoints spring up daily. Three and a half million Palestinians suffer in the West Bank, Hebron, and Gaza, while another three million Palestinian refugees are scattered through the world, unable to return.

"We don't have sovereignty," he continued. "Our eight cities are surrounded by Israeli military. Ethnic cleansing goes on here, and the world ignores it. We need the support of the world community. We want justice and peace. Help us."

At the Applied Research Institute in Jerusalem, the director Jad Isaac pulled out maps. He laid them out before us and traced paths and pointed out landmarks, showing how Israel had set about slowly squeezing Palestinians into ghettos, creating an all-new apartheid system. Jad had led the civil disobedience movement in Beit Shahur during the Intifada, spent six months in jail, and served as a Palestinian negotiator at the Wye River accords. "We should be more outspoken," he said, "but we Palestinians have lost our spirit since the end of the Intifada, even though we have a just cause."

Our next stop was the Israeli Committee against House Demolitions and the Alternative Information Center, a joint Israeli-Palestinian organization resisting Israeli demolitions of Palestinian homes, helping rebuild them, and bringing hundreds of sympathetic Israelis into Palestinian territory. "We are heading either toward a viable, just peace or total apartheid," ICAHD director Jeff Halper told us, "and it looks like it's going to be full-blown apartheid. The new settlements are all part of a master plan."

He thought the majority of Israelis wanted peace. "But all the land and roads around Palestinian cities are controlled by Israel. That's apartheid. That's a reservation. The Palestinians, of course, have lost faith in the peace process. It is a cold, dead peace. There's no discussion about removing soldiers or checkpoints. There will always be war and preparations for war. If Israel wants apartheid, then one day Palestine will explode."

Next stop, Bet Shelem, a human rights research center run by progressive Israelis, where we learned of the foul instruments of repression, such as the rubber bullets used on demonstrators. More than sixty Palestinians, half of them children, have been killed in recent years by these bullets. Israeli soldiers aim at legs in a crowd and end up killing, blinding, or maiming children. We also learned of torture, home demolitions, and settlements. Thousands of Palestinians have been routinely tortured in Israel. More than two thousand Palestinian homes were demolished in the 1990s, making ten thousand Palestinians homeless. And while the settlements, according to international law, are illegal, they continue, as the Israelis deprive Palestinians of their right to build or hold on to what they have already built.

Back in Beit Shahur, Ghassan Adoni, director of the Centre of R'approachment, told us about the extensive nonviolent resistance he organized against the Israeli occupation. "A whole generation of Palestinian male youth has suffered arrest and torture," Ghassan told us. "It's not a healthy society. The Intifada generation is traumatized and defeated. Nonviolent resistance in a society is a sign of health. The outburst is coming. So we are trying to train young people to become leaders, so that our future leaders have vision and a chance for lasting peace with justice."

Later, we visited the Dheisheh refugee camp. Eleven thousand people festered there, half of them children. They had lived for decades under curfew; had been teargassed, tortured, and arrested; and had seen many of their number killed. "We're fed up with the oppression and bloodshed," one said. "We don't care which government rules. We want to decide where we can live. We want our dignity back."

We journeyed next to Hebron, where a handful of Jewish settlers moved into the heart of Palestinian life, and the Israeli army moved in shortly thereafter, ostensibly to offer the settlers protection. But as a practical matter, the army inflicts terror on the natives and nibbles away at their grasp on the land. Ancient olive trees are uprooted, houses demolished, water supplies throttled, livelihoods cut off— all in the name of military necessity. The settlers steal the land, and native Palestinians become homeless.

The settlers are also religious fanatics. They promulgate the claim that God promised the land exclusively to the Jews. Accordingly, they seize it with an iron fist, with the ferocity of Joshua taking Canaan. By the time of our visit, 36 percent of the land in the district had been confiscated. Meanwhile, Israeli authorities nudged the confiscation along by harassing Palestinians in every aspect of life.

We spent the week in Hebron with a contingent of the Christian Peacemaker Teams; the team lived there full-time and monitored the area, a tinderbox ever ready to flare up. When settlers fell upon an isolated band of Palestinians or soldiers harassed them on the street, team members would try to peacefully intervene; sometimes, shame can be a defusing power. Other times, though, the peacemakers themselves suffered attacks.

"One would like to be hopeful and say that peace will prevail," said Khaled Amayreh, a leading Palestinian journalist, from his home on the outskirts of Hebron. "However, with the political reality around us, it's hard to be hopeful." Like all Palestinians, he risks arrest should he enter Jerusalem, a mere thirty miles away.

"The occupation has become more efficient, and Palestinians are more frustrated than ever," he told us. "The situation is bleak. We are living under a mafia, the PLO, with its many security agencies. It's a police state without a state. There is no freedom of speech or press. The people are demoralized. I would like to tell you good news, but I would not be honest if I did."

In the center of Hebron stands the ancient Tomb of the Patriarchs, the purported resting place of Abraham and Sarah and Isaac and Rebekah. Part mosque and part synagogue, it has been a military post since the 1994 massacre of twenty-nine Muslims who died during their prayers at the hands of a deranged Jewish settler from Brooklyn. Those who were not killed rose up and murdered him in a frenzy—and now Jewish settlers regard him as a martyr, and their children sing songs in his honor. He symbolizes the region's insanity.

Each day in Hebron, our little group gathered in a park across the street from the tomb for our interfaith morning prayer. One morning, a school bus pulled to a stop right in front of the tomb. A rabbi in black stepped off and quickly assessed the situation, then hurried the children off the bus and into the synagogue. Under his arm was an AK-47.

On our last day in Hebron, we set off into the countryside for a farewell dinner that several Palestinian families were preparing in our honor. We gathered in a barren hillside under a large tent yards from the rubble of one family's demolished house. There we enjoyed Maq'lube, a traditional Arab feast of rice, vegetables, and spices, a three-thousand-year-old recipe. It had been cooking all day in a barrel over an open fire. Every few hours, layers of rice, vegetables, and so forth were added to the top. When the meal was ready, we sat on the floor of the tent around a large clean plastic sheet. The people carried in the barrel with great ceremony and turned it over. The board that held in the delectable contents was carefully removed, and then, with great suspense, the barrel was slowly raised. Food tumbled out before us, a delicious pyramid, each layer a separate course. It was a memorable feast.

If anything, Israel and Palestine illustrate the failure of violence to solve anything; after decades, centuries, millennia, what has it accomplished? No matter if big guns or little guns are used—no one is secure, everyone is threatened, and all, in effect, are hostages. Their only hope lies in interfaith policies of nonviolence.

回 38 回

The Great
Forty Days
for Peace
(2000)

I returned to Nyack and FOR headquarters and focused on our work, trying to keep things afloat, managing the budget and the finances and the movement itself. My heart was gripped with the possibility of beginning the new millennium with a new Poor People's Campaign, such as the one Dr. King had tried to pull off in 1968. I envisioned thousands of FOR members and friends gathered in Washington, D.C., for forty summer days of conferences, interfaith prayer vigils, and protests on every issue of injustice and war.

I recruited a handful of hopeful and eager activists from D.C. and hired others as consultants and organizers. For the next six months, I labored fifteen hours a day. On weekends, I traveled to speak about peace and describe the campaign; from time to time, I joined others in blocking an entrance or crossing a line and landed in jail. Dreams of sowing the seeds of nonviolence on a wide scale filled my head. I threw myself into corralling other peace-and-justice groups, working on logistics, writing brochures, setting up a Web site, and getting word out across the country.

Finally, the forty days began. On Saturday evening, July 1, 2000, the campaign got under way in the historic Howard University chapel in Washington, D.C. Six hundred people of every faith, all of them inclined toward nonviolence, poured in from every corner of the country, including seventy-five nuns who had arrived on the "peace train" from the Midwest. Shoulder to shoulder, they drank in the reflections and testimony of an extraordinary panel: Mairead Maguire, Daniel Berrigan, Jim Lawson, Arun Gandhi, Helen Caldicott, Jonathan Schell, and Marian Wright Edelman; I served as emcee. Afterward, we all enjoyed free ice cream, compliments of Ben & Jerry's.

For the next thirty-nine days, people from dozens of leading peace-and-justice groups led conferences, prayer services, and public protests—a different group taking the helm each day. The most exemplary people graced us and inspired us: Senator Paul Wellstone, Congressman Dennis Kucinich, Bishop Thomas Gumbleton, Pete Seeger, Jim and Shelley Douglass.

The Dalai Lama spoke on the second day of the campaign, and thousands gathered on the Mall to hear him. On July 3, Mairead, Jim Lawson, and I spoke in Lafayette Park, along with members of the American Friends Service Committee, against the Star Wars missile defense system and the sanctions on Iraq. Afterward, twenty-five of us were arrested for sitting-in, in front of the White House.

On July 4, members of the Nevada Desert Experience and Pace e Bene leafleted at the White House prior to the fireworks celebration. Over the next few days, groups such as the Church of God, the War Resisters League, the U.S. Campaign to Ban Landmines, Physicians for Human Rights, the Presbyterian Peace Fellowship, the

Mennonites, and the Colombia Support Network led protests. Eight congressional representatives joined us in a rally against Star Wars.

The Jewish Peace Fellowship held its first gathering in over fifty years on July 20. The next day, the Muslim Peace Fellowship held its first gathering ever. It was a rare juxtaposition—Jews and Muslims agitating for peace. That alone made all the work worthwhile.

Lutherans held nonviolence training the next day. Jubilee 2000 staged a rally demanding a cancellation of third-world debt. And across town, a women's peace group, featuring Elizabeth McAlister, rallied for nuclear disarmament. North Carolina's People of Faith against the Death Penalty kept vigil in front of the Supreme Court.

And so it went. Pax Christi, SOA Watch, Witness for Peace, the Catholic Worker, the Baptist Peace Fellowship, the Episcopal Peace Fellowship, Families against Violence, the Atlantic Life Community, Women's International League for Peace and Freedom—each carried its vision of the Beloved Community (a new world of peace and justice) before the White House, the Pentagon, or the Capitol.

Things came to a climax on August 5 and 6. We had arranged a daylong teach-in on the fifth focusing on the destruction of Hiroshima and the sanctions against Iraq—all in preparation for the next day, when two scandalous anniversaries would coincide: the ten-year anniversary of the commencement of the Iraq sanctions and the fifty-fifth anniversary of the vaporization of Hiroshima.

August 6 opened with an interfaith prayer vigil and a march of about two thousand hardy souls from the Lincoln Memorial to the White House. As we made our way, the heavens opened, and rain poured down in buckets. Crackling lightning followed shortly, and we stepped up the pace, drenched in rainwater and vaguely demoralized. But somewhere along the way, as the rain fell in sheets and pelted us sidelong, a new spirit overtook us. We regarded it all as a baptism of sorts; we felt renewed, exhilarated, even euphoric.

We arrived at the White House, the rain still pouring down, and heard from Congressman Dennis Kucinich, Ralph Nader, and British Parliament member George Galloway. Then I introduced folk-singer Pete Seeger. I stood close, holding an umbrella over him as he sang beloved songs. What a glorious moment! I sang along with Pete's faltering voice, weaving in a pleasant harmonious line.

A march on the Treasury Department was planned for August 7. There we delivered the thousands of names of those who had signed on for the Fellowship of Reconciliation's Campaign of Conscience for the People of Iraq. Then we stood before the White House in a peaceful demand for an end to the sanctions. The police rounded up 104 of us and hauled us off to the pen a vanload at a time. I sat in jail for the rest of the day, reflective and pleased. The summer's events had buoyed me up. Five thousand had taken part—a modest number for a modest effort, but a beautiful beginning to the new millennium.

On August 9, the anniversary of the bombing of Nagasaki, the campaign drew to a close. Hundreds gathered in a circle on the Pentagon parade grounds and uttered final prayers—Hindu, Jewish, Muslim, Buddhist, and Christian. Then children led us in songs for peace.

Death and the Tombs of New York (2000–1)

The summer of 2000 also occasioned great mourning. Peter Cicchino, my novitiate friend who had been my partner in crime for the Lenten campaign at the Pentagon in the eighties, was dying of cancer.

After leaving the Jesuits, Peter graduated from Harvard Law School, joined the faculty of American University, and became a distinguished professor of human rights law. With a promising life and career ahead of him, he fell sick and was diagnosed with colon cancer. As he lay dying, hundreds of students, relatives, and friends gathered round to lend their support. And he in turn affirmed everyone with love and urged that the work for justice and peace go on.

I visited him in D.C. late one July night and found him confined to his bed, emaciated, and struggling to draw a full breath, his face tinged a wan yellow as a result of his diseased liver. "I have a secret to share with you," he murmured. I leaned in to hear. He told me that on the previous night, God had spoken to him.

So far as I could recall, Peter had never uttered a word one might regard as sentimental or pious. He vetted thoughts and utterances carefully, his mind very much given over to the rational and sensible. He was like his hero, Mr. Spock of *Star Trek*. So for him to claim having heard from God personally was real news. "Tell me," I said.

"A Voice said, 'You have accomplished your mission. Now we want you to come home.' And I said, 'But why do I have to suffer so much and die so painfully?' 'That is the only way to get here,' the Voice answered back, 'to suffer with love.'"

After relating to me that simple, brief exchange between him and the Divine, he began to cry tears upon tears. This was another indication that his testimony was genuine. Peter never cried, much less sobbed.

"Peter," I said, "you did it! You've been faithful to the gospel, to the work of justice and peace. You loved everyone as best you could, you fulfilled the vow of nonviolence we professed long ago. And now you're showing perfect love and grace and kindness to everyone. You really have fulfilled your mission."

I returned to New York but a few days later received the news that Peter was nearing death. I drove from New York to D.C. on a Saturday morning only to find that he had died just five minutes before I arrived. The family bustled about making calls and preparations. Would I sit with the body? they asked. I entered the room and sat by Peter's bed. He looked for all the world like a prison camp inmate: skeletal, wasted, cold and gray and yellow, his mouth agape. For two hours I sat there, praying for him, thanking God for his life, replaying our adventures, and wondering where he was now.

His was the sharpest mind I've ever encountered. And he offered it up for the poor and others in their struggle for justice. He served in soup kitchens, advocated human rights, opposed the contra war, countered bloodletting everywhere, defended gays and lesbians. As South Africa wrote a new constitution, Peter was invited in as legal adviser to Nelson Mandela and helped with the deliberations. His life was one astounding accomplishment after another, but the greatest, to my mind, was his compassionate love as his days dwindled. I've never seen such devotion. His last words to his friends were "I love you all." He was thirty-nine years old.

That afternoon I drove back home, in mourning and exhausted, death very much on my mind. How often I've encountered it—in Iraq, in Central America's war zones, in Northern Ireland and Palestine and Haiti, at the Pentagon and the White House. I've accompanied the dying in death wards, presided at funerals too many to count, sat with the dying and the dead. By now I was familiar with death; I knew well the sudden stillness of the body, the tears of the survivors. I knew enough to resist our government's demonic pursuit of death for the suffering poor, for the whole race. Once again I thought that life is hard enough without us actively bringing death upon one another.

I arrived home late that night and, in the grip of such thoughts, toppled into bed—and in no time slipped into a deep sleep. Later during the night a dream overtook me, one of great vividness and energy, a species of dream that imprints itself on the memory—and more, leaves its mark on one's life and soul, a dream worth telling.

I'm walking around a towering oak tree, so tall as to beg the imagination, some thousand stories high. Outsize bark covers the broad trunk, and overhead are leaves of stunning beauty. Around the tree, millions of people stroll in small groups, conversing among themselves, as if enjoying a peaceful day at the park. All of a sudden it occurs to me that this majestic scene is an image of heaven; the ascending tree is none other than the Tree of Life.

As I move about the tree, someone holds me. It is God the Father. I confess that seldom do I let that patriarchal image seize my imagination; I stay with Jesus. But this is definitely God the Father—and he is a twenty-year-old man. Here is the Creator of heaven and earth, and I'm astonished at his youth. He holds me tight as I weep for Peter. And as I'm held, my mourning increases. I begin to weep for everyone I've ever known who has died, and soon for all who are dying throughout the broken world, in Iraq, Palestine, El Salvador . . . Before long, mourning has completely enveloped me. And God holds me still.

We're walking slowly around the Tree of Life, and this young God, his arms around me, listens attentively. He knows me completely—every detail, every wound, every hope and dream. Waves of unconditional love crest over me. Unlimited compassion, infinite mercy, complete affirmation, measureless, incomprehensible love—all flow mysteriously from God's embrace. He makes the trip with me, around the Tree of Life, and in his arms I come alive.

I woke up from this dream in a daze, groggy, as if coming out of open-heart surgery. I was overcome. I had just experienced a close encounter with the Divine. God had come and touched me in the night, right there in my shabby little New York apartment, and then went on God's divine way.

回　回

I decided that Christmas to step down as FOR director because I did not want to spend so much time on administrative, fundraising, and personnel issues. I wanted to be freer to witness for peace and jumped at the first opportunity.

The year 2001 began with a descent into the Tombs, New York's infamous dungeon. On January 16, I joined fifteen others in blocking the doorway of the U.S. Mission to the United Nations, on First Avenue. On one hand, it was a gesture of honor for Dr. King on his birthday; on the other, an act of opposition on the tenth anniversary of the Gulf War massacre. The action began with a prayer and a meager meal, such as Iraqis endure. Then off to the mission, holding aloft our signs and singing peace songs. It was a small, symbolic gesture, largely ignored by passersby. But the mission employees took note, and the police looked upon us with a truculent eye. They clapped us in plastic handcuffs and carried us away.

Our arrest was a result of an initiative of Mayor Rudy Giuliani. After police emptied their revolvers into an unarmed African immigrant named Amadou Diallo, resulting in daily acts of civil disobedience at police headquarters (Dan Berrigan and I had participated, at the side of Reverend Al Sharpton), Mayor Giuliani decided to crack down. Protesters would be regarded in the same light as criminals. They would be put through "the system." So into the system we went.

For a good long while we cooled our heels at the local precinct, the men in one wing, the women in another. Then, at one in the morning, the police barged in, chained us together, and marched us out into the bitter cold. We hunched close for warmth in the back of the police van and landed finally at central booking, 100 Center Street. More than five hundred people had been arrested that day, a crowd to beat all records. An elderly Muslim subway token distributor accused of stealing, two young people picked up for selling Super Bowl T-shirts without a permit, several men accused of selling drugs or being in the company of people using them—these were our new companions in chains.

At two in the morning, the police led our group in chains down a side street to wait in the frigid night air, because there was no room in the dungeon. Under barked orders, we waddled back to the van and there we sat and froze for an hour and a half more. I glanced over at Dan Berrigan, nearly eighty years old, shackled and chained and blue with cold. Finally, at three thirty, we were prodded back to the Tombs—inside at last, with something passing for heat. We were searched and photographed and questioned. Then we made our precarious descent down flight after flight of stairs, chains rattling underfoot, into the bowels of New York. At last we reached the basement.

An array of cells lay all around. Inside each slouched mostly African-Americans and Latinos. Their eyes bore a look of exhaustion and anxiety. They foresaw their destiny—Rikers Island, the largest prison in the world. Guards shoved us into a small cell, and the great door squealed shut.

In such times as these, every passing minute tests a peacemaker's faith, stamina, and dedication to nonviolence. You quickly learn the limits of your own strength. But support, I've learned, is by no means out of reach. The Gospels, the Acts of the Apostles, the letters of St. Paul—they suddenly come alive, like crocuses in season. Accounts of jails and guards ring familiar, and you remember you are part of a greater story.

The ten of us men sat with our backs against the wall; there was barely enough room for one or two to lie down. Dan endured with characteristic aplomb, never uttering a complaint or expressing discomfort. Instead, he regaled us with stories of his long stint in Danbury prison and sat meditatively for long stretches, a slight and aged Buddha.

At eleven in the morning, sustenance came at last—bologna sandwiches. Vegetarian that I am, I passed the bologna to others and ate the flimsy white bread as though it were communion. That was the only offering of food. However, we had plenty of noise, blazing lights, and foul smells, not to mention incessant harassment, lack of sleep, and rotation from cell to cell.

As the day wore on, weariness and sickness overtook us. Toward noon we felt faint. Heads drooped, backs ached, bellies churned. Finally, around five, we were hauled before a judge. Not guilty, we declared. He mumbled a trial date and released us back onto the arctic streets. We lurched into the night starved, nauseous, and exhausted. The charges were later dropped.

A terrible ordeal, twenty-nine crushing hours in the system. I couldn't have gone much longer—which is precisely the point. Such is the life of New York's disenfranchised. It's also the life of Iraqi children. A day in the Tombs brings a different perspective on life, the empire, and its wars.

That spring and summer I stayed busy on the road, speaking here and there across the country, in places large and small. After reading Gandhi's entire Collected Works, I wrote a lengthy introductory essay and finished the anthology, *Mohandas Gandhi: Essential Writings*. In August, I addressed a large gathering in Los Angeles. The violence that the United States wreaks on the world, I said, will come back to haunt us. I quoted Jesus: "All who live by the sword will die by the sword." I tremble to think on it, but shortly my words would prove prescient.

回 40 回

Life and Death
at Ground Zero
(2001)

On September 7 of that year, I presided over a wedding in New
Jersey, then took the train home. Along the way, for the first time
ever, I spontaneously deviated from routine, making a pit stop for pizza
at the World Trade Center. There I sat during Friday rush hour. The
journey from New Jersey to New York passes right through that lobby,
at the platform of the PATH train. A million people dashed by me in
the lobby of the World Trade Tower. I marveled at the teeming city, its
vast variety of characters and eccentrics, the sinners and saints.

On Sunday, September 9, my parents would arrive for a rare New
York visit. My father made plans to do the town up right: accommodations at the Millenium Hotel next door to the Twin Towers where
I'd sat over pizza, dinner at a fancy Midtown Italian restaurant, lunch
on Monday at the Russian Tea Room, Mass with Dan and dinner
with the community on Monday night. And then, the pièce de résis-
tance—breakfast Tuesday morning at Windows on the World, the
storied restaurant perched at dizzying heights atop the North Tower
of the World Trade Center.

But just before my parents departed for New York, my mother called. "Your father and I don't want you coming all that way downtown, so we canceled our reservation at the Millenium. We'll be staying at the Park Lane Hotel on Central Park."

"Okay." It made no difference to me.

"That means on Tuesday morning, we'll have breakfast there, instead of at the World Trade Center."

Thus, on September 11, 2001—a spectacular day, cool and sunny with a clear blue sky—I sat innocent as a newborn over breakfast in a room overlooking Central Park. Suddenly, there was tension on the air. My father heard the news while checking out of the hotel: "A plane, they think, hit the World Trade Center." We switched on the television and saw the burning tower. My mother began to cry. "All those people are going to die," she said.

My parents and I bade hasty good-byes; they left, and I hopped into a cab for home, where Bob Keck and I watched the horror unfold on TV. A second plane struck; then the towers fell. I cried, said a prayer, and headed downtown to see how I could help.

Like thousands of others, I hoped to lend a hand. I headed south on Broadway, swimming against the tide of the crowd walking up from lower Manhattan. It was an eerie scene, surreal and dreamlike, what you might expect from a disaster movie. The sky was crystal blue except for the gray and pink smoke coming up from lower Manhattan. I pressed toward the smoke, into a growing stench that would linger for weeks.

I walked for hours to St. Vincent's Hospital on West Twelfth Street, where my mother had worked as a nurse in the 1950s. About a hundred medics stood outside along a long row of stretchers, awaiting the arrival of the injured, while a dozen chaplains milled about uneasily. But the injured never arrived. I was shortly informed that there was no need of my services.

I turned away and drifted northward with the crowd toward home. Behind me, a forty-seven-story building fell with a rumble, disappearing almost instantly from the city's notched skyline. A neighbor to the World Trade Center, it was one of several that would fall over the next few days.

I was back on Wednesday at St. Vincent's, but still there was nothing I could do. Finally, that night, I heard that city officials would be opening a center for anxious relatives. The next morning at dawn, I made my way to the hastily assembled Family Assistance Center, a crisis facility set up in the old armory on Lexington Avenue and East Twenty-fifth Street.

Already, thousands lined the street. They waited in worry and tears, hoping to fill out a missing-person report and glean what information they could. Inside, the place was packed with police officers, Red Cross officials, and desperate New Yorkers. I wended my way to the Red Cross chaplains' corner.

There I met Mindi Russell, a bright, charming Baptist minister from Sacramento, California. Mindi was September's on-call national coordinator for the Red Cross's Spiritual Care Program. If an emergency arose anywhere in the country that month, it was her solemn duty to board a plane pronto and coordinate the Red Cross's response. She enlisted me on the spot.

Running on adrenaline and caffeine, she gave me the double-time tour and a speedy lesson on the setup, then handed down my assignment. "Okay, Father John," she said, "go stand over there against the wall, and after everyone has filled out their paperwork, we'll send them to you if they want spiritual counseling. All you have to do is listen and be a compassionate presence." She gave me a smile, turned on her heels, and headed off to attack untold problems. For the next three months, I tried to be that compassionate presence of peace.

During my tenure, I met one-on-one with some fifteen hundred grieving relatives.

As the first day came to a close, Mindi and a handful of Red Cross officials approached me. Would I be willing to serve as a local coordinator for the Red Cross chaplains, here at the Family Assistance Center? And might I be the supervisor? I considered a moment. Yes, I would. Mindi handed me a coordinator's pass, which gave me the highest clearance possible, authorizing me to travel anywhere in the city. It was clear they were desperate—they hadn't a clue who I was, of my criminal record or my unpopular stand for peace.

And so I embarked on my new role. More than 550 chaplains from every religion ministered under my supervision. I worked out difficulties in scheduling and problems of security. I gave orientations to each new chaplain and debriefed each one at the end of every shift, and I taught others to do the same. None of the chaplains were to leave the center until we had gathered together and prayed and shared how we were bearing up. And no one was dismissed before telling the group what he or she planned to do that night for relaxation and rest. I took on no chaplains who refused to participate in those daily sessions. It was a lesson for all, including me, in the fine art of pastoral care and of compassionate listening. You had to take care of yourself if you were going to be of service to others.

On September 14, the day after I had assumed my role as coordinator, I ventured with churning innards and a measure of curiosity to Ground Zero, where my eyes met destruction on a scale beyond imagining. Every block closer struck the senses harder. The television reports simply could not capture the horror. Blocks had been obliterated, sixteen acres all told, with many buildings hit by debris from the two towers. Everything was covered in white ash. At the World Trade Center plaza rose "the Pile," a mound of steel and rubble looming seven stories high. Smoke billowed forth, flames here and there. The stench was overpowering.

Hundreds of rescue workers poked about, tugging on fragments of girders and masses of stone, coming periodically upon a body. In my clerical attire and yellow hard hat, with a security pass slung around my neck, I was an incongruous sight. I marched right up to the edge of the site and stood there overcome with astonishment, nausea, and grief.

Within seconds, a fireman came scrambling down the Pile, ran up to me, and said, "Father, quick, give me your blessing. I'm digging for my best friend." I uttered a prayer and off he dashed, back up the Pile like a squirrel up a tree.

For the rest of the day, workers accosted me—desperate to talk, overwhelmed by grief, exhausted and running on adrenaline. One begged, "Father, please, teach me how to pray. We found the body of my friend yesterday, and I just don't know what to do." No one had ever asked me how to pray. Never had I been pressed for such large answers in such short order, much less before such a sight. God loves you very much, I told him, so just turn to God, ask for help and guidance, and keep on doing that for the rest of your life.

For hours, scores approached me, grief-stricken and tired. I remember one man in particular, Emilio, a friendly police officer. It was his task to sort torsos and limbs, and he suffered terrible distress over his macabre work at the makeshift morgue. He woke up each night after ghastly dreams screaming at the top of his lungs. What should I do, Father? he asked me.

By Monday, the city had uprooted the Family Assistance Center and transported every computer and pencil and stapler to a convention center on West Fifty-fourth Street by the Hudson, a venue typically used for fashion shows and beauty contests. Big enough to accommodate five thousand people, it now served as a center of operations for cooks, nurses, ministers, police officers, city officials, mental health workers, and the grief-stricken throngs. This would be the center's home through Thanksgiving.

In one wing, hundreds of booths were set up with phones and computers; there families could register their missing, submit DNA specimens, pore over lists of the bodies, and complete death certificates. Another wing housed a warren of offices—for the Red Cross, the police, the mayor, translators, and volunteer coordinators. A third wing offered an elegant restaurant that turned out fine meals for the bereaved at all hours, free of charge. And finally, there were the lounges, places of respite where the exhausted could secure child care, watch television, or get a massage. Every day, sacks and sacks of mail poured in. The walls soon filled with letters and bright drawings from children around the country.

I met countless poor souls. Mary, a security guard employed on the seventieth floor of the North Tower, clambered down flights of stairs and broke for daylight just before the collapse—all her co-workers presumably died, and her poor self was trembling still. When I met Neil, a Long Island Catholic, he was clutching a bag of hairs snatched from a comb—a DNA specimen from his missing brother-in-law. In his case, the body had been found, one of the few intact. Neil hunched over hours of paperwork; then, in tears, he placed the dreaded call to the family. I got him through as best I could and sent him on his way with a blessing and a prayer.

Then there was the family of twelve who flew in from Europe in search of a missing son. I bestowed a blessing, and each in turn offered me a hug and a kiss. And the retired New Jersey couple searching for their son; I sat by as their mouths were swabbed for DNA. And the crying and quaking young man who flew in from Italy all by himself in hopes of finding his mother; and the businessman who had lost fifty colleagues. At Ground Zero, I met the dozen firefighters just arrived from Mexico—a gift from the Mexican government—diminutive and scrappy, awaiting their chance to attack the Pile. "Please lead us in prayer, Padre," they said. We joined hands, I murmured a prayer, and they burst into tears. Then off they went, up the Pile.

I harbor images, too, of the working poor—security guards, window washers, restaurant workers—who survived by a hairsbreadth and were now in mourning for friends, in the grips of survivor's guilt, in need of financial help. And I recall, at the other end of the spectrum, the chief executive of ConEdison, dressed in a pinstripe suit and addressing a group of electrical workers two blocks from Ground Zero. He spotted me from across the street, cried out, "Father! Father!" and made his way over. Our eyes met and his sobbing began. "I'm here to dig up wires, but . . . I lost my . . . I can't handle it . . . I lost my brother and my brother-in-law and countless associates. I don't know what to do . . . Don't let them see me cry. What should I do?" "Let's pray," I suggested, "and then you go back and do what only you know how to do: restore power to lower Manhattan." He covered his face. I offered a solemn blessing. Before long, he regained composure, wiped away his tears, ran back to the group, and started giving directions.

So many people, a blur in my battered memory, all of them crying out, "Father, please pray—" I prayed, and more. I saw and touched and listened; I held hands and wiped tears. I answered so many questions, many of a religious sort. Catholics in particular were desperate to know, can we have a funeral Mass even though there's no casket, no . . . body?

▣ ▣

Over and over again, I witnessed the pain of denial. Laura wept as I held her; she tried to tell me between sobs of her husband, Milton, and how she had awoken the night before and heard his whistle, so loud and clear. She knew he was alive. Patricia woke up to the sound of running water and discovered the faucet on—a sign her husband was well. At any moment, he would appear. You don't know my husband (or son, or father), I heard again and again. He can work his way out of anything.

Six weeks into the tragedy, many families were still adamant: You'll be getting no missing-person report from us. Our loved one, by God, will shortly turn up in good health. Wait and see.

By early October, the prime issue became how to help families break out of the denial. City officials decided to offer a ferry ride down the Hudson from the center to Ground Zero to allow family members to take in the devastation, concede their loss, and start the paperwork. A thousand took up the offer, and boatload upon boatload made the trip. Two chaplains were present at every trip. I went along a dozen times, without doubt the hardest task I faced during a bad and mournful time.

Sixty or seventy people would walk solemnly on board. The boat engines would start up, and we would lurch from the pier. Soldiers with machine guns would stand on the deck or trail behind us in smaller boats. Before long, we would pull alongside the site, the Pile a hundred yards off, and silence would invariably fall upon us all. We would huddle close and creep to the ruins, still smoldering. Upon our approach, rescue workers would lay aside their tools, remove their hard hats, and pay their respects with silence. We would come close to the edge of the Pile, and, as every heart was pierced, a loud wail would rise into the air. My colleague and I would move among the mourners, their faces contorted, their bodies convulsed with sobs. Mothers, daughters, wives—we would hold them close, one by one. I felt like the disciple John standing at the foot of the cross and holding the grief-stricken Mary. A sense of helplessness suffused the smoky atmosphere, exceeding that of any war zone or garbage dump I had visited around the world.

We would turn away at last and head back to the boat. But before departing, we would make a lingering stop at the fence around the site. Families would leave flowers and utter last good-byes and take one last look. Finally, we would shuffle back to the ferry. The return ride proved even harder. A dense pall would hang in the air, like the very smoke that rose from the Pile.

Those were strange, unforgettable days. The grief in New York City was palpable and overwhelming. But an unusual spirit descended, something of compassion and unity. People on the street spoke kindly. Even in elevators, where normally all eyes are fixed on the ground, conversation came easily. Passersby exchanged nods, eyes searching out eyes as if to ask, "Have you lost somebody?" A luminous moment—help was freely offered, smiles abounded, kind words issued from everyone's lips. For a week or two, it was a transformed city.

Then, soon after 9/11, the president mounted the pulpit at the National Cathedral, accompanied by his Pentagon courtiers, and announced that he would be a war president. Before long, the bombs started to fall. Overnight, literally hundreds of American flags appeared on the walls and the ceiling at the Family Assistance Center. And just as quickly, the families stopped coming.

The president's speech marked the beginning of the end of the compassion in New York City. Within days, we were told not to grieve but to be patriotic, to support the troops, to cheer the bombers.

Instead of following their hearts, New Yorkers did as they were told. Go to the mall and shop, the president urged.

We were also instructed to hate the people of Afghanistan. We would bring these evildoers to justice, the war president said, "dead or alive." We had enemies, and our job was to kill them. At once, immigrants, dissidents, and those who held an opposing view felt a malign gaze on the back of their necks. I reflected on my own fortune. What, in this climate, might become of me? How would I fare under a spirit of vengeance?

But I reflected for only a moment, because a moment was all I could spare. I was spurred to take action in this dark hour by the anonymous few who had a different opinion from the one that prevailed on the street. I remember one Catholic mother who came to Ground Zero to find closure over the loss of her son, hoping the trip would bear her along. She gazed at the towering wreckage and wept awhile. Then, back on the boat, she looked me in the eye and whispered, "I have no room for anger."

I was astonished at her strength. The ground rules had been set by our president, and the media had made things clear: This woman's role was to call for blood. She was supposed to be angry and vengeful. But no, this mother kept her heart to herself and let it lead the way, a path forged by grief, conscience, and love. "I feel only compassion for the families of the hijackers," she said. "Imagine what suffering they must have known to produce such violence. What must their families be going through?" With that, she rejected out of hand any sort of retaliation. "Bombing Afghanistan will never bring my son back," she concluded, stating what no one else had dared state. "It will only add to my grief." Hers was a greatness I rarely encountered in anyone during those days.

Few people asked the questions this mother entertained: Why did they do it? How is it that hijackers, crazed men, came to carry out suicide attacks? The president and the Pentagon outlawed such questions, and the docile media complied—for reasons manifestly clear. If we scratch beneath the surface and dig just a little to comprehend U.S. crimes across the world, the supposed mystery of September 11 shapes up as a simple matter of cause and effect.

Thousands died at the World Trade Center towers, one hundred twenty-five at the Pentagon, and sixty-four more in the plane crash near Pittsburgh. And with hearts of flesh we mourned, our days overwhelmed by waves of grief. But in Iraq, thanks to U.S. sanctions, mourning had long ago reached a different level altogether. For years in that region, the people had been drowning in oceans of grief. How does one begin to fathom the deaths of half a million children? The psychic ruin of the survivors, their grief? Can one ever dare to hope for anything approaching their psychological healing?

Moreover, in the West Bank and Gaza, parents mourned the hundreds of young people shot by Israeli soldiers with weapons made in the United States. Tens of thousands around the world die daily of starvation, our globalization and hegemony at work, while U.S. companies steal their resources and reap their profits. In other words, many people the world over have many reasons to be angry at the United States. But to make that kind of statement, in some quarters, amounts to treason.

At Ground Zero, my mind often wandered among the Gospels. I pondered Jesus' approach to Jerusalem. When he came in sight of the great city, he broke down and wept, saying, "If this day you only knew what makes for peace—but now it is hidden from your eyes. For the days are coming upon you when your enemies will raise a palisade against you. . . . They will smash you to the ground . . . and they will not leave one stone upon another within you because you did not recognize the time of your visitation" (Luke 19:42–44).

It makes sense, in a world in which violence is heaped upon violence, that anger over U.S policies might surge into some form of retaliation. Somewhere far away, the frustration festered and resources were pooled. And with the same attention to strategy and training practiced by warmakers everywhere, they made their attack. Was it really so improbable? As we begin to comprehend the massive grief we've inflicted around the world, can we deny the possibility that enraged and powerless people, when given the resources and the opportunity, would resort to such insanity? You will reap what you sow, Jesus said long ago. Future attacks, perhaps far worse, are our lot unless we radically alter the way we as a people behave in the world. I believe that unless we make restitution, stop our war-making, feed the world's children, and show respect to the human family, we are doomed to more 9/11s.

The Bible says that overcoming evil requires a different course altogether; it is a matter of active goodness. Active goodness conquers without spilling blood. If we feed the world's hungry, eradicate disease, offer free medicine, and model respect, we will win the world with our love. We had a moment's opportunity after 9/11. Oddly enough, the people of the world clearly felt compassion for us. We could have changed history with a loving, nonviolent response. A few years later, I was with Archbishop Tutu when he asked, "What would have happened if in response to 9/11, the U.S. had built three thousand schools in Afghanistan?" It boggles the mind to consider all that we could build for the public good for the price of one fighter bomber.   .

"Every person in the United States should visit Ground Zero," a firefighter testified before a crowd at a peace rally; it was perhaps his first time ever speaking out. "Then they would see for themselves the horror of war and stand against the bombing of Afghanistan."

回 回

In New York, as the drums grew louder and the days more fevered, I walked in marches, stood in vigils, and spoke at rallies. I served with one hand and opposed war with the other. A basic tenet of the journey to peace is that I love my enemies as well as my neighbors—all of them grieving, Afghans and Iraqis and New Yorkers. This is a promiscuous kind of love, to be sure, gratuitous and undiscriminating. But the Gospel requires it. Jesus calls for, in the words of the Sermon on the Mount, "unusual love."

Mairead Maguire came to visit me in early October, on the day before the United States unleashed its jets over Afghanistan. I toured her through the Family Assistance Center and introduced her to police officers, chaplains, officials, and grieving family members. The next day, some fifteen thousand heard Mairead speak at an antiwar rally in Times Square. "I come here to tell the United States to do what you have been telling us in Northern Ireland to do—not to retaliate, not to bomb, not to kill, but to seek peace through negotiation, dialogue, interfaith cooperation, and nonviolent alternatives." The crowd gave a long cheer.

At a rally in Washington Square with Amy Goodman and Patti Smith the following week, I urged those in attendance to proclaim the gospel truth, distilled to a few unpopular but unassailable tenets: War is not the answer. War does not work. War cannot bring peace. War is not the will of God. War is never justified. War is never blessed by God. There is no security in war—or in nuclear weapons, bombing raids, missile shields, or greed.

I quoted words Gandhi wrote shortly after World War II: "The moral to be drawn from the tragedy of destruction is that it cannot be resolved by counter-bombs, even as violence cannot be ended by counter-violence." I quoted him also at an evening interfaith prayer service a week after September 11: "Hatred can be overcome only by love. Violence can be overcome only by nonviolence."

Gandhi heartened me as I rambled along the streets of New York during those first days after 9/11. More, the nonviolent Jesus impelled me onward. I inclined my heart to his and therein found the courage to agitate for peace, hold peace vigils, love the ones I shouldn't—and do it all publicly. It was a time of grief, but, for me, a time of grace as well.

The Family Assistance Center closed down that Thanksgiving. Like everyone else, I fairly collapsed from exhaustion. But I needed to plod on against the U.S. war on the Afghans. The suicide bombers had not been funded by Afghanistan, pauper among the nations, reduced to rubble already. The more likely benefactor was our oil-rich ally Saudi Arabia, whose ruling family was close friends of the Bushes. This, of course, was never sorted out in the public square, the truth having been clapped in irons and thrown to the bottom of the sea and replaced by a more convenient version of events. Regardless of what had or had not actually happened or who was responsible, one fact was inescapable: once again, impoverished children would die. I had no choice but to denounce U. S. war-making and take considerable heat for doing so.

Six months prior, my Kairos group had begun a weekly peace vigil in Union Square, where we would plant ourselves every Saturday for an hour, holding banners denouncing war. Afterward, we would fold up the banners and repair to a coffee shop. I joined in whenever I was in town. One Saturday that winter, I stood with Bob Keck and Dan Berrigan, a large banner stretched between us that said "Love Your Enemies: Stop Bombing Afghanistan!" The normal flow of pass-ersby eyed us warily or not at all. But one, a tough young New Yorker, marched up to me and let out a stream of abuse in a classic New Yawk dialect. The brunt of it: I was a Communist and a traitor.

Finally, he served up his coup de grâce. "What would you do," he cried, "if I pulled out a gun and killed you right here in Union Square?"

Thanks to all those hours with Jesus and years of learning peace of the heart, I was able to enter a place of detachment. I looked the young man in the eye, took a step beyond myself, and tried to come to some understanding of his rage. From what well did it spring? How might he respond, I wondered, if he knew of my recent stint as chaplain to all those devastated relatives of the dead?

"Well," I answered finally, in a tired voice, "I guess I would go straight to heaven to spend eternity in peace with Jesus and the saints, and you would be arrested and spend the rest of your life in a tiny prison cell, perhaps on death row. And I would grieve for you."

Seconds passed in silence as Dan and Bob looked on. Rattled, the man stalked off in a huff, down the line to set off sparks with someone else. He shortly let loose on one of the Catholic Workers, an intellectual among us who worked his prodigious calming magic and thoughtfully engaged the man in a lengthy dialogue. As our hour wound down, the man returned to me, all apologies.

This was but one small sign of hope, penetrating the New York atmosphere like a blade of grass coming up through the sidewalk. Soon enough, more signs sprang up—for instance, a special gathering of 9/11 relatives who had assembled themselves into an organization, September 11th Families for Peaceful Tomorrows, which spoke against the U.S. bombing raids. They insisted on reconciliation with the people of Afghanistan and Palestine and Iraq. Bravely they issued heart-wrenching statements: Do not kill in retaliation—please, not in the names of our loved ones. Some went so far as to journey in peace to Afghanistan and Iraq, a large and abiding gesture of love.

From among these sublime spirits, I knew Colleen Kelly best. Years before, I had baptized her children. Her brother had perished in one of the towers. Yet off she went to work full-time for September 11th Families, leaving her old job behind. She spoke out of her grief with a sparkling and prophetic eloquence. "No war," she said. "Violence against violence bears nothing but further violence." Her message took deep root in the hearts of many. Drawing from her inspiration, hundreds of people gathered new courage to take a stand.

Meanwhile, the U.S. Catholic bishops had taken matters in hand. But instead of taking that gospel stand for peace, they stood with the Pentagon in its call for war. While the United States bombed Afghanistan and sent some seven million poverty-stricken refugees scurrying to the freezing mountains, the bishops met in a classy Washington, D.C., hotel and held a special Mass for peace at the National Shrine of the Immaculate Conception. There, an admiral of distinction was invited up to the lectern to read the Scriptures. Then the outgoing president of the bishops' conference intoned excerpts from the Sermon on the Mount: "You have heard that it was said . . . 'You shall not kill; and whoever kills will be liable to judgment.' But I say to you, whoever is angry with his brother will be liable to judgment . . ." With that, the good bishop launched into a speech declaring the bishops' full support of the war. The next day, his successor entered the studios of National Public Radio and reiterated the bishop's blessing—in essence, bomb the hell out of Afghanistan; it's the will of God. I heard this myself.

"The bishops have abandoned us," Dan said later that night. Sorrow flickered in his eyes. A week later, he spoke before a packed audience at a Catholic university. We might as well burn our Gospels, he said. We might as well process into our sanctuaries holding aloft the air force manual and offer it billows of incense and recite its supreme command: "Kill your enemy." Then our true fidelity would be revealed—to the false gods of war, the idols of death.

As days shortened and the nights grew longer, theologian Jim Douglass and his wife, Shelley, arrived at our door, all the way from Alabama. A weekend retreat was in the works—just Jim, Shelly, Dan, and me. We needed time to pray over events, compare notes, and reflect again on Gospel nonviolence.

Dan had a quote from Thomas Merton, circa 1962, the Cuban missile crisis then dangling over the world like a sword on a thread: "We are at a point of momentous choice," wrote Merton. "Either our frenzy of desperation will lead to destruction, or our patient loyalty to truth, to God and to humanity will enable us to perform the patient, heroic task of building a world that will thrive in unity and peace."

> At this point, Christian action will be decisive. That is why it is supremely important for us to keep our heads and refuse to be carried away by the wild projects of fanatics who seek an oversimplified and immediate solution by means of inhuman violence. Christians have got to speak by their actions. Their political action must not be confined to the privacy of the polling booth. It must be clear and manifest to everybody.
>
> It must speak loudly and plainly the Christian truth, and it must be prepared to defend that truth with sacrifice, accepting misunderstanding, injustice, calumny, and even imprisonment or death. It is crucially important for Christians today to adopt a genuinely Christian position and support it with everything they've got. This means an unremitting fight for justice in every sphere—in labor, in race relations, in the Third World, and above all in international affairs. Our

social actions must conform to our deepest religious prin-
ciples. Beliefs and politics can no longer be kept isolated from
one another.

We feasted on Merton's challenge and agreed to speak out loudly and
plainly, as best we could. "We have to be a voice for peace and hope,"
Dan said. "The time is dark and dangerous; there is terrorism, blind
patriotism, in the air. But no matter. Our message received or not, our
task is to keep the Gospel alive."

Added Jim: "In order to be hopeful, we need to be hopeful beyond
the United States, to be hopeful for all humanity, to be hopeful from
God's perspective. Our prayer must be, 'Thy will be done'—God's
will being 'Peace on Earth.'"

As a kind of solemnity descended, we turned next to the words of
Dr. King, uttered the night before he died. "The choice is no longer
violence or nonviolence. It's nonviolence or nonexistence."

"We must help others choose nonviolence," Jim said, breaking
the silence. "We must find hope not just for North Americans but
for the whole human race; we must help humanity adopt the way of
nonviolence."

This would be no easy task. But as we later passed the bread and
the cup, we felt consoled and emboldened to do what we could. We
figured that as long as we remained focused on the peacemaking Jesus,
we would not vanish with the dark. There would be light enough for
each new step. We ended feeling more hopeful and more committed
to the mission ahead.

The darkness was dark indeed. By now, we had entered the era of
permanent war, dubbed with all the slickness of Madison Avenue "the
war on terrorism." It was a dirty little rubric under which the government could get away with all manner of monkey business—bombing

raids, election fraud, surveillance, threats, and the removal of civil liberties. The powers that be honored war as raison d'être, as big business, as America's destiny, as global domination, as empire.

And it quickly came home. Dissenters would be monitored and tracked, ridiculed and harassed, arrested on pretext and thrown in jail. Something must be done, and I would do what I could. But I might be a mere voice in the wilderness. Who would listen? Even many U.S. church officials supported war.

A voice in the wilderness. I resolved to write George W. Bush an open letter. It struck a spark, and the Internet carried it around the globe.

> I ask you to stop immediately the bombing of Afghanistan, to stop your preparations for other wars, to cut the Pentagon's budget; to lift the sanctions on Iraq; end U.S. military aid to Israel; stop U.S. support of the occupation of the Palestinians; lift the entire Third World debt; dismantle every one of our nuclear weapons and weapons of mass destruction; abandon your Star Wars Missile Shield program; join the world court; obey international law; and close our own terrorist training camps, beginning with Fort Benning's "School of the Americas."
>
> The only solution to these international crises is to overcome evil with goodness, not further evil. That means we need to win the world over with nonviolent love. We need to change the direction of our country, feed every starving child and refugee on the planet, end poverty at home and abroad, stop all injustices and military aid, create a new nonviolent foreign policy that will serve humanity and support U.N.-based nonviolent international peacemaking teams.

Violence is not only immoral and illegal, it's just down-right impractical. Your global violence is doomed to fail and lead to further suffering because it will only stir up further hostility against us. In the name of the God of peace and compassion, please reverse your destructive course, and start us in a new direction, toward a lasting peace with justice for all people on the planet.

I want you to know that millions of us around the country will continue to oppose your policies and wars. I speak to tens of thousands of students and churchgoers every year, and I find little support for your war. We will continue to pray for peace, march for peace, demonstrate for peace, speak out for peace, work for peace, propose peace, and resist your determined opposition to peace.

You could save us all a lot of trouble and further loss of life around the world by taking the high ground, adopting the vision of nonviolence, exercising true moral leadership and leading us in a better direction toward a world without war, starvation, poverty, oppression or injustice That is the only way to guarantee no more terrorist attacks. In that way, you will help us offer future generations a life of peace.

Winter arrived, and toward January 2002, I sojourned to Block Island for a month, presiding at Mass as my friend Ray Kehew, the usual priest, rested in warmer climes. My month there afforded me a rest after the weary days as a Red Cross chaplain. I reveled in the peace and quiet, spent hours staring out to sea, even spotted a gray whale one cold morning. It was a time of healing and renewal and preparation.

Kicked Out
of New York
(2002)

It was on Block Island that I heard the news: a former Boston priest had been convicted of sexually abusing scores of boys. He was imprisoned and, later, at the hands of a fellow prisoner, killed in cold blood. Other news emerged in fits and starts. As it turned out, he was by no means the only sex offender priest. There were dozens in Boston alone. Church authorities now under duress proceeded to take a grudging inventory. Over the next few years, it came to light: since 1950, more than four thousand U. S. priests had been accused of molesting more than ten thousand young people. And all the while bishops and cardinals had quietly relocated offenders and chosen not to notify public officials.

News of this naturally stirred outrage and pain. And right before our eyes, the institutional church seemed to come apart at the rivets. Many people spoke out in the name of justice and demanded, among other things, reparation for the victims, removal of certain bishops and cardinals—also the end of mandatory celibacy for priests and the ordination of women and married people.

The institutional church clamped down immediately. Damage control superseded the making of amends and reforms. Moreover, those who ventured upon such prickly topics drew a forbidding eye from on high; raising questions was pronounced taboo. Even so, pressure continued to gather behind closed doors, and eventually Boston's Cardinal Bernard Law stepped down. The Vatican relocated him to serve as a church rector in Rome.

The church has a blessed role: to be the peacemaking community of the nonviolent Jesus. And thus, acknowledged or not, it has a solemn charge: to walk in his footsteps, implement his teachings, take up his cross in the struggle for justice, and, finally, witness to his resurrection gift of peace. In a church of nonviolence, we would no longer value power, domination, or control. We would be more concerned with justice and healing than with self-protection. We would be God-of-peace-centered, and thus truly catholic, which is to say universal in our love for human beings and creation itself.

The sex abuse scandal brought to light some critical shortcomings; the church failed to serve our people. Changes were overdue and urgently needed. I offer a simple argument: St. Peter was married, according to the synoptic Gospels. The New Testament brims with hints of women's leadership—as teachers, deacons, and, occasionally, overseers of large house churches. The age is dawning for married priests, women priests, and shared decision making.

The key to this kind of transformed church will be its renunciation of the just-war theory. Then the church will have only the gospel of peace on which to stand. Entanglements with the empire will unknot and fall away, and clarity will descend and bank accounts will close and false peace will evaporate. Once we have extricated ourselves from the culture of war, we will be free at last to embrace the nonviolence— and the transforming love—of Jesus and the early martyrs.

The day the church clarifies its conscience, nonviolence will become a common and accepted requirement of Christian discipleship. And in that attitude and atmosphere, priests and all other Christians will understand at their core that they cannot do harm—to adults or to children. Covering up such violence in the name of protecting reputation and bank balances will not even be an option.

I already had a letter to the president, taking him to task for his murderous policies, under my belt. Why not an essay to the church? In my time of solitude, I discerned the link between the emerging sex abuse scandal and the U.S. bishops' support of the war on Afghanistan; both were cut from the same philosophical, cultural cloth. So I composed an essay titled "The Scandal of the Church's Support of War." It traveled quickly over the Internet and around the world.

▣ ▣

I returned to New York infused with new energy. I planned my itinerary of speaking engagements and put pen to paper for a new book, *Mary of Nazareth, Prophet of Peace*. Then, toward mid-April, I received an unlikely call. It was the New York provincial. Would I be so kind as to drop by tomorrow for a meeting? He had never acknowledged me before or shown interest in my FOR projects. Why now? I agreed to the meeting.

The provincial was all business. He bore an air of equanimity and perfect self-control. He sat back and entered into a lengthy monologue, the aim of which was to discharge accumulated grievances against me. He had received a few stormy complaints from wealthy benefactors over my recent essays. He asked me who I was to say anything about the church, or the president, or peace.

He concluded that I was "not missionable . . . not available . . . not obedient"—at least those are the terms I remember hearing. What I *don't* remember hearing were any questions about my prayer, or how I regarded the call of Jesus in times such as these. Or my take on the Jesuit mission. Or my recent work as a Red Cross chaplain. Or my community life and its support. Or anything else involving my heart and soul.

Such trifling matters as discerning God's will, the mounting sex scandal, war, and the nature of the church never got an airing. And I wasn't really being asked to answer any of the questions directed at me.

The sad conclusion to this meeting was that there were no opportunities for me in New York. The time had come for me to leave the province.

At forty-two years old, I had professed solemn final vows. I had long ago—in prison, in war zones, on the streets—proven my priestly calling. I had addressed hundreds of thousands by now, poured myself out for the Christian ideal of peace, ministered to New York's bereaved. But all that counted for nothing when funding was threatened. I was kicked out of New York by the Jesuits.

Present yourself to the Maryland provincial, he directed me, and receive further instructions. One week later, in Philadelphia, a deadline was set. You have three months, the Maryland provincial told me. Go anywhere in the United States you want, but get out of New York now. If you don't, you will find yourself teaching sophomore religion at St. Joe's Prep in Philly come Labor Day.

Devastated and overcome, I skulked home and wept. Dan regarded me with pity and offered to help. But everything was a shambles and there was nothing anyone could do. I moped about for days even though I really didn't have the luxury. My calendar bulged with planned trips and talks and retreats, so I kept focused on that and dwelled as little as I could on the more dolorous matters at hand. In fact, I pretended it was all a bad dream.

I didn't know where I would go, but as the days proceeded, I decided that I would not leave the Jesuits. Dozens I knew had left long ago over far less provocation, but the calls I had heard at Duke, the call that rang in Galilee—they had lost none of their appeal. Despite being shown the door, I was bound and determined to remain a priest, and a Jesuit at that. Despite rejection, I would try to be faithful. That, I thought, was God's will for me.

I placed calls, including a number to friends in New Mexico, beginning with Father Bill McNichols and Father Tim Martinez, pastors of the adobe Church of St. Francis in Ranchos de Taos, its visage made famous by the artist Georgia O'Keeffe. They had always told me, When the going gets tough, come to New Mexico. There's plenty to do, and it's beautiful. And who cares about you if you are wandering around in the desert?

Tim put me in touch with the chancellor of the Archdiocese of Santa Fe. My status as disgraced Jesuit and notorious peace-maker hung on the air, but he swept it away—he was desperate. In keeping with my sense of call, I offered to take the poorest parish in the state, the one that no other priest wanted. Come out and visit, he said, and let's see what we can arrange. I flew out for an interview. After a lengthy give-and-take, he offered me not one but five parishes. And, on top of that, four missions. It seems I was missionable after all.

That August, I packed up my papers and books and prepared to go. As my time dwindled, I enjoyed many long walks and late-night dinners with Dan and a farewell soiree hosted by my friend the folksinger Dar Williams. But there were no good-byes. Dan and the community counted themselves my friends, and such friendships endure. Being shuffled around was the Jesuit's destiny anyway. To utter good-bye struck us all as vain. We were all in this together, whatever our address. And so I turned and headed toward the sunset.

I decided to drive, welcoming the time to reflect. And I wanted to undergo the journey in stages—from the Upper West Side of Manhattan, through the Great Smoky Mountains of Tennessee and the plains of Oklahoma, under the low skies of Texas, and into the high desert of northeastern New Mexico.

Scenery passed and miles piled up behind me. I put on music—Joan Baez, the Beatles, U2, Jackson Browne—and tried to keep my chin up, my embattled heart seeking a place of repose. You did not betray Jesus, I told myself. You spoke out on behalf of the victims of war; you tried to love your neighbors and your enemies. You tried to help the church reclaim its calling; you tried to be a faithful Jesuit apostle. You tried to announce the good news of the Gospel. You tried to put a stop to wars and the murder of children. I came up with a litany of solid achievements; but still my spirit sagged.

I remembered then those great Beatitudes, first encountered long ago on a hill by the Sea of Galilee. "Blessed are you when they insult you and persecute you and utter every kind of evil against you [falsely] because of me. Rejoice and be glad, for your reward will be great in heaven. Thus they persecuted the prophets who were before you."

Well then. I was in trouble; I had been insulted and excluded, rejected and sent packing, thrown out on my ear. But this was the good stuff, the climax of the Beatitudes, my chance to be like the prophets of old, like Dr. King and Mahatma Gandhi, and Jesus himself. He was put down and dismissed and rejected, and eventually killed. Why, as his disciple, should I expect anything different? "The measure of your discipleship," Dorothy Day once said, "is the amount of trouble you are in for justice and peace."

In a culture of war, those who speak for peace will quickly be shown the door. In a church that turns a blind eye upon child abuse and blesses the murder of children, those who speak out will surely be pushed aside. Such stands have consequences, as Jesus showed us. They are inevitable and painful, but in the end a cause for rejoicing. Suffering such consequences, Luke says, contrary to worldly reason, marks one as blessed. So start dancing for joy.

To endure rejection because of my gospel teachings was part of my job description. I felt a surge of joy. You're right on course, I told myself. As Dan urged long ago, perhaps my story was finally fitting into the story of Jesus.

Pastor in
New Mexico
(2002–4)

Manhattan: island of skyscrapers, sirens, screeching brakes, and screaming adults, the ultimate All-American hustle and bustle. Nothing there could prepare a person for Springer, New Mexico: to the east, vast gray plains as far as the eye can see; to the west, some forty miles away, the postcard-perfect snowcapped Rockies. Located in the middle of nowhere, Springer is home to humans and beasts— deer, horses, cattle, antelope, buffalo, and large, raucous hawks. And draped above, an expanse of turquoise sky.

But poverty holds claim to the place. The 2000 census ranked New Mexico the poorest state in the nation. It's also first in military spending, nuclear spending, domestic violence, drunk driving, hunger, and suicide. There are more nuclear weapons within five miles of Albuquerque than in any other city in the world. If New Mexico seceded from the United States, it would be the world's third-largest nuclear superpower.

Springer is a microcosm of this land of contrasts—grace and beauty juxtaposed with poverty and pain. A gas station, bank, grocery store, and an antediluvian hotel-lined Main Street. Everything else was shuttered long ago. The state's nickname is Land of Enchantment, but locals have emended it: "Land of Entrapment." Once here, a person can never leave. The people are impoverished, struggling, and stuck. About twelve hundred live in trailers scattered out over six or seven blocks where the Santa Fe Trail once led pilgrims westward in search of gold. The remnant left behind—the unemployed, sick, and elderly—get by on little else but Friday night high school football and Sunday morning Mass.

I arrived in Springer on a Thursday morning in late August 2002 and parked in front of the old rectory at St. Joseph's Church, which would be my home base for the next couple of years. A hundred years old, the rectory has a weary antebellum look, a kind of shabby stateliness—columns in front, a second-story balcony with broad wicker chairs, windows six feet high, and everything sinking in the middle. Inside are five bedrooms, four bathrooms, and a gracious front-room parlor for receiving guests. A handful of Jesuits lived here in the 1920s; every morning they took to the trail on horseback to work in the missions. In the 1950s, the place was home to ten nuns. Now it would be refuge for me alone.

I was met by Father John Brascher, the departing pastor, a large man with an easy smile and the gift of gab. He hailed from Springer and had spent his life serving his beleaguered town. He brought me in, sat me down, produced a pot of coffee, and spoke for hours about my new parishioners—their idiosyncrasies and whims and habits and sufferings. And he issued something in the nature of a warning. "The only way you can pastor in this remote desert world is if you have a lot of faith. You're going to need it to get through the long, lonely days." I gulped and nodded.

Later that day, I headed west toward the majestic Rockies and my other parishes and missions. It was my aim to get a feel for the circuit riding that would become my life. First I went to the little Church of St. Vincent De Paul in Maxwell, a village of a hundred so pitiably reduced that the gas station had gone under, then the general store, and finally the post office. From Maxwell, I trundled past the New Mexico detention center for teenagers, many serving decades for rape and murder, to the prison chapel, large and modern, where I would serve as chaplain, celebrate Mass, teach the Bible, and pay visits of a pastoral sort.

Then I headed due west along the gorgeous Cimarron Road, a lonely ribbon weaving through the plains. Endless fields lay left and right, fields of unrelieved flatness, home to hundreds of horses, deer, elk, and buffalo. Thirty miles later, Cimarron came into view, a little town cuddled against the Sangre de Cristo Mountains. *Cimarron* in Spanish means "wild and unruly." Here was a town quintessentially New Mexican, the Old West writ large, a storied place of violence and gunplay. A stone's throw from the church stands the vintage St. James Hotel, host back in the day to the likes of Kit Carson, Wyatt Earp, Annie Oakley, and Jesse James. Bullet holes pock the dining room ceiling, a legacy of the town's lawless days. The proprietors point them out with a certain measure of pride. And on the outskirts of town the "hangin' tree" still stands, a mighty oak reaching a stout limb high over the road, where occasions of frontier justice drew in people from miles away.

Today, nine hundred people reside in the town, most of them Hispanics, most subsisting in a permanent economic depression. It's not at all unheard of to come across homes with dirt floors. Jobs are hard to come by, and good health care is a distant dream. Public health officials estimate that six hundred suffer from cancer or diabetes. But ailing or not, all display deep faith, in large part because of Cimarron's small but dynamic parish, the Church of the Immaculate Conception.

The center of the church and the entire community is Sister Hildegarde Smith, our eighty-year-old pastoral associate, a member of the Sisters of Christian Charity, diminutive but formidable in her full nun's habit. Her ready laugh tempers the image of the stern nun, head to heel in black and white. She spent several decades in heroic labor as an elementary school principal in inner-city Chicago; then she packed up and moved to, of all places, Cimarron. When I arrived, she had been there ten years already, serving the needy day and night, living alone in a small trailer behind the two-room office and rectory next to the church.

Parishioners had added a deck to the trailer, and every morning Sister Hildegarde planted herself there for meditation and gazed upon the magnificent scene. Never leave, I told her. Stay put until the angels call you home. Such a view is a rarity in this world. Millionaires would vie for it; developers would try to sell it. And photographers, if they knew of it, would crowd the deck for a perfect shot. And it was all hers, a gift from Jesus.

Sister was, to my mind, an old-fashioned saint, the kind they don't make anymore. The fact that I—a notorious Jesuit—was thrust into her humble life was itself a sign that Divine creativity was afoot. Every day, she made the rounds, visiting Cimarron's shut-ins, meeting with young people, offering a word of hope. Plus, she arranged the weekly liturgies and ran the community food bank and consoled the grieving and managed a catechism program for the town's vast number of children. Every beleaguered family kept a weather eye for the arrival of her hallowed self, an occasion that invariably imparted a measure of encouragement. She was our own Mother Teresa.

From Cimarron, I drove into Cimarron Canyon, with its sparkling river and sculpted cliffs and enormous evergreens. Deep forests of pine lined the road, a sudden, lavish change from the barren plains.

The road took me to the mission churches of St. Mel's in Eagle Nest and San Antonio in Black Lake, near Angel Fire, a popular ski resort. St. Mel's stood out among my other parishes; it was a tight-knit community of wealthy retired military families from Texas. They had settled here to enjoy the snow and the skiing, and to go to church.

▣ ▣

I had arrived on Thursday; by Saturday I was pastor. Five Masses each weekend, twenty-nine during Christmas and Easter weeks, plus weddings, baptisms, feast day celebrations, parish council meetings, confessions, visits with the sick, anointing services, Monday-night Bible studies, and countless counseling sessions for those in need. I never worked harder in my life.

Two hundred people—most of them tourists—packed into St. Mel's on Saturday night for my first Mass. At the final Amen, I dashed out to my truck and careered through the winding canyon back to Cimarron, nearly an hour and a half away, for the late-night Saturday Mass. Talk about precision timing! I drove safe and fast, like James Bond.

The next morning, I was up with the sun. My first of three Masses was at St. Joseph's in Springer; then I was back at Cimarron, and after that, over to Maxwell. The benediction uttered, I headed back to Springer for a two-hour confirmation class and then a parish council meeting or two as night fell and the desert moon ascended. We often adjourned toward ten.

Thus went my days for the next few years. I arrived at one place and soon hustled off to another. I spurred along my used truck and clocked prodigious miles. I found that I enjoyed cruising the plains; in doing so, I came to know every vista, every horse and buffalo and gazelle, and in particular, one large brown hawk that perched on a barbwire fence on Cimarron Road all day long. I fancied myself a type of Adam in my own private Eden; I could have named every creature.

Communing with nature was one of the perks of the job. I can recall few others. As Father Brascher had warned, the job came with a weight of lonesomeness. No honor or glory accrues to the pastor. He is taken for granted and not taken seriously. Few build a relationship with him as spiritual guide, as a Buddhist might seek out a Zen teacher, or a Hindu a guru.

More often than not, the pastor is kept in the wings, a kind of second-string quarterback, a slumped figure at the end of the bench. Innocuous and familiar, a piece of old furniture—the hydrant, the traffic light, the pastor. But when crisis strikes, his phone rings off the hook and his office gets stormed; the people arrive desperate for help or with blame on their lips for God or the church. In the clutches of a fierce urge, they let off steam, all of it aimed, in lieu of God, at the pastor.

Meanwhile, the pastor endures a curious type of surveillance. Everyone in town keeps an eye on his whereabouts, what he does, who might be paying a visit. It's all of considerable interest and wondrously entertaining. At the post office, the clerk once asked me, "So how are things?" I confessed to a cold coming on. "Well, for goodness' sake," she said, "if you insist on keeping your bedroom window open like that, what do you expect?" My purchases at the grocery store evoked discussions across town—"Father, I understand you like vegetables"—as did everything else: "Morning, Father. You're up a little late today" and "Came by last night and checked your tires, Father. They're looking a little bald to me" and "Father, I wonder if you're getting a balanced diet; we're worried because you don't eat meat." Such are the daily encounters of the desert pastor. I later learned that folks occasionally drove around my block just to see what I was up to. That was their big night out, I guess. I also learned that they even toured the rectory when I was away, to see the pictures and plaques and art on my walls.

The people, however, are salt of the earth. Upon my arrival, I was introduced to Sam and Gloria Roy, St. Joseph's two-person staff. He was the property manager, and she was the parish secretary. They made me feel at home on the spot. Sam, a short, heavyset man with shoulders out to here, was right at home doing heavy lifting and fiddling with imposing machinery and taking care of any crisis. He was utterly down to earth and full of fun.

Gloria, a tiny, dark-haired woman, worked in the office from nine until noon. These were short hours by New York standards, but in a week's time I realized I had a pastor in my midst. A stream of neighbors made its way every morning to her desk, where she would natter about the weather and ease them through their latest problems and pat their wrinkled hands. A presence of unconditional love and compassion, she cast warmth about the place. I had on my hands a part-time secretary but a full-time saint.

There was Louie, a rancher in his eighties, a presence at daily Mass in Springer since he was an infant. Horses were his passion. He asked every day for me to come visit, but I was too busy. So one day, a knock sounded on the back door. I opened it and said, "Yes?" and lurched back, finding myself eye-to-nose with a lanky, brown horse. It issued a loud, snotty snort and stretched forward, looking me in the eye. "What in the world?" Louie emerged from around the corner, laughing his head off. Sufficiently recovered, I suggested we baptize the horse. "Oh Father John," Louie said, "he's already baptized. He wants to attend your confirmation classes."

And then there were Katherine and Paul and Nini and Anthony, of Cimarron. They had few worldly goods, but how they loved life, cherished their families, and served their community. They were hardy and hopeful, and their company was a profound pleasure. There was Martha from Springer, who had suffered the loss of her beloved son from kidney failure and bore concern for others who had the same disease. What resources enabled her to walk so bravely through life? And Odelia, who came to Mass each morning before heading to work at what passed as a grocery store. She bore troubles enough to sink a battleship but was buoyed by faith and joy. How did she do it? I regarded her intently, wanting to learn her secret. She just kept smiling, the perfect Zen master and a true believer.

Accompanying me through every Mass, every funeral, every feast, and every trial were the good Deacon Ed and his wife, Celia. From time to time, they invited me over for dinner. A maestro in the kitchen, Celia whipped up the most delectable meals. After one, Ed eyed me across the table and said that the next time he would prepare his own specialty—prairie dog. "They're plentiful and easy to catch. Basted on the grill or panfried with honey mustard and onions—your choice." My stomach tightened and my gorge rose at the thought. I offered a wan smile and murmured something along the lines of "Well, thank you . . . sounds . . . nice . . . but, you know, I'm a vegetarian." The joke caught me unawares twice. Then I got wise.

One morning a month after my arrival, I badly misjudged how long it would take me to get to a church close to the Colorado border where I was to preside at a funeral. Fearing I'd never make it, I pressed the accelerator hard and headed north at breakneck speed.

Mine was largely the only car on the road. I glanced at the clock and realized I should have been there five minutes ago. I glanced at the speedometer, the needle on a number I need not confess here. Then I glanced at the rearview mirror and saw, to my surprise, a car on my tail—a black and white car, its siren blaring. It took us a hundred yards to come to a stop. A cop I had never met before lumbered over to me. "Morning, sir," he said. "May I see your license?" I fumbled for it, sweating and nervous. He took a quick look and said, "Oh, it's you, Father John. You're late. You better get going; they're waiting for you." As I pulled away, he yelled after me, "Step on it." And off I zoomed.

These were my neighbors, my parishioners, my friends—this was my community. And then there was an altogether different kind of community. One night, heading home down a dirt road along the edge of Cimarron, I came to a halt at a stop sign and saw, out of the corner of my eye, a twitch in the dark. I glanced out my open window to discover, in the light of a big moon, a nose, inches away. It was a male elk, a creature fit for the cover of National Geographic, his headgear big as a mulberry tree, covering half the sky, with antlers that went on forever. He eyed me warily, took a long sniff, and then strolled around the truck as if he were an insurance adjuster. Satisfied finally, he loped on by. I took his departure to mean I was dismissed.

The boundary between nature's domain and ours was blurry indeed. Every morning, for instance, I discovered at the back door of the rectory the "remnants" of a bear. I use the word out of a sense of decorum; Sam lovingly called them "pies." And fresh pies at that, evidence that the bear, who loved the crab apple tree out back, had paid a visit to his local rectory not all that long ago—news this city boy absorbed with ambivalence. Sam told me how during Father Brascher's final homily, only days before I arrived, a bear stood up straight in the open door of the packed church. Evidently, in Springer, the occasional bear comes to Mass. Father Brascher's homily stalled midsentence, and all heads turned toward the back. The bear surveyed the sanctuary and held his ground until Sam courageously charged down the center aisle to run him off.

"You should have let the bear hear the sermon," I suggested, with due pastoral respect. "Perhaps he wanted to receive communion."

"Naw," said Sam. "He's Presbyterian."

回   回

Burying the elderly poor, most of whom had no health insurance, no money, and no medicine, shortly became my primary work. I presided at several funerals a week. Often the people died at home, in their forlorn trailers, in terrible pain, with a relative or two in attendance and Sister or me offering love, prayers, and blessings. My several attempts to interest hospice in our barren remoteness failed.

One day, I received an urgent call. A man from the outlying area, a raging alcoholic who had squandered the family's meager resources and mistreated his wonderful wife and two sons, lay in bed dying of cancer. Would I come and pray with him? asked his wife. "Sure, I'll come," I said. She issued a caveat. One thing you should know, she said: he hates God and despises the church.

I arrived that afternoon, gingerly entered the dim room, and introduced myself, prepared for a summary dismissal or a verbal assault. What I found was a man of seething anger all too ready to get a thing or two off his emaciated chest. His father had left him; his mother had abused him. And recently he had discovered that she wasn't his mother at all. Life had been a cruel hoax, and God was the prime jokester. "I hate the very idea of God. I despise your Jesus," he spat at me. "I don't have any need for them or you; what I need is a beer."

Here was an occasion in which platitudes were useless. Even the word love set off sparks. I steered clear of religious terrain and came up with a simple suggestion. Perhaps he might refrain from doing to his wife and children what his parents had done to him. Perhaps he might spend his last days letting go of his hatred and enjoying the kindness of his loving family. "I would rather spend eternity in hell," he grumbled; then he rolled over—his signal that my pastoral visit had ended.

I offered his wife the sad report of how our conversation had gone. But she expressed delight that it had occurred at all. And it did bear some fruit: a week later, he offered a clumsy word or two of tenderness to his family. He asked their forgiveness in the manner of a man speaking a foreign language for the first time. His wife and sons seized on every word with gratitude and wonder. Two days later, he died, at peace with himself, his family, and God.

I remember another funeral, in Maxwell, of a father of two young boys. Just five minutes before the funeral Mass was to begin, a loud roar filled the air, like that of a squadron coming in for a landing. A fleet of about fifty motorcycles rumbled to a stop outside the church door, and fifty tattooed men dressed head to toe in shiny black leather, with their wives and girlfriends similarly accoutred, strolled in, removing their sunglasses, scarves, and helmets in deference to the sacrament. They took their place right up front. Uh-oh, I thought. This is going to be tricky.

"The Lord be with you," I said, expecting puzzled silence. They returned as one with a lusty "And also with you!" I was among a hundred leather-clad well-practiced Catholics. They moved deftly through the liturgy as if they were bishops, sang songs deep from the heart, and cried like babies.

One after another, a dozen rose to deliver beautiful eulogies, each characterizing their dear friend as a great and beloved man and turning toward the man's wife and boys and praising his kindness. His wife in turn offered words of praise for this gang. During her husband's illness, she later told me, they had offered support and service and never left his side. Was this the gospel playing out before me? I began to suspect so.

The Mass over, they zippered up and mounted their Harleys. Someone grabbed the oldest boy and placed him on the back of a souped-up chopper, all chrome and glitter. Then they hitched the trailer to the bike, put the casket aboard, and made their solemn, if noisy, procession to the cemetery, the ten-year-old boy driving, leading the way. The assembly regarded the serious but smiling boy with great pride, and he himself couldn't help but hold his chin high. I later pondered the scene with astonishment and felt humble indeed. Gospel love breaks out where it will. These were personal friends of Jesus.

How often the example of my parishioners moved me. They always responded to a grieving family with generous love. After a funeral, the exhausted family would invariably return to a beautiful meal in the parish hall, assembled by twenty or so friends who had stayed up all night preparing. St. Joseph's bank account balance hovered around $2,000, and Sunday collections brought in far more coins than bills, but at first news of a parishioner's death, loving hands got busy making a feast to comfort the stricken. Sometimes they'd serve up to two hundred people, and then repeat it twice more that week.

▣ ▣

In Cimarron, six tough high schoolers were studying for their confirmation in a year's time. For my first weekly class with them I ambled in with a priestly air, and they cast me a cold look before turning away with a touch of contempt. Either the novelty of the class had worn off or they were under duress.

Tell me what you have been studying, I asked. "We know every-thing," one snapped, provoking a titter. I navigated as best I could the rapids of teenage angst and defiance. "Well, then, what do you think about the life of Jesus and the Gospels?" I continued. "Have you read the Gospels?"

"No."

"Okay," I said, "let's spend the year reading the Gospels, start-ing with Mark. Let's read it line by line. And you tell me what you think it means, what you like, what you don't like, what you think is true, what you think is nonsense, what doesn't make sense, and what appeals to you."

We started with chapter 1, and how they responded! The evening wore on in our dingy meeting room, and never was there a flagging of attention or energy. The Gospel of Mark astonished them; they in turn astonished me. They made startling connections that rang plain and true. John the Baptist appealed to them especially, "the voice of one crying in the wilderness," desert dweller just like them. And they knew well already the evils of the Roman Empire, and of those who make war—it wasn't a stretch for them to make the connection to the nuclear weapons industry chugging along day and night not far away. Then we came to Jesus' climactic pronouncement in chapter one: "The kingdom of God is at hand."

"What is that about?" I asked. They looked at one another, dis-mayed that I didn't know about the kingdom of God.

"The kingdom of God," said one student finally, "is life." What? Here was a priceless insight, out of nowhere, and it brought me up short. The substance of life itself is the kingdom of God.

I came down from my teacherly heights and looked at them with awe. Why had this never occurred to me before? The kingdom is life— in all its teeming variety and wildness and raucousness, its turns and surprises, its stubbornness and against-all-odds hanging on, its joys and loves and hopes and kindnesses, its peaceableness and simplicity, its music and gardens and parties, its warm sleep and simple work and plentiful food, its devoted lovers and laughing children and contented grandparents and admiring friends, its welcoming hugs and fascinating journeys and reassuring friendships. The reign of God is already here. In ordinary life. In breathing and wonder. The kingdom of God stakes itself in life itself. It is evidenced by our common life.

Such a gift this youth brought to my addled mind—an impoverished kid stuck in New Mexico's high desert, scarcely schooled, his prospects dim. Yet he offered a proposition with genuine authority, one worthy of Thomas Merton or Thich Nhat Hanh. The rest nodded in agreement. I smiled and nodded, too. But on the drive home my heart seized at such spontaneous wisdom. I gave thanks to the God of life that I lived at last to learn such truth. Of course, life itself is the kingdom of God. It's already here, right now.

A Voice
in the Desert
(2002–4)

O ne doesn't enter into the role of pastor in the Catholic Church without some knowledge of the ritual of confession. I confess to a passing knowledge; but practically speaking, this was new territory for me. Before Mass on Sunday mornings, a line would form outside the confessional, fifteen or twenty people long. Ensconced inside, I would ready myself to offer the sacrament of reconciliation. I shortly came to know the community's secrets, its problems and crises. And because I was in a privileged position, I sized up matters fast. Gossip is the commonest sin in a far-flung desert hamlet. People haul themselves through life side by side. Anonymity does not come with small-town life; it's a luxury found in big cities—as is news from the outside world. Consequently, news in a small town derives from neighbors. Everyone's business gets shouted from the housetops, incessantly and sometimes viciously.

From day one, I aspired to become princely among confessors. No matter the transgression, no matter how grave or shameful, I freely tendered forgiveness in Jesus' name. I doled out forgiveness as if it were lemonade at a church picnic. Would that I had written homilies as well as I forgave; in the forgiveness department, I was a worthy successor of the Curé d'Ars.

"You are forgiven; go in peace" was my gentle admonition to their straining ears. This was by no means the conclusion of the sacrament; rather, it signaled that it was just getting under way. "All the sins of your entire life are forgiven," I announced. "The slate is wiped clean. You get to start over." Why? they asked. "Because you are loved. God loves you, you in particular, right here in Springer. God loves you with a wild, infinite, unconditional love. God even likes you." This exegetical word invariably stopped them in their tracks. *God likes me? Is he crazy?*

"The challenge, however," I added, "is that you must forgive in return. Forgive yourself; forgive everyone in your family, everyone in town. Let go of every hurt and anger. Follow Jesus on the path of unconditional love and disarm your heart. From now on, you are going to shower everyone in your family and in town with love."

Many began to forgive themselves after decades of suffering the accusatory inner voice and its heaping up of shame. Many lowered their defenses against relatives and neighbors and put ancient trespasses out of mind. Forgiveness flowed lavishly, and self-esteem rose. People felt happier. In the process, the Good News—namely, that nonviolence resides at the heart of God—dawned in more than a few Catholic minds. There are no angels thirsting for vengeance; there is no lash in the divine hand. Ours is a God of forgiveness and peace. We, too, must be a people of forgiveness and peace. Today, then, is the first day of the rest of our lives.

I found it hard to keep up with the hectic tempo. One homily would see me through the five Masses on a weekend, but each feast, wedding, and funeral required a fresh one. Some weeks demanded I churn out four or five, a constant test. Memo to myself: "Wedding at 10:30 a.m., Saturday morning. Do not mistakenly use the homily from the 9 a.m. funeral."

Parishioners received my homilies as well as could be expected. "I've rarely heard about Jesus in all my years coming to Mass," some told me. "I never thought about him in my whole life, never considered making him the center of my life," others said. They certainly never presumed he cared for them. They dutifully arrived at Mass, said their prayers, followed orders, received the sacraments, obeyed the pope—but Jesus? What did he have to do with any of this? Where was he?

I tried my best to set the record straight. I strove to tell them that the gentle, loving Jesus wanted to live in relationship with each of them. He was available to anyone who wanted to know him and had a way out of every problem. In brief, he was their only way of surviving this cruel world, of surviving these lonesome desert plains. The more they sought him, talked to him, listened to him, walked with him, and lived with him, the more their lives would be blessed.

In the early months, opportunities to hit the road came along once in a blue moon. Catholic Charities surprised me one day with a call. Would I speak at its annual banquet in Albuquerque? Quite a gathering had been invited to the swanky venue, the Crowne Plaza Pyramid Hotel—and quite a distinguished host, the archbishop of Santa Fe himself. This would be my first chance to meet him. Church workers from every corner of the state would be in attendance, many of whom spent their days serving the imprisoned, the homeless, the sick, and the poor. But the rich would be there, too, the principal benefactors of the archdiocese. It would be a night of recognition and awards; our own Sister Hildegarde would come home with an armful.

You might want to preach on Matthew 25, suggested the director, whom I had met years earlier in Oakland: "Whatever you did for one of these least brothers and sisters of mine, you did for me." I pondered a moment; then I replied, in the interest of full disclosure, "I normally speak on Jesus' message of peace. Peace is where my deepest interests lie; it is where I focus my thoughts and deeds."

"That's why we want you," he answered. I wondered if we were talking past each other. But I accepted his invitation and resolved to wait and see.

On the night of the banquet, I drove to the hotel in Albuquerque and entered the luminous ballroom. There I shook the archbishop's hand, mingled easily with the well-heeled crowd, and enjoyed the fabulous meal. The program began, and I came to learn of the people's heroic works. Then came my introduction, and I took the stage. After a good joke to set the audience at ease, I began.

One day, Jesus will surely say to you, "Come, you blessed; inherit the kingdom prepared for you. For I was homeless and you gave me shelter, I was hungry and you fed me, sick and you comforted me, in prison and you visited me. Whatever you did to the least of these, you did to me." You sheltered the homeless, fed the hungry, worked for universal health care, visited the prisoners, and advocated for social justice right here in New Mexico. You have served Christ well.

But more must be done. We need to make the gospel leap from charity to justice, even to disarmament and nonviolence. The time has come to follow the logic of Matthew 25 to its politically incorrect conclusion, to confess, as well, that whatever we do to our brothers and sisters in Iraq, we do to Christ. If we support the bombing and killing of Iraqis, we support the killing of Christ all over again. War not only makes people homeless, hungry, sick, and imprisoned; it kills them. The church in New Mexico needs to stand up publicly and denounce this impending war, and lead everyone along the gospel path of nonviolence. Then we shall truly be blessed by Christ.

I looked up, thanked them once again, flashed a smile, and walked off the stage—to deafening silence. All the way to my chair, I felt their eyes on me; those who weren't gaping had their eyes on their empty plates. Eventually, a few hands offered brief, polite applause. I took my seat, a little crestfallen, my hands shaking and heart racing, but my soul grateful that I had held to my message. I made a quick getaway toward the end of the evening, scarcely receiving a good-bye from anyone.

Such was the beginning of the end for me in the New Mexico church. Nothing had changed; it would always be costly to follow Jesus, to think like him, to speak like him. Even so, I felt like a true pastor, who teaches the gospel to every ear, open or closed. Like it or not, I would speak the Good News, announce the hard word, and tell the truth, letting the chips fall where they may, even if it meant offending everyone. I didn't care anymore.

My mission would in a short time intensify. George W. Bush had by now publicly set his sights on Saddam Hussein. The president's statement—Hussein must be crushed—was so ominous as to send fear even into our remote desert peace. The fever of war, the spectacle and pageantry, the sacred quality of violence, the worship of death— it all crept into town.

I knew it early on when Springer officials hit upon the idea of holding a commemoration on the first anniversary of September 11 at the Springer armory. School would be called off, and the whole town would be there. Father, they said, you must come and offer the blessing. It would be the first official rally for the inevitable war.

In those innocent early days, the city officials presumed I was their kind of chaplain, one who brings the deity's favorable eye upon America's every war. My heart filled with dread, but what else could I do? Jesus never lay low, never skirted a chance to speak. Wasn't I supposed to be his apostle? Hadn't I promised to follow in his dangerous footsteps?

And so I donned priestly attire and off I went to the armory, anxiety-ridden as a man awaiting a root canal. The place was packed with nearly a thousand people. Everyone was smiling but me. I took my place in the far corner, dreading my introduction. Along the side of the room stood the National Guard unit from northeastern New Mexico, at attention, in full regalia. A series of officers took the podium and delivered speeches, all of them bearing the eerie oratorical sameness that the Pentagon has raised to a low art form.

> Americans ... this very day ... are gathering at the Pentagon ... in New York . . . and hundreds of other places . . . united in purpose . . . strong in resolve . . . unflinching under challenge . . . We decry the terrorist attacks against this nation . . . and we remember those in uniform who fight the good fight against those who would harm us . . . because of our standing as a beacon of freedom. . . . The terrorists struck like cowards . . . sought to topple the world's greatest military might . . . the world's most prosperous economy . . . hurting us, yes, but not crippling us . . . never touching the pride . . . the determination . . . of our armed forces.

What power there is in such patriotic cant. Out came the hankies, dabbing at eyes. These poor desert people suddenly found their purpose. They knew they were red, white, and blue Americans, because they supported their military. Here was their common cause.

Then I was introduced.

Dear friends, I was in New York on that dreadful Tuesday morning one year ago. I saw it all, and before long, the Red Cross asked me to coordinate the chaplains program at the Family Assistance Center. I ministered to thousands, including the rescue workers at Ground Zero, and it was horrific. But like you, I follow the nonviolent Jesus, who calls us to be people of compassion, to love our enemies, to seek justice and reconciliation with all peoples. And so, I knew from day one that retaliatory violence was not the answer, that bombing Afghanistan was not the gospel response. We are called to end the root causes of war and win the world over with our loving service, our determination to end hunger and injustice, our relentless loving-kindness, even a new commitment to dismantle our weapons of mass destruction so that no one is ever threatened again. With that in mind, let us pray for all those who died, for the people of Afghanistan and Iraq, for an end to war and terrorism, and for the coming of God's reign of nonviolence, here and now.

I looked out upon a sea of faces showing blank disbelief. I bowed my head and prayed to the God of peace for all who had died— Americans, Afghans, and Iraqis. And I begged for the abolition of war itself. Then I sailed into the final blessing, my hand tracing a cross over the crowd: "God of peace, bless our community, our nation, and our world with the precious gift of peace. May no nation ever again go to war. Make us, like St. Francis, instruments of your peace."

Stunned silence. Shock and awe. It was not the blessing they wanted.

The war shortly invaded my life, my desert peace and soon swayed my homilies. How was I to urge love and forgiveness and discipleship to Jesus while everyone was cheering on the war? How was I to prevent larceny of the Gospels when warfare became, on the lips of most, a moral, gospel duty? This is going to be tricky, I said to myself as I navigated my pastoral duties and searched for clarity.

I found it soon enough. Jesus was a great one for clarity: love your enemies, put down the sword, be compassionate as God is compassionate, blessed are the peacemakers. There are in his words no hemming or hawing, no grand theological edifices, no maneuvering room by which to say, "Yes, but . . ." I resolved anew, gazing at the altar, alone on a pew, sitting in the desert silence: I must speak to these dear people with the clarity of Jesus. Such was my calling as a pastor. I had to preach the Word of God in season or out—clearly out in such days as these. So off I went, week in and week out. I said things plainly. "Christians are not allowed to kill . . . or to send our children to kill Iraqis . . . we must not support this war . . . we must not support any war . . . we are people who love not only our neighbors but our enemies . . . regardless of the wishes of the government . . . We do not follow George W. Bush; we follow the nonviolent Jesus."

The high desert is rife with domestic violence and alcoholism and is rooted in the nuclear culture, but it is also home to a tremendous expanse of sky, red mesas, adobe churches, ancient pueblos, sagebrush and cottonwoods, canyons and mountains. It is, I believe, the last spiritual landscape in the nation. Spirituality ranks high here, thanks to the Native Americans and the Hispanic Catholics. Out here, people still possess their souls.

I just might stand a chance, I thought, if I explained why supporting the war went against every human and sacred instinct they already had. So I let the war bring my sermons into focus. And the battered little towns responded with surprising welcome. At least the war machine would make few inroads into the sanctuary of the crucified Jesus. Parishioners acknowledged the controversy yet stood by the words.

"Nice sermon, Father." "Father John, you're going to make them mad, but I know you're just doing your job." "You're telling us what Jesus would tell us. Thanks."

My parishioners languished at the bottom of the culture, more or less a dispensable people. They were in need of God for the most primal reasons, and in little need of George W. Bush and the false promises of America. I ascended the altar not to speak on behalf of any president, but rather to speak the good news of God's reign, offered extravagantly for such people as these. Their hope lay in God alone, I said. And the political implications of this rang clear: we are going to follow Jesus, which means we are going to be people of nonviolent love, unusual compassion, generous forgiveness, and steadfast peace.

The kingdom of God is at hand, I said with a smile. It's right here, within reach, in your everyday life of peace.

Disturber
of the Peace
(2002–5)

My message of peace was by no means welcomed in all quarters. It penetrated the impoverished parishes in Springer, Maxwell, and Cimarron, but beyond, among the well-intentioned of St. Mel's at Eagle Nest, it was another matter altogether. There, I observed a darkening of mood and watched stony faces in the pews turn red. Many of these parishioners were military retirees and fans of George W. Bush. They had settled here with their wives for a life of horseback riding and skiing and, toward evening each day, repairing to the deck for a martini.

I did not change my homilies one iota in deference to this demographic. What I spoke at St. Joseph's in Springer I echoed at St. Mel's. Not even two months after my arrival, I quoted Dorothy Day's exegesis of the verse "Give back to Caesar what belongs to Caesar—and to God what belongs to God." Said Dorothy, "Once you give to God what belongs to God, there is nothing left for Caesar."

We are Christians, I said. We pledge allegiance to God's reign of love and nonviolence. It requires all of us, leaving nothing that the president can claim for his conquests and wars. The God of peace, for the purpose of peace, claims our lives and the lives of our children. The Pentagon cannot legitimately make a counterclaim, taking our lives for the purpose of war.

I felt that I had come clean; they may as well know from the get-go who I was and how I intended to pastor. The benediction uttered, I stood by the door to greet people as they left. A young mother marched up to me, her face red. Her husband, fairly high-ranking in the military, was deployed in Iraq, where he served as pilot of a fighter bomber. This woman's family had long standing in the church, and she took me to task, none too gently, for my lack of patriotism.

I immediately understood her quandary. She was a good Catholic who, all of a sudden, was given no place to stand. My homily had flung her on the wrong side of the chasm, and a crisis of conscience had emerged. She was now faced with a decision that had never before come up: whom to honor—the God of peace or George W. Bush?

She fought off the decision tooth and nail. "What are you saying? That my husband shouldn't fly, shouldn't serve his country?"

"That's right, ma'am."

"But you allow that police officer to stand at the back of the church with his gun; why can't my husband fly and still be a good Catholic?"

The police officer in question patrolled the region on the weekends, driving all night through the canyons. I learned that he came to Mass regularly while on duty—in full uniform, with his trooper hat, striped pants, and holstered gun dangling off his belt. My first day at St. Mel's, I approached him after Mass and engaged him in the usual introductory conversation—I thanked him for coming, inquired about his family, and offered my services. Then I made a request:

could he perhaps leave his gun in the car? "The sanctuary is a place of peace and prayer," I explained. He agreed without any argument.

So now I could turn to the woman and say, "Your point is well-taken. And in fact, I asked him to leave his gun in his car because we do not support violence or weapons, and he agreed." With no answer to that, she left, still upset.

The confrontation didn't end there, however. Other parishioners approached me with a glare. One said, with tears in her eyes, "I want you to stop speaking against our military and our great country. I've studied the bishops' statement. And they support the war." Yes, I knew all about that unfortunate statement.

"I've prayed over this," she continued, "and Jesus told me he wants us to bomb Iraq. You've got no right to say otherwise." Some dozen others lingered by in angry silence. They reflected the town's general mood. I was, in sum, invited to shut the hell up.

That night was the first of many sleepless ones for me. My initial reaction was one of piercing pain at the rejection. But over the next few weeks, the pain mellowed into a kind of hazy disappointment, a steady sadness.

Here were good people, players by the rules, upstanding citizens, devout churchgoers—a sign of God's favor, right? But now this—a contrary word, the intrusion of the Gospel of Jesus. The Gospel, to their minds, was exclusively a private matter, never a matter to govern social or national ethics. The idea of it governing international life lay quite off the map.

By no means do I place blame on the parishioners. Any responsibility lies with our spiritual leaders, who we hope would teach us to love our enemies. Too often, though, even these people who know the Scriptures turn a blind eye to the cities set aflame, the civilians going under, their homes coming down around them, the shrapnel tearing flesh, the bloodied children left to die. And thus the war is endorsed by the silence of bishops, priests, preachers, and pastors, and supported in turn by their churchgoing faithful.

As best I could discern, the priests in New Mexico did not speak against the war. I learned later that the archbishop had urged his priests away from controversy. I never received that memo.

But controversy does not so easily die. Many in New Mexico had contempt for the war and a message for its makers—specifically, to Donald Rumsfeld. He owned thousands of acres near beautiful Taos and visited there frequently on weekends. A few Taoseanos gathered and resolved to make a stand. Organizing got under way, and later that autumn some three thousand New Mexicans gathered and stood alongside the foot of Taos Mountain. There they rallied, within shouting distance of the Rumsfeld estate, and under the pressing heat of the sun heard from the leader of the Taos Pueblo, the mayor, and me. "God is a God of peace," I said. "God does not bless war. Each Catholic and every Christian should act against Bush's war on Iraq."

I made little ado about this rally among my parishioners, none at all among those at Eagle Nest. But the media reported the event widely across the region, and my words came unbidden and unwelcome into the dens and parlors of Eagle Nest. For some at St. Mel's, this was the final straw.

I regarded myself a minor voice crying out in the desert, but not at all the only one. I stood among many saying, "Make straight the way of the Lord." And, as I reflect on it now, I simply repeated what Pope John Paul II said every day. In January 2003, for example, he met with Tariq Aziz, Saddam's number two, whom I'd met in Iraq. Around that time, he said, "War is not always inevitable. It is always a defeat for humanity. War is never just another means that one can choose to employ for settling differences between nations. Everything can change. It depends on each of us."

Each week, he took President Bush and Prime Minister Tony Blair to task and leveled strong rebukes at warmakers everywhere. "War should belong to the tragic past, to history," the pope said on Valentine's Day 2003. "It should find no place on humanity's agenda for the future." When U.S. bombs fell in March, he said, "The whole world is calling on Pharaoh to 'let my people go.'"

Bush as modern-day Pharaoh—here was an analogy I hadn't the wherewithal to make, and one that would surely have made Christians sit up and take notice. But by then the U.S. media had been vetted and cleared and embedded where the Pentagon wanted them, and the pope's clear denunciations were largely ignored in the press.

Despite my conformity with the pope, the people of Eagle Nest shouted me down Mass after Mass. There I stood at the door, moments after communion, my hand extended idly, as they stormed out. "You Jesuits!" said one. "You're so smart and intellectual. You know just what you're doing, giving us your political agenda under the guise of Scripture." Then, leaning forward, this parishioner said, "Better watch yourself, Father. Something might happen to you."

My devout St. Mel's parishioners and other faithful churchgoers across New Mexico had been penning missives full of brimstone for weeks, especially after a profile of me appeared in the newspaper at Christmas. The message of their letters was fairly consistent: We love America. We support our troops. We have every good reason to bomb Iraq off the face of the earth. And to hell with you, Father.

After Mass another day, a parishioner cornered me again. "I have so much anger against you," she said to me, standing in the sacristy. "We come to Mass to praise the Father, not to hear your opinions. No one is interested in what you have to say about the

Gospel. You hurt us when you criticize President Bush. He's a good Christian. I doubt you're a Christian at all."

I reached deep for patience and explained matters again: Jesus commands that we love our enemies; we are not allowed to kill them. The president plans to massacre them in untold numbers. We have to follow Jesus—it's as simple as that. I'm so sorry, but I will not change my position.

Finally I said, "If this is so unbearable, if you hate me that much, go ahead and write the archbishop." Her letter, the first of many, was in the mail that evening.

A few days later, a phone call came out of the blue—from an air force chaplain, a lieutenant colonel, if memory serves, out of a base in California. He had received an urgent call or two from my region and was made privy to the whole sorry matter.

You are, he solemnly explained, a terrible pastor. You mustn't preach against the war. You must show sensitivity. There are parents at St. Mel's with sons in harm's way.

Our disagreement erupted quickly. I'm sensitive to everyone, I returned, including the people of Iraq, whom these sons are killing. Perhaps it is you, I suggested gently, who lack true pastoral skills. You should be urging your Catholics to quit the military, to love their enemies, and to join in protests against this slaughter. And then, I pressed, you might be so bold as to resign your commission. That, as I see it, would greatly improve your own prospects of being a good pastor.

The chaplain conceded a point or two. Alas, he said, war always bears a measure of sin and evil. But we need to minister to Catholics even as they kill. "They're undertaking a necessary evil, and someone has to minister to them," he insisted. "They deserve our ministry; they need our support. It's not easy dropping bombs on Iraq."

回 回

Some weeks later, a few high school seniors in the confirmation class confided to me that they planned to join the army or the National Guard. I turned to face them with urgency and concern. Don't do it, I said. I know of your quandary, your grim future, the lack of options. But don't be manipulated by false promises into sacrificing yourselves—or killing someone. That will end your future and theirs. You have your whole lives ahead of you; think long and hard about how best to spend them.

To my surprise and relief, none of them joined up. For once, someone had listened to me. I regarded my action as good pastoral care—keeping these kids far from murder and mayhem. What good comes of sending them off and watching their consciences disappear and their bodies get killed or maimed? I regard it as supremely pastoral to hold aloft the gospel of Jesus and draw out the social and political implications of the cross, whether anyone wants to hear or not.

As for St. Mel's, a useful word had come by way of the chancellor of the archdiocese. "To be a pastor," he said, "is to be loved and hated, just like Jesus. Some will always be mad at you, even hate you, but it goes with the territory." His wisdom guided me through the turbulence.

In April 2003, just after Bush had begun his war on Iraq, I returned from leading a retreat at Kirkridge to find a message from the chancellor. He had bad news. The people at Eagle Nest had held a series of meetings and had asked to meet with the archbishop to express their dissatisfaction with me.

The archbishop agreed to meet with one person who would represent the group. The gist of the communication was this: Father Dear is no pastor; rather, he's a political activist, a divisive presence. He has no place in an ecclesiastical setting. No doubt he is a lover of peace, but he brings peace in a violent way. And, finally, "John Dear is a vessel of harm, a virus who could bring down the entire archdiocese"— the man's exact words, as quoted to me later by the chancellor.

At issue, it seemed, was a single difference of opinion. Was it a sin to drop bombs on Iraq? I plainly stated that I believed it was, and the folks at St. Mel's just as plainly believed it wasn't. The archbishop assured the man that wars aren't sinful, and some are just. Not to worry: sometimes killing others is a holy duty.

Thusly assured, the man had one last request: have Father Dear removed.

The archbishop agreed—without hearing my side. I guess this is what you would call frontier justice. But the chancellor told me the archbishop wanted to know, did all my parishioners feel this way? No, I said. As far as I can tell, the discontent lies exclusively at St. Mel's. The chancellor said he would inform the archbishop.

Deeply wounded, I placed a call to Sister Hildegarde, a friend of considerable compassion. She cried at the news but wasted precious little time starting a letter-writing campaign, urging everyone for miles to assess my work and send their assessments to the archbishop. In short order, more than a hundred letters arrived; parishioners from Cimarron, Maxwell, and Springer submitted words of appreciation at hearing the gospel preached with clarity and verve. Such glowing testimony, remarked the chancellor. He told me days later that, in all of its history, the archdiocese had never received so many letters of praise for a priest. In light of that, I would keep my remaining parishes.

This was cold comfort. I had been shown the door, and it took a while for me to shake the feelings of shame and disgrace. Worse was the injustice: my departure resulted not from some sensational impropriety, but from my preaching the gospel of Jesus. I had been called a bad pastor. This sent me into a funk, but it also motivated me to explore what it really means to be a good pastor. Beyond institutional definitions, what are the bounds and demands? And what light might conscience and Scripture shed on things? I studied what Jesus had to say about the matter.

Jesus, the ultimate pastor called himself "the good shepherd"—the one who leads his flock to pastures of peace and defends them from the wolf and the fox. The wolf in John's version, the antagonist and villain, is the one intent on wreaking death; in Luke's Gospel, the fox is King Herod. A hired person who is not a shepherd turns tail and runs when the attacker comes for the flock. The good shepherd, by contrast, stays put and risks life and limb and good name to protect the flock from violence and death.

I tried to do likewise—to protect my parishioners from the gathering forces of death, from the lure of warfare, which would only leave their children dead. And, riskiest of all in a hawkish town, I tried to afford a measure of protection for our sisters and brothers in the desert of Iraq.

I had often wondered why the thousands of diocesan priests didn't ever speak out. Why this silence in the face of national crimes? One scarcely heard a word anywhere about war, poverty, or nuclear weapons. I could count on one hand the priests who dared speak out.

As I pondered this, I began to see the reason: they feared rejection. If my example proved the rule, congregations would storm bishops' offices everywhere and demand new pastors. The notion has been drummed into the head of every priest to *unite* the congregation. Division and rejection are the ultimate signs of failure, and what pastor wants that?

On this matter, Jesus offered a sharp word. He didn't advise anyone to avoid division; in fact, he noted that division would follow closely upon the work of the disciple. Brothers and sisters, mothers and fathers would turn against you because of Jesus. Indeed, such division would play a role in his death. Jesus the unpatriotic, the unspiritual, and the unholy was denounced, threatened, rejected, abandoned, and killed outright.

Uniting the congregation was not on his list of priorities. "Do you think that I have come to establish peace?" he asked. We can imagine that no one dared answer that one. So Jesus answered for them: "No, I tell you, but rather division."

How long I labored over that question and answer. Of course, Jesus wanted to bring peace. How many times—before his death and after—had he said to his disciples, "Peace be with you." His very purpose was set on peace; his desire for peace ran deep. "Peace on earth," the angels sang when he was born. "Blessed are the peacemakers," he taught. "If this day you only knew what makes for peace," he said through tears. Now, for the first time, I understood. "Do you think that I have come to establish peace?" was a lament.

He had realized that his message would not be accepted. And thus, heavy of heart, Jesus made a realistic assessment: "My very presence is divisive." And the presence of his disciples would be as well—especially in a world gone mad, filled with war and injustice. No matter what the bishops and cardinals wish, divisiveness is a fact of life. The gospel forever forces the issue—people must choose between God and money, peace and country, service and selfishness, love and fear. The gospel comes down to this: Jesus takes sides, and so must we. And so must pastors.

回　圓

I was now a parish short, but in Cimarron, Springer, and Maxwell, I carried on, busy as ever. On Thursdays, I took to the road, my weekly venture into the world. I headed for some university or church around the country, arrived at a packed auditorium with notes in hand, and stirred the people to take a stand against the war, to follow the non-violent Jesus. Interest in the subject percolated everywhere.

At least to an extent. During Bush's reelection bid, an invitation arrived by mail from Messiah College. Would I consider offering the annual pastor's lecture to the student body? The college, of Anabaptist roots, lies a few miles beyond Harrisburg, Pennsylvania. I arrived to find the gymnasium flung open and some two thousand students streaming in. The proceedings opened with a beautiful prayer service. The music shimmered, and then a reverent hush settled over the students, the Beatitudes projected onto a large screen. I came to the lectern.

"Now let's get this straight," I said. "Jesus says, 'Blessed are the peacemakers.' Which means, he doesn't say, 'Blessed are the warmakers,' which means, maybe he's saying, 'Cursed are the warmakers.' Which means if we want blessings, and not curses, we must make peace. Which means we need to stand up and speak out against this evil, immoral, sinful war on Iraq." With that, the place exploded. Yells and howls and hollers and boos. In short order the voices converged into a roaring chant: "Bush! Bush! Bush! Bush!" Hundreds of students stormed out. The rest stood and shouted. Commotion and pandemonium. The faculty looked on in shock. Speech over; the assembly ended in record time. So much for the Beatitudes.

Division? It had become my specialty. I made my way out through the crowd, a sort of Via Dolorosa, all eyes furiously avoiding mine, looking at the ground. When I finally neared the exit, two young women ran up to me. "You did it," they exclaimed, thinking of that last line of the Beatitudes. "Everyone hates you. Rejoice and be glad."

"Thanks a lot," I murmured.

But not all was lost. February 15, 2003, had been a great day of hope. That day, some fourteen million marched for peace around the globe—on 6 continents, in 60 nations, in 430 cities—an unprecedented show of solidarity for peace, the single largest day of protest in history. Close to home, some eight thousand gathered at the Round House, the state capitol in Santa Fe. My speech this time found a receptive audience.

"Today," I said, "in the name of nonviolence, we say, 'Don't bomb Iraq.' The way to end terrorism is by ending the real axis of evil, which is poverty, starvation, the degradation of the earth, the proliferation of weapons, and the existence of nuclear weapons; because we were created to be nonviolent with one another and with everyone on earth. Keep on speaking out against this war, and working for peace!"

Richard McSorley, my friend and elder, had died the previous October. He had gone to the hospital to have a chronic heart condition tended to and had never come home. "If and when we go to war," he had written shortly beforehand, "it may be in the service of oil, or the flag, or money, or power, or any number of worldly allegiances, but not in the service of Christ." When the news arrived of Richard's death, my stricken heart conjured Edna St. Vincent Millay's inspiring words "I shall die, but that is all I shall do for Death." Richard was a saint; I hope he keeps me in his prayers.

Meanwhile, the Bush administration set off on a hunt for "weapons of mass destruction." In the spirit of Richard, my friends and I countered by announcing in New Mexico papers, "We've found the weapons of mass destruction. They're not in Iraq. They're right here in our backyard. Tell the president he does not need to bomb

New Mexico. Just come and dismantle them." This was not well received.

Renounce the culture of war, Richard had said. Just before the Bush administration began its massive assault on Baghdad and the destruction of Iraq, a notice made the rounds: a march on Washington would take place, and all were invited. I received a summons: Please come and address the crowd. That crowd turned out to be about three hundred thousand strong—the largest gathering against war since the early 1970s. I shared the stage with Jesse Jackson, Elizabeth McAlister, Ron Kovic, and actors Jessica Lange and Tyne Daly. "Today," I began, "in the name of truth, we say, 'Don't bomb Iraq,' because bombing Iraq will not bring democracy."

> It will not bring nuclear disarmament or peace to the Middle East or prevent terrorist attacks or help the international work of peacemaking or the United Nations' weapons inspections or fund jobs or feed the hungry or pay for health care, education, housing, or environmental cleanup or uphold international law or solve our problems. Bombing Iraq will only make the oil companies richer, sow the seeds of further terrorism, and lead to the deaths of thousands of innocent Iraqis. If you agree with me, let me hear you!

A cheer rose on the frigid air. And I continued, receiving after each statement a great cheer of solidarity.

> Today, in the name of the innocent children of Iraq, we say, "Don't bomb Iraq," because they have died by the hundreds of thousands from our sanctions. They live in terror from our bombs when they only want to live in peace with us.

Today, in the name of Martin Luther King Jr., we say, "Don't bomb Iraq," because Dr. King said the night before he died that "the choice is no longer violence or nonviolence. It's nonviolence or nonexistence"; because he calls us to love our enemies, not bomb them; because he calls us to renounce violence and become people of nonviolence; because he teaches that peaceful means are the only way to a peaceful future and the God of peace.

Today, in the name of the God of peace, we say, "Don't bomb Iraq," because war is not the will of God. War is never blessed by God. War is the ultimate mortal sin. There is no such thing as a just war. War cannot end terrorism, because war is terrorism. War is not the way to God. The God of peace calls us to beat our swords into plowshares and live in peace with everyone on the planet.

A final cheer rose up, loud enough to set the monuments trembling.

Dear friends, in these days of war, we have to create days of peace. We have to take a stand for peace, speak the words of peace, and walk the road to peace. From now on, every one of us must make the journey to peace. And as we do, the God of peace will bless us.

Sackcloth and Ashes
in Los Alamos
(2002–5)

I tried devilishly hard to practice what I preached. So I went back to New Mexico with a view to confronting weapons close to home. These days, business at Los Alamos is booming. The Bush administration has unabashedly filled its coffers for a whole new generation of weapons. Throughout the Southwest, beyond Albuquerque and its storehouse of nuclear weapons, reside millions of discarded drums of nuclear waste, giving off radioactive emissions for a lifetime of lifetimes.

Another risky venture was calling my name. It was one thing to cast an accusatory eye on warmakers inside the Beltway, but quite another to bring a rebuke upon New Mexico's bread and butter.

I had journeyed to Gallup some months before to meet Marcus Page, a young Catholic activist. Together we plotted the formation of Pax Christi New Mexico. Within a few months, a dozen groups had sprung to life and attracted more than five hundred members. Our first order of business was to plan a vigil for nuclear disarmament in Los Alamos itself, the birthplace of the bomb. We set the date: Hiroshima day, August 6.

Los Alamos and I had a relationship of sorts already. My arrival to New Mexico had attracted a modicum of media mention, particularly in the conservative *Albuquerque Journal.* The paper dispatched a reporter to Springer, hot on the trail of controversy. He dogged me for an afternoon, keeping close, snapping photos, and asking questions. On his way out, he inquired, "Oh, by the way, what's your opinion of Los Alamos?"

"Los Alamos? Why, that place is demonic." And he was gone. The article soon appeared, along with my description of Los Alamos. My notoriety soared. The great debate was under way. Letters to the editor poured in, and the editorial staff soon joined in. I quote:

"Does he believe that had we just shown love to the Nazis, they would have ceased their murderous rampage?"

"There is nothing wrong with a desire for peace, but it appears Rev. Dear would have peace at any price."

"Jesus said that man has no greater love than to lay down his life for his fellow man. Is this not what soldiers do when they defend innocent victims and their fellow soldiers by sacrificing their own lives?"

"That Rev. Dear sees no difference between nuclear weapons in the hands of a murderous despot and in the U.S. suggests moral myopia."

"If Rev. Dear cannot support his opinions without resorting to intellectual dishonesty, perhaps he should reexamine those views."

The most fevered objections, of course, bellowed forth from Los Alamos employees, indignant that the nature of their work had fallen under the scrutiny of church people. After all, most of the employees were faithful Catholics—and generous benefactors. Didn't the church bless their work, offer a kind of dispensation?

As it happens, Los Alamos sits far above Bandelier National Park, where the Anasazi Native Americans lived from the 1100s until the 1500s, hidden away in a spectacular canyon surrounded by richly colored cliffs sculpted by time. There the people shared everything in common, cared for their children, honored the landscape, and lived together in peace. Each day they ascended a high cliff toward a large niche to worship the Creator. While St. Francis strived to teach nonviolence in Europe, these holy people had formed a community of nonviolence already, according to a local historian. Today their spirit of peace remains in that canyon; you come away from it knowing that you've stood on holy ground.

But just beyond the canyon, on top of the cliff, stands Los Alamos, cradle of the bomb, the most destructive place on earth. The churchgoers of Los Alamos fatuously praise Christ, then, come Monday morning, design massive systems to vaporize his creation. Peaceableness and omnicide, a half millennium apart, but occupying the very same terrain—a contrast so vivid as to exhaust the imagination.

Soon, the Los Alamos parish priest entered the fray. In advance of the vigil, he penned a letter to the editor in his parishioners' defense. For starters: "John Dear is wrong." I could not but notice how he chopped up and reconstituted my thinking: "Rev. Dear reasons that since the United States has nuclear weapons, we have no right to deny Iraq's—or, I assume, North Korea's—right to the same." In closing, he wrote, "Personally, I'll sign up for pacifism when the other 6.2 billion folks on this earth make the same choice."

The vigil approached, and controversy swirled. It required effort to maintain a measure of poise. Then word came from the archbishop's office that I was to present myself. I figured I was still due a reprimand over the imbroglio at Eagle Nest, the whole thing up to this point mediated by the chancellor. It made sense that sooner or later the archbishop would have something to say to me. I made an appointment, prepared to be brought on the carpet. Then I resumed work on the vigil.

We finely crafted our message: The nuclear age started in New Mexico, and it needs to end here. New Mexico must be made new again—a new New Mexico. We would name nuclear weapons immoral, sinful, evil, and demonic. We would argue for production to cease, for the cleanup to begin—because nothing that puts the world at such risk can make us safer.

And hereupon we entered biblical ground: Whatever unseats the God of peace must bear the ancient name of idol. Nuclear weapons are our modern-day idols. They are honored, served, relied upon, and paid tribute. We might as well say, "In nuclear weapons we trust." But in them our future ends. There remains but one solution: to dismantle them to their nuts and bolts, as Moses dispatched Aaron's golden calf. South Africa and Ukraine have disarmed; we need to as well. Remember: they shall beat their nuclear swords into plowshares of peace. The churchgoing employees of Los Alamos would know the words well.

We took the message further, beyond mere theology to practical action: "Quit your jobs. Find life-giving work." Such a simple gesture would get the process of dismantling well on its way, for an idol not served is an idol on its last legs.

This idea nearly always elicits the question: But where else would I work? In any spiritual struggle, fear is usually a key player. With some creativity, all sorts of jobs could be created for good—work cleaning up the environment or creating alternative energy resources. But there is always the bottom line, too. And greed is as much behind Los Alamos as any other factor. Greed goes hand in glove with nuclear warfare. There are more millionaires per capita in the tiny town of Los Alamos than anywhere else in New Mexico, or the whole planet.

In the 1980s, the bishop of Amarillo, Texas, had issued a similar challenge, calling upon Catholics to quit their jobs at the Pantex nuclear facility. They returned immediately with hue and cry. They would never, they complained, be able to find other work. To that, he responded in a sensible way. He raised a massive fund and laid it on the table: tens of thousands of dollars, plus assistance in the job search, for anyone who would leave. The church would support their families for a year. In tendering this offer, he urged them toward more life-giving work and, in the process, helped the church fulfill its vocation. But interestingly, there was no rush to his door. Only one of thousands of Catholic bomb makers took up the offer. The others, as the bishop judged the matter, stayed put for the status and the big bucks.

Despite the disheartening precedent, we stuck to our message. Most at Los Alamos were followers of Jesus and thus forbidden to support war; they were commanded to put down the sword and to love the enemy. But something went terribly wrong along the way, and some reminding was in order—namely, that one can't serve both the God of peace and the idols of war. One can't follow the way of Jesus and work at Los Alamos. One can't sing praises to the Creator and design weapons that could put the earth into an eternal winter.

In seven days, out of the formless void, God laid the foundations of the world, an achievement no doubt of great pride in the heavens. But we have created the means to crack the foundations of the earth and hurl it again into formless void. Scientists say it would require but seven minutes.

As the vigil neared, I went for my scheduled appointment with the archbishop. I prepared to defend myself in the matter of Eagle Nest. But Eagle Nest was not even on the agenda.

"Stay away from Los Alamos," he said. "I forbid you to be there on the sixth of August." He issued a comprehensive ban: I was not to speak or even pray publicly for peace. Finally, I managed an objection. Other priests would be there, and hundreds of Catholics. This makes little sense—why could they attend and I couldn't? Evidently, my high profile was of concern to him.

Then he read a quote from a letter he had received—from a local priest: "John Dear is at it again. He is stirring people up and organizing church people around the state to stop the work of Los Alamos. You brought John Dear to New Mexico. You, therefore, must support his stand for peace. It seems that even Pope John Paul II supports him. I'm beginning to realize I no longer belong in this church. Perhaps I should resign."

"I refuse to lose a good man over this," the archbishop said. "I forbid you to go."

August 6 arrived, and I stayed put. Shortly, there was buzz on the air. What of John Dear? asked the media. Friends promptly informed them that the archbishop had forbidden me to attend. The headline read, "Protestors Gather at LANL; Priest Says He Was Barred from Peace Demonstration." As it turned out, there was a huge turnout of ordinary New Mexican citizens—greater than that of any protest in the state in sixty-five years.

◧ ◧

I stayed home that year, but in years to come I would join the vigils, speak out against nuclear weapons, and call for the conversion to

Gospel nonviolence. Over time, my Pax Christi friends and I decided we needed an innovative symbol, some fresh way to draw attention to our call for repentance, conversion, and disarmament. Finally, we settled on an image from the book of Jonah: sackcloth and ashes.

The biblical story names Jonah, however reluctant he might have been, as the only prophet to have converted an entire community, the fearsome people of Nineveh. Jonah stalked the city and cried out a message of woe and hope. The Ninevites weighed his words and, against the odds, took them to heart, repenting of their violence. Here, we thought, was a story to inspire hope and action.

And so, on the sixtieth anniversary of Hiroshima, August 6, 2005, we would converge on Los Alamos and put on sackcloth and sit amid ashes. We would lay no blame on our sisters and brothers in the town but embrace it ourselves. We would refuse to point fingers at anyone. We would instead point them at our own hearts and begin the process of conversion there.

"The atom bomb," Mahatma Gandhi once said, "resulted for the time being in destroying Japan. What has happened to the soul of the destroying nation is yet too early to see." Some sixty years later, what happened is all too plain, if you dare look. As a people, we've lost our soul. We deny what we did and rush full steam ahead toward global annihilation. In light of this, we would meditate on Hiroshima, face the great evil as best we could, and in the process reclaim ourselves, our souls, our minds, our hearts.

We gathered for Mass the night before the vigil; then, the next morning, hundreds of us came together on Los Alamos. We marched through the streets, and at the appointed hour we sat down in spiritually charged silence. For thirty minutes, the whole town fell silent, and for a moment, we felt the peace we longed for. Perhaps we even showed Los Alamos the way to peace. The 325 marchers had donned sackcloth, scattered ashes on the sidewalks along Trinity Drive and Oppenheimer Road, confessed our sins to God, begged that the world be spared, and promised a new life of nonviolence. The occasion bore an air of sacrament and harmony; we felt mercy descend from the skies.

We were learning to take the Word of God seriously and the gospel personally. I first heard the latter phrase from Martin Sheen, as we marched through the streets of Baltimore on the occasion of Phil Berrigan's death. "Phil took the gospel personally," Martin said. The words took me by surprise and became my manifesto. I decided right then to embrace the gospel all the more, as if Jesus had uttered my name, as if he had addressed every word personally to me. Once again, I heard the call to conversion. Life was beginning anew.

I received word of Phil's illness in October 2002. He told me the news himself: cancer of the liver, kidney, pancreas. The physicians shook their heads; little could be done. During the following week, I perceived Phil's image and words and example everywhere I turned. What an immense impact this man had had on my life. He had condemned every war, every weapon, every injustice—he was our very own Jeremiah. I recalled those painful days when he and Bruce and I bided our time in our tiny cells. Phil had spent more than eleven years of his life behind bars for his work for peace.

I had to see him one last time. In early December 2002, I arrived at Jonah House, in the heart of Baltimore and on the edge of an ancient cemetery. That very night, Phil took a turn for the worse, and a five-day deathwatch began. I stayed there with Phil's wife, Liz; their children; Dan; his other brother, Jerry, and his wife, Carol; and about two dozen community members and friends. We uttered prayers in shifts around his bed. We held him, cared tenderly for him, tuned our breathing to his. Elsewhere, people cooked and planned the funeral. In the basement, Phil's son, Jerry, crafted a casket.

Toward afternoon one day, I sat before a computer as Dan dictated the homily for Phil's funeral. "If Philip's patience was marmoreal, his impatience was a lifted hammer," Dan concluded. "The blow struck marble, repeatedly. What we had at the end was a masterwork of grace, of human sweetness. We gazed on him with a kind of awe. . . . Dying, Philip won the face he had earned at such cost."

Phil wanted to offer a last message, and he asked Liz to take it down. "I die," he murmured weakly, "with the conviction held since 1968 and Catonsville that nuclear weapons are the scourge of the earth. To mine for them, manufacture them, deploy them, use them is a curse against God, the human family, and the earth itself." Suddenly exhausted, he fell silent. We let those last words stand as they were, unfinished.

Phil's dying was a time of misery and great blessing all at once. From the grief sprang a community of love and grace—a togetherness, a fullness, and a wholeness one can only ascribe to the Holy Spirit. On Friday night, December 6, 2002, with family and friends in bustling solicitude, Phil died peacefully, the center of a true community of peace.

Hundreds of mourners walked for blocks through inner-city Baltimore singing hymns of peace as Phil's handmade casket rode in the back of a pickup truck. We gathered at the African-American Catholic church where Phil had tended the flock some thirty-five years before.

More than six hundred filled the sanctuary, including great friends such as Martin Sheen, Dar Williams, Ramsey Clark, and Howard Zinn. I presided over the Mass with its uplifting music, loving eulogies, and tears and joy. Peace banners hung everywhere. It was supposed to be a funeral, but it was instead a true experience of resurrection. As friends in El Salvador might put it, Phil Berrigan had risen in these peacemaking people.

A homeless man, bundled and chilled, wandered by and gazed upon the departing crowd. "I'm glad to see they sent him off in style," he said.

▣ 46 ▣

Soldiers at
My Front Door
(2003)

It happened on Thursday, November 20, 2003. A grand announcement had been made the week before: the 515th Regiment of the
New Mexico National Guard, based in the Springer armory, would soon
depart for Iraq. Yellow ribbons sprang up overnight all over town.

As far as I was concerned, this was not an occasion to celebrate. It
was so typical of the empire to send its poorest off to kill and wage its
wars—the impoverished of New Mexico set against the impoverished
of Iraq. Dying to escape the desert, these young men and women were
now destined to die in a desert across the world. As usual, mine was
the dissident viewpoint; most everyone in town, parents and neighbors, all of them parishioners, swelled with pride. They knew no other
response.

On Wednesday evening, I turned off the alarm clock, intending
to sleep until noon the next day, my first day off in a month. But at
six the next morning, a racket outside caused me to jump straight
up in bed. The shouting and screaming seemed to be coming from
right outside my window, from right in front of the rectory. I listened

carefully: "Swing your guns from left to right; we can kill those guys all night."

What in the world was going on? I got out of bed and peered out the window. And there they were, some seventy-five soldiers double-timing right in front of the house, on the street where I lived. They turned a corner and went out of view.

Soldiers in formation in the middle of town—it was a curious sight. It had something to do, I supposed, with their impending departure. Perhaps they wanted to drum up the town's support, perhaps psych themselves up for the combat ahead. After all, they would soon be marching in front of houses in Iraq—and blasting their way in and killing everyone in sight. I heard this report later from some of my parishioners, who had received calls all the way from Iraq from these same young soldiers, crying and scared.

I figured that their chanting made it easier for them to take another life. I considered returning to bed, but minutes later they were back again. They seemed to be on a circuit of some kind, marching in front of the rectory, down Main Street, around the corner, down the street parallel to mine, around another corner, and past the post office, finally ending up back in front of the rectory, the volume of their chanting rising and falling.

I put on some coffee and settled into a chair by a window on the second floor to begin my morning prayers. Round and round they went, shattering the palpable morning stillness of the desert. The clamor rankled my soul. But after a few minutes of prayer, my irritation was replaced by compassionate sadness. They were just kids, probably no older than twenty, and probably—behind their bravado—really scared. Many had gone to some community college with the military footing the bill. Not in a million years were they prepared for this. Iraq? To their youthful minds, it lay far off the map.

The chants persisted, in and out of earshot. An hour went by. I sipped my coffee and read my Bible. Then, at seven, all of sudden the screaming and shouting increased dramatically. It sounded as if the soldiers were in the house. I walked over to the window and saw that the entire company now stood at my front door, spilling out onto the street.

A handful of officers stood in front, urging the soldiers to chant the battalion's slogan: "One bullet, one kill! One bullet, one kill! One bullet, one kill!" But these young people were new to war, and quite out of sync. All that emanated was an unrelieved series of commandments: "Kill! Kill! Kill! Kill! Kill!"

It was a sight worthy of a horror film or, worse, some Latin American dictatorship. What should I do? They didn't move an inch but stood at attention and screamed until they were blue in the face: "Kill! Kill! Kill!"

For the first time in modern U.S. history, as far as I can tell, U.S. soldiers were marching against a private citizen—and the local parish priest to boot, in front of his church. As I stared out the window at the scene, it seemed to me that we had turned a corner. This looked like Chile under Pinochet. Or Reagan's contras marching on Nicaragua. Or the death squads I had witnessed long ago in El Salvador and Guatemala. Some soldiers are dispatched overseas to kill in the name of democracy. Others harass and menace dissenters at home. I thought, I don't need to go to Iraq. The war has come right to my door.

I looked on those poor young people, doomed to the horrible chaos of warfare, many of them already doomed to death. I thought about the many funerals I had presided over already. You will have to preside at their funerals, I told myself. But I didn't want to. I was the town's pastor. It was my job to defend them from the forces of death.

I reached for my old blue winter coat, flung open the door, and walked outside, right into the middle of their ranks. The chanting came to a halt. As I stood there in their midst, the desert silence returned. All eyes were on me. I pointed a finger to the sky.

"In the name of the God of peace, I order all of you to quit the military, not go to Iraq, not kill anyone, and not to be killed. Go home, all of you, and refuse to go to Iraq. Disobey your orders to kill. God does not want you to kill so that Bush and Cheney can steal more oil from Iraq. God does not bless war. God does not support war. God wants us all to live in peace. I want none of you to get killed. Stop all this right now and go home, and start practicing the nonviolence of Jesus. God bless you."

Stunned silence. They looked at me as if I were crazy. For five long seconds, we stood there in the street. Then they burst out laughing. An officer barked, "Dismissed!" and they walked away, shaking their heads.

Within a few days, they were on their way to Iraq. Meanwhile, some of my parishioners placed calls to National Guard officials. Why, they demanded, had the guard targeted Father John? No such incident ever happened, officials insisted. But, said various parishioners, I heard the soldiers myself. I live down the street. I saw it happen. This was an unforeseen problem—witnesses, people awakened at dawn for blocks. Officials shortly trotted out another version of the facts. This was retaliation, they said. Apparently, I had disrupted exercises at the armory. It was a blatant falsehood; I hadn't been back to the place since my blessing there on September 11, 2002.

The Progressive asked the National Guard for a statement and was offered a blanket denial: The incident to which you refer never occurred. The *Albuquerque Journal* placed a few calls. This time, the officials proved more forthcoming. Yes, they had marched by, but it had nothing to do with John Dear. The backpedaling intensified, all par for the course.

The whole episode set me thinking. Perhaps this assault was a sign of hope. Perhaps when soldiers are compelled to march to our doors, they do so precisely because we are making a difference. Perhaps we are more powerful than we realize. Maybe this is a sign of things to come—the end of the empire, the last gasp of its military might, the last repression of those who point the way toward a future of peace.

There is reason for hope. Jesus showed us long ago: love is stronger than fear or hatred or indifference. Life is stronger than death. Nonviolence is more powerful than violence. A new day is dawning, and the reign of God is at hand. It's right here, right now, in this moment of life. All we have to do is take another step forward on the long road to peace, and the blessings of peace are ours. All we have to do is be persistent in our stand for peace.

回 EPILOGUE 回

I'm up early this morning, out on the edge of the wind-scoured
mesa where I now live. I find myself a comfortable boulder, pen
and paper in hand, and watch the sunrise—a riot of colors breaking
out low in the sky. Violet gives way to red and red to orange. The
rugged terrain and far mountains, along with the junipers and desert
flowers, come slowly into view. And far below on the desert floor, slen-
der as a thread and slanting toward the horizon, stretches the Santa Fe
Railway, on its way to L.A. or New York.

I sit awhile and reflect on that momentous occasion, the morning
the National Guard arrived at my door. And I ponder the intervening
years since—a quagmire of a war, our young squandered, Iraqis going
under, their cries never reaching our ears, and in our own plagued
neighborhoods, social programs gutted and the poor growing poorer.
And everywhere the hastening of global warming. Death upon death.
A culture of perpetual war. Empire as a way of life.

Against such a backdrop, one does what one can. As for me, I
travel east and west, north and south, speaking to any audience that
will have me, to stir up resistance to the war. I teach Gospel nonviolence and nurture as best I might a new culture of peace. And the
yearning for it takes me by surprise; invitations come in at a rate faster
than I can respond. So many that my Jesuit provincial, Father Tim
Brown, urged me to step down as parish pastor and take to the road

full-time, like the early Jesuits, he says, traipsing through Europe, announcing the reign of God. This has been a kind of a turnabout for me, being an itinerant preacher.

I inaugurated my new vocation by taking a month-long pilgrimage to India with Gandhi's grandson Arun, there to see where the Mahatma lived and worked and to imbibe his spirit. Now I crisscross the United States and beyond, having become an apostle of Gospel nonviolence. I deliver the good news of peace before tens of thousands each year and journey to places such as Colombia to investigate human rights abuses and Australia to encourage the peace movement there.

Closer to home, I keep my feet to the fire and endure arrest for opposing Bush's war on Iraq. On September 26, 2006, nine of us entered the federal building in Santa Fe bearing a copy of our "Declaration of Peace," part of a nationwide effort to mobilize actions at every local congressional office to push for an end to the U.S. war on Iraq, and to insist on making reparations to the Iraqi citizenry. We were headed to the senator's office on the third floor, hoping to get his signature on our petition.

Our arrival caused some consternation and back-and-forth in the lobby. We milled about as time dragged on, and we decided to enter the elevator (we couldn't take the stairs because one of our number was an elderly gentleman with a walker). A policeman jabbed his foot in the door, forcing it open, then cut the elevator's power, the doors full open. That's where we stayed for six hours.

Before long, I produced a list with the names of the killed—American and Iraqi—and to pass the hours we recited them out loud for all to hear. In the meantime, various bureaus dispatched officials—the Federal Police, the FBI, a SWAT team. And as we recited, they murmured and placed calls and scratched their heads. Toward the end of the day the local director of Homeland Security took matters in hand and placed us under arrest.

A year later, on September 6, 2007, we stood trial in Albuquerque, in Federal Court. We were found guilty and each sentenced differently to a small or large fine and / or community service. This episode shows the breadth of destruction caused by war. Young men and women die, but so do imagination and independent thinking and conscientious government and simple justice. War has declared it a crime, prima facie, to insist on peace. War has declared the tenets of the Constitution an inconvenience. War has criminalized trying to sway one's senator on matters pertaining to itself. The real crime, of course, is war. And the true criminals persist in their high crimes and misdemeanors and get away with mass murder.

Thus has Lady Justice gone doubly blind. The war burns on, and in Iraq, Afghanistan, Palestine, and Colombia, life is cheap. The U.S. government hurries after global empire and every day sinks further into repression and hubris and global destruction. All traces of right order are banished, with the full backing of the courts.

So we give thanks for our modest gesture, and for all humble acts for God's reign of peace. Perpetual war must be countered by perpetual nonviolent resistance—non-cooperation in the Gandhian sense and cooperation always with the God of peace. Instead of Bush's surge for war, we organize a surge for peace, an uprising of peacemakers marching for peace, holding vigils for peace, praying for peace, crossing lines for peace—people who, if judged guilty nonetheless regard such a judgment as a blessing. For they share the fate of Jesus, who himself suffered arrest and trial and humiliation and jail, and worse, capital punishment by the empire.

Outside my rustic hermitage, some four miles from the nearest road, I dwell in the spare style of Gandhi, Merton, and Thich Nhat

Hanh. And I gaze in awe again upon the spectacular vista. The solitude warms me like wool and I center myself in God's perfect peace. "Blessed are the meek," said Jesus. "They shall inherit the earth." It is as if I'm receiving the blessing myself, the earth stretched out before me, the God of peace comforting me. The blessings multiply, my share overflows—friends, community, peacemaking actions, opportunities to speak and serve. I survey the years, amazed and grateful. So much grace despite a bitter trove of mistakes and wrong turns and setbacks.

But I look forward, too. I want to keep always faithful to the journey, to go the distance. My heart burns to follow the nonviolent Jesus all the way to the cross and beyond, to the new life of resurrection. My heart has set itself on the long road to peace.

And what has the road taught me? That Gandhi, Dorothy Day, Dr. King, the Berrigans, and Merton were right: Gospel nonviolence holds the key to personal, social, and global transformation. The future will be a future of peace, if we dare seek it, sacrifice for it, and enact it—a new world without war, poverty, or nuclear weapons, where God's reign abounds freely and all accept its abundant grace of love and peace.

This is a precious hope. But realizing it requires a few things. First, that our hearts and minds fill with a new mystical awareness, namely, that each one of us is a beloved son or daughter of God. The God of peace loves us infinitely, loves us wildly, crazily—hovers over us like a doting, devoted mother, her infant on her knee. Our first step requires that we claim and embrace that divine love. All we have to do is let God love us, and live in that love more and more every moment. Proffered freely, it empowers us, fills us with happiness, meaning, and purpose—and sends us forth on the road to peace.

This truth leads to a second realization. Because each one of us is the beloved, apple of God's eye, then east to west, north to south, each one of us is a beloved sister and brother to one another. Every human being on the planet is equal to every other human being. We are all children of the God of peace, already one, all united and reconciled long ago. As a family, we are called to live in peace and nonviolent love, and to share that common unity with all creatures and with creation itself. Peace will descend when we see the world this way—when we admit that all are redeemable, not only you and me, but one and all, that all life is sacred, lovable, called into God's reign of nonviolent love. Then things will come naturally to us, beginning with the practice of universal, all-inclusive, unconditional love. It will lengthen, broaden, widen for one and all, and become our shared, common vocation.

Finally, from this vocation of love, a new culture of peace and nonviolence will flower and grow and multiply. We know who we are: God's beloved sons and daughters. We know who everyone else is: our beloved sister and brother. And so it follows precisely—we will never hurt another again. Moreover we will renounce every trace of violence and war. We'll forsake corporate greed and nuclear weapons. We'll refuse to be silent or passive or afraid or complicit with the world of violence. We'll get involved, and give our lives so that every human being on the planet can live in peace with justice, with food, housing, healthcare, education, employment, and dignity.

We'll turn our compassion toward the earth itself and halt its warming, purify its noxious waters and heal its scarred land. No one will be classified as an enemy. Instead we'll work to end oppression itself and starvation and all manner of needless suffering, to cut the roots of war and terrorism. We'll abolish our nuclear weapons and stop spending money on instruments of death and greed, and use those resources to institutionalize and erect a new culture, one of nonviolence and peace.

So each day we pray: "Your reign of peace come. Your will of peace be done." We don't wait for some far-off future, some eschaton beyond imagining. The promise is for now, today, this very moment. We are already there. The reign of God is at hand, right now, in this very moment. We pledge to live with the God of peace, follow the Christ of peace, breathe in the Holy Spirit of peace. We are already citizens—beloved sons and daughters—of God's reign of peace. We can easily love one another and our nation's enemies come what may, and love confidently, because the God of peace loves us all and sends us into the world as emissaries, ambassadors, spokespeople of the divine reign—servants, disciples, apostles, teachers, prophets, visionaries, champions—each of us a saint of Gospel nonviolence.

I trudge back to the house. There I answer the mail, make a few calls, write a sermon, say a few prayers, pack for the next trip—and prepare myself for the next nonviolent action. Always the journey is just beginning. The vista of peace spreads out before me. A new horizon of nonviolence is ours for the asking. It awaits our pilgrimage, our embrace, our acceptance. All we have to do is welcome the gift, stay the course, be persistent in our peacemaking, and live in faith, hope, and love. All we have to do is follow the nonviolent Jesus, wherever he wants to lead us.

And so we walk the narrow path of Gospel nonviolence. We are becoming Beatitude people, Sermon on the Mount people, a new breed of Christians. We go forward filled with hope into the new life of resurrection, the promised land of peace. Each step forward brings blessing upon blessing upon blessing.

◙ ACKNOWLEDGMENTS ◙

I thank all those who helped me with this book, my many friends. First of all, I thank my friend Ted Gordon for his tireless assistance and hard work on the manuscript. This book has been years in the making. When I began the project in earnest in 2005, I mentioned it to Ted and he offered to help. He tightened every page, rearranged some chapters, talked me through various episodes, and made the final manuscript a much better book. Thank you so much, Ted, for your persistent peacemaking.

Thanks also to other great friends: to Martin Sheen, for his encouragement, especially over the course of several late night phone calls during the early months of writing, for his support and his foreword; to Daniel Berrigan, for his steadfast support and letters of encouragement; to Jim and Shelley Douglass, for their calls and e-mails encouraging me to finish the project; to Harry Geib and Jim Martin, for all their help and support; to Bruce Friedrich, my jail-mate, for his suggestions; and to Mairead Maguire, for her help particularly with the section on Northern Ireland. And special thanks to my dear friend Natalie Goldberg for looking at the early draft, offering comments, recommending me to her agent, and encouraging me to keep at it. To you, great friends, every blessing of peace, love, and joy.

Thanks also to my parents for their comments and support, and my brother David, for his feedback and comments. I thank my friend and assistant Ellie Voutselas for her hard work arranging my endless speaking schedule and seeing me through various projects and crises—all of which not only made my life easier, but gave me time to write this book. Thanks, too, to Mat Crimmins and Renea Roberts, friends and neighbors, for giving me the peace and space, literally, to write. Thanks to Wendy Chmielewski and the Swarthmore Peace Collection at Swarthmore College, for managing my papers and manuscripts, and to Geri Thoma, my agent, for supporting me through this project.

I offer all my thanks and blessings to Joe Durepos, Michelle Halm, Brett Nicholaus, and the team at Loyola Press for accepting this book and seeing it through to the light of day, and for walking the road to peace with me. Most especially, I thank Vinita Wright, my editor, who labored long and hard on the manuscript to shorten and improve it. Thank you so much, Vinita—you're the best!

I thank my friends and relatives who have helped me on my journey over the years, especially: Steve Kelly, Bill McNichols, Sister Hildegarde Smith, Sister Helen Prejean, Sister Margaret Maggio, Jack Marth, Miriam Ford, Bud Ryan, Megan McKenna, Richard Deats, Liz McAlister, Bruce Friedrich, Lynn Fredriksson, Scott Nash, Jim Wallis, Joe Cosgrove, Sam and Gloria Roy, Davida Coady, Jackson Browne, Joan Baez, Sue Mosteller, Patrick Hart, Phil Cousineau, Edwina Gately, Kathy Kelly, Tom Gumbleton, Walter Sullivan, Bob Keck, Ben Jimenez, Bill Sneck, Jane Ferdon, George Murphy, Frank McAloon, Joe Schmidt, Mary Anne Muller, Simon Harak, Danny Muller, George Anderson, Mark Deats, Patrick O'Brien, Gerry Straub, Jeremy Seifert, Ed and Celia Olona, Marcus Page, Tom Roberts, Michael Lerner, Jerry and Carol Berrigan, Ken Butigan, Anna Brown, Anne Brotherton, Frida Berrigan, Robert Ellsberg, Dorothy Cotton, Ramsey Clark, Eavl Crow, Trace Murphy, Nancy

Cusack, Susan Sarandon, Roy Bourgeois, Dar Williams, Janet Sheen, Emilio Estevez, Adolfo Perez Esquivel, Toshi and Pete Seeger, Patty Smythe, Sister Joan Chittister, Sister Jose Hobday, Sister Roni Daniels, Billy Neal Moore, Lisa Goode, Jeff Dietrich, Catherine Morris, Jim Corkery, Terry Howard, Paul Farmer, Arun Gandhi, Anne Germino, Bob Hunter, Hildegard Goss-Mayr, David Hartsough, Tom Hoffman, David Hackett, Stanley Hauerwas, Jeff Putthoff, Franziska Jägerstätter, Don Moore, Marietta Jaeger Lane, Dennis Kucinich, Judith Kelly, Janet Chisholm, Mary Lou Kownacki, Jim Lawson, Art Laffin, Chas and Ysabel McAleer, Colman McCarthy, Ched Myers, Joe Markwordt, Barbara Mikulski, Cecilia Zarate Laun, Jim Reale, Maggie Ritz, Richard Rohr, Jonathan Schell, Susan Sherman, Joe Sands, Thane and Neva Hascall, Terry Taylor, Thich Nhat Hanh, Pema Chödrön, Archbishop Desmond Tutu, Mordechai Vanunu, Louie Vitale, Janice Vanderhaar, Lorry Wynne, Carolyn Whitney Brown, June and Walter Wink, Howard Zinn, Javier Giraldo, Pacho de Reux, Jon Sobrino, Joe McVeigh, Des Wilson, Ciaron O'Reilly, Matt and Amanda Deloisio, Katherine Behrenson, Chris Boles, Bruce and Valerie Kent, Dennis Coday, Mary Burton Riseley, Pat Gaffney, Dave Robinson, Bill Bichsel, Blase Bonpane, Nancy Blackman, Rick Malloy, Bill Pickard, Mindi Russell, Patrick O'Neill, Jerry Zawada, Senan Timoney, Ed DeBerri, Mary Donnelly, Tim Brown, Carol Powell, Brendan McKeague, Simon Moyle, Gill Burrows, and last but not least, Jarrod McKenna of Perth.

I dedicate this book and my life to Jesus of Nazareth. When I applied to join the Jesuits, I decided to try to follow the nonviolent Jesus consciously for the rest of my life. I'm still trying, still just beginning, still very much on the journey. Jesus remains for me the greatest person who ever lived, to say the least, and his universal love and persistent peace still offer the only solution to our problems. I consider Jesus the embodiment of the God of peace, the incarnation of nonviolence, the Way, the Truth and the Life. This book is my poor testimony to the effect of Jesus on my life and the hope he offers me and the world. Every grace and miracle in my life I credit to him; every failure at peace, love, compassion, nonviolence and understanding is my own.

May we all walk in the footsteps of Jesus, practice his creative nonviolence, radiate his light and hope, and persistently pursue his resurrection gift of peace for the coming of a new world without war, poverty or nuclear weapons—God's reign of peace at hand. Amen.

Index

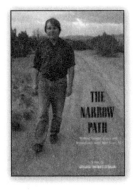